AMERICA
HELD HOSTAGE:
The Secret Negotiations

By Pierre Salinger

(Non-fiction)

AMERICA HELD HOSTAGE: THE SECRET NEGOTIATIONS
AN HONORABLE PROFESSION: A TRIBUTE TO ROBERT F. KENNEDY
WITH KENNEDY

(Fiction)

ON THE INSTRUCTIONS OF MY GOVERNMENT

PIERRE SALINGER

AMERICA HELD HOSTAGE:
The Secret Negotiations

ANDRE DEUTSCH

PHOTO CREDITS

Photos supplied by:

WIDE WORLD PHOTOS: numbers 1, 2, 3, 10, 11, 13, 14, 26, 27, 28, 29
UNITED PRESS INTERNATIONAL: numbers 4, 5, 6, 7, 8, 9, 15, 16, 17, 18,
19, 20, 21, 22, 23, 24, 25
Jerome Chatin of GAMMA/LIAISON: number 12

Library of Congress Cataloging in Publication Data

Salinger, Pierre.
America held hostage.

1. United States—Foreign relations—Iran.
2. Iran—Foreign relations—United States. 3. Iran
Hostage Crisis, 1979–1981. 4. Salinger, Pierre.
I. Title.
E183.8.I55S25   327.73055

First published in Great Britain 1982
by André Deutsch Limited
105 Great Russell Street London WC1

Copyright © 1981 by Pierre Salinger

Printed in Great Britain by
Ebenezer Baylis and Son Limited
The Trinity Press, Worcester, and London

ISBN 233 97456 3

To Roone Arledge and the ABC News team
and
To those brave Americans who spent 444 days in captivity in Iran and those who devoted so much of their energy and intelligence to try and free them.

acknowledgments

I OWE MUCH TO MANY PEOPLE FOR HAVING BEEN ABLE TO WRITE THIS book. My first and most heartfelt thanks go to the devoted men and women at ABC News who worked with me in producing the ABC News Special "America Held Hostage: The Secret Negotiations" from which I have taken the name for this book. I owe a special debt of gratitude to Roone Arledge, who always believed in me, and whose commitment to this project was extraordinary. Nor can I forget Av Westin, Bob Frye and Bob Roy, all men of exceptional talent, who supervised the production of the show and made it what it was. When we finally decided to go ahead with the show in November of 1980, the core of material I had accumulated in almost a year of reporting needed verification and amplification all over the globe. Bill Blakemore, Lou Cioffi, Liz Colton, Frank Manitzas, Chris Powell and Bill Redecker provided that reporting with high professionalism and selflessness. Frank Manitzas and John Lower also made an important contribution to the production of the show. Nor can I forget those in the Paris Bureau of ABC News, with whom I work side by side every day, and who in one way or another made a contribution to the show. Finally, while I cannot name every one of the more than eighty persons involved in the project I want to thank Dick Kuhn, Rudy Boyer, Jerome Slattery and John Cordone, who lived with me almost day and night for five weeks in Suite 1001 of the Plaza Hotel in New York, always good-humored in moments of high tension and pressure. Nor can

I neglect to thank the many videotape editors and post-production editors who often worked around the clock to prepare the show.

When I agreed to do this book, my thoughts went immediately to an old friend, Leonard Gross. Leonard and I worked together as young journalists on the San Francisco *Chronicle* and later shared a tiny cubicle at *Collier's* magazine in the great days before that marvelous magazine died. Leonard has been invaluable to me in producing this book. As an author of national repute in his own right, he graciously agreed to be part of a team, helping me get to the heart of thousands of pages of documents and interviews I acquired—a great many of which I did not have at the time the ABC Special went on the air in January of 1981.

I am also particularly grateful for the help of Diane Seligsohn, a talented young American journalist living in Paris, who worked around the clock on the research for the book, assisted by Susan Blaine and Elizabeth Frawley in the United States and Linden Gross in Paris.

Every author needs a critical and unbiased observer to read the manuscript and point out the errors. This time we had two: my wife Nicole and Leonard's wife Jacquelyn.

Finally, I want to thank Maurice James of the Paris Bureau of ABC News, whom I dispossessed of his office for four months so that we could have a central working place.

A number of the people who play key roles in this book agreed to be interviewed. I cannot name them all, but I would particularly like to thank Hamilton Jordan, Christian Bourguet, Héctor Villalón, François Cheron, Mohammed Heikal, Robert Armao, Lloyd Cutler, Warren Christopher, Harold Saunders, Henry Precht, Cyrus Vance and Edward Brunner of the Swiss Foreign Office. Their perceptions were invaluable in helping me to enlarge my own understanding of this colossal event.

Pierre Salinger

Les Pins, France
July 4, 1981

contents

prologue

"MR. SALINGER?"

The man at the bottom of the ramp had been watching me since the moment I stepped through the door of the press plane that had accompanied President Jimmy Carter to Teheran. He was obviously an officer in the Iranian Army, but the exaggerated lines and heavy decorations of his uniform gave him the appearance of a soldier from an operetta. He handed me an envelope, which I opened as soon as I was seated in the press bus that would take us to the city.

By Command of Their Imperial Majesties
The Shahanshah Aryamehr and the Shahbanou of Iran
in honour of
The President of the United States of America and
Mrs. Jimmy Carter
The Minister of the Imperial Court requests the pleasure of the company of Mr. Pierre Emil George Salinger, L'Express at dinner on Saturday December 31st, 1977, at 20.00 hours.

Dress: Dark Suit
Ladies: Long Dress   Niyavaran Palace

I was, it developed, one of only four journalists of the two hundred accompanying President Carter to be invited to the dinner. The others were the representatives of the three American television networks.

The reason I found myself in such august company was that I had met the Shah sixteen years before when I was press secretary to President John F. Kennedy.

The Shah had come to Washington in 1961 on a state visit. He was forty-two at the time, and he struck me then as a man who looked exactly like the person he was: rich beyond counting, handsome, alert, virile, healthy—a consequence of an unrelenting passion for vigorous sports—self-possessed and serene, a monarch among mortals, exuding a near-mystical belief that, although born a commoner, he was the present representative of a 2500-year-old Persian dynasty. That he considered himself superior to other men had been unstated but obvious sixteen years before; now, as our press bus moved out of the Mehrabad Airport and sped along the main route to Teheran, I saw that he had converted that thought to stone. "The Shahyad Monument," I read in my press kit, "serves as the 'Gateway to Iran,' a symbol of the nation to all visitors to the capital. The monument, a 45-meter-high tower, was dedicated in 1971 to remind future generations of the Shah."

But on this brilliant winter day there were indications as glaring as the sun's reflection bouncing off the snow-capped Alborz mountain range behind the city that the memory of the Shah would not be as he wished it. There were charges of corruption within his regime, repression by the Savak, his secret police, and a lack of respect for the strict traditions of Shiᶜism, the religion of more than 90 percent of his subjects. There were cries for political democratization and demands for greater respect for the country's constitution. Thus far, the Shah's police and Army had muted the opposition within Iran, but Iranian exiles in Europe and the United States were becoming increasingly strident. Only the month before, the smell of tear gas used to quell Iranian rioters had drifted across the south lawn of the White House as Jimmy Carter greeted the Shah. On that day, masked demonstrators had cried, "Death to the Shah!" In Teheran, the day before Carter's visit, a bomb had been placed at the door of the American Cultural Center. The day before that the freeway from the airport to the city had been declared off limits to the public.

I have traveled in twenty-three countries with five Presidents of the United States. Rarely have I seen, in dictatorships or democracies, security as heavy as that which I observed as our motorcade sped into Teheran. Armed soldiers stood at intervals of five yards on either side of the road. Soldiers and police manned all the overpasses, as well as the rooftops of apartments and houses. There seemed little doubt on this last day of 1977 that, despite the gathering signs of protest, Mohammed Reza Pahlavi, His Imperial Majesty the Shahanshah, now a graying but stately fifty-eight, was still very much in control.

That feeling was emphatically reinforced during the New Year's Eve banquet for President and Mrs. Carter.

Niyavaran Palace, a complex of three pavilions in a park, is in the city's northern suburbs. It had been constructed for a king of the Kajar dynasty one hundred years before and refurbished in the 1960s by the Shah and Empress Farah for use as a residence, office and reception. The banquet was held in the largest of the three pavilions. Its opulence stunned the senses. I had the feeling that a wing of the palace at Versailles had been transported to Teheran and then redone in Persian style. The rooms were heroically scaled, many with mirrored walls. Marble floors were covered with Persian rugs. Chairs of red velvet were threaded with strands of gold. The Shah, who had been raised by a French governess and spoke French perfectly, was an unabashed admirer of the French; to commemorate the 2500th anniversary of the Persian Empire, he had flown in 165 chefs gathered by Maxim's, as well as 25,000 bottles of vintage Bordeaux. The service was Ceralene Limoges china, the glasses Baccarat crystal.

The Shah greeted me warmly now. His grip was firm, his skin smooth. He smiled and turned to President Carter and said, "I read Mr. Salinger every week in *L'Express* and I learn so many things about what is going on in the United States."

I thanked the Shah for his graciousness, paid my respects to the President and Mrs. Carter and moved into the crowd of 120 persons, most of them high-ranking Iranians and foreign diplomats and their wives. The Iranians, richly dressed, seemed like the modern equivalent of the bewigged French men and women who had filled the halls of the Palais de Versailles in the days of Louis XIV, an illusion reinforced by the dozens of liveried waiters who passed among us, offering Dom Pérignon champagne. Although I knew almost no one in the room, I didn't feel as though I was among a crowd of strangers; many of the guests approached me to share some memory of John F. Kennedy and his thousand days in the White House.

After an interval, several towering doors opened and we walked into a dining room where six tables had been set perpendicular to the head table in the configuration of a rake. My companions at dinner were equally amiable Iranians, and one of them, Houshang Navahandi, the rector of the University of Teheran and a member of Iran's moderate opposition, promptly invited me to give a series of lectures on the role of the press in society.

It amused me that the menu was printed in French and Persian, neither of which the guest of honor could read. But the dinner itself needed no description. It began with Pearls of the Caspian, a special caviar reserved exclusively for the Shah. There followed kebabs, splendidly garnished, a Russian-style pilaf with diced partridge and salad. Soon the dining-room lights dimmed and dozens of waiters marched to the tables with ice cream aflame with cherry sauce. For those with any stamina left, there was a final course of fruit salad. Throughout the dinner, an orchestra serenaded us with compositions by Verdi, Chopin, Bernstein, Sandjari and Matesky.

And then it was time for the two leaders to exchange toasts—which, in the context of subsequent events, are freighted with ironies.

The Shah, as host, began:

"In our country, according to ancient tradition, the visit of the first guest in the new year is an omen for that year. And although the annual new year is celebrated with the advent of spring, nevertheless, since the distinguished guest tonight is such a person of good will and achievement, naturally we consider it as a most excellent omen."

The Shah extolled "distinctive qualities of the great American nation" that had always been "highly regarded by us," among them humanitarianism and liberty. And he thanked the United States for its "unforgettable" role during past Iranian crises, an allusion, perhaps, to his own return to power in 1953 with the help of the CIA.

And then it was Carter's turn to speak, and he did so in that same flat unexceptional manner that by now had become so familiar to millions of Americans. His words, however, were startling.

"Iran, because of the great leadership of the Shah, is an island of stability in one of the more troubled areas of the world. This is a great tribute to you, Your Majesty, and to your leadership and to the respect and the admiration and love which your people give you . . .

"As I drove through the beautiful streets of Teheran today with the Shah, we saw literally thousands of Iranian citizens standing beside the street with a friendly attitude, expressing their welcome to me. And I also saw hundreds, perhaps even thousands of American citizens who stood there welcoming their President in a nation which has taken them to heart and made them feel at home . . .

"The cause of human rights is one that also is shared deeply by our people and by the leaders of our two nations . . .

"We have no other nation on earth who is closer to us in planning for our mutual military security. We have no other nation with whom we have closer consultation on regional problems that concern us both. And there is no leader with whom I have a deeper sense of personal gratitude and personal friendship."

The moment Carter concluded his remarks, the Shah was on his feet. The guests rose with him and joined in the hearty applause. Then the Shah took the President's right hand in both of his and shook it vigorously. He was beaming; no foreign leader—certainly no American President—had ever hailed him so warmly.

But the American diplomats in the audience were dumbfounded by Carter's speech, and well they might be, because Jimmy Carter had campaigned for office on an unequivocal policy of human rights for all. Iran, by this point, had been condemned by Amnesty International for many specific acts of torture. If the President chose not to accept Amnesty International's evaluation, he knew, nonetheless, that his own country's diplomats had reported a widespread conviction among Iranians that torture was being routinely used to deal with opponents of the Shah.

I myself was astounded by the fulsomeness of Carter's remarks—but not by his support for the Shah. From the day the President had enunciated his human rights policy, I had felt that the time would come when it would conflict with the national interest. It had been my experience that whenever such a conflict occurs, it is the special policy that gives way, no matter how sincerely it was initiated. That phenomenon was never more evident than on the night of December 31, 1977, when Carter's human rights policy was confronted by the need of the United States to maintain a strong ally in the Middle East. That ally was Iran.

The importance of Iran to Western strategy is an undisputed fact. Thirty percent of U.S. oil imports come from the Persian Gulf. Western Europe derives sixty percent of its oil from the same area, Japan seventy percent. For the United States and its allies, an independent Iran is, in effect, a guarantor of oil supplies for their industries, and a protector of Western interests in the Middle East. An Iran dependent on or dominated by its next-door neighbor, the Soviet Union, would be a catastrophe for the West.

Beyond questions of strategy and security, there was the simple matter of business. Military expenditures aside, Iran was buying well over $2 billion worth of American goods each year, making that country one of America's ten leading overseas customers. The sale of U.S. nuclear technology to Iran was expected to increase the value of exports to Iran by as much as $12 billion during the next decade. Given the country's precarious balance of payments, no American President could afford to discount this aspect of Iran's importance.

One possible reason for Carter's effusiveness that evening in Teheran was the knowledge that the Shah felt less certain with Democratic Presidents than he did with Republicans. It was during the Republican Administration of Dwight D. Eisenhower that the Shah was brought back to power after he was deposed in 1953. The military buildup of Iran occurred during the Administration of Richard Nixon and after, when, between 1973 and 1978, some $20 billion worth of U.S.-made weapons went to Iran—nearly seventeen times the amount that had been sent in the previous twenty years. Democrats, contrarily, were usually suspicious of the Shah's infatuation with arms, and they were always pressing him to democratize his country, and asking questions about human rights.

Whatever Jimmy Carter's motives that evening, he had—for better or worse—thrown in with the Shah. The next hours, the last of 1977, seemed almost an orchestration of the new and sudden harmony. After dinner, we adjourned to a salon to enjoy the swirling movements of the Mahalli Dancers of Iran and the melodious voices of the National Choir. At some point, unseen by the other guests, the Shah led President Carter and King Hussein of Jordan to another room. It was the Shah's hope to act as a peacemaker in the Middle East. He had been working behind the scenes to resolve the differences between Jordan and Israel. It was he who had invited Hussein to the dinner, and he who had pressed for a meeting between the President and the king.

The three leaders reappeared just as the entertainment ended. We were taken then to still another room. Moments before midnight, dozens of waiters appeared, champagne was poured and glasses raised to toast the new year. The Shah kissed Mrs. Carter, and the President kissed the Shahbanou. As an orchestra struck up a fox-trot, the Shah swept Mrs. Carter into his arms. The President danced with the Shahbanou. Soon all of the guests were dancing. At 1:15 A.M., Rosalynn Carter walked up to the President and took him by the arm. Two minutes later, he was gone. But the Shah danced on.

It was the monarch's last state dinner—and his last official exercise in illusion.

The next morning, the Shah accompanied President Carter back to Mehrabad Airport, from where the President would depart for India. They drove through streets of Teheran that had been completely cordoned off by the Army. Unseen by the leaders, thousands of Iranian teenagers in the side streets were pelting the soldiers with rocks.

Within two weeks, antigovernment demonstrations would become so visible that no military force could hide them. Before the year was over, rioting would pulverize the nation.

On January 16, 1979, Mohammed Reza Pahlavi, Light of the Aryans, His Imperial Majesty the Shahanshah, became a man without a country, confused, bitter and sick. On November 4, 1979, he suffered a fate that, for a monarch who held himself above other men, may have been truly worse than death. For history records him from that day forward not as a king but as a pawn—whose single move set off a struggle that, for 444 days, would hold much of the world in thrall.

Although no one could conceive it at the outset, the seizure of the American Embassy and sixty-six of its American occupants by Iranian student militants on November 4, 1979, was destined to become the most trying and suspenseful and widely reported episode in the history of diplomacy. But what appeared on television and in the newspapers and magazines was only the visible portion of the story. There was another portion that went unreported during this entire time. It was the story of the secret negotiations to free the hostages—a tale of intrigue, double crosses, aliases, disguises, surreptitious messages, clandestine meetings and missed opportunities played out against an international panorama.

That is the story it was my good fortune to follow from its outset and disclose to the world on January 22, 1981, two days after the hostages were released, in a special three-hour broadcast on ABC. But even a broadcast of that length could only hint at the rich drama inherent in the narrative. That story, amplified substantially by information I have subsequently acquired, is the one I have attempted to tell in this book.

chapter one

Into the Trap

THE HOUSE IN CUERNAVACA, A LANGUID AND FRAGRANT COMMUNITY sixty miles southwest of Mexico City, was known as the Villa of Roses. Since the death of its owner, an architect, four years before, it had remained unoccupied, its rooms stripped and shuttered and collecting must, its grounds overgrown. But the scale of the house was ample, and the promise of the gardens substantial. There were many flower beds and terraces, and there was a swimming pool as well. Most impressive of all was the location. The Villa of Roses stood at the end of a cul-de-sac, and backed onto a river. For good measure, it was enclosed by a high wall. No stranger could come near the villa without being observed. To Robert Armao, the isolation of the villa was the all-important factor, and he rented it on sight. He knew it was far from perfect, but these days everything was relative.

Before the day was over, Armao, a tall, slender, dark-haired man in his early thirties with a brisk manner and a tendency to speak in bursts, had recruited two dozen strangers—most of them Americans from the city's sizable colony of expatriates—and, with their help, collected the beds and bedding and kitchen utensils he would need for his client and the client's family. Some of the strangers loaned furniture they were using themselves. One dotted the house with antiques. Another gave up his own desk. A third even loaned her servants. In two days, the house was ready for occupancy, and Armao signaled his client to come along.

Armao's client was the Shah of Iran. Since early January, when the

Shah was preparing to fly into exile, no move he had made had been without the counsel of Armao. It was, perhaps, the most curious aspect of an opulently bizarre odyssey, because Armao was an American, not an Iranian, and nothing in his previous life had prepared him to serve anyone as shepherd, let alone a deposed monarch with a presumable price on his head.

Armao was a lawyer by training who had drifted into public relations consulting, with a specialty in government and politics. His forte was labor law, and it was as an adviser on labor relations that he had served Nelson Rockefeller—for whom he had begun to work as an apprentice while still in his teens—when Rockefeller was governor of New York, and, later, Vice-President of the United States. His proximity to Rockefeller had, in turn, put Armao in touch with the problems of the Shah, because the former Vice-President and the Iranian leader were friends of long standing, and the Shah frequently called on Rockefeller for advice. One day, as Armao was ushering several labor leaders into Rockefeller's office to discuss a dispute, Rockefeller informed him that he had just finished talking by telephone with the Shah, who was having some labor problems of his own. Skilled workers were at such a premium in Iran that those employed in the construction of a new building would be hired away by another firm before the first building was finished. In August 1978 the Shah had telephoned Rockefeller to ask for advice on how to handle an outbreak of violence in his country. But beyond attempting to bolster the Shah's sagging morale, Rockefeller could not be very helpful.

Early in November, Armao, who operated out of New York City, received a telephone call from Princess Ashraf, the Shah's twin sister and the head of Iran's delegation to the United Nations. For years, the princess, a tough and spirited woman totally dedicated to her brother, had served him unflaggingly as confidante and adviser. Now she asked Armao to come to her Manhattan townhouse, which he did. "The people never understood what my brother was trying to do for his country," she complained bitterly, slipping unconsciously into the past tense. She told Armao that a well-financed propaganda campaign, involving, she said, hundreds of millions of dollars, had been organized in Paris by Iranian exiles, who were smuggling cassettes into Iran containing denunciations of the Shah by the Ayatollah Ruhollah Khomeini, an exiled religious leader and, for many years, an implacable foe of the Shah. Princess Ashraf asked Armao if he could launch a public relations counterattack, spreading the word throughout Iran about what the Shah had done for his people.

"It's rather late in the game for that," Armao said regretfully. "We'd have to play catch-up ball."

Nonetheless, Armao reported his conversation with the princess to Rockefeller, and the former Vice-President, after conferring with Henry Kissinger, Secretary of State under Presidents Nixon and Ford and a friend of the Shah as well, asked Armao to go to Iran to see whether he could counsel the Shah on how to counteract the propaganda attacks against him.

But by the time Armao arrived in Teheran in early January, the situation had deteriorated so greatly that the Shah had determined to leave the country. His departure was advertised as a vacation for a much-needed rest, but everyone knew that he was going into exile.

His decision to leave was about all that the Shah could manage. He seemed to be incapable of marshaling any effort to extricate himself. Nor were the members of his entourage who were to accompany him into exile, and who were supposedly to care for the monarch, able to muster themselves to prepare the Shah's departure, let alone their own. Many in the Shah's party were so distraught by the turn of events that they needed help themselves.

It was at this point that Armao took over, for lack of a practical alternative. He quickly organized a team to take charge of day-to-day affairs, as well as the logistics and security that would be involved in the Shah's exile. The Shah, who could well understand the bewilderment and helplessness of his staff, and who trusted no other Iranians by this point, welcomed the American, and quickly came to lean on him.

On January 16, 1979, the Shah and his party flew to Egypt. Seven days later they moved to Morocco, where they would remain for two months. Meanwhile, Princess Ashraf, operating out of her townhouse, worked diligently to find a permanent exile for her brother. Late in March, with the help of David Rockefeller, she found one: the Bahamas. She immediately contacted Armao and asked him to fly there to make arrangements with the Foreign Ministry.

The Bahamian Government had agreed to let the Shah in, but there remained the sizable question of where he and his party would live. Because of the approaching Easter vacation, space was at a premium. The Shah's party needed not one room but forty. The foreign ministry suggested that the Shah's party take up residence at Resorts International on Paradise Island. Armao wasn't happy with the choice because of the security problems it imposed, and he was secretly relieved when the resort could turn up no more than three rooms. But then the resort management proposed that the Shah might lease the house of the chairman of the board of Resorts International, James M. Crosby. The house had never been rented before, but it was on the ocean, it had three rooms and a swimming pool. A call to Crosby confirmed the rental, at $1000 a day, which, considering that it was high season in the Bahamas, Armao thought was fair. But when he went down to the beach to inspect the house, he could not disguise his disappointment. It was not simply that the house was much too small, it was that the security would be impossible. Tourists on the beach could look right up into the terrace.

But Armao was without an alternative, and when he agreed to take the house, the hotel managed to find a few nearby dwellings for the Shah's children, as well as rooms for his staff, by dispossessing a number of paying guests.

From the moment the Shah arrived at his Bahamas beachhouse, he found himself staring into the lenses of several hundred tourists' cameras each time he stepped out for a walk. Had an assassin been among the tourists, the Shah would have been defenseless.

The Shah's vulnerability, as well as his discomfort, soon became academic; his application for an extension of his tourist visa was rejected by the Bahamian Government, due, he was certain, to pressure from the government of Great Britain. He left the island on June 10, 1979.

After the Bahamas, the house in Cuernavaca seemed like a godsend. When the Shah arrived, he went on a tour of the house with Armao and then said with a sigh, "At least we can live again."

The Shah's invitation to Mexico was, in part, a consequence of a friendship he had developed with President José López Portillo during a visit in 1975, when López Portillo was Mexico's Finance Minister. Now, in Cuernavaca, the Shah could relax for the first time in months. There were stories in the newspapers that the imperial family was under heavy, around-the-clock police protection, particularly after the Ayatollah Sadegh Khalkhali made it known that he had sent a special commando to Mexico with instructions to "shoot the demon." But only a few policemen in civilian clothes reinforced the Shah's own security guards at the Villa of Roses, and only one police car followed him when he drove his car to the center of town.

Through the summer, the Shah received numbers of visitors, including David Rockefeller, Henry Kissinger and Richard Nixon, whose visit, he said, particularly cheered him. In addition, he busied himself with his memoirs, which he dictated each day. He finished on September 16. Outwardly, he seemed calm and stately. He read copiously, particularly biographies of great historical figures, and one Saturday he even played tennis, first singles, then doubles. That evening, as usual, he watched a film on a videocassette. The next day he went to an outdoor luncheon at the police club as the guest of Cuernavaca's chief of police. His entire entourage accompanied him. When the invitation was first tendered, the Shah had wanted to turn it down. But then he thought better of it, speculating that his refusal might offend some of the very people who had made his stay in Cuernavaca possible. At the party, a small orchestra played a number of Iranian songs, creating amused speculation among the Iranian guests as to where they had obtained the music. Sitting with the policemen and their wives, the Shah found chitchat difficult, but did his best to be charming. At the end of the meal, he excused himself, saying that he did not feel well.

That evening, a guest of the Shah's suggested that the conversation at the luncheon must have worn him out. "No," the Shah replied, "they were very kind people. I really felt sick. I'm ill, you know."

In fact, the Shah had been ill for a very long time. For seven years prior to his flight into exile, he had been under the care of two French cancer specialists, Jean Bernard and Georges Flandrin of the Hôpital St. Louis in Paris. They had diagnosed his illness as a mild form of lymph cancer, but their diagnosis was kept so guarded that not even the Shah's most intimate friends were aware of the problem. Remarkably, the secret seemed to have been kept from the various foreign intelligence services as well, even though two readily identifiable French cancer specialists made many trips to Teheran to see the Shah, in full public view.

In March 1979 Dr. Flandrin had traveled to the Bahamas to see the Shah. A biopsy by vacuum revealed lymphoma of the white blood cells, for which he was given three chemotherapy treatments.

In July, about a month after his arrival in Mexico, the Shah was examined by several Mexican doctors. They diagnosed a new condition, malaria, a disease he had once had as a child. When the Shah's condition failed to improve after two months of treatments by the Mexican doctors, Armao got in touch with Benjamin H. Kean, a New York City physician and specialist in tropical diseases.

Kean is a tall, robust man with white hair and a perpetual suntan who dresses a somewhat flamboyant personality in three-piece suits. While he can play the role of the conservative Manhattan physician, his students know him as a cigar-chomping raconteur with a dossier of anecdotes about some of his more illustrious cases.

Kean had previously treated the Shah's twin sister, Princess Ashraf, as well as Armao himself, after he had taken ill on one of his trips to Mexico. When Armao learned from Mark Morse, a member of his staff whom he had posted to Cuernavaca, that the Shah's illness had been diagnosed as malaria, he immediately thought of Kean. But rather than call the doctor himself, he went through Joseph Reed, executive assistant to David Rockefeller. Kean was the Reeds' family doctor. Armao wanted to have Kean's visit seem unofficial and, if possible, pass unnoticed as well. He felt it would not do for an American physician to challenge the diagnosis of the Mexican doctors so long as the Shah was, in effect, a guest of Mexico.

But almost from the moment he examined the Shah in Cuernavaca, Kean was certain that the monarch had not contracted malaria. The Mexican doctors were giving the Shah the classical treatment for malaria, but he wasn't getting better; had malaria been the problem, the Shah would have responded to the treatment. It had to be something else. The Shah's complexion was yellow; he was suffering abdominal pains, chills and high fevers, was frequently nauseous and had begun to lose weight. Kean could see that the Shah was jaundiced.

To confirm his analysis, Kean asked the Mexican doctors to let him look at the slides on which they had based their diagnosis. His appraisal of the slides only reinforced his suspicions. But was the jaundice obstructive or non-obstructive? An example of non-obstructive jaundice is hepatitis, a definite possibility because one of the men guarding the Shah had contracted that disease. Obstructive jaundice can occur when something—perhaps gallstones, perhaps a tumor—is blocking the bile duct. Kean suspected obstructive jaundice, and so reported to the Shah at midnight, during their second meeting. The two men decided to sleep on the problem posed by the doctor's evaluation.

When they met the next morning, Kean told the Shah that he wanted to make some blood tests that could help him sharpen his diagnosis. There were two hospitals in Mexico City whose laboratories he trusted, Children's Hospital and Social Security Hospital, the doctor said, and he would send samples to each of them. For good measure, he would take a third sample back to New York.

But the Shah refused to let Kean take any blood. He explained that he was already receiving large doses of cortisone, prescribed by French doctors. He preferred to continue with that treatment.

Kean was piqued and perplexed. He considered the use of cortisone in the Shah's case dangerous, perhaps fatal. He could not understand the Shah's refusal to let him take blood. Whatever the Shah's reason, it was clear to Kean that he was not going to be in charge of the case. He suggested to the Shah that he send for his French doctors and let them take over. Then he went back to New York.

Three weeks after Kean's visit, Robert Armao flew to Mexico to meet with his client, whom he had not seen in more than a month. Armao had been told that the Shah had not been feeling well, but nothing had prepared him for the sight he encountered when he went to the Shah's bedroom. The Shah was lying in bed. It appeared to Armao that he had lost twenty pounds. His face was black. He complained of fierce abdominal pains and nausea, especially during the night, and he said that for several weeks he had scarcely been able to eat. When Armao asked the Shah what he thought the problem was, the Shah replied, "Maybe malaria. Maybe jaundice."

A few minutes later, Armao emerged from the bedroom. The first person he saw in the hall was Mark Morse, his man in Cuernavaca. "What the hell's going on here?" Armao demanded. "He looks like he's dying."

The first thing Robert Armao did after seeing the Shah that October day was to get in touch with Benjamin Kean in New York and ask him to return to Cuernavaca. "They haven't leveled with us," the public relations man said. When Armao told Kean the names of the two French doctors treating the Shah, Kean was sure that he was right. He knew the work of Professors Bernard and Flandrin—they were specialists in lymph cancer—and the mention of their names was like the hoisting of a flag.

By the time Kean arrived in Cuernavaca a few days later, Armao had finally learned the truth, and so informed the doctor at a meeting at his home, two hundred yards from the villa. The Shah had had cancer for many years; it had been kept under control for all that time, but was now in relapse.

When Kean and Armao arrived at the Shah's residence, Dr. Flandrin was there. He handed Kean a thirty-page document detailing the course of the Shah's disease during the previous seven years. For good measure, the French doctor summarized its contents orally. The Shah, he said, had spleen and blood cancer. But the disease had until now been controlled with one pill a day. Whether the disease had spread or not the physicians could not be certain, because the Shah had refused to permit them to make a definitive diagnosis. If he had, they would surely have operated by now to remove his spleen. For six years, all had gone well. Then the Shah developed a tumor in his neck. Again, the Shah would not permit exhaustive tests on the tumor, so the doctors had started Mopp therapy (an acronym for four different cancer chemotherapeutic agents). The first four treatments had worked perfectly; the Shah's spleen had reduced in size, and the tumor had almost disappeared. Now, Flandrin said, the treatment was no longer working; the spleen had enlarged and the tumor had returned.

Kean and Flandrin were joined by the Mexican doctors, and all of them examined the Shah anew. Then Kean confronted the monarch with the results: he had five serious medical problems, all of them potentially fatal. One was surely jaundice, the American said, for which the Shah would have been admitted to a U.S. hospital within a matter of hours. "When you have obstructive jaundice, you operate in forty-eight hours," the doctor said. "Here you've been in this condition for seven weeks." Kean, now clearly in charge, told the Shah that his obstructive jaundice—if that, indeed, proved to be the problem, as he was all but positive it was—had to be treated first, before anything could be done about the Shah's spleen or the tumor in his neck or his blood condition. They discussed a number of alternatives for the surgery, including Mexico and the United States. The American favored the United States; he told the Shah that there were at least six different centers in the United States where the right kind of medical team could be assembled to treat him.

But the Shah did not want to go to the United States. "I've never gone where I'm not welcome," he said flatly. By that point, he had good reason to believe that he wasn't.

When the Shah had left Iran nine months before, it was, he thought, with a firm invitation from the U. S. Government to enter the United States. The government had arranged with Walter H. Annenberg, the publisher and former ambassador to England during the Administration of Richard Nixon, to lend his home, an estate called Sunnylands in Rancho Mirage, California, to the Shah for several months. For the exiled monarch, the home would have been ideal. It was in the desert, and on a piece of land so vast that it even contained a private golf course. And, for good measure, the house and its grounds were enclosed by a wall. The Shah wanted to accept the invitation, but within days after he had left Iran, he began to suspect that the United States really didn't want him to come. The idea was first conveyed to him in Egypt a few days after his arrival by Ardeshir Zahedi, Iran's ambassador to the United States. There had been demonstrations linked to the announcement of his pending admission to the country—among other things his mother's house in Beverly Hills had been stoned—and the Administration was getting worried, Zahedi informed the Shah. That concern may have been further conveyed to the Shah when he arrived in Morocco in late January and met with General Vernon Walters, the retired former deputy director of the CIA.

By January 26, just ten days after he had fled Iran with a sack of his nation's soil, a clear sign to his followers that he was never going to return, the Shah had determined to seek sanctuary elsewhere than in the United States—or so, at least, he privately informed me. These were the golden days of his exile; he had lived for a week in the palace of the ancient kings of Egypt on the upper Nile in Luxor; now he was in residence in the palace of the king of Morocco, just outside the desert capital of Marrakesh. That day, the Shah had agreed to have his picture taken by the press, my own ABC crew among them. But no microphones were permitted, and there were to be no questions from reporters. After the photo session had ended, the press was invited over to a table for a glass of orange juice, but the Shah remained standing near a cluster of trees, talking to his advisers. Suddenly, seeing me, he beckoned for me to come over. As I approached, I was struck by how drastically his appearance had changed in the year since our meeting in Iran. His face was thin and sallow, and his expression suggested the existence of a fierce struggle within him, as though the regal person he believed himself to be could not accept the ordinary mortal he had become.

We made small talk for a few minutes. And then I asked him, in as offhand a way as I could, whether he had made any definite plans. For just a moment, the Shah seemed to struggle. Then he said abruptly, "I'm not going to the United States. I'll stay here for a while."

Before two months had passed, the Shah would change his mind once again, principally because demonstrations against him in Moroccan universities had compelled his host, King Hassan, to ask him politely to find another sanctuary. But when the Shah finally asked point-blank if he could go to the United States, the U. S. Government balked. Conditions in Iran were still uncertain, U. S. Ambassador

Richard B. Parker told him, and the United States was concerned about what might happen to its people in Iran if the Shah were admitted to the United States. The embassy was particularly vulnerable as it was being guarded by three different groups of revolutionary guards, all of them antagonistic. Moreover, Parker told the Shah, there could be legal complications for him. While he enjoyed diplomatic immunity from any actions undertaken while he was chief of state, he would not be immune from lawsuits filed subsequent to his departure from Iran. Finally, Parker said, there was the ever-present problem of demonstrations and harassment. For all these reasons, the United States now felt that it would no longer be "convenient" for the Shah to come to the United States.

Although the Shah himself may have suspended direct efforts at that point to gain admission to the United States, others, notably his sister, Princess Ashraf, pursued the cause in his stead. On August 10, 1979, she sent an impassioned letter to President Carter.

"I am taking what may appear to be a great liberty in writing directly to you in regard to the increased difficulty and the traumatic situation in which my brother, his wife and their son find themselves in their search for a relatively stable place of residence, a place where they can find some continuity in their family life. Since his exile, I know that it has always been his desire to find a suitable residence in the United States where he could be with his family and where appropriate arrangements could be made for the much needed education of his children . . . There is another factor, as his sister, which is becoming of increased concern to me. This is the quite noticeable impairment of his health in Mexico . . . One of the best-known traditions of the United States throughout the world has been its record of hospitality and refuge to those who are forced to leave their own countries for political reasons . . . It will not be long before the problems of new plans for moving will be upon him and I firmly believe the added strains are bound to result in further inroads in his health . . . I believe that at one time your government was concerned over the possible harm to American citizens in Iran which might result from his being given refuge here. I do not believe that reasonable cause for this continues to exist. But I cannot believe that means could not be taken by your country to assume the essential safety of the United States citizens in Iran, rather than to submit to any such type of blackmail."

alistic government in Iran took over the country's sizable oil enterprise, which until then had been owned jointly by British and Iranian interests. It was not simply the nationalization of the Iranian oil fields that disturbed foreign companies with investments in the Middle East, the Rockefellers' companies among them. It was the precedent Iran had set. If the seizure were to go unchallenged, other countries in the Middle East might also nationalize their companies.

It is generally conceded that the plot to oust the nationalist Premier, Mohammed Mossadegh, and return power to the Shah, who had prudently left the country in 1953, was masterminded—with an assist from British intelligence—by the CIA, which then, as now, had difficulty in distinguishing between the nationalization of a country's productive resources and a Communist takeover. While the oil companies themselves gave no marching orders, it is well known that they exerted all the pressure they could to force the United States to act.

From the moment the Shah regained power, his business connection with the Rockefellers began to grow, until it finally became all-embracing. Every official deal that the Shah made, whether it involved bank loans or acquisitions, the country or his own Pahlavi Foundation, was handled for him by David Rockefeller's Chase Manhattan Bank.

There was yet another connection to the Rockefeller family, albeit an indirect one, that was now being brought to bear, and that was the pressure by Henry Kissinger, the former Secretary of State, to admit the Shah to the United States. Kissinger, who is presently the chairman of the advisory committee of the Chase Manhattan Bank, was associated with the Rockefellers long before he went into government, and when he did, it was because of Nelson Rockefeller's recommendation to Richard Nixon that Nixon appoint Kissinger as his National Security Adviser.

In a sense, it was Kissinger who made the Shah the world figure he became. Kissinger believed that for the United States and its allies the Middle East was the most dangerous zone in the world. Soviet intervention in the Middle East, he felt, would cut off supplies of oil to the West. To prevent any possibility of such a cutoff, it behooved the West to have a well-armed policeman in the Middle East. It was during the Nixon administration, and because of the prodding of Kissinger, that the United States turned Iran into a surrogate American power.

But the idea that direct intervention by Rockefeller and Kissinger caused the Carter administration to admit the Shah does not stand inspection. The pressure both men attempted to exert was, if anything, irksome and counterproductive. It was certainly not decisive. Whatever influence they possessed derived from their membership in the country's "old boy network," that small group of men at the highest levels whose judgments are taken into account in any important decision. Rockefeller, for example, is the founder of the Trilateral Commission, a young but influential group formed several years ago to study the relationships between the United States, Europe and Japan. In addition to Rockefeller and Kissinger, its members include Zbigniew Brzezinski, Carter's National Security Adviser, Harold Brown, Carter's Secretary of Defense, and Carter himself.

Even that connection, however, was of small account when the decision to admit the Shah was finally taken. That matter had been under study ever since the Shah had taken flight.

Although the United States had told the Shah in March 1979 that it would not be "convenient" for him to come to the United States from Morocco, it assured him at the same time that it would help him find a place somewhere else. That proved to be a difficult undertaking, for no country, by that point, was willing to let him in. The invitation to the Bahamas came about not only through the efforts of the Shah's sister, Princess Ashraf, and David Rockefeller, but also through the intervention of the United States. When the Shah could no longer stay in the Bahamas, he turned once again to the United States; once again, the United States said it would not be "convenient." The subsequent invitation from Mexico also came about, in part, because of the urging of the United States.

Always in the background, however, was the notion that, for lack of any alternative, the Shah might eventually have to be admitted to the United States. To that end, on July 25, 1979, Secretary of State Cyrus Vance sent the following top-secret cable to Bruce Laingen, the American chargé d'affaires in Teheran, and the ranking U.S. diplomat in Iran since the recall of Ambassador William H. Sullivan a few weeks before.

CHEROKEE, LITERALLY EYES ONLY FOR CHARGE LAINGEN SUBJECT: SHAH'S DESIRE TO RESIDE IN THE U.S.

1. WE ARE AGAIN CONSIDERING HOW TO RESPOND TO THE SHAH'S CONTINUING QUERY TO US THROUGH VARIOUS CHANNELS REGARDING ESTABLISHING RESIDENCE FOR HIMSELF, THE SHAHBANOU, AND HIS

FAMILY IN THE U.S. (HE CAN REMAIN IN MEXICO AT LEAST THROUGH
OCTOBER.) I WOULD LIKE TO HAVE YOUR PERSONAL AND PRIVATE
EVALUATION OF THE EFFECT OF SUCH A MOVE ON THE SAFETY OF
AMERICANS IN IRAN (ESPECIALLY THE OFFICIAL AMERICANS IN THE
COMPOUND) AS WELL AS ON OUR RELATIONS WITH THE GOVERNMENT
OF IRAN.

2. WOULD YOUR ANSWER TO THE QUESTION POSED IN PARA 1 BE DIF-
FERENT IF (A) THE SHAH RENOUNCED HIS CLAIM AND THAT OF HIS
HEIRS TO THE THRONE, OR (B) THAT HE AGREED TO FORSWEAR POLITI-
CAL ACTIVITY OF ANY SORT AND THAT THIS BE CONFIRMED PUBLICLY.

3. WE CLEARLY UNDERSTAND THAT THE KEY TO MINIMIZING THE
IMPACT OF THE SHAH'S ADMISSION WOULD BE IN BAZARGAN AND THE
GOVERNMENT'S WILLINGNESS AND ABILITY IN SUCH A SITUATION TO
CONTROL AND COMMAND THE SECURITY FORCES GUARDING OUR PEO-
PLE AND TO MINIMIZE ANY HOSTILE PUBLIC REACTION AGAINST OUR
PEOPLE OR OUR RELATIONS.

SINCE THIS QUESTION IS BEING VERY CLOSELY HELD IN WASHINGTON, I
WOULD APPRECIATE YOUR NOT SHARING THIS MESSAGE WITH ANYONE
ELSE ON YOUR STAFF. PLEASE SEND YOUR REPLY NODIS/CHEROKEE,
FOR THE SECRETARY. WITH BEST REGARDS.

VANCE

Laingen's precise reply is not known, but that it advanced the
Shah's eventual admission to the United States a notch is indicated by
a scenario drafted on August 1, 1979, by Henry Precht, head of the
Iranian desk at the State Department.

Labeled "Secret/Sensitive," the scenario envisaged a postponement
of any action until the new Iranian Government had consolidated its
position, which Precht estimated would occur by the end of 1979.
Then, he wrote:

"we should inform the new government that we wish to clear our decks
of old issues on the agenda. One of these old issues will be the status
of the Shah. We could inform the government that we have resisted intense pressure to allow him to come to the U.S. because we did not
wish to complicate the PGOI's [People's Government of Iran] problems or our efforts to construct a new relationship. Now with the new
government firmly established and accepted, it seems appropriate to

admit the Shah to the U.S. The new government may not like it, but it
is best to get the issue out of the way. This discussion with the new
GOI [Government of Iran] should take place after it is in place some
2–3 weeks and some few days before the Shah would come here."

At the end of his memorandum, Precht dealt with the question of
protection for the American Embassy, in the event the Shah were admitted to the United States. He had good reason to be concerned; only
the previous February, the embassy had been occupied by 150 guerrillas wearing Iranian Army and Air Force uniforms and armed with
military-issue rifles. An unarmed Iranian employee of the embassy had
been shot and killed, a Marine had been kidnapped and embassy personnel, including Ambassador Sullivan, had been taken hostage. Only
skillful negotiating on the part of the Iranian Government had resolved the issue without further bloodshed.

"We have the impression that the threat to the U. S. Embassy personnel is less now than it was in the spring. Presumably the threat will
diminish somewhat further by the end of this year. Nevertheless, the
danger of hostages being taken in Iran will persist.
"We should make no move towards admitting the Shah until we
have obtained and tested a new and substantially more effective guard
force for the embassy. Secondly, when the decision is made to admit
the Shah, we should quietly assign additional American security guards
to the embassy to provide protection for key personnel until the danger
period is considered over."

That memorandum could not have been an easy one for Precht to
write. His own experience as a diplomat in Iran from 1972 to 1976
had convinced him that the Shah's government had not only been cor-
rupt but had used repressive measures, torture included, against its political opponents.
In the hierarchy of the State Department, Precht, a tall, clean-
shaven man in his late forties with salt and pepper hair, was not a
major figure. But in the absence of most of his superiors, who were
preoccupied with Camp David and SALT negotiations, he had found
himself, willy-nilly, the virtual overlord of American policy in Iran. It
is not often that a career foreign service officer at his level becomes so
well known to the White House, but by the end of 1978, when the
Pahlavi dynasty was crumbling, Precht had become very well known

indeed. His interpretation of what was going on in Iran did not square at all with the one held by the White House and, in particular, by the President's National Security Adviser, Zbigniew Brzezinski. There were times when the Brzezinski faction accused Precht of hating the Shah. Precht did hold definite ideas, and he was sometimes abrupt and emotional in the way he conveyed them, but his emotion in those days did not stem from any feeling for or against the Shah; it came from his frustration at being unable to make anyone see what, in his eyes, was really going on in Iran, how deep-rooted the emotions of the Iranians were and how those emotions were gathering force and what all this portended for the Shah.

Whatever residues of feeling about the Shah still existed in Precht, he had a professional responsibility to acquit and he prided himself on his ability, as a career foreign service officer, to rise above his emotions in the exercise of his duties. So he had written the memo outlining a possible scenario for the admission of the Shah to the United States.

But Precht's memo had been written with the conviction that no action would be taken until after the new year; it had not envisaged the precipitous march of events. When the matter of admitting the Shah came to a head, no appreciable action had yet been taken on his recommendations.

Once the State Department had confirmed to its satisfaction that the Shah was, indeed, gravely ill and that the proper medical care could not be organized in Mexico, Secretary of State Vance recommended to President Carter that the Shah be admitted to the United States. Vance stressed that admittance should be for the sake of medical treatment and not be construed as a permit to take up residence.

The decision to admit the Shah was made October 19, 1979, at Carter's weekly Friday morning foreign policy breakfast. The sense of the meeting was that, yes, there was a risk involved, but they owed the Shah this consideration because they had treated him so shabbily in the past months when he had tried to enter the United States and they had passed the word that he wasn't really welcome.

Carter himself felt that the United States should do something in the Shah's behalf. His reluctance was keyed to his fear that something might happen to the U. S. Embassy in Teheran. Before making his decision, he polled the regulars at the breakfast: Vice-President Walter Mondale, Vance, National Security Adviser Zbigniew Brzezinski, Secretary of Defense Harold Brown, and Hamilton Jordan, White House chief of staff. The recommendation was unanimous: let the Shah enter the United States.

Carter went along. Then he said, "What are you guys going to recommend that we do when they take our embassy and hold our people hostage?"

Although the decision had now been taken, it was not immediately made known. Before the actual permission was given, the Administration wanted to make certain about the very concerns expressed in Precht's memo. Precht, who was in Iran on an inspection trip, was immediately instructed, along with chargé d'affaires Bruce Laingen, to inform the Iranian Government of the likelihood of the Shah's imminent arrival in New York on humanitarian grounds. The Americans asked for help in protecting the embassy in the event of any problems. Mehdi Bazargan, the Prime Minister under the new revolutionary government, and Ibrahim Yazdi, the Foreign Minister and adviser to the Ayatollah Khomeini, were clearly not happy with the news. They requested that Iranian doctors be permitted to examine the Shah, in order to certify his illness. Precht and Laingen told them that this would not be possible. Then the Iranians told the Americans that there probably would be problems, but nothing they couldn't handle.

Great stock was put in Yazdi's assurances in particular. He had lived in the United States for a number of years, and he still held an American passport even though he was now the Foreign Minister of Iran. Whether his past associations with the United States had been a factor or not, it was Yazdi who had successfully negotiated with the armed Iranian terrorists the previous February and gained the hostages' freedom.

A final consideration for the Americans in believing that the Iranians would be responsible for the security of the compound was that there were regular contingents of police on duty now, not just revolutionary guards.

Once the Shah had received permission to enter the United States, he wanted to leave at once, but he was instructed to wait for twenty-four hours. When Kean, who had made arrangements at New York Hospital to receive the Shah, asked for an explanation, he was told that the government had ordered Marine reinforcements posted from Frankfurt, Germany, to half a dozen American embassies, and needed an extra day to get them in place.

The Shah and his party finally left Mexico on Monday, October 22, aboard a chartered jet. They were to fly to Fort Lauderdale on Florida's Gold Coast, where immigration formalities could be accomplished discreetly, and then on to La Guardia Airport in New York. But by the time the plane reached Fort Lauderdale, it was twilight, and the pilot landed at the city airport instead of the private airfield where he had been expected. Officials who had been awaiting the Shah at the smaller field needed an hour to get to the city airport. In the interim, the only government official to greet the Shah's plane was an agricultural inspector who wanted to know whether there were plants aboard or whether the crew planned to dump any garbage.

Two hours after it landed, the plane took off again for New York. It arrived a little before midnight, and taxied to a remote part of the airport, where a small army of New York City police had been assembled. The story of the Shah's flight to the United States had been leaked to the press in Mexico, and photographers had recorded his departure. But there were no TV cameras at the airport to cover his arrival, for which he expressed his gratitude. By this point, he was exhausted and feverish. As soon as he arrived at the hospital, he was taken to a two-room suite on the seventeenth floor. He recognized it at once. He had occupied the suite in 1949 when he checked in for a routine medical examination during a trip to see President Harry S. Truman.

On October 23, some thirty thousand infuriated Iranians marched past the American Embassy in Teheran, screaming and waving their fists. Three days later, five Islamic students at the Teheran Polytechnical College, who had been among the demonstrators, met to discuss what they might do in response to the admission of the Shah to the United States. All five were members of the Society of Islamic Students, an organization that was usually behind any concerted student action. Since the Shah's departure nine months earlier, such action had been considerable, because in that time the students had become the militant acolytes of the violent society that had coalesced around the Ayatollah Ruhollah Khomeini, who had returned to Iran on February 1 to passionate outpourings of joy by the multitude, following a fifteen-year exile.

That day, the students decided to organize a demonstration for November 4 to protest the latest obstacle in returning the Shah to Iran to stand trial on charges that he had stolen money from the country and tortured his political opposition. They chose November 4 because it would be the first anniversary of an invasion of the campus of Teheran University by Iranian soldiers, who killed several students in the process.

To dramatize their cause, the students decided, they would make the most dramatic gesture possible. They would seize the American Embassy.

Approximately half of the persons admitted to New York Hospital for treatment are private patients. Five floors, the thirteenth through the seventeenth, are reserved for them. The most expensive facility is the two-room suite occupied by the Shah, who, in addition to the suite, took over several additional rooms for his entourage. The hallway leading to the rooms was blocked off and put under permanent guard, and only those with the highest clearance were admitted.

Security around the hospital was tight as well. Police patrols were posted at each entrance to the hospital twenty-four hours a day. Normally the hospital's regular security guards make only a halfhearted check of the ID cards of staff entering the hospital, but that procedure tightened up the moment the Shah arrived. And because of a number of telephoned threats, all packages and parcels were examined before their bearers could bring them into the hospital, no matter how long they had been employed there.

The hospital's staff doctors were more annoyed than outraged by the Shah's presence. Some of them felt that he should not be treated there; most thought that he was seriously ill and considered it a medical responsibility to respond. But a number of doctors voiced the opinion that after the Shah had been treated and cured he should be sent back to Iran to stand trial. On the other hand, a few of the doctors wondered if a "nice" donation might not result from the Shah's stay. The Shah had, in fact, once made a $1 million donation to the Memorial Sloan-Kettering Cancer Center, where New York Hospital's cancer patients have their radiotherapy, after the institute's director and another oncologist had gone to Teheran to treat the Shah's mother.

The morning after the Shah's arrival, he was given a thorough examination and a series of tests, which confirmed Benjamin Kean's diagnosis of obstructive jaundice, which, the doctor now knew, was caused not by a tumor but by gallstones. Kean was all for removing the Shah's gallbladder, stones and spleen during the same operation, but the surgeons who would be operating on the Shah told him that would be too dangerous. The Shah still had a fever and chills; if the spleen were removed, that would leave a dead space in his body susceptible to infection. So the doctors agreed that they should do the gallstone operation, and save the spleen operation for later.

The next morning, the Shah's gallbladder was removed.

The Iranian students who had decided to attempt a seizure of the American Embassy had enlisted several hundred fellow students for the effort, but they had not identified their objective. All that they had announced was that there was to be a demonstration against the admission of the Shah to the United States. A secondary objective of the organizers by this time was to embarrass the government of Prime Minister Mehdi Bazargan, who, along with Ibrahim Yazdi, the Foreign Minister, had committed treason, in the militants' eyes, by meeting with Zbigniew Brzezinski, President Carter's National Security Adviser, in Algeria on November 1 while attending anniversary celebrations for Algerian independence.

The one person to whom the student organizers had disclosed their objective was their spiritual mentor, the Hojatolislam Moussavi Khoeiny, who gave them his blessing. Only when the student battalion had been assembled on Sunday morning was the battle plan revealed.

All of the students selected for the demonstration had been trained in the use of pistols and automatic weapons. There were only ten pistols among them, but they were certain that they would find plenty of arms once they were inside the embassy compound.

The group assembled a block east of the embassy, near Roosevelt Avenue, on a drizzly Sunday morning. At 10:30 A.M. they marched east, along Taleghani Avenue, toward the embassy gates, the young women among them in front. The women marched past the gates, then suddenly wheeled about and faced the embassy. Instantly, several of the most agile young men raced to the gates and scaled them. Four armed policemen watched them for a moment, dumbfounded, then fled without firing so much as a warning shot; they had been told, in any case, not to shoot at anyone, no matter what the provocation.

Inside the compound, armed revolutionary guards helped unchain the gates, which had not been padlocked. Once the gates were opened, the student brigade poured into the compound and took up prearranged positions. At the main chancery building, they were met by Marines firing tear gas canisters, but the effect of the tear gas was minimized by the mist.

Within an hour and a half, the compound was under the students' control. The Americans were blindfolded and, with their hands tied, taken to various buildings around the compound.

Some of the Americans were laughing, and treated the whole operation as a joke.

Hamilton Jordan was asleep in a friend's home on the Maryland shore when he was awakened at four-thirty Sunday morning.

"This is the situation room," a voice said without further identification, "and the President asked me to call you. The embassy in Iran has been overrun, and a certain number of our people have been taken captive."

"Was anyone killed?" Jordan asked.

"We don't know. We don't think so," the caller said.

As Jordan returned the receiver to its cradle, he said, "Oh, my God." He had two immediate thoughts: were we going to war? and what the hell was this going to do to the campaign?

Robert Armao was awakened at eight o'clock by a call from Empress Farah, who told him about the seizure of the embassy.

"Have you told the king?" Armao said.

"Yes. He was up early, and I talked to him. I think you'd better call him."

When Armao reached the Shah, the monarch's first reaction was not surprise that the embassy had been taken but that the American Administration's position had become so weak that the students would dare to do what they had done. He had underestimated the depth to which the weakness of the Carter administration had been felt in Iran, the Shah said. "My people are like children," he went on. "If you let them take one piece of candy and you don't scold them, they'll take another and another until they soon have the whole bowl. And that's exactly what happened. They perceived the Carter administration to be so weak that they could just slap it and slap it and slap it."

President Carter returned to Washington that morning from Camp David, where he had first learned the news. That afternoon the President met in the cabinet room with his foreign policy group. Two questions were put before the group: what can we do? and whom can we talk to?

The most obvious answer to both questions was to contact the Iranian Prime Minister, Mehdi Bazargan, and Foreign Minister, Ibrahim Yazdi, both of whom had assured the Americans that they would be able to handle any problem that arose. On the next day, the Americans did just that, and the answer they got back from Bazargan was reassuring. The action of the militants was like a 1960s sit-in at an American university. It would soon end.

There had been difficult moments since he had become Prime Minister in February 1979 when Mehdi Bazargan could not get people to obey his orders, and on each of those occasions he had gone to the Ayatollah Khomeini and said, "I resign." And each time he did so, the imam would reply, "Mr. Bazargan, you must not resign. You are a man of great stature, and we need you." And when Bazargan would return to the people with the imam's renewed support, the people would obey. Now, faced with the illegal action of the students, which, contrary to his expectations, did not soon end, Bazargan prepared to "resign" again. But this time, instead of going to see the imam personally as he always had in the past, he sent his teenage nephew to tell the imam he was resigning. And the imam, despite all the respect he had for Bazargan, concluded that if the Prime Minister hadn't come himself to present his resignation, it was either because he did not attach much importance to the matter or because he truly meant to resign. So this time the imam accepted Bazargan's resignation.

Had Bazargan gone to see the imam himself, the imam, in the opinion of his closest counselors, would have once more refused the Prime Minister's resignation, and under those conditions, he could have liberated the hostages.

Because Bazargan did not go himself, what ended on Tuesday, November 6, was not the seizure of the hostages but the power of the present government. Both Bazargan and Yazdi were out—and now the Americans had no one to talk to at all.

chapter two

Wrong, Wrong, Wrong

HOW IS IT THAT A COUNTRY WITH THE TECHNOLOGICAL POWER TO send men and ships to outer space and back could not get anyone to answer the telephone in Teheran? Only when that question has been answered can the magnitude of the problem now confronting the suddenly resourceless Carter administration be understood. To ask that question is to ask, as well, how the greatest power in the world could suddenly find itself at the mercy of a country in revolutionary disorder.

When Harry S. Truman was President of the United States, he kept a sign on his Oval Office desk that said, "The buck stops here." Jimmy Carter kept no such sign on his desk, but that is where the buck stops in the case of the United States versus Iran.

Few people, the former President least of all, would dispute the statement that admitting the Shah of Iran to the United States was the one decision of Jimmy Carter's presidency that he would regret the most. But Carter's problems with Iran went back much farther than that decision, and traced to an ambivalence in his makeup that plagued him throughout his Administration.

In matters of foreign policy, Jimmy Carter was really two persons. There was a public and a private Jimmy Carter. The result of any foreign policy negotiation depended on which Jimmy Carter you were dealing with. Almost to a man, the heads of state who had private dealings with Carter came to admire him. They considered him highly intelligent, and found him better prepared than almost anyone else at the negotiating table. And yet, some of the public pronouncements Carter would make five or six days after the meetings were seen by these same leaders as erratic in the light of the agreements they had reached, and would all but annul the high regard the leaders had developed for Carter in private.

Carter's foreign affairs record had marked positive and negative aspects, as well. During his four years in the White House, he made several courageous foreign policy decisions. Several Presidents had toyed with the idea of negotiating a new Panama Canal treaty, and some had even gotten involved. Carter not only negotiated the treaty, he got it confirmed by the United States Senate. Years from now, when the jingoism surrounding the "loss" of the Panama Canal is forgotten, the United States will still be profiting from the good will that the treaty created in the country's behalf throughout Latin America. Similarly, Carter's decision to attempt personally to bring about an accord between Egypt and Israel was a crucial development for the Middle East. While the accord reached at Camp David created tensions among the Arab nations that had not previously existed, it did bring peace between Israel and the most important Arab power. Both of these germinal accomplishments came about because President Carter demonstrated a genius, in these instances, for sticking to a central idea. Camp David, in particular, was a study in patience, as the President sat for endless hours listening to each side, then led each of them one more step down the path to agreement.

But Carter's foreign policy failures were as spectacular as his achievements, and when they occurred it was usually because he would *not* stick to a central idea. Rather, he would say one thing and do another. His campaign to sell Western Europe on the neutron bomb is a case in point. Carter set out to convince the West Germans that they should accept the bomb as a means of offsetting the overwhelming superiority of the Soviet Union over the NATO forces in the ability to wage conventional warfare. For Helmut Schmidt, the West German Chancellor, such a policy was loaded with political explosives; his Socialist Party has a large and powerful left wing that is opposed, in general, to any kind of military buildup in Western Europe, and specifically opposed to the placing of neutron bombs on West German soil. But when Carter convinced Schmidt that the neutron bomb was the only way to restore military equilibrium, Schmidt courageously endorsed the policy—only to have Carter decide not to build neutron bombs after all. Schmidt came to hate Carter intensely. It was the end of any effective relationship between the Carter administration and West Germany, and created grave problems between the United States and the other countries of Western Europe as well, because it demonstrated such a lack of sensitivity on Carter's part to their problems.

Nothing Jimmy Carter could have done would have saved the regime of the Shah. But the inaction and blundering of the Carter administration assured the succession of a revolutionary government profoundly hostile to the United States. The choice was not—as some have portrayed it—solely between the Shah and the Ayatollah Khomeini. There were other alternatives, which, if backed by the United States early enough, could have produced a moderate government not hostile to the United States. Let us state it bluntly: the Carter administration didn't know what to do about Iran. And this indecision led directly to November 4, 1979, the day the hostages were seized. In the fateful months of the Shah's waning rule over what would soon be transformed from America's strongest ally in the region to its bitterest enemy, United States policy ran down two widely diverging tracks.

On one track was the U. S. State Department led by Secretary of State Cyrus Vance, which had finally come to believe, despite faulty intelligence and tardy reporting from its embassy in Teheran, that the Shah was doomed and that the United States must move with all speed to establish contact with the Iranian opposition. There had been virtually no such contact for twenty years because the Shah had made it known that it would displease him.

On the other track was the small but potent contingent led by Zbigniew Brzezinski, the President's National Security Adviser, which wanted the Shah to stand and fight and the United States to help him.

In a sense, these two divergent approaches were reflections of the wide differences between their respective advocates.

Cyrus Vance is the epitome of a successful Wall Street lawyer—cautious, guarded, articulate, precise, cool. He is, additionally, a man of great principle whose sense of duty drew him to service in the administrations of John Kennedy and Lyndon Johnson and who, like numbers of others in those administrations, was all but burned alive by the Vietnam war, and deeply troubled ever after by the question of whether he might have changed the course of events had he spoken out at the time. Because of his Vietnam experience, Vance did not want to get America into any entanglements anywhere.

Brzezinski, too, operated out of a deeply felt set of principles, but of a totally different sort. He was a Polish-born immigrant who had married the niece of Eduard Beneš, a Czech leader overthrown by the Communists after World War II. Given that history, it is not surprising that he would take a fierce confrontational view of the world. A fervent anti-Communist, he was always the advocate of the tough line inside the foreign policy apparatus of the United States during the Carter administration.

Carter's decision to embrace two men of such opposite persuasions is only surprising if one assumes that he had his own well-articulated notions on foreign policy at the time he took office. But that was not the case at all. He plunged into the presidency with no experience in foreign affairs, and almost no background. Such preparation as he received was in his studies with the Trilateral Commission. It was at the Trilateral Commission that he met Vance and Brzezinski, both of whom became his mentors.

Although Carter probably never consciously told himself that he would be protecting his own inexperience by bracketing it with men of totally opposite persuasions, it does not seem farfetched to speculate that such a consideration was a part of his unconscious processes.

But what happened as a consequence was a disaster. If he had set out deliberately to do so, Jimmy Carter could not have constructed a situation in which two opposing forces would pull more strongly on his ambivalent center.

The history of the kings of Persia is a turbulent one in which monarchs rarely reign for life and seldom die in peace. By the summer of 1978, there were abundant signs that Mohammed Reza Pahlavi would not be an exception to history. How he had managed to set his people against him will be detailed in a later chapter; what is important at this moment is to understand the American response to his predicament as the harbinger of the hostage crisis.

The Americans had been slow to understand the significance of those signs, a fact attested to by their response to a warning from the Israelis that the Shah's days were numbered. The Israelis maintained a full embassy in Teheran that the Iranians, to avoid troubles with their Arab neighbors, pretended didn't exist; no public contacts were made, and no Israeli diplomats were invited to official functions. Privately, it was another matter. In April 1978 the Shah asked Uri Lubrani, the chief of the Israeli mission, to visit him on Kish Island, an ultramodern exclusive resort in the Persian Gulf where he was vacationing. In Tel Aviv a few weeks later, Lubrani, who had correctly predicted the downfall of Emperor Haile Selassie when he had been ambassador to Ethiopia, told Moshe Dayan he was convinced that the Shah was finished. This intelligence was immediately transmitted to the American Government. When Lubrani returned to Tel Aviv a month later, he was shown the American response. His fears, the United States said, were "poppycock"; the Shah would last another ten to fifteen years.

It was in their reading of the political timetable that the Americans erred; they *did* understand by this point that the Shah was running into trouble with his own people, in good part, ironically, for his ambitious but disruptive reform program—landholders and religious leaders who had lost their properties, merchants who believed they had been neglected in the drive for industrialization, workers uprooted by expectations that did not then mature, social democrats suppressed in the 1953 coup, radical Islamic groups, separatists, tribal chieftains, Communists and the Shi^{c}ite mullahs. "All of these opponents of the Pahlavi dynasty, for their own individual reasons, were willing to band together for the negative purpose of overthrowing the Shah," William Sullivan, the American ambassador to Iran during this period, would later write.

Sullivan, a man of soldierly bearing who during thirty-two years as a foreign service officer became accustomed to difficult foreign policy problems, was the U.S. ambassador to Laos when the Vietnam war was beginning to heat up and the United States was sending troops to South Vietnam over the Ho Chi Minh trail, which ran for miles and miles through the forests of eastern Laos. In Paris in 1972 and 1973, he was the principal negotiator, under Henry Kissinger, of the Vietnam accords. He is a no-nonsense diplomat with little capacity for small talk, and a man to be taken seriously when he analyzes a situation in a foreign country. In January 1979 Sullivan would report to Washington that if a massive confrontation were ever to occur between the revolutionary cadres of the Ayatollah Khomeini and the armed forces, the armed forces would disintegrate. That turned out to be one of the most accurate predictions ever made by an American foreign service officer.

When Sullivan and other American diplomats left Teheran on vacation in the summer of 1978, they were sure that trouble was coming, but they thought of the trouble in terms of years, not months. By late summer, when they returned, they could see that the troubles were maturing much faster than they had predicted. Public outrage was focused chiefly on a fire at a movie house in Abadan on August 18, when some four hundred persons were killed. There was no question that the fire had been set by arsonists, but there was grave question as to who had employed the arsonists. Despite inconclusive evidence, the public had decided that it was the work of the Savak.

A second major indication of unrest was the series of demonstrations by Shiᶜite mourners, occurring with clocklike regularity every forty days since the previous January 9, when half a dozen demonstrators were killed while protesting the publication of an article defaming the Ayatollah Khomeini. By now, hundreds of thousands of Iranians were participating in the demonstrations. The next one was scheduled for September 7. Late the night before, the Shah, pressed by his generals, approved the institution of martial law. But few of the demonstrators who assembled early the next morning in Jaleh Square knew that. When soldiers told them to leave, they threw brickbats. The troops then opened fire. According to the most reliable reports, some two hundred to three hundred persons were killed that day, but reliability was of no consequence. What mattered were rumors, and these had it that thousands had been massacred.

September 7, 1978, would be known henceforth as Black Friday.

Ironically, the Shah had begun the year before to democratize his regime, on the theory that he could not maintain an authoritarian rule unless he chose to repress the discontent. "I can repress," he said at one point. "I can control as long as I'm alive. But when I'm gone, the situation will blow up in the face of my son." By then the Shah was mindful of succession because he knew he did not have long to live. So he relaxed restrictions against the press, and on October 26, the day before his fifty-ninth birthday, pardoned some 1500 political prisoners. But these efforts had anything but their desired effects. Instead of improving the Shah's image in the eyes of his opponents, the measures only confirmed how much ground he had lost. In addition, they set off a sequence of events unforeseen by the Shah, which further discredited him with his people and forced him to revoke the very freedoms he had been determined to allow.

Although the Shah had never said that he was freeing *all* political prisoners, it was nevertheless interpreted that way. Families who did not find their relatives among the 1500 that were freed assumed they had been killed. Those who were liberated immediately held outdoor meetings in which they described their years in prison. All of them, regardless of age, sex or religious fervor, swore they had been tortured. Numbers of these torture stories were picked up by the newspapers, giving the added stamp of veracity. Suddenly, the rumors and suspicions that had permeated the society for years could no longer be denied. A week later, the Shah clamped down on the press once again.

It is a further irony that the man who is accused, with good reason, of sanctioning brutal methods against his political opponents would not order his troops to shoot to kill. As the discontent mounted, he sent orders for them to shoot into the air. Each time the people tested the troops and found that they weren't being shot at, they became increasingly bold. On November 5, a major riot broke out. The Shah toured Teheran by helicopter. He saw disorder everywhere. The British Embassy was sacked. Burning autos dotted the city. That day, Ambassador Sullivan received an urgent summons from the Shah. Miraculously, his driver was able to find a way through the raging fires and get Sullivan to the palace. The ambassador found the entry unguarded and the door to the palace unlocked. He wandered in and ran into Empress Farah, who escorted him to the Shah.

"There's no alternative," the Shah began. "We've got to have a military government. I want to know what Washington thinks of that option."

"Your Majesty, I foresaw the possibility. I've already asked Washington and Washington does not object," Sullivan said.

But a military government that is not prepared to shoot into mobs is not a military government—and the Shah, who as a young ruler might not have hesitated to use whatever means were required to put down an unfriendly manifestation, was no longer prepared to do this. Again, the soldiers received orders to shoot into the air, and again, the mobs responded by becoming ever more aggressive.

At that point, the newly appointed Prime Minister, General Gholam Reza Azhari, telephoned Ambassador Sullivan and told him it was "crucial" that they meet. Their rendezvous was set for the following afternoon at the Prime Minister's office. When Sullivan arrived, he was ushered not into the office but into a side room. The room was totally dark. Finally, a weak light was put on, and Sullivan saw the general. He was lying on a cot in his pajamas, under an oxygen tent. He had suffered a heart attack. He motioned the ambassador to come near. "I am not sure I can carry on this job because of the Shah's indecision," Azhari whispered. "The Shah will not permit me to use military force—and if I cannot use military force, this country cannot survive. You'd better tell that to your government."

It was the first of many reports that the Shah no longer had the will or the strength to maintain himself in power.

In mid-November of 1978, Michael Blumenthal, the Secretary of the Treasury, made a swing through the Middle East to "hold hands," as he later put it, with the leaders of several countries that might have dollars to invest that they had earned from the inflated price of oil. Blumenthal was hoping that the leaders would agree to purchase U.S. treasury bonds in sufficient quantities to arrest the slide of the dollar. A second purpose was to twist the arms of these same members in an effort to get them to hold down oil prices. A third purpose of the trip was to stop off in Iran at President Carter's request to appraise the position of the Shah.

Blumenthal had in his possession a National Security Council briefing paper that said "the Shah remains in firm control and has stated that he will not step down." That appraisal coincided with the impression the Treasury Secretary had gained the year before on a similar swing through the Middle East. The Shah had struck him then as every bit the Imperial Majesty. He spent most of their time together lecturing his visitor about the need for law and order in affairs of state. "You in the United States don't understand how a country should be run," the Shah said.

When Blumenthal reached Iran a year later, however, he had reason to wonder whether the Shah himself knew. Street riots were an almost daily occurrence. Reassurances by members of the Cabinet did not seem persuasive. By the time Blumenthal was to see the Shah, he had the feeling that he was dealing with a government that was doomed to failure. When he saw the Shah on November 21, that feeling became a conviction.

William Sullivan had told Blumenthal that the Shah had gone through a "tough" period but was now improving. The man Blumenthal confronted at lunch that day did not seem to be improving. The robust, handsome Imperial Majesty of 1977 was, exactly one year later, a haggard, befuddled ruler without command of the situation. "I don't know what to do," he told Blumenthal in a shaky voice. "I don't know what they want me to do." He repeated the same phrase, or variations, many times during their luncheon. In between such statements, there were long, embarrassing silences when the Shah would stare glassy-eyed at the floor.

At last the luncheon ended and Blumenthal walked to the street with Sullivan, who had accompanied him to the meeting. When he was certain that no one would overhear him, Blumenthal said, "This man is a ghost."

Blumenthal was closer to the truth than he could imagine.

The true extent of the Shah's illness was a secret so closely guarded that it was conveyed only privately and at the highest levels of government, and only because affairs of state were involved. Even today, I am still not at liberty to disclose the names of the people involved in the following incident, but I am positive about the information because it was given to me by one of them. This person, a high-ranking official of a major foreign power, was at a reception at the residence of the nation's chief executive one day in June of 1978 when he was approached by one of the country's most famous doctors. "I must see you urgently," the doctor said, at which point he pulled the government official into a quiet corner. "You must communicate to the President that the Shah is very, very ill. Not only is he ill, but his illness renders him incapable of making decisions."

Decisions were coming hard these days for Jimmy Carter as well.

Logically, Carter could not ignore what the State Department was telling him, based on information from its representatives in Iran—that the Shah was losing his grasp. But intrinsically he couldn't accept it because that's not what he wanted to hear. And so he listened appreciatively to the assurances of Zbigniew Brzezinski that the Shah could be maintained.

In October 1978 Carter had made an unorthodox move, the effect of which was to ensure that he would start receiving information more congenial to his wishes. Carter asked the Iranian ambassador to Washington, Ardeshir Zahedi, to return to Teheran to offer counsel and moral support to the Shah. "I will represent Iran's interests in Washington," Carter said with a smile as he bade Zahedi farewell.

Zahedi was a swashbuckling diplomat known more for his lavish parties and gifts of caviar and champagne than for his astute analyses of the world situation. It was his father who had pulled off the 1953 coup in which the Shah regained his throne. Carter's mission appealed to Zahedi, an unconventional diplomat himself, who regularly dealt with the Shah instead of working through his foreign office as ambassadors are supposed to do.

The removal of Zahedi to Teheran was the idea of Zbigniew Brzezinski, who by this point no longer trusted the advice coming from the
State Department. Carter's National Security Adviser believed that the
State Department had been so blinded by the human rights abuses of
the Shah's regime it had lost sight of the larger picture, the battle between East and West. When Zahedi went back to Iran, it was with the
advice of Brzezinski ringing in his ears: "The Shah should use force
to preserve his power." That message was conveyed again and again to
Zahedi once he was in Iran, and he, in turn, conveyed it to the Shah.
Finally, Brzezinski began calling the Shah himself to offer the same advice.

But when the Shah would ask Ambassador Sullivan what instructions he had received from Washington to back up Brzezinski's counsel, Sullivan would reply, "Nothing."

Despite Zahedi's assurances that the Shah was still very much in
command, neither the State Department nor the CIA believed that the
Shah, by this point, had a chance.

On November 12, 1978, Ambassador Sullivan sent a long and
gloomy message to Washington, which said, in effect, that the U. S.
Government must now face the fact that the Shah was not going to
survive. In the strongest terms, he urged his government to look at the
alternatives—meaning that the United States must immediately make
contact with the people who were going to come to power when the
Shah's regime collapsed.

Sullivan never received an answer to his cable, nor even so much as
an acknowledgment. He was flabbergasted.

In late November, Sullivan took it upon himself to make contact
with opposition leaders. He believed that a moderate opposition group
could survive with the support of the military. Sullivan also persuaded
the State Department to begin to send people back to Teheran who
had been there in the early seventies and had contact with the opposition—the very people who had been withdrawn by the State Department at the request of the Shah.

But what most preoccupied Sullivan was how he would evacuate
thirty-five thousand American residents in Iran if and when it no
longer became safe for them to live there, and how he would safeguard
the American Embassy in the event of an attack. Such an attack actually occurred on Christmas Day, when Marine guards used tear gas to
repel student demonstrators.

Then, at long last, the Administration decided to send an emissary to the Ayatollah Khomeini in Paris: Theodore Eliot, the inspector general of the U.S. foreign service, a seasoned diplomat who knew the Middle East, had served in Iran and spoke fluent Farsi. The message from the United States to the Ayatollah Khomeini via Ambassador Eliot was to be simple and direct: the United States was not unfriendly to the Iranian people; the United States respected the right of Iranians to govern themselves in whatever way they saw fit; it was important, considering the potential of Soviet intervention, for Iran to move toward a new kind of government—if that's where Iran was going—in an orderly way.

But just as Eliot was preparing to leave on his mission, word suddenly came that it had been canceled on the order of the President.

Not even the Shah could understand such an order. He had not objected when Sullivan had informed him of the planned contact with Khomeini. When it was canceled he said to Sullivan, "How can you expect to have any influence with these people if you're not even willing to meet with them?"

The only possible answer to the question is that Jimmy Carter had decided that sending a high-level emissary to the opposition would be interpreted as a sign that he had given up on the Shah. And this he hadn't done.

That these were Carter's views, despite all the contrary advice he had received from the State Department and the CIA, is strongly indicated by the private remarks of Valéry Giscard d'Estaing, then the President of France, on his return from his meeting with Carter in the first days of January 1979. The occasion was the Guadeloupe Summit Meeting, also attended by Prime Minister James Callaghan of Great Britain and Chancellor Helmut Schmidt of West Germany. "At last, Carter's made a decision on Iran," the French President told his aides. "He's going to support the Shah to the end, and he's going to put the whole force of America behind keeping the Shah on the throne."

At that conference, even Giscard d'Estaing had urged Carter to make contact with the opposition, because by that point, the French themselves had decided, on the basis of private information, to write the Shah off.

A week before the Guadeloupe conference, a man who will figure strongly in this narrative received a call from the French Foreign Office, asking if he would come over for a chat. His name was Sadegh Ghotbzadeh, and he was an Iranian exile who had lived for years in Paris. The French wanted to talk to Ghotbzadeh because he was very close to the Ayatollah Khomeini, so close, in fact, that he was known as "the son-in-law of the prophet." What the French wanted to know, in preparation for the discussion of Iran that was sure to occur at Guadeloupe, was what kinds of policies the Ayatollah would institute if he came to power. Ghotbzadeh, who is usually a somewhat disorganized person, was absolutely brilliant that day. In three hours, he presented an entire exposé of the political and economic policy of the new Iran.

Shortly after the French President left for Guadeloupe, the Ayatollah called Ghotbzadeh to inquire whether the French President was going to bring up the question of Iran at the conference, and whether the notes of the Foreign Office meeting with Ghotbzadeh had been shown to him. Within an hour, Ghotbzadeh had learned the answer in a roundabout way from the Quai d'Orsay. Yes, the President was going to present the Iran case, and yes, he had seen the report of the conversation with Ghotbzadeh. Moreover, the Quai d'Orsay person said, Ghotbzadeh's remarks had made such an impact that Giscard would recommend to Carter that he look to the possibility of doing business with the probable new government of Iran—whose spiritual leader would be the Ayatollah.

Many months later, after he had gone into exile, the Shah would remark to a friend that he had been betrayed at Guadeloupe by Giscard d'Estaing, a certain indication that the French President did pursue his agenda. So Jimmy Carter knew that not only his own, but French diplomats as well, had determined that the Shah could not survive. And yet, forty-eight hours after the Guadeloupe conference ended, he canceled the last chance the United States would have to create a direct link between the United States and the future government of Iran. Those forty-eight hours coincided with a deep-sea fishing trip Jimmy Carter took after the conference ended. His only companion on that trip was his National Security Adviser, Zbigniew Brzezinski, arguing that if the United States "abandoned" the Shah its word would be discounted in the future by every country in the world.

Six days later the Shah was gone. By mid-February, following a murky U.S. effort to support the caretaker government of Shahpur Bakhtiar appointed by the Shah, the armed forces of Iran had collapsed, proving, as Ambassador Sullivan had predicted all along, that in a revolution army troops will not fire on their own brothers and sisters. (For his prescience Sullivan would be recalled in April 1979.)

No army so highly touted had ever collapsed so rapidly. And, suddenly, the people took up their arms. Bands roamed the streets, exacting vigilante justice. The Ayatollah Khomeini refused to object, lest his own position be weakened. For months, Iran would experience a fractured and violent time—the kind of time in which student militants of a country in revolutionary disorder can seize the embassy of the most powerful nation in the world, as well as sixty-six of its people.

There were two men the United States might have called in Teheran on November 6, 1979, the day the regime the Americans had counted on was overthrown. Their names were Abolhassan Bani-Sadr and Sadegh Ghotbzadeh. Both men had been in exile for years. Both were principal advisers to the Ayatollah Khomeini. Both were mature, sophisticated and worldly. Both were aghast at the seizure of the hostages, knowing the price Iran would pay in the international community. Both had direct access to the Ayatollah, as well as important positions in the revolutionary government. Bani-Sadr ran several ministries; Ghotbzadeh directed the state-run radio and television services. Both men would probably have answered the telephone that day, had prior contact with the Ayatollah by the Americans made it politically possible for them to do so. But both knew that unauthorized communications with the Americans was now political suicide. Witness the abrupt ouster of Bazargan and Yazdi for daring to talk, on November 1, with Zbigniew Brzezinski.

Had the Americans been able to talk directly with the Ayatollah's two most trusted aides, the hostage crisis might have ended in days. But the Americans couldn't talk to them now because they hadn't done so when they should have.

chapter three

Casting the Net

No one was pushing any panic buttons at the White House on the afternoon of November 4, 1979, the day the hostages were taken. There were, after all, the assurances of Iran's Prime Minister and Foreign Minister that they could handle any problems. And communications hadn't been broken; Bruce Laingen, the American chargé d'affaires in Teheran, had taken refuge in the Iranian Foreign Office, along with two other American diplomats, and from there he was able to be in direct touch with the State Department by telephone. But just as a precautionary measure, the foreign policy group agreed that some qualified American should be readied to go to Teheran to negotiate with the Iranians as a representative of the President, in case such an effort became necessary. Which single American, they wondered, was most qualified to take on such an assignment? There was a moment's reflection, and then Warren Christopher proposed Ramsey Clark.

Given the nature of the opposition, Clark was an inspired choice. Attorney General of the United States during the Administration of Lyndon Johnson, he had, since his departure from government in 1969, moved far to the left on the political spectrum and been active in the cause of human rights both in the United States and abroad. His feelings about the government of the Shah of Iran were well known; he considered it a tyranny with an enormous capacity for violence, and he had been publicly opposed for a long time to U.S. support of the Shah's regime. Clark had had extensive contacts with Iranian exiles in the United States; many members of the new government were, in fact, former exiles who had heard him speaking out against the Shah at various U.S. campuses. Clark had already made three trips to Iran that year; his first arrival had coincided with the departure of the Shah, and the outpouring of emotion he had observed that day by some two million Iranians parading through the streets had been permanently imprinted on his mind. In addition to having the right sensibilities for his mission, Clark was the one American who had had the good sense to pay a call on the Ayatollah Khomeini in Paris. He had done so on January 22, the Monday following the Shah's flight into exile.

In that encounter, strangely enough, Clark had established that the Ayatollah still had an open mind about Jimmy Carter. "Do you think Carter is sincere about his human rights policy?" the Ayatollah had asked him. Clark answered that while the Ayatollah's question was a complex one, he, Clark, found Carter to be a man of good will with basically good intentions. Two hours later, Clark departed from the meeting believing that the Ayatollah, despite everything that had happened, possessed a pragmatic understanding of Iran's need, eventually, to side with the United States.

Once the decision to send Clark had been made, the foreign policy group was eager to determine if he would be willing to go. But it wasn't until early Monday morning, thirty hours after the hostages had been taken, that the Administration found its man.

Clark had been out of the country and had returned late the previous evening. The telephone rang in his Manhattan apartment at 7:30 A.M. It was Christopher. "What do you think of the news?" he said.

"Tell me what the news is and I'll tell you what I think of it," Clark joked.

"They've taken our embassy in Teheran."

For a moment Clark was silent. "I hadn't heard," he said then.

"Can you help?" Christopher asked.

"Of course. I'll do anything to help."

Clark had no idea what he would be asked to do, but that day he attempted to get what information he could from private sources. The next morning, he received a call from Ben Reed, an Undersecretary of State. There was a trace of tension in Reed's voice that had not been present in Christopher's, and Clark would soon learn why. His mission was no longer a precautionary one. It was now the only card the United States had left. Two developments had turned a gray situation black. In Teheran, earlier that day, the Prime Minister, Mehdi Bazar-

gan, had resigned, and his government with him, leaving the United
States without contacts of any kind in the Iranian hierarchy. And the
Ayatollah Khomeini, alluding to the American Embassy as a "nest of
spies," had endorsed the seizure of the hostages in an address carried
over Teheran Radio.

From the U.S. point of view it was debatable as to which development was worse.

"Will you go to Teheran as the President's representative to negotiate for the release of the hostages?" Reed asked Clark.

Clark agreed at once, but qualified his consent. For his efforts to
have any prospect of success, he said, he would have to have the prior
agreement of the Iranians that he could come to discuss the situation,
as well as an agreement from the United States that he and the Iranians could discuss all matters of interest and concern between the
countries. If he were to go simply to talk about the hostages, Clark
said, he wouldn't get to first base.

"When can you get here?" Reed said.

"Whenever you need me."

Reed told Clark to pack a bag and come at once. Three hours later,
Clark was at the State Department, meeting with Vance, Harold
Saunders, Assistant Secretary of State for Near East and South Asian
Affairs, and Henry Precht, head of State's Iran desk. Vance himself
was handling the attempt to make certain that Clark could enter Iran
and would be received once he did. That assurance eventually came
through from Bruce Laingen, still able to function from his sanctuary
at the Foreign Office.

Meanwhile, State Department aides drafted a letter for the President's signature that expressed the sense of Clark's conditions.

After lunch in the secretary's dining room, Clark went to see the
President. It was, he felt, a pointless meeting whose only function was
a cosmetic one, to be able to say that he had personally discussed the
crisis with the President. Clark was anxious to be off. He finally left
Washington at seven that evening, aboard a U. S. Air Force plane big
enough to carry the hostages away in the event that he succeeded in
obtaining their freedom. Aboard the plane with Clark were Precht,
William G. Miller, staff director of the Senate's Select Committee on
Intelligence, and a State Department doctor.

After the plane was airborne, the White House announced that
Clark had departed as the President's special emissary aboard an Air
Force 707. The announcement proved to be a mistake. To the Ira-

nians, it looked as if Carter was trying to play the hero. The very idea of an American Air Force plane setting down on Mehrabad Airport at this moment in Iranian history struck them as all wrong.

By the time the 707 landed in Spain to refuel, the Iranians had sent word that they would not let a big U.S. plane enter their territory. By the time the 707 got to Ankara, Turkey, where the Clark party was to transfer to a smaller plane, the word was, "No U.S. planes at all."

At that point, Clark and Miller booked on an Iran Air flight that was to fly to Teheran late that evening. They went to dinner at the home of the U.S. consul. At nine o'clock, as they were getting ready to go to the airport, they received word that they had not been cleared for the commercial flight. They drove to the airport anyway, and after much difficulty got a call through to Teheran before the flight departed. The Iranians they contacted told them that everyone was so upset by Carter's premature announcement and the fanfare attached to it that they were not to come at all.

For a few moments, Clark considered getting on the plane anyway. But he decided that if he were to do so, he might destroy his chances to have communications with the Iranians in the future. All they're saying at this point, he thought, is that you're not cleared for this flight.

For the next ten days, Clark and Miller remained in Ankara, booking space on every flight available, even those leaving from nearby cities. But permission to enter Iran never came.

No nation in modern times had ever confronted such a problem as the United States now faced. Its diplomats were held hostage in a bitterly hostile and unpredictable country, with the approval of that nation's putative leader. Worse yet, the normal manner of resolving conflicts, dialogue between the two disputants, was no longer available to the Americans, because the only people with whom they had had previous experience and on whom they had counted in the event of any problems had suddenly left the government. Many times in the following weeks, the Americans would wish that they had done something more to cultivate the Iranians who had come to power when those people were exiles in Paris. They had finally initiated some low-level contacts after the Shah had left Iran; Warren Zimmerman, the political officer of the American Embassy in Paris, had met on seven separate occasions and in the greatest secrecy at a small auberge outside the city with a member of the Ayatollah's group at Neauphle-le-Château. But the man the Americans had selected to cultivate proved to be an unfortunate choice. He was Ibrahim Yazdi, who subsequently became Deputy Premier and Foreign Minister of the interim government appointed by the Ayatollah, but who was pressured from office, along with Mehdi Bazargan, two days after the hostages were seized. The Americans had selected Yazdi because, by virtue of his longtime residence in the United States, he would have presumably developed a more realistic view of the country than others closely connected to the Ayatollah—notably Abolhassan Bani-Sadr, rejected because he was too anti-American, and Sadegh Ghotbzadeh, who was suspected of being a Communist. Now, in the face of the total breakdown in communications, all the Americans could do was to cast a wide net across the world, seeking anyone, anywhere, to help resolve the problem.

One of the first persons they set out to find was Habib Chatty.

Chatty, in his early sixties, is a veteran Tunisian diplomat who had once been his country's ambassador to Iran. In October 1979 he had been elected secretary-general of the Islamic Conference, which, in effect, gave him a second strong connection to the Iranians, who were members of the Conference. He was in Paris on the day the hostages were taken. The next day, at the request of U. S. Ambassador Arthur Hartman, he called the Iranian ambassador in Paris to offer his good offices in negotiating with the United States for the hostages' release.

About a week later, Chatty, who had gone to Jidda, Saudi Arabia, the headquarters of the Islamic Conference, received a message from the Iranians. It said that the taking of the hostages had to be viewed in the context of the long relationship between the United States and Iran; that the seizure had been a direct retaliation for the arrival of the Shah in the United States; and that the Iranians were convinced the Americans were plotting to overthrow the present government of Iran, just as they plotted to oust the government of Mohammed Mossadegh in 1953.

What the message didn't say but nonetheless implied was that, inasmuch as the Americans had refused to let Iranian doctors examine the Shah in order to confirm that he was ill, the Iranians could only conclude that the Shah had entered the United States not for medical treatment but to conspire with the Americans in a new CIA-led coup.

In addition to attempting to find qualified intermediaries, the United States had to deal with the practical matters raised by the seizure of the hostages. The two countries had not severed diplomatic relations— the taking of the embassy had been a student action and not an official government one—and Iran's embassy in Washington was able to remain open, therefore. But the Americans, with no functioning embassy in Teheran, needed some representation. For this, they called on the government of Switzerland.

The Swiss were well placed to help. They were in the good graces of what they referred to as the "Occidental wing" of the revolution, Bani-Sadr and Ghotbzadeh, because in 1976 they had discovered and closed down an office in Geneva of the Savak, the Shah's secret police. With the seizure of the hostages, the Swiss decided to take a scrupulously fair position. They would not apply sanctions against the Iranians, as the United States had asked other nations to do, because that would disqualify them as intermediaries, but at the same time they would not be used as a way station for the shipment to Iran of sanctioned goods.

In his private meetings with the Iranians, Erik Lang, the Swiss ambassador, was not nearly so restrained. An outspoken man, surprisingly aggressive for a diplomat, he had quickly become the spokesman for a group of ambassadors representing neutral Western nations who had protested the seizure of the Americans to the Iranian Government. Speaking for his own country, Lang told Bani-Sadr, at that time the Foreign Minister, "The Swiss cannot accept such arbitrary behavior from a bunch of unruly students. Iran must respect international laws and the principles of human rights."

Publicly, however, Lang had to remain quiet, so that he and his embassy could function in the Americans' behalf.

On November 9 the U. S. Embassy in Bern, Switzerland, asked the Swiss to charter a Swissair plane to be ready to go to Teheran at any moment to pick up the hostages in case there should be a break. The next day, the United States asked the Swiss to arrange the evacuation of U.S. citizens still in Iran. In addition, Swiss diplomats were asked to go to the homes of the American hostages, see if any papers of importance were lying around, close up the houses and pay the bills and salaries of the domestic help. Three days later, the Americans asked the Swiss if they were ready to take over the interests of the United States in Iran if and when diplomatic relations between the countries were cut off. The Swiss said they were.

There were several conventional responses available to the Americans, and they made use of them all. On November 9 President Carter ordered a halt to the shipment of spare parts for military equipment so long as the hostages were held. The following day the President ordered the Justice Department to deport Iranian students in the United States who were not in compliance with visa requirements. Two days later the President cut off oil imports from Iran—a measure that hurt the United States as well as it did Iran, since Iranian oil accounted for nearly 4 percent of daily U.S. consumption. At the same time, Carter asked America's allies to abandon all exports to Iran except food and medicine. "If this should fail to prod Iran toward releasing the prisoners," the President said, "the allies should join us in strong diplomacies against Iran to show them that we all stand together in this condemnation of terrorism."

By far the biggest economic move against the Iranians came on November 14, when the President ordered all official Iranian assets on deposit in American banks to be frozen. No one knew the exact amount, but educated estimates put it in excess of $10 billion.

On the legal front, U. S. Attorney General Benjamin Civiletti went before the International Court of Justice at The Hague to lodge an official complaint against the Iranians—who boycotted the session.

In a final action, the President ordered all permits for demonstrations by Iranian students revoked. The President feared that Americans might attack the Iranian students and thereby precipitate retaliations against the hostages.

And then there was the question of force.

From the outset, the military men called into the U.S. discussions were pessimistic about their ability to do anything. The situation, they said, could not be likened to Entebbe, when Israeli commandos succeeded in liberating 103 hostages taken by Palestinian guerrillas. Entebbe was an isolated airport. The American Embassy, where the hostages were being held, was in the center of a densely populated city.

Nonetheless, Zbigniew Brzezinski pressed for some kind of contingency plan to be used in case the Iranians put the Americans on trial and then began to execute them. In addition to a rescue mission, possible naval blockades, the mining of Iranian waters, as well as air strikes, should also be organized, the group concluded. But the feeling was that no military option of any kind should, or would, be exercised.

The best possible strategy was to attempt to isolate Iran diplomatically, to apply pressure in the form of economic sanctions and to continue to search for people who could intercede with the Iranians on behalf of the United States.

Each day that the hostages were held, Vance, Harold Saunders, Henry Precht and David Newsom racked their brains for new channels and new emissaries. They brainstormed and forced themselves to think untraditionally. It was in this way that they came up with the name of Yasir Arafat.

A more unlikely intermediary in behalf of the United States than the head of the Palestine Liberation Organization could scarcely be imagined. And yet, it made a certain amount of sense. Despite his public truculence and belligerence, Arafat, they knew, was always looking for ways to ingratiate himself with the United States in an effort to dispose the Americans more favorably to his cause. And there was no question that the PLO leader was superbly connected with the new revolutionary government. For years, he had operated guerrilla training camps for Iranian exiles. Moreover, he was a good friend of Sadegh Ghotbzadeh, the Ayatollah's adviser and director of the state-run television and radio operation in the new regime. When Hilarion Capucci, the Catholic Archbishop of Jerusalem, was arrested in 1974 for running arms to the Palestinians, it was Ghotbzadeh whom Arafat had asked to find a good Western lawyer.

It would not do for the Americans to go to Arafat directly; they would need an intermediary who might contact him in their behalf. They chose two. The first was Bruno Kreisky, Austria's Chancellor, who, although a Jew, is an anti-Zionist and a friend and admirer of Arafat. The second was a Lebanese newspaperman believed to have close links to the U. S. Embassy in Beirut.

Within days after the hostages had been seized, both men contacted Arafat on behalf of the United States. Arafat's response was immediately positive. He had been trying for years to get the United States to talk directly with him; if he were to solve the crisis, he reasoned, the United States would have to do so.

Arafat asked Hani al-Hassan, the PLO's representative in Teheran, to see what he could do. But Hassan ran into unexpected resistance. The Iranians, he found, were resentful of what they felt was the PLO's effort to take too much credit for the success of the Iranian revolution.

c

When Hassan informed Arafat that the situation was not opportune for PLO mediation, an impatient Arafat flew to Teheran himself. His reception was not cordial. Militants at the American Embassy let it be known through channels that his services weren't needed. And Ayatollah Mohammed Beheshti, the secretary of the Revolutionary Council, told him that under no circumstances was he to bring up the subject in a forthcoming audience with the Ayatollah.

But somehow Arafat got his message to the Ayatollah—probably through Sadegh Ghotbzadeh, who saw in his proposal an opportunity to reclaim some lost goodwill in the international community. When the first hostages were released, the United States as well as Bruno Kreisky said that it was the PLO leader who had made it happen.

On November 19, the Iranians freed a female embassy employee and two black Marines from the embassy. They were immediately flown to Copenhagen and then to Rhine-Main Air Base outside Frankfurt, Germany. The next day, the Iranians released ten more hostages, four women and six blacks, who flew off to Paris, and then on to Frankfurt. That day, the Ayatollah Khomeini himself explained the release of the hostages. Islam, he said, respects women, and because he felt American blacks to be oppressed, he had ordered the release of all women and blacks among the hostages whose spying had not been proved. (Kathryn Koob and Elizabeth Ann Swift did not come under the Ayatollah's exemption and would stay until the end.)

At 4 A.M. on November 19, I was awakened by a call from John Herrick of ABC's foreign desk in New York. "Three hostages are being released right now," he said. "Charter a plane and fly to Frankfurt with a crew to meet them."

"I can't fly to Frankfurt today," I said, "because there's an air controllers' strike. Every airport in Paris is closed."

"You just have to find a way to get to Frankfurt in four hours," Herrick said. "How you get there I'll leave up to you."

I hung up and, still half asleep, tried to figure out how to do that. First, I called a charter company I'd used frequently in the past. "If I can get permission to fly, can I get a plane?" I asked.

"We've got plenty of planes, but we can't fly," a company official said.

"Give me the number of the tower at Le Bourget Airport."

Le Bourget is the airport used by private planes flying in and out of

Paris. When I reached the tower, I said, "Who controls the situation as to whether planes fly or not?"

"The air controllers' union."

"Do they have a permanent headquarters where they're working around the clock?"

"They do."

Within another minute, I was speaking to the man in charge of the strike committee. Luckily for me, he was familiar with my name. "Here's my problem," I said. "In the United States the biggest story in a long time is the story of the American hostages in Iran. Three hostages have been freed this morning in Teheran and are flying to Frankfurt. My office has asked me to go to Frankfurt to meet them. I cannot fly out of Paris because there's an air controllers' strike. Would you give one exception—an order of one exception, one plane—to take off from Paris this morning to go to Frankfurt to meet the American hostages?"

The man on the line was silent for what seemed like an hour. "Just a moment," he said at last. In the background, I could hear a small meeting going on. Then he came back on the line and said, "You have permission to fly."

I called the charter company, and then got my television crew out of bed. At eight o'clock, we taxied to the end of the runway. The pilot called the tower to file his flight plan and ask permission to take off. "You must be kidding," the tower said. "There's an air controllers' strike on. You can't fly."

For ten seconds there was silence. I doubt that I breathed. Then the tower said, "Are you the one flying Mr. Salinger to Frankfurt?"

"Yes."

"Okay. Take off."

We landed in Frankfurt five minutes before the hostages, and filmed their arrival.

The next day, the group of ten hostages arrived, and was immediately taken to the U. S. Army Hospital in Wiesbaden, where the first three hostages had also gone. The following day, they all met the press. Twelve of them sat together on a makeshift stage, staring straight ahead, while their spokesman, Lloyd Rollins, a general services officer in the State Department, read a statement issued by their former captors. The statement said the Iranian students holding the embassy demanded the return of the Shah for trial. Were the Shah to be transferred to a third country, it would be "detrimental to the welfare of the remaining hostages," the students were quoted as having said. Beyond this, the thirteen former hostages would say nothing, answer no questions, lest they jeopardize those still in captivity.

After Habib Chatty, the secretary-general of the Islamic Conference, had delivered the message of the Iranians to the Americans, he was asked to tell the Iranians that the United States was open to all dialogue, and had the greatest faith in the Islamic Conference to generate such dialogue. Chatty contacted the Iranians anew. A week later, he received a second Iranian message that, for the first time, officially spelled out the demands for the release of the hostages.

"It is the opinion of the Iranian Government that the hostage question is only a very minute part of the dispute between Iran and the United States, that this question cannot be treated separately, it can only be dealt with within the general framework of Iranian-American relations. That, in any case, for a release of the hostages, the Iranians demand:
First: That the Shah be given up to the Iranian Government
Second: That his wealth be returned to Iran
Third: That the United States recognize all the harm it has done to Iran
Fourth: That the United States commit itself not to intervene any more in the internal affairs of Iran
"So long as these conditions are not met, no release of the hostages should be hoped for, and any new request without these conditions having been met would be useless."

Several days later, a special envoy of the President, Hermann Eilts, a professor at Boston University and former U.S. ambassador to Egypt, finally caught up with Chatty in Jidda, Saudi Arabia. Eilts asked Chatty to try again to mediate the dispute. Chatty now realized that no dialogue was possible and was reluctant to try in his official capacity. He agreed to make another effort, but only on a personal basis.

If Habib Chatty had come to a dead end for a moment, Sean Mac-Bride had not.
MacBride is an elderly, French-born Irish diplomat, former Foreign

Minister of Ireland, whose thick brogue is compounded by a French accent to the point that an American can scarcely understand his English. He has won both the Nobel and the Lenin peace prizes, and had been one of the founders of Amnesty International, which had investigated and then condemned the violation of human rights by the Shah of Iran and his secret police, the Savak. He was currently the chairman of a special committee studying worldwide communication problems for UNESCO. One week after the seizure of the hostages, he received a call from Amadou Mahtar M'Bow, director-general of UNESCO. M'Bow, from Senegal and a Moslem, had made some sounding in Teheran at the urging of the United States; he asked MacBride now if he would be willing to go there to act as an intermediary. He was, M'Bow assured MacBride, eminently acceptable to the Iranians.

MacBride arrived in Teheran at 3 A.M. on November 22. That morning, in a brief meeting with Abolhassan Bani-Sadr, the Foreign Minister, he presented a letter from M'Bow. The letter pointed out that while it was not UNESCO's role to act as a mediator in international disputes, M'Bow was nonetheless offering his good offices to attempt to restore a dialogue between Iran and the United States. At lunch the next day, MacBride and Bani-Sadr got down to cases. Bani-Sadr assured MacBride that he respected international law, including the protection of diplomats. But at the same time, he said, he understood the action undertaken by the Iranian students who had occupied the American Embassy. It was the students who had most suffered from the repressive acts of the Savak, which they associated with "certain services" of the American Embassy. That, said the Foreign Minister, explained the occupation of the embassy, an occupation that he could regret but that he understood as well, even more because it "translated" the opinion and reaction of the entire Iranian people. Then Bani-Sadr brought up the question of the extradition of the Shah. He understood the difficulties, he said. Nonetheless, he felt that the government of Iran had the right and the duty to raise the question of the guilt of the Shah. No country, not even the United States, could deny Iran's a priori right to do so. For its part, the United States should be the first to question itself in regard to the guilt of the Shah, and should do so through its legal processes.

When Bani-Sadr had finished, MacBride set forth a three-point program that he felt would respond to the Iranians' desires.

First, he said, the Iranians should create a financial commission to identify the Shah's assets around the world. This would anticipate what would surely become a major issue between Iran and the United States.

Second, the Iranians should establish another commission to investigate the wrongdoings of the Shah. Once this commission was established, the hostages should be released on bail.

At this point, Bani-Sadr interrupted. The hostages would surely never come back to appear before such a commission, he protested.

"The commission wouldn't have to hold its hearings in Teheran," MacBride countered. "It could hold them in Paris or New York or some other location outside Iran."

Then MacBride offered the third point of his proposal. The United States, he said, would assure the government of Iran that the U. S. Congress would investigate the links between the United States and the Shah. The record of the Congress in this regard was exceptional, MacBride argued. It was just such a congressional investigation that had led to the resignation of President Nixon.

Bani-Sadr nodded, but made no reply. The next day MacBride met with the ambassadors of Algeria, France, Sweden and Syria, the group that had been selected by the students to visit the hostages. That evening he received a call from an aide of Bani-Sadr, who told him that Bani-Sadr wanted him to visit the embassy as well. MacBride waited in his hotel room through the next day for someone to fetch him. But no one came.

As soon as he returned to Paris, MacBride met with Arthur Hartman, the U.S. ambassador to France, and Dr. Barbara Newell, the U.S. ambassador to UNESCO. He told them that the solution he had given Bani-Sadr was, in his opinion, "possible."

But by this point the United States could only wonder. It had now been three weeks since the hostages had been seized, and there wasn't the remotest sign of a break in the crisis. In spite of the good efforts of MacBride and others and the release of thirteen of the hostages, fifty-three Americans still remained captives in their own embassy, contrary to all rules of international law. Nor did the Americans feel that they were yet in touch with the Iranians in a manner that would eventually lead to the release of the hostages. While there was no official indication of despair, the U. S. Government slipped word to the Swiss to arrange for Christmas services for the hostages, a sure indication of the Administration's assessment that they were in for the long haul.

It was at this precise moment that I received a telephone call that would plunge me into the most exciting journalistic enterprise of my life.

I was at my home in Paris, just off the Place de la Concorde, on Saturday afternoon, December 1, when a man who identified himself as François Cheron called me. He said that he was a lawyer, and that he had obtained my telephone number from my sister-in-law, Christiane Gillmann, who is also a member of the French bar. He had an important matter to discuss with me, Cheron said, that had to do with the hostages.

"Why don't you come tomorrow morning?" I said. I gave him my address on the Rue de Rivoli. As I hung up, I said to my wife, Nicole, "This could be interesting. This guy wants to see me about the hostages. Maybe he knows something that could be helpful."

It did not even occur to me to telephone my sister-in-law to verify Cheron's credentials. He seemed credible enough on the telephone, and if she had given him my number, she would undoubtedly vouch for him.

The next morning Cheron arrived, a well-dressed, amiable man whom I judged to be about forty. He began at once. "First, I have to tell you something about myself. I am a lawyer in Paris, associated with two other lawyers, and we are old friends of Abolhassan Bani-Sadr and Sadegh Ghotbzadeh. We have, in fact, been their lawyers since they came to Paris to live in exile fifteen years ago. And when the Ayatollah Khomeini came to Paris in 1978, we also became his lawyers."

In less than thirty seconds, Cheron had won my undivided attention.

He and his partners were friends of the Iranian revolution, Cheron explained. One member of their firm belonged to a Franco-Iranian friendship committee that occasionally sent lawyers into Iran to do studies of human rights violations. He and another of his partners had once made such an investigation for the Association of Democratic Lawyers in France. That partner's name was Christian Bourguet.

Nine days earlier, Cheron went on, he had been in Rome, where he had had dinner with an old friend, a lawyer named Dario Piga. Piga had told him that a friend of his, Giulio Andreotti, a former Italian Prime Minister, had been asked by the American Government if he knew any responsible people who had contacts with the revolutionary government of Iran. Andreotti was just one of many people the Americans had contacted during the last few weeks throughout Western Europe, Piga said. He told Andreotti that he did know someone: Cheron. "Would you be willing to meet with Andreotti?" Piga asked Cheron.

Cheron told Piga that before he could answer he would have to discuss the matter with his partners.

Back in Paris, Cheron and Christian Bourguet reflected for a long time about whether they could accept the responsibility without compromising themselves with their clients. They agreed that Cheron should at least talk to Andreotti, to see what was on his mind. When Cheron relayed this information to Piga, the Italian lawyer said that Cheron would hear from Andreotti. Within the hour, Cheron did. Andreotti asked Cheron if he would be willing to contact the Iranian Government in behalf of the United States. Cheron said he would have to let him know.

At this point, Cheron and Bourguet decided to sound out Bani-Sadr and Ghotbzadeh in Teheran. The response was surprisingly positive. Both Iranians were, indeed, interested in getting some messages back to the Americans, and comforted by the knowledge that two old, trusted friends might be the couriers.

The next day was Sunday. That morning, Cheron accompanied his daughter to a gymnasium where she was participating in a fencing competition. During the competition, he was called to the telephone. It was Andreotti, so anxious for Cheron's answer that he had tracked him down. Yes, Cheron said, the Iranians were ready to hear what the Americans had to say.

Elated, Andreotti invited Cheron to fly to Rome and have dinner with him on Tuesday evening, November 27.

The following day, Andreotti had lunch at the American Embassy in Rome with Richard Gardner, the ambassador. The Americans asked Andreotti to develop his contact with Cheron.

But when Cheron arrived in Rome for dinner on Tuesday evening, he found a furious host. "I'm sorry I bothered you and had you come down here," the former Prime Minister said, "because I've just gotten a call from the American Embassy thanking me for my services and informing me that they're no longer needed."

Back in Paris the next day, Cheron called Richard Murphy, a political officer at the American Embassy, to find out why the United

States was not using the channel that had been opened up. Murphy called back later to tell him that the United States would be in touch. But nothing happened.

"And now," Cheron said to me, "I find myself in this most difficult situation. I've alerted Bani-Sadr and Ghotbzadeh that the Americans want to have contact with them, and now I have no contact. But I have Bani-Sadr and Ghotbzadeh who have things they want to say to the Americans." He smiled lightly. "What do I do? How do I make contact with the Americans? That's what I want you to do for me."

"Where will you be in an hour?" I said.

"I'm going directly home."

"Okay," I said. "Stay there. In one hour, you will get a phone call."

As soon as Cheron departed, I telephoned Arthur Hartman, the American ambassador to France, a man I know well and admire immensely. I recounted the story Cheron had just told me. When I finished, I said, "It sounds to me like these people could be an extremely valuable contact to the American Government in dealing with the Iranians. I think it's unfortunate that this channel has been dropped, and I think we ought to pick it up immediately. There ought to be some reaction from the American Government today, so that these men know that they're back on the track."

"Let me look into it," Hartman said.

Before long, I received a call from Warren Zimmerman, the political counselor at the American Embassy. "How do I contact Cheron?" he asked.

At seven that evening, Cheron called me. "You've done it," he exulted. "I've had a two-and-one-half-hour meeting with Warren Zimmerman and I've already given to Zimmerman some thoughts of Bani-Sadr and Ghotbzadch. I'm extremely grateful."

I expressed my own pleasure that I had been able to help. And then I asked a favor in return. Could he keep me abreast of developments? He promised to do so.

That night I slept very well.

chapter four

"We've Run Out of Countries"

ON NOVEMBER 22, 1979, THANKSGIVING DAY, MY COLLEAGUE BARbara Walters of ABC interviewed the Shah of Iran in his suite at New York Hospital—the first journalist to talk to him directly since she herself had interviewed him in Morocco eight months before. The Shah received Walters in his hospital room, wearing a paisley robe and pajamas. He appeared to her to be fifteen pounds lighter than the last time she had seen him; he still had a tube in him—placed there by his surgeon so that a gallstone in his common bile duct not removed in the initial surgery could be extracted later by a semisurgical process—and was experiencing some pain. Nonetheless he seemed alert, and he even smiled from time to time. Someone had brought him a poster of a gorilla and taped it to a wall. A caption under the photograph said, "Don't be hard on me. I've had a bad day."

While the interview was not taped or filmed—the Shah had vetoed that on the prospect that it might somehow be used against him in Iran —he did respond readily to Walters' questions. By far the most important response was the one he made in regard to the question that, since his trip to the United States on October 22 for medical reasons had disturbed a great many people: had this trip really been necessary, or could the Shah have been treated just as well in Mexico or some other country—thereby, presumably, avoiding the series of events that had led to the seizure of the American Embassy in Teheran and the taking of the hostages?

The gist of the Shah's response was that if he had not come he would have died.

Later that day, Walters was interviewed herself by Hugh Downs, another of my ABC colleagues, and their dialogue was aired on *20/20*, the network's newsmagazine.

DOWNS: He had to come here? He couldn't have stayed in Mexico and got good treatment?

WALTERS: Well, what he said is, and he keeps saying: he said that he had pills—chills, forgive me, I'm a little excited because I just left him a few hours ago—chills and fever the whole time he was in Mexico. He was being treated for malaria, and that made his condition worse. Then he had intense pain and jaundice.

The reason he had to come here was for the diagnosis. They didn't know whether it was the gallbladder itself, or whether it was the tumor pressing on the gallbladder, and he had to have a very new and sophisticated instrument called a body scanner. They didn't have that there. They do have it here, and in order to find out whether it was the cancer or the gallbladder, he had to come to this country.

DOWNS: I see.

WALTERS: He did not want to, he said, his doctor said—

DOWNS: He didn't want—

WALTERS: And the Empress, and they all said: you must, you must come. There are very few of these scanners in the world. They're very, very new.

What the scanners do is "image" tumors in the organs and certain body spaces that are invisible on conventional X-ray films. They can also discover whether the bile ducts of jaundiced patients like the Shah are obstructed. Where a tumor is suspected, the scanners can reveal not simply whether it exists but the extent to which it has spread.

Did the Shah need to come to the United States to avail himself of a scanner? Although he told Walters that Mexico didn't have scanners, the fact is, *Science* magazine noted in a story analyzing the Shah's assertions, that there were eleven such instruments in the country, three of which were as good as any existing in the world; where older scanners take up to six minutes to complete a scan, the new machines do the work in less than five seconds. If Mexico were somehow unsuitable, Australia, Korea, Japan, Canada, Argentina, Colombia, Brazil, Norway, Sweden, Germany, France, Spain, Italy, Russia and

Syria all had scanners identical to the one at New York Hospital. No one knows which of these countries might have offered to admit the Shah for treatment, because none of them was considered.

The matter of equipment, then, was not an issue. The only real issue was whether those using the machines in other countries would have diagnosed as competently as the American doctors. On this point, at least as regards Mexico, *Science* was unequivocal. "Nothing done by the doctors at New York Hospital or at the Memorial Sloan-Kettering Cancer Center was any trickier than what doctors in Mexico do routinely."

Why, then, was the Shah admitted to the United States when the capacity to treat him presumably existed in Mexico? One reason was that for the U. S. Government, the scanner question was much more narrowly defined. The government had not attempted to challenge the diagnosis of Benjamin Kean, particularly since it was supported by the Shah's French doctors. It seemed like a reasonable diagnosis in the absence of a scanner report. But to the State Department, the question was not whether there was a scanner anywhere in Mexico that could be used for further diagnosis, it was whether such a scanner was in a hospital that was practicable in terms of who the patient was. The Americans did not want the identity of the patient to be revealed. The only facility at which they felt their concerns could be managed was the American-British-Cowdray Hospital in Mexico City. Was there a scanner there? Eben Dustin, the State Department's chief medical officer, put that question to Dr. Jorge Cervantes, the medical adviser to the American Embassy in Mexico City, who happened to be in Washington at the time. "No," Cervantes replied, "but we can achieve the same results with ultrasound equipment." His answer wasn't good enough; it was a scanner that was wanted.

But was a scanner *needed*? The question remains. In the minds of the people who made the decision to admit the Shah to the United States, the scanner was an important issue. None of them were doctors, so they knew little about disease. But they could all understand the magic of machines.

A body scanner was used during the diagnostic process within hours after the Shah arrived at New York Hospital. But according to Dr. Kean, the scanner was "not at all essential" for what he needed to know—the cause of the Shah's jaundice. A sonogram study done the same night, he says, showed the jaundice was caused by gallstones and led to the operation the next day. But for the cancer specialists treating the Shah, the scanner was essential. But, again, there were scanners in Mexico.

Did the Shah *have* to come to the States? The Administration certainly thought he did. "We were convinced that he could only get the treatment he needed in the United States," Hamilton Jordan says. A case can be made that the reason they thought so was because of Robert Armao, the Shah's adviser, who put out the story that he needed a body scanner and there were none in Mexico. But what would have happened had Armao not told such a story? Would the Shah still have been admitted to the United States? The evidence strongly suggests the answer to that question is yes. Both the Shah and the U. S. Government were worried about the language problem, the security problem and the lack of equipment in the right facility. The Shah was undeniably sick and needed immediate treatment, and with or without external pressure from the Shah's friends David Rockefeller and Henry Kissinger, there was a deep-down feeling among President Carter and his associates that they had treated the Shah poorly since he left Iran, and they owed him a favor. "It ultimately was a matter of principle," Hamilton Jordan says.

For the Americans, there was one galling irony to the entire episode that they could not even make public. A month earlier they had admitted another Iranian to the United States for exactly the same kind of medical treatment. The same surgery was performed—at the Mayo Clinic in Rochester, Minnesota—as was subsequently performed on the Shah. The Iranian, Sheik-Ul Shirazi, was a member of the inner circle of the Ayatollah Khomeini, but he begged for, and was granted, anonymity, so that he could go back to Iran.

That knowledge did not help the disposition of Jimmy Carter, whose admission of the Shah for humane reasons a month before had precipitated the hostage crisis. In the weeks after the hostages were seized, Carter's popularity had shot up among the electorate. But the professionals around Carter, as well as Carter himself, knew that the response was a reaction against the Iranians more than a positive response to the President, and they all knew it wouldn't last.

Meanwhile, there remained the problem of finding a new haven for the Shah, if that became necessary, following his expected return to Mexico. What the Americans wanted was a permanent sanctuary that was both safe and accessible to excellent medical care. They had cast out many feelers, but not even the Shah's former allies had responded. No one really wanted him.

For the moment, however, the Shah was not as concerned with where he would eventually find a home as he was with the state of his health. The mild lymphoma from which he had been suffering for six years had suddenly turned into a more severe form of the disease called diffuse histiocytic lymphoma. He had developed a growth on his neck the size of a handball, for which he had received ten radiotherapy treatments at the Memorial Sloan-Kettering Cancer Center just across the street from New York Hospital. The treatments had been performed in the middle of the night to minimize security problems, but the irregular routine had disturbed his sleep and tired him considerably.

As to his fate after his discharge from the hospital, the Shah was certain that he would be welcomed back by Mexico. On two occasions in the past, President López Portillo had told him to consider Mexico his home. For good measure, he had been in contact with the office of the President and been assured that everything was in order for his return, which was scheduled for Sunday, December 2. His aide, Robert Armao, had dispatched Mark Morse and other members of his staff back to Cuernavaca. The house had been reopened and fully stocked, and was already being watched by the Mexican secret service. The Shah's own security force was back in place as well.

On Friday, November 30, two days before the Shah's scheduled departure, Robert Armao received a telephone call from the Mexican consul general in New York. He told Armao that he had an urgent matter to discuss with him. Armao, who was at New York Hospital, agreed to meet the diplomat at three that afternoon at a restaurant on Fifty-seventh Street. They were no sooner seated than the diplomat said, "The Shah can't come back to Mexico. Two or three days, okay, because he's got that much time left on his tourist visa. But that's all."

Armao, who is rarely at a loss for words, was rendered momentarily speechless. When he finally recovered, he said, "I don't believe you. We had confirmation from the Presidential Palace this morning that everything was 'go.'"

"I'm telling you, Bob, this supersedes all previous communications," the Mexican said. "The Shah cannot stay in Mexico. You don't believe me? Let's get the ambassador on the phone. He's the one who received the message from Mexico."

The two men went to the consul general's car, from which they telephoned the Mexican ambassador, Hugo Margain.

"That's right," Margain said. "I received a communiqué. The Shah is not welcome in Mexico. You have to understand—his presence is becoming a threat to our national interest."

What the ambassador did not say at the time, but Armao could deduce, was that the Mexicans were worried about what might happen to some of their embassies if the Shah were readmitted to Mexico.

Crestfallen, Armao returned to New York Hospital. For an hour, he sat in the room adjoining the Shah's bedroom, wondering how to break the news. Then one of the Shah's guards came in. "There's a bulletin on television. He's got his set on. You'd better go in and tell him."

The channel the Shah was watching hadn't yet carried the news, so it was Armao who informed him. For a moment the Shah stared uncomprehendingly at Armao. "But why?" he said at last.

"The Foreign Ministry was never in favor of us going there anyway. I guess they finally won out."

The Shah was still scheduled to quit the hospital on Sunday, December 2. If he couldn't return to Mexico, where could he go? There were no real options, and the Shah himself could not negotiate with the governments of foreign countries, because he no longer had diplomatic status. The only place the two men could think of was the townhouse of his twin sister, Princess Ashraf, on Beekman Place in midtown Manhattan.

At that point, Armao left the room, went to a phone and, for the first time since the Shah had gone to Mexico, spoke directly with a U. S. Government official. The man he called was David Newsom in the State Department. When Newsom heard what the Shah had decided to do, he said that was impossible.

At that point, Robert Armao, the Shah's unlikely shepherd for almost eleven vexatious months, blew up. "I'm out," he shouted. "There's only so much a public relations firm can do. We are now making an official request to the White House. You have to assist him in finding another place. You have to provide him with safe haven. You have to provide him the transportation there, and the medical care. Otherwise we're going to Beekman Place."

At about the time that Robert Armao was delivering his ultimatum to David Newsom, a naturalized American of Cuban descent named Bernardo Benes was repeating for the benefit of a State Department official a conversation he had had two days earlier with Ricardo de la Espriella, the Vice-President of Panama. Benes, president of the Continental Bank of Miami, had met at the Miami International Airport with de la Espriella on a business matter. They had spoken in passing of the seizure of the hostages as well as the predicament of the Shah. Benes had become well acquainted with Cyrus Vance and other State Department officials because of the major part he had played in negotiating with Fidel Castro for the release of political prisoners in Cuba. He remembered that shortly after the Shah was deposed, Panama had invited the exiled monarch to move there, believing that he might make some timely investments. Prince Reza, the Shah's son, had even toured the country, piloting a Panamanian Air Force plane, to inspect the prospects.

"The Americans are looking for a place for the Shah," Benes told the Vice-President of Panama in Miami. "Is that invitation of yours still good?"

"I think so," de la Espriella said.

In Washington that evening, Peter Tarnoff, a special assistant to Secretary of State Cyrus Vance and executive secretary of the State Department, put in a call to the American ambassador in Panama, Ambler Moss, and told him of the exchange between Benes and de la Espriella. Would he follow up right away? Tarnoff asked.

Moss said he would.

Then Tarnoff put the importance of the matter into one short sentence: "We've run out of countries," he said.

Early the next morning, Lloyd Cutler, the chief White House counsel, flew to New York to meet secretly with the Shah. That Cutler had drawn the assignment said something for the delicacy with which it was viewed by the Carter administration. His soft, grandfatherly appearance and easygoing manner are deceptive; he is, in reality, one of Washington's movers and shakers, a member of that small pool of the city's lawyers frequently tapped for advice by successive administrations.

Cutler brought with him an invitation from the United States to the Shah to recuperate at Lackland Air Force Base, a military installation with excellent medical facilities. In addition, Cutler said, the United States would be looking for a more permanent home for him in some other country. Perhaps Paraguay. Perhaps South Africa. South Africa was where the Shah's father had once lived in exile.

In her interview with the Shah, Barbara Walters had asked him if he had ever considered returning to Iran to stand trial.

"I have been called many things," the Shah replied, "but I have never been called stupid."

His return to Iran would have been a major step toward resolving the hostage crisis, but the Shah did not even consider sacrificing himself in the hostages' behalf because he did not feel responsible for their predicament. He believed that the Ayatollah Khomeini had perpetuated the crisis with his endorsement of the militant students' actions in order to divert attention from the problems and failures of his revolution.

On November 8 the Shah had issued a statement deploring the action of the students, and had offered to leave the United States if it would help resolve the crisis. But his doctors had told him that travel at that time could be fatal. He was still extremely anxious to quit the United States, however, because he knew he wasn't wanted. How much that knowledge had gotten to him became apparent when Walters asked him if he would give her a Thanksgiving message for the hostages. "I've already said everything I want to say about the hostages," the Shah replied brusquely.

His reply took Walters aback. After a moment, she tried again. "Perhaps you don't understand, Your Highness. Thanksgiving is an important holiday in the United States, and it will be important for the hostages—"

The Shah cut her off. "I don't want to talk about it anymore," he said.

Walters did not bring the subject up again.

The Shah had been watching television and reading the newspapers. He was aware of the tremendous anger and bitterness toward him being reported in the media, but he had anger and bitterness to match. He considered media reports totally distorted because they emphasized the protests against him—some of them, he was certain, staffed by paid non-Iranian recruits—and ignored demonstrations in his favor. He recalled the thousands of friendly letters he had received during his stay in the hospital, and the plane that had flown along the East River, past his bedroom window, trailing a banner that said, "Long live the Shah." What really got his back up were the reports about his wealth. He had heard one estimate that he was worth twenty-five billion dollars. "Don't people realize even what one billion is?" he asked Barbara Walters plaintively. "Look, I'm not a poor man. I would say that I have about as much as an American millionaire." But, he went on, reports that he was living selfishly and like a king were simply not the case.

But these concerns were transient compared to others that reached to his marrow. A new growth had festered within him, as destructive as the one that would eventually kill him. It was the galloping suspicion that those he had considered his friends in the international community had used him so long as he was of value and discarded him when he wasn't. These people had asked him to serve the world as the guardian of the Middle East, and were now holding court and currying favor with the people who were now ruining his country. "Every day reports had come of murder, bloodshed, and summary executions, the death of friends and of other innocent people," he would write before many months had passed. "All these horrors were part of Khomeini's systematic destruction of the social fabric I had woven for my nation during a thirty-seven-year reign. And not a word of protest from American human rights advocates who had been so vocal in denouncing my tyrannical regime. It was a sad commentary, I reflected, that the United States and indeed most Western countries had adopted a double standard for international morality: anything Marxist, no matter how bloody and base, is acceptable; the policies of a socialist, centrist or right-wing government are not."

Of all the statesmen he had counted on, the one who had most disappointed the Shah was Jimmy Carter, who in a toast on New Year's Eve, 1977, had declared "there is no leader with whom I have a deeper sense of personal gratitude and personal friendship." It was Jimmy Carter, the Shah had concluded, who had abandoned him—and caused thereby the predicament in which he now found himself.

In spite of the medical treatment he had received, the Shah knew that he was probably going to die before many months had passed. The greatest pain he bore was the belief that he would go to his grave a colossally misunderstood man. "I know that one day history will understand," he told Barbara Walters. "History cannot be so unjust."

chapter five

Monarch Versus Mullah

HISTORY WILL HAVE A DIFFICULT TIME WITH MOHAMMED REZA Pahlavi. He is not an easy man to judge. He was an autocrat by any measure. By most standards, he may have even been a tyrant. But he ruled a volatile, fickle and capricious people with a turbulent history, and so to some extent it might be said that it was not his disposition so much as the expectations of him that made him the man he became.

Iranians—Persians before they were rechristened by the Shah—display the kinds of feelings in both the secular and religious realms for which there is no equivalent in Western culture. They are incredibly sensitive to shifts in power, and will change sides on a whim, usually with an explosion of emotion. No one who witnessed, via television, the street scenes in Teheran during the hostage crisis need be reminded of the intensity of the participants; what is less well understood, perhaps, is the ease with which such mobs can be aroused by the idea of the moment.

There is one constant about the Iranians, however, and that is their need for a symbolic figurehead, not simply for psychological reasons but to hold together fiercely independent tribal groups in the context of a nation. In a sense, all Persian history is organized around its shahs, or kings, to whom the populace ascribed divine powers.

A Persian shah, historically, has not been a descendant of royalty, but almost literally a king of the hill—a man who through strength or force of will or connivance has ascended to the throne. Once there he is as vulnerable to ouster as is the "king" in the children's game. His

rival may be an individual, or it may be a group that has banded together for the sole purpose of tossing him off his throne. Much of a
shah's time, as a consequence, is invested in maintaining his position.
He comes to believe that the maintenance of power is a devious process. Authority must be centralized, with all lines leading to him, in the
manner perfected by Napoleon and practiced by the French to this
day. Checks and balances must be instituted, not to better orchestrate
government but to neutralize any person or body that collects too
much power. Anyone who becomes too proficient must be disarmed,
be he friend or foe. A shah not willing to rule dramatically and
decisively is quickly discarded by his people. The stakes are high and
the end often violent. It is not a game for the timid.

In many ways, Mohammed Reza Shah fulfilled these historical and
cultural expectations. He came to power not because he was of legitimate royalty, but because his father, Reza Shah, who began his career
as a fourteen-year-old foot soldier, ascended to the throne through an
extraordinary mixture of courage, daring and hubris, plus an ability to
ingratiate himself with the British forces then occupying the country
under a protectorate agreement. Reza Shah's son, Mohammed, over-
came childhood illnesses, survived an airplane crash and escaped so
many assassination attempts—in one of which he was shot several
times—that he came to consider his own life as divinely protected. His
success, particularly with the Americans, seemed to vindicate his concept of himself as a man apart from other men, with a special mission
in life, not only to lead his country to a new position in the family of
nations but to act himself as the linchpin holding the world together.

The Shah was a patronizing ruler who thought of his subjects as
children. He was so devious a politician himself that he could not understand how the democratic process could thwart an American President; so conspiratorial, it seemed at times as though his objective was
to neutralize more than accomplish. In this he was very much like his
people. "It's impossible for Iranians to believe that an event occurs as
it appears to occur," a man who knows them well observes. "They
have to have some sort of conspiracy behind the scene. I've had highly
intelligent Iranians tell me that the hostage crisis was really a British
plot to destroy American influence." The Shah himself viewed any
contact with the opposition by U.S. diplomats as proof that a plot
against him was being hatched behind his back. In the last months of
his rule, he became convinced that the United States and the Soviet
Union had conspired between them to divide up the Persian Gulf, and

he was certain that no mere mullahs could organize the kinds of demonstrations that were being mounted against him. It had to be the CIA.

But for all the ways in which he validated expectations, the Shah also went against the grain. Whereas few shahs in the past—his father a notable exception—had thought beyond their own situations, Mohammed Reza Pahlavi, whatever else he may have been, was a paternalistic ruler with an incontestable desire to make life better for his subjects. While he was not timid, he was a worrier and brooder long before he fell from grace with his people, an indication, perhaps, of a sensitivity to their moods. The very insecurity that made him seem not that impressive a monarch to the foreigners taking his measure early in his regime made him that much more responsive to the desires of the populace. And there is no doubt whatever that when it came to that moment when he might have saved himself by shedding his people's blood, the Shah, who in his younger and more virile days would not have hesitated, now refused to do so. In November 1978 Senator Robert Byrd of West Virginia, whose daughter is married to an Iranian, went to Iran with a message for the Shah from President Carter. The message said, in effect, that the Shah should get tough, and the United States would support him. Prior to his meeting with the Shah, Byrd was briefed by U. S. Ambassador William Sullivan. When the senator told Sullivan what the message from the President said, Sullivan replied, "The Shah is going to ask you, 'Does that mean you're for shooting people?'" That is exactly what happened.

So it is too simple to portray the Shah as a singularly cruel and mendacious tyrant, as his detractors have attempted to. For all his arrogance and vanity, he did have his saving graces. In the end, however, it was the traditional forces within him—the zest for power for its own sake and the refusal to relinquish even a portion of it—that proved the Shah's undoing.

As the former press secretary to President John F. Kennedy, I might be accused of partiality for what I am about to say. But I truly believe that had the Shah of Iran taken the advice of President Kennedy when Kennedy took office in 1961 the Pahlavi dynasty would still be on the throne in Iran and Jimmy Carter would never have been confronted with a hostage problem. Kennedy tried to persuade the Shah that he should begin to democratize Iran, but the Shah dismissed the idea. He believed that the West's ideas of democracy were unfeasible in a country like his own, and he considered efforts by Western powers to influence him as attempts to clip his wings.

The Shah did begin, at his own pace, to bring his country into the twentieth century. In 1963 he launched a program known as the White Revolution, which included rights for women, a campaign for literacy, agrarian reform, nationalization of forests, the sale of state-owned enterprises to the public and profit sharing for workers. Intellectuals both within and outside of Iran were optimistic that the economic and social modifications the Shah was calling for would, of necessity, produce democracy as a by-product. And in fact, despite the continuing authoritarianism of the Shah, the late sixties saw impressive economic and social gains. Iranian women were given the vote and allowed to study at the university. The traditional black veil was outlawed. The political control of the feudal landowners and aristocracy crumbled under the onslaught of land reforms. The founder of Savak, the secret police, a man considered by many to be a sadist, was replaced by a soldier believed to have a more sympathetic character. Young men were brought into government and the old guard professional politicians were dismissed, creating at least the illusion that the future would be a fresh one. By the early 1970s, living conditions in Iran had improved remarkably for a portion of the population. Then was the time, thought many political observers, for the Shah to temper his authoritarianism and move toward a true constitutional monarchy. But nothing of the kind transpired.

Ironically it was an American administration that not only reinforced the Shah's autocratic tendencies, but actually gave credulity to his view of himself as an Aryan Napoleon. On May 30, 1972, President Nixon and his Secretary of State, Henry Kissinger, made a side trip to Iran in between official visits to Russia and Poland, to instruct the Shah on the new role they envisaged for him. Kissinger, it should be remembered, had structured virtually his entire global strategy on the conviction that the most dangerous zone in the world was the Middle East, and the most serious threat to the Western world the prospect of Soviet intervention in the Middle East. The Western world needed, in Kissinger's view, to have a number of Middle East allies clearly identified with American policy and willing to support it, a need made all the more urgent with the British departure from the Persian Gulf in 1971. The United States, already involved in an unpopular and expensive war in Vietnam, could hardly declare itself the new policeman in the Middle East, at least not directly. And so when the Shah agreed to take responsibility for the defense of the gulf, and what's more, foot the bill, Nixon and Kissinger were elated. For their part, they promised to sell the Shah unlimited quantities of arms—which elated the Shah, in turn. Sure enough, as the price of oil quadrupled in 1973—following an Arab embargo on oil to supporters of Israel in the wake of the Yom Kippur War—the revenues of Iran began to swell, and the Shah, a man enamored of arms, was able to pour more and more billions into the purchase of military supplies.

Like his French hero, the Shah came to believe that it was his divine destiny to move on to new frontiers. Sitting on his pot of black gold, backed by the most powerful country in the world, he asked himself why he should delegate authority when it was his inspired vision that was changing Iran from puppet to puppeteer.

With a military support system well under way, the Shah began to dream of transforming Iran into the fifth industrialized nation of the world after the United States, West Germany, France and Japan. In order to reach his goal, he instituted a crash program, but because Iran lacked both technology and know-how, the country had to import foreigners to build its steel and aluminum plants.

The Shah was counting on the growing demand for oil to finance his industrialization program as well as the reforms he had initiated with the White Revolution in 1963. What he hadn't counted on were the massive efforts by Iran's customers to conserve oil and the subsequent drop in sales.

Something had to give. The military establishment, which required 25 percent of the national budget, would not. As a consequence, there were insufficient resources for the development of a sound infrastructure. Many of the promises the Shah had made turned into pipe dreams. His efforts had not provided adequate housing for the people, nor had his programs produced energy and transportation to stimulate the growth of industry. In 1975, despite still substantial oil sales, Iran had a deficit balance of payments. Yet the Shah stuck to his guns, and foreign manpower continued to pour into Iran. This influx of foreigners, especially Americans, began to have a destabilizing effect on the people. The presence of a wealthy foreign class, whose cars, clothes and habits were in stark contrast to their own, underscored the Shah's failure to deliver on the basic amenities, let alone the constitutional equality they had expected.

When the rumblings of discontent begin in Iran, they emanate first from the bazaars. From them now there came rumblings that would soon turn to roars. As the resentment of his people mounted, Mohammed Reza Pahlavi came more and more to validate historical expectations—trusting no one, dividing authority, tightening control to the point that either he or his family had to be involved in any new project if its advocates wished to move forward. Always before under such conditions, corruption had flourished; the reign of Mohammed Reza Pahlavi was no exception.

In every possible way, the Shah was burning the bridges that connected him to his countrymen. The most important bridge of all was the one leading from the secular to the spiritual realm. And this one could not be destroyed.

However history eventually records the Shah of Iran, it will include the remarkable story of how he was eventually toppled from his throne by an aged mullah of the Shiᶜite faith who had not set foot in Iran for the sixteen years preceding the monarch's downfall.

To understand how this can happen, one must understand the hold that religion has on the people of Iran. Broadly speaking, they are Moslems, believers in an all-embracing system of public and private conduct whose foundations are in the words spoken by Allah to Mohammed the Prophet, and then recorded in the Koran. Ninety percent of Iranians practice the Shiᶜite faith, a branch of Mohammedanism whose followers believe that leadership passed from the Prophet Mohammed to his son-in-law Ali. The Shiᶜites anticipate a second coming. They expect a spiritual descendant of Mohammed who disappeared in the ninth century to reappear one day and establish the kingdom of Allah on earth.

If the supporters of the Ayatollah Khomeini one saw in the streets of Teheran seemed fanatical, if they paraded under the guns of government troops, if they took up arms following the collapse of the Army without regard to their own safety, all of this was with an underlying purpose. Martyrdom—death in defense of the religion—is one of the basic tenets of Shiᶜism. Shiᶜites are willing, often eager, to die for their ideals because they have been taught since childhood that martyrdom is the highest expression of religious existence. A milder form of the same ideal can be seen on the great holy days, when the Shiᶜites march through the streets beating themselves with chains and whips.

Nominally, the Shah was a Shiᶜite. But from all accounts he did not practice the faith. His feelings about the hold the mullahs had on his people were critical to everything he did. The view of the mullahs was that all authority—and, indeed, all competence—flowed from them. Government should simply be an expression of divine judgment—in effect, a theocracy run by the holy men. The Shah's view was that the government should be run by civilians and the mullahs should stay in their mosques and pray. For a man who governed a religious society, he might have appeared, on the surface, to be insensitive to the beliefs of his people. That was not the case at all. What he sensed was what his father had believed—that in the mullahs and their conviction that all power resided with them lay the one great obstacle to the modernization of Iran.

Part of the legacy the Shah inherited from his father was an abiding enmity on the part of the mullahs. Shiᶜism decrees a secondary role for women; Reza Shah, the father of Mohammed Reza Shah, offered education to women and campaigned unsuccessfully, as it turned out, for the outlawing of veils. Through land and legal reforms, he attacked the power of the mullahs. When zealots protested his reforms, he sent troops into a religious shrine to kill them.

But if Mohammed Reza Shah was the bearer of a legacy, so was the man who would orchestrate his downfall. Ruhollah Khomeini was born in 1900, the youngest of seven children. His father and his father's father before him had been ayatollahs, as was his eldest brother. The ideas on which he was raised were the Moslem counterpart of Christian fundamentalism—a society absolutely and irrevocably controlled by an all-embracing moral code and a body of enforcers, the mullahs.

But there were important secular components to the future ayatollah's formation as well; he grew up during a series of foreign occupations and became a fervent xenophobe. He was equally anti-Semitic; one of his great quarrels with Mohammed Reza Pahlavi was over the latter's surreptitious support of Israel.

The specific enmity between Mohammed Reza Pahlavi and the Ayatollah Khomeini traces to the Shah's return to power following the 1953 coup. Numbers of persons were killed in the process of putting the Shah back on the Peacock Throne; in response, the Ayatollah sent letters to leaders of Moslem and Arab countries, asking for help for the victims of what he described as the atrocities of the Shah. Of all the leaders the Ayatollah contacted, only one responded: Gamal Abdel Nasser, the Egyptian army colonel who, the year before, had overthrown King Farouk. The Egyptian leader sent $150,000 by courier to the committee that was responsible for the relief of the victims. But the Savak arrested the courier at Mehrabad Airport as he was bringing in the money. The Shah seized upon the incident to rebuke the Ayatollah publicly, who even then was identified as a leader of the opposition. In a widely publicized speech, the Iranian monarch questioned both the source of the money and the use to which it was to be put. The next day, the Ayatollah replied: "Everybody knows I did not ask for the money for myself. I asked for it for the committee for the relief of the victims of what you have done—the children you have orphaned, the wives you have widowed."

The tension between the two men continued unabated, but did not visibly manifest itself until 1963, when the Shah undertook his White Revolution, an extension, in a sense, of the reforms begun by his father. There is some question as to whether the religious protests that ensued were part of a general reaction against the Shah's reforms by his opposition, or were specifically directed against a government decision to exempt U.S. troops, whose numbers were already growing, from local laws. The Ayatollah perceived such an exemption, which he construed as illegal under Islamic law, as a sign of the encroachment of the hated foreigners. He and his followers began to refer to that action of the Shah as "the capitulation."

Whatever the cause, the results were violent. The Shah ordered the Ayatollah arrested. Protests followed. Government troops put down the rebellion at a cost of many lives. The Ayatollah was exiled. He went to Turkey for a year and then to Iraq, whose western border adjoins Iran. There he was kept under strict surveillance and was not permitted to see foreign journalists.

But rather than destroy the Ayatollah's dream for a religious revolution, exile eventually made it real. Until his troubles began, Khomeini had not been a prominent spiritual leader. The top ayatollahs promoted him into their ranks only to keep him from being arrested. In those days, he was perceived as more an advocate than an original. But the Iranian ayatollahs who were more powerful and respected were in Iran, where they couldn't speak, whereas Khomeini in exile could. As the years passed, he learned to speak with increasing effect, and to deliver his message to Iran in a variety of ways. There came a point where his life path and the path of events in Iran converged. A revolution was building. The revolution needed a leader. He was available.

Even then, the Ayatollah might not have been in a position to assume leadership had it not been for a set of extraordinary circumstances. The first of these was the death of the Ayatollah's son in
1977, presumably at the hands of the Savak. From Iraq, the Ayatollah
issued a scathing attack against the Shah, blaming him for his son's
death.

The attack angered the Shah beyond all reckoning; he vowed retribution at the first possible opportunity. By one more of those accidents
of history, that opportunity may have presented itself—at least in the
Shah's mind—as a consequence of the visit to Iran of President Carter.

There were plentiful signs by this point that his regime was in trouble, but the Shah seemed indifferent to them. The bedrock of his
power was his relationship with the United States, and by now he had
the assurances of Jimmy Carter that the support he had enjoyed during the three previous administrations would continue unabated.
Buoyed by Carter's assertions, feeling the American power at his
back, the Shah apparently decided that there would never be a better
time for him to do what he had wanted to do for so long—destroy the
Ayatollah Ruhollah Khomeini. Immediately after the new year, the
Shah ordered Amir Abbas Hoveida, Master of the Royal Court, to
prepare an article attacking the Ayatollah and plant the article in a
Teheran newspaper. When a draft of the proposed article was given to
the Shah, he complained that it was too weak, and ordered it to be
strengthened. By the time the article had been rewritten to the Shah's
satisfaction, it was so scurrilous that no newspaper wanted to publish
it. Darioush Homayoun, the Minister of Information, reinforced by
the Prime Minister, Jamshid Amouzegar, finally compelled the daily
Ettela'at to do so.

The article, entitled "Iran and the Red and Black Imperialism," was
published on January 7. It accused the Ayatollah of a catalog of
sins, including allegiance to foreign powers, religious ignorance and
even homosexuality, and suggested that the mullahs of Iran were
conspiring with the Communists to destroy the existing order.

Every Moslem in Iran, even those moderates opposed to Khomeini,
was offended by the article, which provoked an immediate bout of
rioting, especially in the religious city of Qum. On January 9, government troops fired into the crowds, and at least six persons were killed,
some of them religious students. The irreversible tide of the Islamic
revolution was unleashed.

The Shah, worried about his health and thinking of the day when his son would succeed him, had wanted to crush the mullahs while he had time and external as well as internal support, so that his heir could take the throne in peace. He did not immediately see the magnitude of his error. When a trusted aide warned him that he would have to do something at once to placate the opposition, the Shah replied, "This is not something to be repeated, but as long as the Americans support me, we can do and say whatever we want—and I am immovable."

No assessment could have been more wrong. Before the year was over, the situation would change dramatically, partly because of a gross miscalculation on the part of the Iranian Government, but mostly due to the timely intervention of an exiled Iranian who, as an early victim of Savak torture, had been working for years to overthrow the Shah. That exile was Sadegh Ghotbzadeh.

For some time now, the Ayatollah had been taping denunciations of the Shah and then giving the cassettes to supporters, who would smuggle them across the Iraqi border to Iran under the label of Oriental music. The tapes were then copied and distributed to mosques throughout Iran, where they were broadcast to the multitudes, to the increasing dismay of the regime. In September 1978 Iran's newest Prime Minister, Jafar Sharif-Imami, decided that he would try to frustrate the Ayatollah's efforts by moving him away from the Iran-Iraq border. He asked the Iraqis to expel the Ayatollah, and the Iraqis obliged.

The Ayatollah's first choice of a new sanctuary was Kuwait, but he was no sooner in the country than he was arrested and sent back to Iraq. It was at this point that he received a visit from Ghotbzadeh, who had been coming to Iraq periodically since 1965 to visit the imam. Ghotbzadeh proposed to Khomeini that he come to Paris. It was far removed from Iran, true, but there he would be among friends —a group of Iranian exiles, like himself intent on overthrowing the Shah, as well as French men and women sympathetic to their cause.

The Ayatollah did not respond enthusiastically to the idea. Ghotbzadeh had to convince him. His success would prove to be the turning point in the Ayatollah's struggle against the Shah, because forces would now coalesce that could not otherwise have been marshaled. With his move to Neauphle-le-Château on the outskirts of Paris, the Ayatollah would suddenly have free access to the media, and would be such marvelous copy that he would be turned almost overnight into an international celebrity. He would be able to produce his cassettes with greater frequency and smuggle them back to Iran more systematically in the garments of couriers leaving from different cities each day. And he would have the use of a newly installed direct dial telephone service between France and Iran, which would permit him and his aides to make untapped calls to supporters throughout the country and give orders for manifestations. Most important, the Ayatollah Khomeini would finally come under the management of a group of bright Iranian exiles—Sadegh Ghotbzadeh, Abolhassan Bani-Sadr, Ibrahim Yazdi, Hassan Habibi and Sadegh Tabatabai—who had been waiting for years for the right leader to come along, and who would convert his frenzied but solitary cries into the crescendo of protest that would destroy the Shah.

One day in 1973, shortly after I had joined the staff of *L'Express,* France's leading newsmagazine, a tall and slightly pudgy Iranian exile in his middle thirties presented himself at my office with a ream of documents that, he said, offered irrefutable proof of the existence of torture and corruption in the government of Iran. Nothing about him corresponded to my mental image of an exile. There was no air of deprivation about him; rather, he was well dressed and groomed, with a carefully combed head of hair to set off his handsome, rugged face. He had also identified himself as a student, but he seemed much too old to be one.

My visitor offered to leave the documents with me so that I could study them at my convenience. As he was departing, I asked him to write down his name and telephone number, so that I might be able to find him if I had any questions. After he left, I glanced at his name, and was struck by its singularity. The name was Sadegh Ghotbzadeh.

Over the next five years, Ghotbzadeh came to my office half a dozen times, always with the same story and a collection of documents to support it. And gradually his story emerged, both from what he told me and what I learned about him from various sources as my curiosity enlarged.

Ghotbzadeh, born in 1938, was the son of a well-to-do lumber merchant. He became a militant before he finished high school. He was fifteen when Mohammed Mossadegh was overthrown in the CIA-led coup, an event that caused him to identify at once with the opposition to the Shah and in particular with the Islamic liberation movement led by Mehdi Bazargan. When he entered university, Ghotbzadeh founded the Association of Islamic Students. For this he was arrested and tortured by the Savak, and it was only through family connections that he was released and allowed to leave the country. By the time he was twenty-four, Ghotbzadeh had become a political vagabond, roving from country to country in search of some kind of connection that would give purpose to his hatred of the Shah. For a while, he lived in Washington, D.C., where he attended Georgetown University, but his political activities made life constantly precarious. At a reception at Washington's Hilton Hotel one evening, he insulted Ardeshir Zahedi, Iran's ambassador to the United States, and avoided expulsion from the country only because of the intervention of Robert Kennedy, then the Attorney General of the United States. Ultimately, Ghotbzadeh's activities proved too much for the immigration authorities and they sent him packing.

Wherever he located, Ghotbzadeh was given the task of organizing and leading the local Islamic student movement. In 1964, with the help of the Algerians, he organized an embryonic guerrilla movement in Iran. The next year he met the Ayatollah Khomeini, and life suddenly gained the focus he had been seeking. Ghotbzadeh concluded that the only organized force in Iran capable of ultimately overthrowing the Shah and his regime was that represented by the mullahs.

It was, in many ways, a strange alliance. A good Moslem, Ghotbzadeh didn't drink, but he was scarcely an ascetic. His enthusiasm for Paris nightlife was well known to French authorities, who watched him closely because of his associations with Communists. For a while, the authorities believed that Ghotbzadeh was a Communist himself, but then decided that he was simply interested in cultivating anyone who might possibly help him in the pursuit of his objectives.

In the ensuing years, Ghotbzadeh, traveling on a Syrian passport, kept moving, now to Syria, now to Lebanon, now back to France. He passed himself off as a journalist, but his real work was as a courier for Khomeini, carrying money and ideas throughout the network of exiles and their supporters.

There were many Iranian exiles Ghotbzadeh's age living in various parts of Europe and the United States at the time. Many had known one another in Teheran, most had been charter members of the Islamic student society founded by Sadegh Ghotbzadeh and all of them had been expelled during the same period.

One of them was Ibrahim Yazdi, who had spent his exile in the United States. Another was Abolhassan Bani-Sadr, who left Iran for France after spending four months in jail for his part in the 1963 anti-

Shah riots, during which he was wounded. The son of a wealthy and prominent ayatollah, Bani-Sadr was a scholar specializing in economics, which he hoped to adapt one day to an Islamic society in Iran.

How was it that young, left-wing intellectuals like these three men, Westernized to a great extent from long sojourns abroad, would rally around a seemingly archaic religious fanatic like the Ayatollah Khomeini? What convinced them—rightly, as it turned out—that Khomeini was the man capable of providing the strong leadership necessary to carry off their revolution?

Khomeini's Islamic opposition ideology, in their view, wove itself perfectly into the cultural fabric of Iran. As political scientist Barry Rubin observes, "To create a liberal or Marxist in the Islamic world takes much time and experience, but almost every citizen carries a Muslim orientation within himself. Even—one might say especially— the illiterate masses receive the bulk of their intellectual experience through the mosque, the mullahs and the Koran."

The Shah had, like his father, been at often violent odds with the mullahs throughout his regime, but while the antagonism had occasionally erupted and blood had flowed, he had never dared to take on the entire religious establishment in a showdown confrontation, sensing, perhaps, that this was one battle he would never win. The clergy in Iran was the one group well enough organized to attack the Shah in a systematic way; better to mollify them wherever possible, and to continue to support them financially, as the state did.

So here was the sanctuary and the common bond that the men who came to back Khomeini considered indispensable to their objectives. Iran, they knew, would always need a strong leader. The Ayatollah was the only one in sight. Under him, if they succeeded, Iran would have a religious government, but it would be one, they hoped, in which he would be the religious figurehead and they would be at the head of a predominantly civilian apparatus, incorporating the religious element, that would make the country run.

Beneath the surface, never expressed, was the question of which of these men would be at the controls. They never discussed it themselves, but those who were familiar with them and their work sensed a tension between Ghotbzadeh and Bani-Sadr, in particular, as though both men, putative friends, recognized the inevitability of a confrontation if they ever made it back to Iran. If it came to that, these bystanders favored Ghotbzadeh to emerge the victor. He was the militant, the one who had fought relentlessly against the Shah. Bani-Sadr was an opponent of the Shah as well, but he was an intellectual and a dreamer and too far to the left. Ghotbzadeh, despite the rumors, was a centrist at heart, those who knew him felt.

Both men were at Orly Sud to meet the Ayatollah on the October evening he arrived in France. With them were eight others, including three French attorneys, Christian Bourguet, François Cheron and Nuri Albala, who had come armed with documents and citations in case the Ayatollah had trouble with the immigration authorities. But the Ayatollah and his party—his son Ahmed and Ibrahim Yazdi—sailed through passport control.

The party walked outside the terminal, where Ghotbzadeh stood with the Ayatollah, waiting for the Peugeot 504 of Christian Bourguet in which he expected to take the imam to the apartment where he would spend the night. Just then a maroon Mercedes sped up to the entrance. The doors were flung open and Bani-Sadr half shoved the imam into the car and got in beside him, while Ahmed Khomeini took the front seat. To François Cheron, a friend of Ghotbzadeh, it seemed like a blatantly political move. "Get in the car!" he urged Ghotbzadeh.

But Ghotbzadeh didn't move. He had watched the maneuver in surprise but with an expression of mild amusement. When the Mercedes sped away, he turned to Cheron and said, "Don't worry. You know the story of the son-in-law of the Prophet."

Ghotbzadeh said no more, and only when Cheron saw the affection with which the Ayatollah treated his longtime supporter in subsequent weeks did he understand what Ghotbzadeh had meant.

The arrival of the Ayatollah Khomeini in France caught both the French and the Americans by surprise. French President Valéry Giscard d'Estaing, in Brasília on a state visit, was incredulous when he heard the news. "But how did he get in?" he asked. As soon as Giscard returned to Paris, he ordered the Ayatollah expelled. But the night before the imam was to leave the country, the Elysée Palace received a frantic telephone call from the palace of the Shah. "Don't expel the Ayatollah," a spokesman for the Shah begged. "If you do, we'll have riots in Iran." Nor, for the same reason, did the Iranians want the Ayatollah muzzled, as the French proposed to do.

The Ayatollah spent three days in Bani-Sadr's cramped Paris apartment. Then he was moved to a small villa in Neauphle-le-Château, in the western suburbs of the city. But no one in his new command post

expected any quick miracles. There was still the Iranian Army to consider, which, as far as they knew, would fight to the last man to bar
their return. That same appraisal was still in vogue at the White
House. Within weeks, however, the Ayatollah and his people began to
receive reports from inside Iran that important military leaders were
willing to desert the Shah and make their peace with the religious leadership. And suddenly the quick miracle they hadn't dared expect was
at hand.

Three months later, the Shah was gone. On February 1 the Ayatollah Ruhollah Khomeini flew to Teheran aboard an Air France
jet that had been chartered for $100,000 with a rubber check.
The check was signed by Sadegh Ghotbzadeh, who then sold tickets at
the airport to members of the press who wished to accompany the
Ayatollah on his triumphant return. Payment was in cash only, which
Ghotbzadeh stuffed into a plastic shopping bag and then turned over
to the wives of the French lawyers Christian Bourguet and Bernard
Valette, with instructions to deposit the money the moment the banks
opened the following morning. Then Ghotbzadeh boarded the plane
and flew with the imam to Iran.

D

chapter six

Panama Pays Its Bill

AMBLER MOSS, THE AMERICAN AMBASSADOR TO PANAMA, WASTED NO time in following up on the report that Panama might be willing to offer a home to the Shah of Iran. The morning after he had been alerted by Peter Tarnoff, the executive secretary of the U. S. State Department, Moss called on Vice-President Ricardo de la Espriella. Would Panama admit the Shah? Yes, the Vice-President said, provided President Carter asked Panama to do it. Moss immediately relayed that advice to the State Department.

That same morning, December 2, 1979, the Shah of Iran left New York Hospital, traveling a route through hospital corridors so heavily guarded it reminded him of a getaway scene from a 1930s gangster movie. Later that day, the Shah and his party landed at Lackland Air Force Base in Texas, a facility where many Iranian pilots had been trained. Lackland is not a "secure" facility; no pass is needed, either by military personnel, their dependents or visitors, to enter or leave the base. There are few fences or restricted areas. As a consequence, the only place the post commander had thought to take the Shah on such short notice was to the psychiatric ward of the base hospital.

As soon as he saw the bars on the windows, the Shah recoiled. He refused point-blank to remain there. The commander, General Acker, moved the Shah and his party to the visiting officers' quarters as soon as they could be readied.

Overnight, the Shah's disposition improved. He was back in a realm that he understood. The officers with whom he came in contact, some of whom had served in Iran, were extremely sympathetic and did everything they could to make him feel at home. They briefed him on military affairs around the world and discussed the newest developments in weaponry. It was the kind of talk the Shah enjoyed. Little by little, he could feel the pressure lifting.

And then, on Friday, December 7, the Shah was brutally reminded, once again, that he was a hunted man.

Shortly before 1 P.M. that day, the Shah's nephew, Shahriar Moustapha Shafik, thirty-four, son of Princess Ashraf, was returning to his home at 30 villa Dupont in the fashionable Sixteenth Arrondissement of Paris. He had been out to do the morning errands, carrying a plastic shopping bag and wearing a sport coat and blue jeans. Just before he reached the gate of his home, a young athletic-looking man wearing a beige jacket and white motorcycle helmet came up behind Shafik, followed him for a few steps, then drew a pistol and shot him at point-blank range in the neck. Shafik fell to the ground. The assassin bent over and fired a second shot into his head. Then he fled on foot.

Shafik, Moroccan-born, had held a French residence permit. Although he had been the deputy commander of the Iranian Navy and was considered to be the one man capable of crystallizing an opposition to the new regime, he had not requested special protection, nor had the French Government thought to provide it.

In Teheran, shortly after the shooting, Islamic judge Ayatollah Sadegh Khalkhali announced that Moslem assassins had been searching for Princess Ashraf when they found and shot her son. The judge claimed responsibility for the assassination of Shafik, whom he described as "one of the filthy and mercenary agents of the sinister Pahlavi dynasty."

It was 7 A.M. in Texas when Robert Armao learned of the shooting. Once again, he dreaded being the bearer of bad news, and waited until nine o'clock before going up to the Shah's bedroom.

The Shah had just gotten out of bed. For a minute after Armao told him he simply stared in silence. Then he said, "He was a very dedicated officer. He was a patriot."

Later that morning, the Shah was told that a childhood friend of his had been one of the planners of the assassination. He was crushed. "I can't believe anyone that close to me would be so low as to do a thing like that. If I believed that, I would have to lose faith in all humanity."

Armao thought that, deep down, the Shah knew it was true but didn't want to accept it.

By the second week in December, the Americans had come to the conclusion that there was little chance to resolve the hostage crisis peacefully so long as the Shah remained in the United States. The Shah was well aware that the Americans felt this way, and was more than ready to leave. But of all the countries the United States had canvassed, only Egypt had agreed to extend an invitation to the United States; all the others were concerned about what would happen to their own embassies in Iran and elsewhere in the event that they admitted the Shah. The Americans didn't want the Shah in Egypt; they didn't want to cause trouble for the Egyptians with other Arab countries in a way that might upset the delicate balance they had sought to achieve in the Middle East. The Shah, for his part, knew the troubles he had caused his friend Sadat when he went there on leaving Iran—there had been violent demonstrations in the universities—and he was unwilling to subject Sadat to that problem again if there was any way to avoid it.

So, if only by the process of elimination, Panama was elected.

President Carter did not want to telephone directly to General Omar Torrijos, the commanding officer of Panama's armed forces and the country's real ruler. Too much was riding on the Panamanians' response for so casual an approach. Instead, Carter decided to send his White House chief of staff, Hamilton Jordan.

Superficially, Jordan would seem an unwise choice for so delicate and important a mission. Nothing in his aspect suggests a diplomatic bent; to the contrary—and in total contrast to the overt Puritanism of his boss—he has an undisguised zest for wine, women and life in general. If anything, he gives an impression of the good old Georgia boy— a tad roly-poly, good-natured and with a grain of self-deprecating humor. But the impression is deceptive; Hamilton Jordan is a serious and effective political strategist who, still in his twenties, helped Jimmy Carter gain the presidency. What most commended Hamilton Jordan to Jimmy Carter, despite their differing life-styles, was that his political brilliance was contained within a framework of absolute loyalty to the man he served. Every President must feel that he has a few people around him who are totally loyal to him and him alone. It is this sense of trust that gives the President a feeling of security in dealing with the many others in his administration whom he has not known well but has appointed to top government posts.

For this new mission, Jordan had one other important qualification: personal knowledge of General Torrijos. The two men had come to know one another well during negotiations on the Panama Canal Treaty, and developed a friendship based on mutual respect.

Jordan flew to Panama on December 11, under security so strict that not even the personnel at Howard Air Force Base where he landed knew who he was. At nine-ten that evening, he and Ambassador Ambler Moss met with Torrijos in "the Bunker," the office the general maintains in his home. On one wall of the office, across from shelves loaded with books and trophies, hung a framed copy of a *Time* cover of Torrijos and Carter.

"The message you're bringing must be very important, judging from the importance of the messenger," Torrijos said.

"Given that criterion, you should expect a foolish message," Jordan joked. Then, abruptly, he turned serious. "In the name of world peace, in the name of the American people, in the name of President Jimmy Carter, I wish to present you with a request: that Panama receive the Shah temporarily to surmount one of the most serious crises the world has suffered since the Second World War." Jordan assured Torrijos that the American Government would provide Panama with all the help it might need in the event of problems, and that it would continue to look for a permanent asylum for the deposed monarch. American intelligence sources and certain secret contacts had allowed them to hope that the crisis would resolve itself favorably with the exit of the Shah from the United States, Jordan said.

The response was immediate: the Shah could come to Panama. Everything would be ready for him on his arrival. There were no conditions to the offer.

From the first, there had never been any doubt about the Panamanian response. Torrijos had already discussed the anticipated request with the Panamanian President, Arístides Royo. Neither man had forgotten that it was Jimmy Carter who had given them the Panama Canal Treaty they had wanted, after three previous Presidents had failed them. It had taken courage to do that, they believed; what a shame it was that no country had the courage—*cojones* is the word they used in Spanish—to help the Americans now, when the Americans had helped so many countries in the past. More, Panama's experience with the United States had shown the world how a small country and a power-

ful one could reach agreement, and perhaps in this experience there
was a lesson for Iran. The Panamanians knew they were assuming a
risk. They could be isolated by the Islamic world and deprived of oil
to an extent that would create serious problems for the Panamanian
Navy and thus the operation of the Canal. These were not just theoretical assumptions; Panama had just negotiated a highly favorable contract with Iran for the purchase of oil at two dollars a barrel below
market prices, and there was talk of building an oil refinery in the
country with Iran's help. Both the new contract and the refinery prospect could be out the window if they took the Shah in, the Panamanians knew. But they owed Jimmy Carter, and they were prepared to
take the risk.

As soon as Torrijos had indicated that Panama would go along,
Hamilton Jordan telephoned President Carter to inform him of the decision. He spoke to him in code. Then Torrijos suggested to Jordan
that when he conveyed the invitation to the Shah he speak in the
strongest terms. "We offered him asylum once and never got an answer," the general recalled.

Jordan assured the general that the Shah, by this point, had lost his
arrogance, particularly since he'd been spurned by Mexico.

Then Torrijos asked Jordan about the true state of the Shah's
health. Jordan replied that confidential sources had indicated the Shah
had widespread cancer, and did not have long to live. Moreover, he
appeared to have lost the will to do so.

As he was preparing to leave, Jordan received a gift from Torrijos—
a quantity of Cerveza Panamá, a beer he esteemed. Holding the beer,
Jordan joked that someone should take his picture and send it along to
Time. Torrijos joked as well; he told Jordan to be sure to thank the
President for the Christmas present he was sending him.

At the door, Jordan became serious again. He told Torrijos that
Carter's reelection could well depend on the outcome of the hostage
crisis. Then, thanking him for his help, Jordan said he was sure that
the general was one of the greatest men he had known.

Jordan left Panama very late that evening and flew to Kelly Air Force
Base near San Antonio, which adjoins Lackland. He arrived early the
following morning, December 12. At 3 P.M., he met with the Shah,
along with Lloyd Cutler, who had flown in from Washington, and
Robert Armao, the Shah's adviser, who had come from New York.

The Shah was not feeling well. He was already bothered by the malignancy in his spleen. He listened quietly as Jordan presented the case for Panama, but Armao was hostile from the outset. He pointed out that the invitation was "nothing new," that they had been invited months before and had scarcely considered it. Panama was run by a strong man with an unsavory reputation, Armao said. Moreover, he didn't believe the Panamanians could provide adequate medical care. Finally, he was worried about the possibility of extradition. "Based on those considerations," he said, "I would rule Panama out."

Jordan, who had left Panama in a state of euphoria, could scarcely believe what he was hearing and seeing. Here he was, the emissary of the President of the United States, dealing with the Shah of Iran on a matter of surpassing global importance, and the Shah's decision turned on the assessment of a Manhattan public relations man. He said nothing of these feelings, however. Instead, he worked hard to reassure both men. There was no possibility of extradition, he said, first because Panama and Iran did not maintain diplomatic relations, and second because the United States wouldn't permit it. As to medical care, the United States would provide it at its military hospital in Panama. Jordan extolled the climate of Panama, the beauty of its mountains and islands and the grace of its people. When he had finished, he and Cutler left the room so that the Shah and Armao could talk.

"My best advice is no," Armao said. "You can't trust the Panamanians. It's unfortunate, but that's the reputation of this regime."

"Where else?" the Shah asked. "You have nothing else to offer. They're offering Panama."

For another several minutes, Armao continued to argue. Finally the Shah cut him off. "Regardless of what you say, I'm going to Panama."

"Your Majesty, you're crazy," Armao blurted.

For a moment, the Shah was nonplussed. No one had ever spoken to him like that. Then he said, "I would feel remorse if I knew my children had to go through life with our American friends believing that I was responsible if any harm came to the hostages."

In his discussions with Cutler, Jordan had proposed that Armao return with him the next day to Panama to meet Torrijos and reassure himself about the available facilities before the Shah made his final decision. Now the Shah said to him, "If you don't want to go to Panama, I'll send someone else. I'd like you to go, but I'm not going to force you."

"No," Armao said. "If you've made up your mind, I'll go."

Early the next morning, Jordan, Armao and the Shah's senior security man, a former Iranian colonel, flew to Panama aboard a U.S. DC-9. They were met by Manuel Antonio Noriega, the head of the secret police, who took them on a tour of possible homes for the Shah. There were three: a mountain retreat, a city residence and an island. The mountains were beautiful, as advertised, but the retreat the Panamanians had in mind was an hour and a half from the nearest airport, and from that airport to Panama City was another forty minutes. That was too much of a gamble if the Shah were suddenly to become ill. Panama City was too crowded and noisy. That left Contadora, an island in the Pacific thirty miles off the mainland with its own small airport, from which one could fly to the capital in fifteen minutes.

The house that the Shah was being offered belonged to Panamanian ambassador Gabriel Lewis, who the previous spring had traveled to the Bahamas to offer the deposed monarch asylum. Armao didn't like the house at all. It seemed more like a vacation retreat than a permanent residence. There were four bedrooms, but all but one were tiny. The kitchen was equipped for the preparation of snacks, rather than meals. The dining area was so small that if six persons were at the table a dog could not pass behind them. Worst of all, the house lacked privacy. Its terrace faced the beach; once again, as in the Bahamas, the Shah would be subjected to the stares of tourists each time he wished to come out. Yet for all its shortcomings, Armao considered Contadora the least of three evils.

Before returning to Lackland, Armao went to Torrijos' house for a meeting with the general. Torrijos reaffirmed his desire to have the Shah in Panama as his guest. "When I invite you into my house for a drink, I don't make you pay for it," he emphasized. "If anyone tries to take money from you, come to me and I'll put them in jail."

Then Torrijos gave Armao a letter to the Shah, written in both Spanish and English on the stationery of the Commander of the National Guard. In the letter, Torrijos formally invited the Shah to Panama, promised that he would be treated in a manner befitting a man of his high station and indicated that he was looking forward to a long and lasting friendship.

Jordan called President Carter to tell him he believed that the matter was settled. They would be returning to Lackland that night, he said, to discuss it with the Shah; Armao would recommend approval.

On the flight back to Lackland, Jordan and Armao went over medical provisions as well as the problems of a telephone for the Empress, who, the Shah had said, had to communicate with people in order to preserve her sanity.

Jordan and Armao arrived back at Lackland at 12:30 A.M. on December 14. Armao, tired and eager to retire, figured he would speak to the Shah in the morning. But he was told that the Shah had waited up for him. So he went at once to the monarch's quarters. "I'm not particularly satisfied," Armao reported, "but it can probably work out."

"Fine," the Shah said.

That morning Jordan presented Torrijos' letter to the Shah. The Shah was pleased; it meant something to him to receive an official invitation from a state. Several times that morning he remarked, "I'm officially invited."

There was still one grave problem to overcome, however. By this point the Shah's spleen had enlarged so dangerously that the Air Force doctors attending him had alerted Benjamin Kean in New York. Kean flew to Texas the next day on a plane with Lloyd Cutler, the White House counsel, William Jackson, the Shah's attorney, and Hibbard Williams, chief of medicine at New York Hospital. He, Williams and five Lackland physicians examined the Shah. All of them agreed that the spleen should be removed, an operation that for a man the Shah's age and in his condition carried a 10 to 15 percent risk of mortality. Then Kean laid the facts before his patient in private.

"How long would it take for me to recuperate?" the Shah asked.

"About two to three weeks," Kean said.

"No," the Shah said at once. "I want to get out of the United States fast. I've been told it may help the hostages. I don't believe that, but I don't want to stay where I'm not wanted." The Shah told Kean that his spleen had been this large before, but had been reduced by drugs. Kean told him that drugs would probably work this time as well.

"Let's get out, then," the Shah said. "We'll try the drugs, and if they fail, we'll do the operation in Panama."

Under normal circumstances, Kean would have counseled immediate surgery. He wasn't thrilled with the Shah's decision, but he accepted it, and he was somewhat comforted by his personal knowledge of Panamanian medical capacities as well as the facilities at Gorgas Hospital in the former Canal Zone, where he had been stationed for seven years. After seeing the Shah, he returned to the room where Jordan, Cutler, Armao and the other doctors had assembled to await the deposed monarch's decision. "Every bit of medical evidence we have tells us we should take the spleen out," Kean said. "We're not going to at this moment—but I want it done at Gorgas Hospital with doctors of my choice."

"When can he leave?" Jordan said.

"In half an hour."

Jordan started for the telephone.

"Not so fast," Kean said. "I want an agreement on Gorgas Hospital."

Jordan turned to Cutler. "Is there any trouble on meeting that condition?"

Cutler said there wasn't.

"Okay," Jordan said. Then he went to the telephone to advise the White House of this latest development.

Now all that remained to remove the Shah from the United States— and presumably remove, thereby, a major obstacle to the freeing of the hostages—was the matter of what would come to be called the "Lackland Agreement." The agreement, worked out principally by Jordan, Cutler, Armao and the Shah's attorney, William Jackson, was an oral one; it provided that the United States would assist the Shah with any medical or security problems that might arise; that the White House would acknowledge its full support for the move to Panama; that the Shah would be given access to Gorgas Hospital; and that, in the event of any emergency that couldn't be handled in Panama, the Shah would be returned to the United States, in a fully equipped medical B-52. And the Empress would have her telephone; a mobile unit with radar beam was promised.

After agreement had been reached, Carter called the Shah, wished him good luck and endorsed the assurance his aides had given. It was the first time the two men had spoken since Carter had called the Shah from Camp David in September 1978 at the behest of Anwar Sadat.

As the government representatives prepared to depart the Shah observed that he would leave the United States for Panama within the next two days.

"Actually," Jordan said, "we'd like you to leave tomorrow morning —as early as you can."

At 6 A.M. in Panama the next morning, General Torrijos awakened Ambassador Gabriel Lewis with a telephone call. "Get up and get out," he said. "The Shah is coming."

The ambassador did not ask questions or discuss terms; he did not expect to be paid. By midmorning, his house was ready for occupancy.

The plane bringing the Shah from Texas arrived at the military base in the former Canal Zone with a flotilla of helicopters—five Panamanian, five American—flying escort. As the Shah was debarking, an Air Force medical officer who had accompanied him on the trip walked over to the Panamanian physician who was waiting to receive him. The American doctor saluted smartly, and then said, "He is in good health and good condition. He is now your responsibility." That son of a bitch, thought General Torrijos, who was standing nearby. We know that the Shah is dying, but this doctor washes his hands with a salute.

It was a momentary pique that quickly passed. Torrijos was genuinely pleased by the turn of events. He wanted to help solve the hostage crisis, and with the Shah now in Panama he believed that he could do it. We have the kingpin, he thought, the most important piece in the problem.

The Spanish word he used was *tornillo,* which also translates as "screw." Screws were very much in the news, because one that held a motor to a wing of a DC-10 had recently come loose, precipitating a disastrous crash.

Prior to the Shah's arrival, the United States and Panama had agreed to a code word for the Shah. They called him the "DC-10 screw." Now the word went back to the United States: "The DC-10 screw has arrived."

It was late that same day in Teheran when Sadegh Ghotbzadeh learned that the Shah had left the United States to take up residence in Panama. He immediately dialed an unlisted telephone number in Paris, but the man he wanted wasn't there. Then he dialed the number of his lawyer and longtime Parisian friend, Christian Bourguet. "Find Héctor," he said.

chapter seven

Something for Panama

OF ALL THE IMPROBABLE PEOPLE WHO WOULD BECOME INVOLVED IN the secret negotiations to free the hostages, the most unlikely was Héctor Villalón. He was an Argentine expatriate living in Paris, with no formal legal or diplomatic credentials, but with a record of success as an entrepreneur attesting to a profound understanding that, regardless of the leftist or rightist persuasions of his clients, at the center of everything was business.

Villalón had started professional life as a protégé of Evita Perón, had maintained contact with her husband, the Argentine dictator Juan Perón, after he was deposed and expelled, and had even helped plot his comeback. He had developed a talent for identifying and ingratiating himself with political figures on the way up in countries throughout the world; people meeting him for the first time suspected he was a name-dropper until they discovered that he really was on a first-name basis with the powerful men he discussed. During the first years of the Cuban revolution, he had worked hand in glove with Fidel Castro, advising the nation's planning commission, organizing the country's sugar and tobacco industries and trying to maintain the country's ties with the United States while at the same time diverting its leader from his drift toward Marxism and close ties with the Soviet Union. It could almost be said that Villalón was a revolutionary *manqué*, perpetually frustrated in the fulfillment of his political aspirations. In his personal life, however, he was anything but a failure. His quick wit and wheeler-dealer talents had gained him a small fortune. Dark and dapper, with a neat mustache and Latin looks, he traveled the world over, making contacts here, negotiating agreements there, and always finding adventures.

Until this moment, Villalón's biggest adventure had been one he would have preferred to have skipped. In 1977 he was arrested by the French police for his alleged complicity in a sensational kidnapping. The victim was Luchino Revelli-Beaumont, the head of Fiat France. Before coming to France, Revelli-Beaumont had been the head of Fiat Argentina, where he had developed close links with the Perónist groups, one of whose members was Villalón. After the kidnapping at the hands of Argentine Montoneros and for a large ransom, Villalón, at the request of Mrs. Revelli-Beaumont, tried to track down the kidnappers. But Argentine police, who had been after him for years because of his efforts in behalf of Perón, intercepted his telephone calls and reported them to the French. Acting on the theory that Villalón might be implicated in the kidnapping, the French arrested him and held him in jail for three months before declaring him innocent. The attorney who secured Villalón's release was Christian Bourguet.

But the Argentine's troubles weren't over. The following year, he was once again under legal pressure as a consequence of a request from the government of General Jorge Rafael Videla that he be expelled from France for carrying on anti-Argentine activities on French soil. Once again, Villalón was defended by Christian Bourguet. By coincidence, Bourguet was also defending Sadegh Ghotbzadeh against efforts to expel him from France.

It was at Bourguet's Left Bank office that the two men met, and they hit it off at once. The similarities in their lives were obvious—both of them globe-trotters, both political adventurers, both of them enamored of charismatic leaders. While they were not similar in appearance, each man cut a striking figure. Before the day had ended, they had discovered a host of mutual friends, and developed an affinity for one another based on a common sense of vocation.

But while Héctor Villalón warmed to Sadegh Ghotbzadeh's forceful personality and passion for his cause, he found the Iranian's naïveté in the sphere of political strategy jarring. He was especially concerned about Ghotbzadeh's dealings with Communists.

"I find my help where I can get it," Ghotbzadeh replied. He assured Villalón that he himself was not a Communist.

Villalón satisfied himself that Ghotbzadeh was telling the truth, but the young Iranian's attitude left him restless. It wasn't realistic. You didn't get help for nothing from the Communists.

Over the next months, the Argentine expatriate schooled Ghotbzadeh in the finer arts of achieving one's objectives. The first lesson Villalón attempted to teach the Iranian was that two fights are one too many. His meaning was clear: pit yourself against the Shah, and make peace with the Americans. "You cannot imagine going back to your country without starting a dialogue with the Americans," he argued. "You can't fight against the Shah and against the Americans too. You must start a dialogue with the Americans."

"Okay. I accept that," Ghotbzadeh said.

Villalón turned first to Ambassador Esteban E. Torres, the representative of the United States at UNESCO. But Torres was unwilling to see Ghotbzadeh, let alone pass him on to the State Department. Then Villalón sought out Irving Brown, the European representative of the AFL-CIO, a fierce anti-Communist and old-time trade unionist with many contacts throughout the world. Brown was interested. A longtime opponent of the Shah, he had disapproved of the 1953 coup d'état that had unseated Mohammed Mossadegh and brought the Shah back to power. He was aware of rumors within the U. S. Government that Ghotbzadeh was a Communist and conceivably an agent of the Soviet intelligence agency, the KGB. Brown undertook a discreet inquiry with sources he refuses to reveal to this day, and satisfied himself that Ghotbzadeh was not a Communist, let alone a secret agent for the Russians. When he finally saw Ghotbzadeh, Brown confined the discussion to what a new Iranian revolutionary government might do to limit the power of the Tudeh Party—the Iranian Communist Party—in the oil fields of Iran.

Brown passed the substance of these discussions on to members of the American Government whom he will not identify either. But when Villalón attempted to use the Brown connection to promote Ghotbzadeh further with U.S. officials, he was unsuccessful.

Several years had passed since those efforts. The exile the Americans wouldn't see was now the Foreign Minister of Iran and a candidate for the Iranian presidency. The Americans would have very much liked to see him, but he would not see them.

The news that the Shah had gone to Panama was especially dismaying to Héctor Villalón. Just weeks before he had been the broker on an oil deal between Iran and Panama that would be extremely helpful to the Panamanians. The deal, signed on December 1, provided for the shipment of $32 million worth of light and heavy Iranian oil to Panama at prices well below the market. But money and goods had not yet changed hands, and Villalón was certain the deal would fall through.

He was at the Hôtel du Rhône in Geneva on the night of December 5 when he learned from Christian Bourguet that Ghotbzadeh wanted to talk to him. He immediately telephoned his friend and former "pupil." Ghotbzadeh wanted to know everything—who had organized the move, how it had been accomplished, even whether it was true. "What will be absolutely necessary to find out," he said, "is whether I myself can go to Panama immediately."

Villalón begged Ghotbzadeh to be patient, and asked for a little more time to reflect on the best strategy to pursue.

As soon as he returned to Paris, Villalón conferred with Christian Bourguet at the attorney's office. Both men agreed that it would be a mistake for Ghotbzadeh to go to Panama—the trip was fraught with political hazards—and so informed him in a call to Teheran. "Come to Teheran," Ghotbzadeh said.

In Caracas, Ali Akbar Moinfar, Iran's Oil Minister, who was attending the OPEC meeting, was so infuriated by Panama's action in admitting the Shah that he announced the abrogation of the oil deal between Iran and Panama. It was a unilateral decision; Moinfar had not even cleared his announcement with Teheran.

It was an abrupt end to a deal that had more to it than business. The contact with Panama had been initiated by the Iranians at the suggestion of Héctor Villalón; the idea was to give favored treatment to underdeveloped countries by selling oil directly to them, rather than have them buy from the big, multinational companies. In addition, the Iranians had promised to help the Panamanians construct their own refinery, which would have made the tiny country a major distributor of petroleum products. Panama had been chosen as the first country for the program because, to the Iranians, it had, for years, suffered the consequences of American imperialism.

When news of the cancellation reached Panama, government officials estimated the cost of their generosity to Jimmy Carter, when the value of the prospective refinery was included, as something in excess of $100 million.

Sadegh Ghotbzadeh, who had scarcely had a home to speak of during his two decades in exile, now lived around the clock in the Foreign Minister's office in Iran. The office was a suite, with a big room in the center where he worked, a small dining room and a minuscule bedroom. Despite his newly won eminence, he remained a vagabond in spirit; he kept his clothing in a suitcase, as if to suggest that after all his years of wandering, he could not take permanence for granted. If something were to happen, he would be prepared to move at once.

There was a big desk in the central office, but Ghotbzadeh never used it. He did all his work while seated in a black leather reclining chair at the other end of the room, next to a couch and a set of chairs. It was there that he met on December 19 with Christian Bourguet and Héctor Villalón, who had arrived that day from Paris.

It was clear that Ghotbzadeh's desire to resolve the hostage crisis was as strong as it had always been. From the outset, he had believed that the crisis had created a grave problem for Iran, discrediting the country and its revolution with governments and people throughout the world. The student militants, he was certain, had been infiltrated by Communists who were using the situation for the good of the party and not the country. There was, in addition, his complex personal reaction to the situation. In one respect, he didn't give a damn about the Americans being held hostage. His view was that if for once some Americans suffered a bit, after all the harm their country had caused his, so much the better. On the other hand, he had been a prisoner himself, and had never forgotten the experience. What the Americans were undergoing could scarcely be compared to incarceration by the Savak, but their situation troubled his conscience, nonetheless. For more than twenty years, he had fought against the Shah's repressions; how could he countenance the holding of hostages now, without formal charges, when he had been so opposed to that very procedure for all these years? The hostages could be held for months, even years, with no way to extricate them. The thought of anyone being held prisoner without trial was humanly unacceptable—one more indication to him of politicians playing at politics and using human beings as their tools.

All this Ghotbzadeh had conveyed to the Ayatollah, but he had not been successful in swaying the imam. Others were saying that the hostage question could be used for the benefit of Iran, a means of gaining attention throughout the world for the country's grievances against the Shah, and possibly of recovering the Shah's wealth and even the Shah himself. The imam had been effectively neutralized by the conflicting information.

Over the next two days, Ghotbzadeh's two old friends and counselors, Bourguet and Villalón, reiterated their advice that he should not make the trip to Panama. He had no assurances that things would work out there, and any unexpected misfortune could ruin his chances for election.

Finally, it was decided that both men should go in his stead, and to help pave their way Ghotbzadeh gave them copies of two letters that were being sent to Panama through diplomatic channels. One was addressed to President Royo, the other to General Torrijos. The letters assured the Panamanians of Iran's respect for the integrity and political independence of Panama, but proposed that perhaps the country had received the Shah under pressure from the United States. In any case, the Iranians wanted to develop legal initiatives to achieve the Shah's extradition.

"Look," Villalón said, "these letters are all well and good, but the Panamanians aren't going to make a political concession without getting something in return. We have to arrive with something in our hands, so that we can say, 'Here's what we're bringing you on behalf of Iran.'"

"Like what?" Ghotbzadeh said.

"You've liberated most of the blacks and the women, as a political gesture. I'm told that there are two Chicanos and an Indian. Why not liberate them? That would have an impact not only in Panama but all over Latin America."

Ghotbzadeh thought for a moment. Then he said, "Good idea. But to do it, we'd need three agreements—from the Revolutionary Council, the imam and the students." He thought for another moment; those three, he realized, should have been released with the other blacks and the women; their release now shouldn't be much of a problem. "I'll take care of it," he said abruptly.

Ghotbzadeh saw Bourguet and Villalón again that evening as they were about to leave for the airport. "Okay, it's done," he said. "I have the three agreements. You can go to Panama and say those three people will be liberated."

The three hostages picked for release were William Gallegos and James Lopez, both of Hispanic origin, and Frederick Lee Kupke, an American Indian.

What amazed General Torrijos and other Panamanian officials about the Shah as they got to know him in the early days of his stay was his insistence on "imperial protocol," one example of which was that the Shahbanou could not sleep in the same room with him. Doesn't he know he's an emperor without an empire? Torrijos mused. He's down to seven persons, a Dalmatian and a French poodle, and he thinks he's still a king. The strong man of Panama could not understand that protocol was all the former occupant of the Peacock Throne had left.

"My father left me a country—my inheritance," the Shah would repeat again and again. Right there was where they separated; Torrijos could not accept intellectually that a person could inherit a country.

"Weren't you aware that your people wanted a change?" the general asked the Shah in one of their conversations.

"Yes, I was going to make a change. I was going to leave the throne to my son."

Again, Torrijos could scarcely believe this man. Did he really consider passing the rule to the crown prince a change? "Do you want to save the monarchy, or save the people?" the general asked.

"Saving the monarchy is saving the people," the Shah replied.

The general studied the Shah. It's incredible, he thought. He really does believe that.

After the conversation Torrijos gave up on trying to reason with the Shah. Pahlavi was a cultured man, he decided, but he didn't have his feet on the ground. He was superstitious; for him everything was macumba: black magic. It was as if the Shah was talking in A major and Torrijos himself in A minor. It was easier to stick to neutral subjects like the weather.

The Shah told his host that the heat and humidity of Panama had been good for his throat, which was sore from chemotherapy. He slept in an overheated room filled with five steamship trunks—Torrijos called them *baúles,* or packing boxes—and the two dogs guarding them. Torrijos suspected that the trunks contained masses of important papers.

For his part, the Shah found life on Contadora Island "pleasant enough" in the beginning. In addition to the climate's salutary effect, the dramatic view of the ocean from his beach house calmed his nerves. Both General Torrijos and Panamanian President Arístides Royo were friendly and their attentions reassured him. He liked the way they called him "Señor Shah."

But Robert Armao saw things differently. Within a few days after their arrival in Panama, he began to develop suspicions that all was not as it seemed. He felt that all the niceties, such as the lunches with Royo and Torrijos, were nothing but a front and that in fact, the Panamanians had no respect for the Shah. His every movement was monitored, which gave Armao the impression that they were treating his client more like a prisoner than a guest. There were a number of bearded men in front of the house, wearing bathing trunks and carrying machine guns. Were they guards or jailers? In addition, they were spending the Shah's money wildly, with no authorization from the deposed monarch or from Armao, who handled all disbursements.

At last, Armao decided to confront the issue. He approached the chief security officer, and said, "I don't understand why you needed to rent fifteen cars to watch over a two-block island."

"Mind your own business," the officer snapped. "It's none of your affair."

Armao reported the story to the Shah. "We're not the guests we were cracked up to be," he said. The Shah tried to play down Armao's fears. A few days later, however, he had an encounter with the chief of the secret police, Manuel Antonio Noriega, that seemed to confirm Armao's suspicions.

"Get rid of the Americans," Noriega instructed the Shah. "They're interfering with security, and leaking things to the press."

The Shah held his ground. "No, I need them, and my children need them."

But the police chief's tone had unnerved the Shah. When he got back to Contadora he told Armao, "Tell your staff to stay in the background, and not use the telephones. I'm sure they're tapped. And let one of the Iranian colonels be the liaison with the Panamanians."

Armao followed his client's instructions, but he was increasingly disturbed by the Panamanians' hostility toward himself and his staff. Finally, he couldn't take any more; he told the Shah that he would take a vacation in order to calm the situation.

For the first time in a long while the Shah laughed. "I tried that once. It doesn't work," he said.

General Torrijos wanted badly to solve the hostage crisis for his friend Jimmy Carter. He had proved that already by accepting the Shah and thereby exposing Panana to a punishing reprisal. In addition, for the first time in ten years, Panama was now experiencing daily rioting in the streets. In spite of this, Torrijos was determined to press on. He would negotiate with the Iranians in a manner that would not only be diplomatically impossible for the Americans but was beyond the reckoning of the ingenuous gringos.

The idea taking shape in Torrijos' mind was to make a hostage of the Shah.

Shortly before Christmas, Hamilton Jordan received a call from General Torrijos in Panama. He had a notion, the general said, that the presence of the Shah in Panama might be used in some manner to help secure the release of the hostages. What Torrijos had in mind was a "delaying" action, he said, in which he would appear to go through the motions of extradition.

The idea chilled Jordan. It seemed to him unrealistic, even farfetched, and he said as much to the general.

It wasn't all that farfetched, however. The Panamanians had a law and legal process by which anyone whose extradition is requested by a foreign power must be detained while the charges are studied. The Americans had made it known to the Panamanians that under no circumstances would they permit the Shah to be extradited. If and when that became a real possibility they would remove the Shah from Panama at once and return him to the United States. But arrest was another matter. If the Iranians requested extradition, as everyone expected them to, and if some kind of symbolic detention could be arranged that might facilitate the release of the hostages, perhaps that option ought to be considered. Despite Jordan's own negative reaction, and although no American would admit it, either then or subsequently, a good many of them now began to think of the arrest of the Shah as a definite possibility.

The week before Christmas, a French parliamentary delegation made a visit to Qum, the religious capital of Iran and the site of the Ayatollah Khomeini's headquarters. The delegation was led by a French senator, Brigitte Gros. All of the legislators represented districts that included Neauphle-le-Château, where Khomeini had lived while in exile in France. The parliamentarians were received by Khomeini, and also by Bani-Sadr, who told them in confidence about the forthcoming release of the three American hostages.

The news proved irresistible to the French legislators. When they landed in Paris on December 23, they called a press conference at which Madame Gros announced the forthcoming release as a gesture to the country that had provided sanctuary for the Ayatollah.

Within hours, student militants were demonstrating so vociferously in front of the American Embassy in Teheran that the plans to release the hostages were dropped. Because of a French senator's indiscreet disclosure, William Gallegos, James Lopez and Frederick Lee Kupke would spend an extra thirteen months in captivity—and Christian Bourguet and Héctor Villalón would have no Christmas present for Panama.

Bourguet and Villalón arrived in Panama on December 24, at almost the same moment that Robert Armao was leaving the country in disgust for a brief vacation. When the two men tried to make contact with government officials, they received a cool reception. The government officials were not completely persuaded that a French attorney and an expatriate Argentine entrepreneur could be the bona fide representatives of a nation not their own. A call to Washington only confirmed their suspicions; Washington had never heard of them.

But then Bourguet and Villalón placed a call to Ghotbzadeh in Teheran to prove that they were well connected. In the end, Iran's unorthodox Foreign Minister not only confirmed the legitimacy of his uncharacteristic envoys but used the call to emphasize his desire to develop close relations with Panama, particularly because Panama's close relations with the United States might permit them to act as intermediaries to solve the hostage problem.

At eight-thirty on Christmas morning, Bourguet and Villalón met with President Arístides Royo and Marcel Salamin, the political counselor to General Torrijos, in the presidential suite of the capital's Holiday Inn. As they delivered the letters they had brought from Iran, the two emissaries said that the Panamanians would never understand the real meaning of the letters if they didn't first get a feedback on what was happening in Iran.

What Bourguet and Villalón tried to explain to the Panamanians during the next three hours was the dilemma confronting the country's leaders in attempting to deal with the hostage crisis. It was this: as much as many of them might be embarrassed by the student action, or acknowledge that it had placed Iran in an untenable situation, or even that it was costing the country millions of dollars a day, none of them, with the exception of Bani-Sadr and Ghotbzadeh, was willing to take on the students, whose action had electrified the people. The people wanted the Shah back in Iran to be judged for his crimes.

For the Panamanians, the most perplexing factor was that the students were under the control of the Ayatollah Khomeini, and yet could not be brought to heel. "How is it possible that the Ayatollah, with his leadership within the country, can't help to solve the problem?" Salamin demanded.

"This is precisely the crux of the problem," Bourguet said. "If the Ayatollah solves the problem it will cost him his political head."

To the Panamanians, it was now clear that the American hostages were in the middle of a decisive struggle for control of the revolution in Iran.

chapter eight

Foreign Complications

BY NOW THE CAST OF CHARACTERS ASSEMBLED TO NEGOTIATE AN END to the hostage crisis looked more like the product of a fiction writer's imagination than a representation from real life. The scenes themselves had an aspect of fantasy about them. But there was nothing unreal about the event on which the hostage crisis next turned—the invasion of Afghanistan by the Soviet Union on December 27, 1979.

There is a theoretical, but strong, link between the Russian invasion and the American dilemma in Iran. Certainly, the Russians had their motive, independent of any American involvement; in the sixty-two years, to that point, since the revolution of 1917, no country that had gone Communist as a consequence of Soviet efforts had ever dropped from the fold. Had events in Afghanistan been left to run their natural course, it is more than likely that anti-Communist forces would have overthrown the government of Nur Mohammed Taraki and Hafizullah Amin. Given the Soviet record in Hungary and Czechoslovakia, it is conceivable that their move into Afghanistan might have occurred regardless of the Americans' preoccupation with the hostage crisis. But the vulnerability of the Americans at this moment made the decision for the Kremlin that much easier. To add to the Russians' inducement, the hostage crisis had precipitated a power struggle within Iran, thereby rendering that country incapable of concerted action. Finally, there was the conviction, in the Russians' minds, that the Americans would have to carry out a military action against Iran. If that was the case, then the occupation of Afghanistan by the Soviets would be a quid pro quo for the future American intrusion in Iran.

For the Americans, the Russian action produced one immediate and encouraging consequence in regard to the hostage crisis: it pulled all of the Arabs together in their desire to see the crisis ended. The Arabs had been uneasy enough about the prospect of an armed intervention by the United States to free the hostages; in the Soviet action, they saw a redoubled danger. There was the added prospect of a military response by the United States to thwart a possible Soviet adventure in Iran itself; the United States would occupy Iran on the assumption that it had to be protected from the Russians. But to the Arabs, the most dangerous possibility was the one they could see just by looking at a map. Afghanistan lies in a landlocked pocket below the Soviet Union and between Iran and Pakistan; the occupation of the country put the Russians within four hundred miles of the Persian Gulf. One more grab for land, either the southeastern tip of Iran or the southwestern corner of Pakistan, would give the Russians command of the gulf itself—and control over the shipment of oil from most of the Middle East.

But as much as the Arab countries might want to see the hostages freed in the wake of the Soviet invasion of Afghanistan, their sudden zeal had little or no influence with the new revolutionary government installed in Iran. The outside pressure the United States had hoped would materialize failed to do so. And so the United States was suddenly forced to change its tactics in the struggle to free the hostages, because the Soviet invasion of Afghanistan had dramatically and fundamentally changed the power game in the Middle East. If the United States had hoped to encourage the disintegration of authority in Iran as a means to free the hostages, it could no longer afford to think in that way, let alone encourage such an event. The fear that preoccupied the Arabs was equally felt in Washington—that the Soviet Union might take advantage of Iranian internal disorders and march to the warm waters of the Persian Gulf.

From this point forward, President Carter had to deal delicately with the Khomeini regime, firm enough to free the hostages, not tough enough to push Iran into the Soviet orbit. Part of that delicate dealing was an added effort to understand the Iranians' sensibilities.

The clue to those sensibilities was a big one. It had been all but explicit in the message that Abolhassan Bani-Sadr and Sadegh Ghotbzadeh had conveyed to the Americans early in December via François Cheron, the French attorney I was fortunate enough to put in touch with U.S. diplomats in Paris.

Bani-Sadr and Ghotbzadeh, neither of whom approved the seizure of the hostages as much as they might understand the students' sentiments, wanted the United States to give a clear and unmistakable signal that it respected the people of Iran and comprehended their concerns. It was to be a signal more of symbolic meaning than of substance. What the Iranians proposed was that the Americans treat "seriously" the Iranian request to extradite the Shah. Let the question be taken at once before the United States Supreme Court, the Iranians proposed. Let the Supreme Court rule on the constitutionality of Iran's request. The Iranians had no illusion about the result; they were certain that if the justices were to hear the request, they would find it unconstitutional. Nonetheless, the *effort* would say to the people of Iran: "We take you seriously."

The scheme of the two Iranians showed how little they understood about either American law or sensibilities. A request such as they envisaged had no practicality whatever; the United States had no extradition treaty with Iran, and there wasn't a lawmaker in America who would take it upon himself to sponsor a demand for the extradition of the Shah. Nonetheless, that desire for serious acknowledgment was still the underlying force of the Iranians' present demands. What they wanted, above all, was some kind of international forum in which they could put their grievances before the world.

For once, the United States responded with flying colors. Three days after François Cheron saw Warren Zimmerman in Paris, the United States sent a top-secret message to the Iranians via the Swiss Foreign Office and its embassy in Teheran. The message, designed to make certain that the Iranians had not missed the significance of a statement by U. S. Ambassador Donald F. McHenry before the UN Security Council, was unsigned and on blank stationery—the diplomatic manner of dealing with communications between adversaries who cannot—or will not—deal directly.

MESSAGE

A l'intention de S.E. Monsieur Sadegh Ghotbzadeh, Ministre des Affaires Etrangères de la République Islamique de l'Iran.

TOP SECRET

Citation:

1. Ambassador McHenry's speech in the UN Security Council was written to signal to the Authorities in Iran that the US recognizes

that the Iranian Authorities seek a hearing for their position. Ambassador McHenry said:

"None of US is deaf to the passionate voices that speak of injustice, that cry out against past wrongs and that ask for understanding, there is not a single grievance alleged or spoken in this situation that could not be heard in an appropriate forum. The US took the position in the Security Council debate that both the Secretary General and the Council itself should remain seized of the problem in order to help Iran and the US find a solution.

2. The Shah has not yet left the US but has moved to a US Government Hospital for a period of further recuperation. He is seeking an alternative residence outside the US. His status remains that of a private person in the US for medical treatment. The US continues to recognize the Provisional Government of Iran as the legitimate Authority in Iran.

3. If the US could be assured of the release of all the Americans held hostage in Teheran and of all official Americans there, the US Government would be prepared to discuss the future of the US-Iranian relationship and other matters, including the possibility of cooperation with an International Tribunal established by the UN Secretary General.

4. The US is prepared to send to Iran Mr. Charles Kirbo, close personal friend and Advisor of President Carter, for discussion at the highest Government level of a precise course of action, provided such discussion could take place in complete security and safety. He would prefer to meet in a neutral place but would be prepared to come to Teheran or Qom. The US leaves to Iranian Authorities the judgment on how best to proceed to a decision but wants to make this possibility known, should it be useful."

Fin de citation.

Téhéran, le 5 décembre 1979.

Charles Kirbo was Jimmy Carter's most trusted crony, used as a troubleshooter in particularly difficult situations. This was the first time his name had come up in connection with the hostage crisis.

The Iranians' desire for a forum continued to be evident in both the public and private realms.

In late November an Egyptian journalist respected throughout the Middle East, Mohammed Heikal, had had dinner with Bani-Sadr at the home of the Iranian's sister. At the dinner, Bani-Sadr told Heikal that while the Ayatollah Khomeini was not against the release of the hostages in principle, he did not want to release them until some kind of international tribunal had been held. There had been speculation that the United Nations might be the agency for setting up such a tribunal, but if the UN failed, Bani-Sadr said, the Iranians themselves would have to organize one.

Bani-Sadr thought that Jean-Paul Sartre, the French philosopher, should head the tribunal. All of the hostages would be permitted lawyers, and these lawyers, in their clients' defense, would call as witnesses all of the Americans the Iranians held responsible for the injustices they believed the United States had perpetrated on their country—Richard Nixon, Henry Kissinger, Richard Helms, the former director of the CIA, Kermit Roosevelt, the CIA agent who had masterminded the 1953 coup, and so forth.

Bani-Sadr reasoned that the attorneys for the hostages could compel such people to come—either by subpoena or moral force—if their presence at the tribunal would assure the release of the hostages. The hostages themselves would be released on the condition that they remain in Teheran until the tribunal had finished its work.

It was a dreamy idea that reflected its author's scholarly background, but it was important in what it said about the Iranians' desire for consideration by the rest of the world. As it turned out, the students holding the hostages would not accept Bani-Sadr's formula.

At this point, however, Khomeini himself decided that the proposal for a tribunal should be accelerated. The Ayatollah requested that three separate dossiers be prepared and presented to the tribunal. The first, prepared by Hojatolislam Ali Akbar Hashemi Rafsanjani, the Minister of the Interior, would deal with the Shah's alleged repressions and the role of Savak. The second, by Bani-Sadr, would deal with the "rape" of the Iranian economy by the Americans. The third, by Sadegh Ghotbzadeh, would deal with the foreign policy of the Shah, the bribes he was said to have paid to foreign leaders and journalists, and his links with foreign intelligence agencies. The three dossiers were to be completed and ready for presentation by the end of January 1980.

But their own proposal for a tribunal was only one of three in which the Iranians were actively involved in the first months following the embassy seizure.

The second proposal, a United Nations commission, had been mentioned informally almost since the day the hostages had been seized. Kurt Waldheim, the Secretary-General of the United Nations, had been, from practically the first day, solicited by the United States Government to do everything in his power to aid in the freeing of the American diplomats. For Waldheim, the hostage crisis was a superb opportunity to render a service to the United States that would assure the support of the American Government for his reelection when his second term as Secretary-General came to an end in late 1981. But the United States had limits on what it was prepared to allow the United Nations and its Secretary-General to do. The United States would accept the idea of a UN commission to investigate the alleged crimes of the Shah and U.S. involvement in Iran, but only *after* the release of the American hostages.

In early December Pakistani Foreign Minister Agha Shahi, who had gone to Teheran at the instructions of his country's President, General Zia ul-Haq, to see what he could do about the hostage problem (a way for Pakistan to gain favor with the United States), flew to New York to see Waldheim. He persuaded the UN Secretary-General that what the situation needed was a personal visit by Waldheim to Teheran. Waldheim was reticent. The veteran Austrian diplomat is not a man who likes to walk into a situation full of unknown factors. He sent Agha Shahi to Teheran to receive assurances from the Iranian Government that he was welcome, that he would see the hostages and be received by the Ayatollah Khomeini. The Pakistani Foreign Minister found a frigid reception to these ideas in Teheran. Where, he was asked, was the voice of the UN Secretary-General during all the years the Shah was oppressing his people? By what right did he think that the UN could intervene in the hostage matter when it had been absent from Iranian affairs in the past? Despite the rebuff, Agha Shahi was convinced that if Waldheim came to Teheran, things would work out, and he finally convinced the Secretary-General to make the trip. On the evening of his departure, Waldheim received an aide-mémoire from the United States Government, written by Harold Saunders, Assistant Secretary of State for Near East and South Asian Affairs, in which he was reminded that the position of the United States Government was for prior or simultaneous release of the hostages before the United States would approve the creation of a United Nations commission. Saunders was merely underlining the points made to the Secretary-General by Secretary of State Cyrus Vance.

From the moment that Waldheim arrived on January 1, 1980, until his hasty departure on January 4, his mission was doomed to failure.

The Iranians, under the direction of Foreign Minister Sadegh Ghotbzadeh, had organized a brutal welcome for him he would never forget. It was a way of reminding Waldheim that the UN had been absent from the struggle for human rights in Iran. The Iranians had arranged to present him with a sampling of the violence that had allegedly been committed during the Shah's regime. Hundreds of crippled and maimed Iranians were paraded before him. "He appeared shocked and moved by the victims, who waved crutches and artificial limbs and displayed stumps as they chanted support for the Ayatollah Khomeini," Christopher Wren reported in the New York *Times*. At one point, Wren went on, a father held an armless child before the Secretary-General, who was told that the child's arms had been cut off by interrogators for Savak to make the father talk.

Visibly moved, Waldheim spoke through an interpreter: "I wish to extend to all those people who I see here, whether they are grown-ups or children, my warmest sympathy and deepest feeling for them. My heart is with them." He promised those present an investigation of alleged human rights violations.

On January 3 Waldheim flew by helicopter to a revolutionary martyrs' cemetery south of Teheran, intending to decorate a grave as a symbolic act of sympathy. Here is Christopher Wren's account of the scene:

"Small clusters of mourners walked among the stone slabs and several women draped in black chadors fussed over one gravestone. The morning serenity was broken when about fifty men in symbolic white burial shrouds that looked like butchers' aprons paraded into the nearby shrubs bearing portraits of Ayatollah Khomeini and shouting in English, 'Death to Carter, Death to the Shah!'

"The Secretary-General was flown from his hotel in an American-made military helicopter to a nearby asphalt-paved lot, where he climbed into a Mercedes limousine. Another helicopter carried in a large red and white floral wreath for him to lay at the grave of Ayatollah Mahmoud Taleghani, who had died last summer [September 10, 1979].

"But when Waldheim arrived at the cemetery, several hundred shouting Iranians rushed at his car, pushing past the young Revolutionary Guards assigned to protect the entourage. The Secretary-

General had started to climb out, but an Iranian security man pushed him back in and shut the door. The limousine sped off."

All of this seriously upset Waldheim. To compound matters, Ghotbzadeh informed the Secretary-General there had been threats against his life, a fact which was subsequently broadcast by Teheran Radio. Waldheim would later tell a news conference in New York he never knew whether the security forces in Iran "were there to protect me or attack me" and that he was glad to be back alive. That was Waldheim's state of mind when he showed up for his tough session with the Revolutionary Council.

That state of mind was clearly reflected by his opening remarks to the Council:

"X: As I said at the beginning I was really deeply moved by what I saw this afternoon when I visited the center for rehabilitation. It was a terrible experience for me. It was a heartbreaking experience. I have myself three children and I can imagine what the mother or father feels if a little boy has his arms cut off. There was this one boy which I took in my arms was horrible. —You see I have seen many things. I was in the war 6 years, and I have seen a lot of bloodshed, and cruelty—but this was really heartbreaking. Little children mutilated in that way and also the grown-ups had lost their legs and their arms, their eyes—be assured that this was a good experience and I shall never forget it in my life . . . And this morning as you know I visited the graveyard—the cemetery of the victims of the revolution. Again, a very moving experience. Thousands and thousands of graveyards of people who had fought for their freedom, for their dignity and for their human rights . . .

"X: You see I have a great understanding for your suffering because I myself I am coming from a small country which has suffered a lot. I was born in 1918 when the first world war ended . . . I grew up then in a terrible situation. There was a civil war in Austria . . . the two main groups in Austria fighting each other. I remember I was a young boy when I saw in Vienna the bodies of my compatriots lying in the streets, dead, mutilated. It was a horrible impression. Then we had the war and I was a young man of nineteen years of age. I went through the whole war. I was wounded in the war. Then I came back and my country was partitioned by the big powers in four different parts. This tiny little Austria, which has not more than, not even 7 million inhabitants, was partitioned in four parts and we were living for more than ten years under the occupation of the big powers. That was the life I went through and I can assure you that this has taught me a lesson, about the big powers especially but about many other things in life. So I mention this just to show you what kind of life I have behind me and therefore I have so much understanding for your own suffering."

Prior to his meeting with the Revolutionary Council, Waldheim had spent five hours with Sadegh Ghotbzadeh. When Waldheim put forth the U.S. proposition of a UN commission in exchange for the simultaneous release of the hostages, Ghotbzadeh brutally cut him off. "That's not even discussable," the Foreign Minister said. "There's no way the mere creation of a commission will lead to the release of the hostages." When Waldheim tried a second time with Ghotbzadeh the second day, he got the same negative response. Waldheim apparently understood, because at no point during his subsequent meeting with the Revolutionary Council did he present the American plan for the establishment of a UN commission with prior release of the hostages. Instead, he went on at length to disassociate himself from American policy and American tutelage and announced that his own homeland, Austria, would not participate in any UN sanctions against Iran for the taking of the hostages.

"Then what I hope to say before I answer the questions put to me, is that I did not come here on behalf of the Americans. Because I saw here and there in some of the newspapers all kinds of things about my visit two years ago for instance. I took six years after I had to come because this is the mission of the Secretary General visits all the Member States. But I waited for six years and it was really not more than something which is part of the job of the Secretary General. I wish to assure you of this. But what is in my opinion important is to make clear that I didn't get orders from the Americans and I would never receive orders from the Americans. I'm an independent man. I come from a small neutral country and maybe you have by chance read in the newspapers that in my own country there is the question of economic sanctions against your country was raised in the United Nations . . . My small country was one of the first saying it would never participate in sanctions against Iran. I don't know whether you heard this statement, but I can convey it to you. So I just want to stress I come from an independent, neutral, small, but independent country and this is my whole attitude—I shall never accept orders any of the big powers whether it's the Americans or whether it's the Russians or anybody else. And I have insisted again and again in my talks with the Americans . . . that this problem has to be solved peacefully, and in no other way. And I shall continue especially after my visit to your country in the light of my talks I've had with you and what I have seen of the people—your courageous people in this country."

The Secretary-General stressed his and the UN's attachment to independence movements like the PLO, the South West Africa People's Organization (SWAPO) and the Polisario in the Western Sahara.

"X: We are also the strongest supporters of the liberation movements in the world . . . The liberation movements—we are the forum for them. We have in New York in the United Nations the PLO—the Palestinian Liberation Organization—I was one of the first personalities of the international community who visited Chairman Arafat, in Damascus first, then in Beirut, in his headquarters, then I met him on most of the African and non-aligned summit meetings around this globe. So I'm really a defender of the interests of the right to self determination for oppressed people and this is well known by the PLO for instance . . . by SWAPO . . . I have conceded also the liberation movement of the Western Sahara."

The Secretary-General then outlined for the Iranians the kind of inquiry commission he would seek United States approval for. It corresponded closely to what the Revolutionary Council had been pushing for, and it didn't once mention the release of the hostages as a condition of the inquiry.

"So then I tried to find out what could be done, I discussed with the foreign minister some of the possibilities. An international inquiry commission which would examine the misdeeds, the violation of human rights by the shah and his regime. And this type of such an inquiry commission would then present it either to the security council or the General Assembly directly so that the Assembly can decide . . . Of course this would have to be done in a sort of a package . . . Such a settlement should certain other elements like for instance . . . the ending of economic measures against Iran, normalization of the relations in general . . . of course the release of the financial assets of the shah which were taken out of the country . . . And I shall certainly convey this to the members of the Security Council and the membership of the United Nations. It will help to create more understanding between the national community who have no grievances. But we have also to see how can we set up an apparatus to . . . take note of your grievances, elaborate on them, look into it, and make then a judgment of the situation as such an international commission which would then include all the elements which were mentioned and then the assembly could take the necessary decisions. Of course for this one would have to try to begin as strictly as possible with the setting up of such an international inquiry commission and so that we do not lose too much time and in this way I think we could make a practical beginning of our efforts to find a solution of this . . . problem.

"I think I should after these general ideas which I expressed at the beginning say that you know better about my approach to the problem . . . what can we do to get out of this situation . . . I am very grateful to you that I had the opportunity to see what the country has suffered, you see the people in the West. They don't know this . . . So I am extremely grateful that I have seen this with my own eyes."

And in a final gesture to the Iranians, Waldheim promised not to reveal what had happened in the meeting.

"I too agree with the following step. I think that really we should not go into details as far as the public is concerned—the press especially—the western mass media. They are behind us all the time, and so in fact (he laughs) you are in the same situation. It's incredible how many press people hang around here. And I think it is in the interests of the cause—what we discussed today—that we do not make it public until we have reached a point where it is useful to make it public. I would limit myself to say that we had a hopeful and helpful exchange of views on the situation and its aspects. And that I shall continue in my efforts now after my return to New York for a peaceful solution of this crisis."

All of this could be regarded as normal diplomatic practice. It is true that the Secretary-General of the United Nations represents the international community, not any one country. But this situation was different. The United States was the aggrieved party trying to bring about the release of its own diplomats. It was entitled to set the

E

parameters for negotiations on that point. In any case, the problem
that ensued came from a failure in communications. The Secretary-
General reporting to the United Nations Security Council on January
7 told them that Ghotbzadeh said the hostages could be freed after an
international inquiry had been set up and that he had told the Iranians
the release of the hostages would have to come simultaneously or prior
to the creation of the commission. In Washington some American
officials interpreted this to mean that the conditions under which a
commission could be created were still negotiable—but not for the time
being. The idea of a UN commission was put on the back burner. Attention then turned to possibility number three.

In Paris on January 6, 1980, a French lawyer named Nuri Albala was
interviewed on Europe One, a privately owned radio station, about a
plan to organize an international inquiry into the crimes of the Shah,
and the American involvement in Iran. That same day a story ran in
Le Monde, under Albala's byline, propounding the same idea.

Both the interview and the story were plants, deliberately contrived
in terms of both content and placement to arouse attention among a
handful of people, in the hope that these people might be attracted
enough to the idea of an international inquiry to want to support it
and even associate themselves with it.

Albala was following a time-honored ritual by which political
figures who want to communicate with others don't just pick up a telephone and call them. In certain instances a more subtle approach is
required—when the origin of the message or the identity of the courier
needs to be masked, or when it is feared that the person at whom the
message is being aimed won't come to the telephone.

Albala planted the idea for an international inquiry out of a fear
that neither he nor the inquiry's initial proponent had sufficient clout
to sell the idea alone. To the contrary, they felt that they were too con-
troversial. Albala was a Communist, which made the project vulnerable to charges that it had been sanctioned by Moscow; and the father
of the idea was Sean MacBride, the former head of Amnesty International and former Irish Foreign Minister, hardly a neutral when it
came to the Shah. It was Amnesty International's and thus MacBride's
contention that the spread of systematic torture among certain governments in the world had actually started in Iran before spreading to
Greece, South America and East Asia; and that the American CIA

helped train the Iranian secret police, Savak, in the use of torture methods, and then supervised their implementation. For evidence, MacBride cited a statement made to him in Teheran by then Prime Minister Amir Abbas Hoveida, "All right, yes, it is true we are using torture, but you don't have to worry, it's being done under the supervision of the Americans."

It had been six weeks since the Irish diplomat had gone to Teheran at the request of Amadou Mahtar-M'Bow, the Secretary-General of UNESCO, to meet with Bani-Sadr, then the Foreign Minister of Iran. In his report to M'Bow on that mission, MacBride had written in a covering letter: ". . . the replacement of Mr. Bani-Sadr by Mr. Sadegh Ghotbzadeh, coupled with the decision of Mexico not to permit the Shah to return, are new elements that make the situation more difficult. I would suggest that you should inform the U.S. authorities that in the event of the Security Council failing to provide a forum for a dialogue you would be prepared to send me on a further mission to Teheran in order to maintain at least an indirect dialogue . . ."

Three weeks after writing that letter, MacBride was back in Teheran, but not at the behest of UNESCO, or even the United States, whose request for help had been responsible for his initial mission. Rather, MacBride was there because Ghotbzadeh wanted to pick up the threads of the idea the Irishman had left with Bani-Sadr. Rather than call MacBride directly, Ghotbzadeh had contacted Nuri Albala. The two men had known one another in Paris, where Albala, in addition to a long association with the cause of the exiles—he had gone to Iran to investigate charges of political torture and co-founded the French Association for Friendship with the Iranian People—had been a friendly witness at a trial in which Ghotbzadeh was suing a French writer for implying that he had publicly expressed his desire to kill all the members of the Iranian royal family. And finally, Albala had worked behind the scenes with Christian Bourguet to quash attempts by the French Government to deport Ghotbzadeh for engaging in political activities. In this effort, they were helped by the French ambassador to Teheran, Raoul Delay, who cabled the Quai d'Orsay, "Why throw him out? His people are coming to power in the near future anyway."

Ghotbzadeh had called Albala four weeks after the hostages were taken, and shortly after he had become Foreign Minister, to ask him to come to Teheran to explore ways in which the Iranians could "get out of this situation." Albala did have some notions, particularly the formation of a private association of families of the victims of the Shah, as well as an inquiry into the crimes of the Shah in the association's behalf. It was a means of finessing the hostage issue entirely; since the people asking for the inquiry had no power over the fate of the hostages, they couldn't be asked for a quid pro quo in exchange for the inquiry. As Albala envisioned the scenario, the Iranians would realize what they so desperately wanted, an international forum for airing their grievances against the Shah, and then liberate the hostages as an act of goodwill. After organizing a group of Iranian lawyers to do the groundwork, Albala went back to Paris to await word from the Ayatollah Khomeini, whose approval Ghotbzadeh would have to secure.

But the Ayatollah did not approve the idea, or so Ghotbzadeh informed Albala on December 15 in a call to Paris. The Foreign Minister wanted Albala back in Teheran, however, and said he would send him a ticket. Albala, who knew of MacBride's earlier trip, suggested to Ghotbzadeh that he bring the diplomat along.

A few days later, Albala and MacBride went to Teheran along with Robert Dossou, dean of the law faculty of the University of Cotonou in Benin.

In addition to their meetings with Ghotbzadeh, the three men had long discussions with the Revolutionary Council. By the time they returned to Paris, they had a clear idea of the kind of international inquiry they wanted; their ideas resulted in a memorandum dated January 3, 1980. A "Nuremberg-type" international commission would be appointed "to investigate the extent to which there is reason to believe that acts committed by or on behalf of the Shah and his administration during the period 1953–79 amounted to violations of human rights, as defined by the universal declaration of human rights in the UN international covenants on human rights." The commission would also investigate charges of plundering, misappropriation of private property, fraud and embezzlement. If the commission found that there were grounds for putting the Shah and members of his administration on trial, it would seek a Nuremberg-type tribunal under the auspices of the United Nations to try the accused. If the commission found reasons to believe that any suspected illegality on the part of the Shah and his associates had been performed with the aid or counsel of the United States, the commission would recommend to the United States Congress that it undertake an investigation.

One critical element of the proposal was that no international commission could be set up unless the American hostages were first released. The release, in turn, should be made conditional on the hostages' agreement to appear before the commission if requested to give evidence.

On December 24 MacBride left Teheran for Dublin, pleased with what he had accomplished. There was only one disquieting element to the visit. Throughout his meetings with Sadegh Ghotbzadeh, MacBride had the feeling that the Foreign Minister was not so much interested in the hostage problem as he was in the responses Bani-Sadr had made during his and MacBride's encounter, almost as though Ghotbzadeh were trying to discover whether Bani-Sadr, whose initial disapproval of the seizure of the hostages was well known, had in any way compromised the official Iranian position as defined by the Ayatollah Khomeini. The Irishman was very careful to avoid any remarks that might have embroiled Bani-Sadr in internal political problems.

MacBride promised Ghotbzadeh that he would write a draft of the commission proposal, and did so over the Christmas holidays. Oddly enough, Albala, whose name appears at the end of the report, would later insist that no solution to the hostage crisis had ever been discussed during the meetings in Teheran. The idea, he maintained, was to look into the crimes of the Shah—which might then lead to a solution of the hostage crisis. His interpretation was in line with the proposal he himself had made in Teheran a month before. How Albala could have made such an interpretation, given the specific statement about prior release of the hostages in the MacBride report, was never made clear, but his interpretation was an instructive clue as to what was really on Albala's mind.

In the coming months, much would be made of Albala's motive. He would be charged with deliberate attempts to disrupt legitimate efforts to free the hostages. It would be pointed out that he was the legal counsel for Tudeh, the Communist Party of Iran, which gets its orders from Moscow. And Moscow did not want the hostages released.

Whatever Albala's subsequent game became, he, MacBride and Dossou all agreed on their return to Paris after the new year that the report should be planted in the media in the hope that it would arouse the interest of Kurt Waldheim, the UN Secretary-General.

The strategy worked. Waldheim called MacBride and asked him to come to New York.

MacBride found Waldheim in a state of nervous tension, still feeling the effects of his experiences in Iran. Although the Secretary-

General reasoned that a bad time had been planned for him, he was nonetheless very upset about it. In any case, Waldheim wasn't interested in MacBride's idea for an international commission. It was in direct competition with the idea of a UN commission that Waldheim still favored, despite the rough treatment he had received in Teheran. The one good result of his trip to Teheran had been a three-hour interview with Sadegh Ghotbzadeh, the Foreign Minister, in which his ideas had been discussed.

After Waldheim told MacBride that he was pursuing another line with Ghotbzadeh, MacBride telephoned this information to Albala. Albala was shocked. He wondered whether Waldheim was lying, or whether his old friend and client Ghotbzadeh was giving him the runaround.

MacBride did no better in Washington. He received a sympathetic hearing from the Iran task force at the State Department, and spent a short time with Secretary of State Cyrus Vance. But Vance concluded that MacBride's commission wasn't a worthy channel to pursue. For one thing, he found the notion implicit in the proposal that some hostages had been guilty of crimes and others not totally unacceptable. For another, he bridled at the description of a "Nuremberg-type" investigation.

"Well, we can easily change that," the Irishman told him. "I merely used the words 'Nuremberg-type investigation' to indicate what I had in mind."

Vance's overriding concern was that the MacBride proposal had, without its author's knowledge, been seized upon by the Communists. He didn't want any part of it.

chapter nine

Contact

OFFICIALLY THE AMERICANS WERE DEAD SET AGAINST THE "PANA-manian track," as Harold Saunders referred to the efforts under way to extradite the Shah. They advised strongly against it, believing that the extradition efforts, even if they were nothing more than a charade, would complicate what they were trying to do. What they most feared was that the Iranians would eventually see the maneuver for the sham that it was and become so incensed that they would then be unap-proachable at any level. If the Americans were not going to be a party to the extradition of the Shah, and if the Panamanians weren't going to be either—or so at least they were telling the Americans—what did that leave? A move that would quickly be perceived as transparent. For all these reasons the Americans repeatedly urged that this track not be used.

But the Panamanians persisted nonetheless, sincerely believing that they could be helpful and that the Americans' intransigence proved that they did not have an understanding of the subtle diplomatic ma-neuvers by which problems between nations can sometimes be re-solved. In this, the Panamanians had the encouragement of Christian Bourguet and Héctor Villalón, the two emissaries *extraordinaires* of Iran, who were looking for some kind of dynamic development that they could present to the Iranian leadership as a tangible sign of prog-ress. The most dynamic sign they could present was one that involved the prospective extradition of the Shah to Iran.

The Panamanians assured the Americans that Ghotbzadeh knew

they would not permit the extradition. All the same, he wanted the official process to begin so that he could show that something was being done to collar the Shah. Only in this way could he create a climate in which the release of the hostages could begin to be discussed. It was a new version of that earlier refrain: "Take us seriously."

Regardless of the Americans' feeling, or their apparent lack of understanding, the Panamanians pressed on. On December 28 President Royo of Panama wrote a formal letter and General Torrijos a private one to President Carter in which the possibility of a request for the extradition of the Shah was broached, even though, at the moment, no initiative had yet been taken. Then the Panamanians sent a letter to the Iranian Revolutionary Council hinting that they might be helpful. The letter was strictly a trial balloon, meant to test the Iranians' reaction. The Panamanians could not have been more pleased when, a few days later, the Revolutionary Council issued an invitation to Royo, Torrijos or their representatives to visit Iran as soon as possible, in order to establish direct contacts.

Hamilton Jordan was eating his dinner at Camp David on Friday, January 11, when he received a call from General Torrijos. Through an interpreter, the general said, "I need to see you right away." He did not explain why.

Jordan was heavily involved in the presidential campaign; his first instinct was to decline. "I'm very busy," he said. "Can it wait?"

"No," Torrijos replied, "it's very important."

"Very important?"

"*Very* important."

Jordan did not want to put Torrijos off; he had been too good to the Americans to warrant such treatment. He also respected the general's judgment; if he was insisting, then it had to be a matter concerning either the Shah or the hostages, possibly both. "I'll get back to you," he said. Then he telephoned President Carter, reported the call and told him he thought he should go.

"That's what I'm thinking," the President replied. "He's taken the shot for us. If he thinks it's that important, we ought to hear him out."

The President told Jordan he would send his helicopter for him the next morning.

A while later, Jordan received a second call from Panama. It was Gabriel Lewis, the ambassador who had relinquished his Contadora

Island house to the Shah. "You've got to come," Lewis said. If Jordan had had any lingering doubts, they vanished with that call. Torrijos had a way of dramatizing events, but Lewis, a cool diplomat, wouldn't do that. In all their prior dealings, he had never called before to say, "You've got to come."

The one suggestion Jordan made was that they meet somewhere other than Panama. If either his arrival or departure were noted and the Shah heard about it, he would surely begin to think that something was going on behind his back. There was no telling what he might do at that point.

That night arrangements were made to meet at Homestead Air Force Base in Florida. The next morning the President's helicopter flew Jordan to Andrews Air Force Base near Washington, D.C., where Henry Precht, the Iran desk officer at the State Department, was waiting to give him the latest word on the hostage situation, in case that was the subject the Panamanians wanted to discuss. Although they had been intimately involved in the same affair for more than two months, it was the first time the two men had met.

Later that morning Jordan rendezvoused at Homestead with Marcel Salamin, political counselor to General Torrijos, Jorge Illveca, Panama's ambassador to the UN, and Gabriel Lewis. The meeting, which took place in the base commander's office, lasted three hours, with Salamin and Jordan doing most of the talking, and Lewis the interpreting.

What the Panamanians had wanted so urgently to tell the Americans was that they had just returned from a visit to Iran, and now had intimate knowledge of the situation there. In addition, they had identified effective representatives of Iran who might talk to the Americans. "It is our personal impression that there is a way to achieve the release of the hostages without military confrontation," Salamin said.

Before he could go any farther, Jordan asked to be excused. He went to a telephone and called President Carter. When he returned, he told the group that a UN Security Council meeting, scheduled for 6 P.M. that day to discuss sanctions against Iran, had been postponed at the request of the U. S. Government.

Jordan was ready to hear the Panamanians out.

Salamin and Romulo Escobar Betancourt, Panama's chief negotiator on the Canal treaty, had gone to Iran at the invitation of the Iranians ostensibly to advise them on how to handle their request for extradition, but in reality to develop a feel for the situation with a view to helping the Americans. "You Americans don't really understand what's going on in Iran," Salamin told Jordan. "With our experience in Latin America, living in the middle of disturbed areas and revolutions, we think we understand a situation like Iran's."

Jordan nodded, but said nothing.

"You have to start off from the point of view that you can't qualify all Iranian political forces with the same adjectives," Salamin went on. "You have a very difficult problem here. Either you head straight for a war, or you play a very clever diplomatic and political hand. This will imply that you understand the internal drama that each of these men is living and the power struggle that is going on in Iran right now."

Salamin was convinced that however much of a simple figurehead Khomeini appeared, he was more involved in political decisions than the Americans realized. "I think that he really wants to solve the problem, but unfortunately he is engaged in a politico-ideological confrontation that obliges him to take positions contrary to his thinking."

Nonetheless, Salamin said, all of the Iranians recognized that the problem had to be resolved eventually. "These people depend on you; if tomorrow or the next day a problem arises within the area, there may be a possibility to find a way to come to an agreement. You have to think strategically."

And in this game of political chess, Salamin reminded Jordan, Panama held the only pawn.

Salamin then argued a pet Panamanian thesis, that the Iranians really didn't want the Shah and wouldn't know what to do with him if they got him. His presence would create further unrest among the populace. They would then have to decide whether or not they should execute him. They were already isolated from the rest of the world for an act that transcended all diplomatic rules and traditions. If they were to execute the Shah, they would be damaged still further. On the other hand, if they did not execute the Shah, there was always the prospect that his return would rally those persons in Iran still loyal to him. "The specter of 1953 still hangs over the people's heads," the Panamanian said.

When they met with the Iranians in Teheran, he went on, there was not a single document ready nor was a presentation made in behalf of the extradition of the Shah. That alone should prove that they really don't want the Shah, he said.

Then Salamin got down to cases. While none of the Iranians would deal directly with the Americans, there were two men, one a Frenchman, the other an Argentine, who had been commissioned by the Foreign Minister to deal with the Panamanians, and with whom the Americans might also conceivably deal. The two men had spent several days in Panama, where they had made an excellent impression, and another several days with the Panamanians in Teheran, where they had proved beyond any doubt that they were well connected.

As Salamin continued with his presentation, Jordan silently marveled. The United States had been turning the world upside down in search of some person who could be their bridge to the Iranians, and now, at last, here was a man who had actually been to Teheran and met with the key people.

Jordan's reverie was suddenly interrupted by what Salamin was now saying. Both Bani-Sadr and Ghotbzadeh, the Ayatollah's two most trusted confidants, had read a story in *Time* about how Jordan had negotiated the transfer of the Shah to Panama without any public notice. It had occurred to the Iranians that a man who could work so silently and successfully might be a good person to contact. Moreover, he was close to the President, and he had no connections with the State Department, which they considered to be dominated by Henry Kissinger and David Rockefeller.

What a series of crazy accidents, Jordan thought. It was only because of his previous dealings with Torrijos that he had been asked to go to Panama to negotiate with the general. And then the Iranians had read about him in *Time*. And, finally, after Salamin and Escobar had reported on their trip to Torrijos, the general had decided not to go through channels, calling either Cyrus Vance, the Secretary of State, or Zbigniew Brzezinski, the President's National Security Adviser, but calling his friend Hamilton Jordan.

Now Jordan proposed to Salamin that the Panamanian return to Teheran and tell the Iranians that the United States was willing to negotiate directly for an agreement that would be pleasing to both parties.

Salamin never made it back to Teheran. He started off for London, via San Juan, but fell ill from nervous exhaustion and had to turn back. After a day's rest, he determined to try again, but at the Panama airport he received a call from General Torrijos, who ordered him not to risk his health any further. They would send someone else.

In the end, no Panamanian went to Teheran, nor was it necessary, because the groundwork had already been laid during the several days that Salamin and Escobar had spent in Teheran earlier that month with Bourguet and Villalón. No formal discussions were held on the question; nonetheless the Panamanians managed to float the idea of a high-up meeting with some American. Bourguet and Villalón were for it, but they wanted to take no chances. Before they would even consider such a meeting, they had to gain approval from all the power centers. The reply they got was passive, but not negative: "We're not against it." But the Iranians, especially Ghotbzadeh and Bani-Sadr, ever mindful of the political risk of any contact with the Americans and deeply involved in the presidential campaign, made it clear that it was Villalón's and Bourguet's idea. They weren't asking them to go.

In mid-January Gabriel Lewis, who had been in Paris for further talks with Christian Bourguet and Héctor Villalón on the plans for extradition and had then gone on to London, called Hamilton Jordan in Washington. "Why don't you come over here and see these guys?" he said.

Jordan agreed at once. He told Lewis, however, that he would bring someone from the State Department with him. He did not want to do any negotiating whatever without an expert on his side.

As soon as the two men had finished talking, Jordan called Harold Saunders, the Assistant Secretary of State for Near East and South Asian Affairs, and told him to prepare for the trip. Then Jordan asked the CIA for dossiers on Bourguet and Villalón. Bourguet's dossier held no surprises; it was a classic profile of a French attorney enamored of progressive causes. But when Jordan started to read Villalón's dossier he let out an involuntary whistle. Among his many eye-popping global adventures, the man had been deeply involved in Cuba, and was a friend of Fidel Castro. Well, Jordan figured, you can't pick your mediators. But he decided that he wouldn't tell either the President or the Secretary of State about what he had learned.

On January 18 Jordan and Saunders boarded the Concorde in Washington for London, using assumed names.

Seventy-seven days after the seizure of the American hostages in Teheran, two top-level representatives of the government of the United

States finally got into the same room with two emissaries of the government of Iran. They would soon discover, to their distress, that a great deal of time had been wasted; Christian Bourguet was the law partner of François Cheron, the man who had come to my home in Paris on Sunday, December 2, 1979, forty-seven days earlier, to ask for help in making contact with the Americans.

It had taken almost two months and three separate contacts to click in the Americans' minds that a French law firm representing the government of Iran, the national bank of Iran, the spiritual leader of the Iranian revolution, the present Finance Minister and likely next President of Iran and the Foreign Minister of Iran was, indeed, close to the Iranian leadership and men with whom they could deal. The first contact had been through Giulio Andreotti, the former Italian Prime Minister. The second contact had been through me, when I passed François Cheron to the American ambassador in Paris. Neither contact had really done the job. Only because of the persistence of the Panamanians had the Americans at last come to believe that these were serious people.

Believe it they did, before the day had ended. As Bourguet and his ally, Villalón, spoke, it registered on Harold Saunders that they were men with authentic knowledge of the scene in Teheran—who were the principal actors, what were the relations between them, where the real power resided. It was invaluable information because, for months now, the Americans had had no clue whatever as to the political realities inside Iran.

Jordan, for his part, could only wonder in amazement, as he had at Homestead, at the unlikely series of circumstances that had led to this meeting. Since November 4, the United States had made countless attempts to Third World countries, to Islamic nations, to individuals who might conceivably have good enough relations with the revolutionary government of Iran to put its representatives in direct contact with representatives of the United States. The Americans had even tried to initiate direct discussions themselves. Each and every one of these efforts had proved unsuccessful. And now, out of the blue, as if they'd been sent by God, appeared two people who seemed to have the right credentials and contacts.

That he, of all people, should be in charge of the negotiations for the Americans was what most overwhelmed the young Georgian. It had never been intended on the American side that he be the key man. It had happened only because he was the person the Iranians had identified as someone they might be able to deal with. The assignment filled him with trepidation and anticipation in equal measure.

The meeting took place in the drawing room of a comfortable London townhouse whose tenant was the deputy chief of mission of the American Embassy. Jordan and Saunders sat on a sofa with their backs to the window. To their right sat Christian Bourguet and an American interpreter, and the two Panamanians, Gabriel Lewis and Rory Gonzales. To their left was Héctor Villalón.

The discussions went on for twelve hours. From time to time the participants would adjourn to the dining room on the other side of the entry to help themselves to the buffet of cold chicken and sandwiches that had been prepared for them, as well as whiskey, beer and fruit juice. But the dialogue would continue as they stood at the table, eating and drinking.

The discussions had begun on the morning of January 19 with Villalón alone, because Bourguet, who was flying in from Paris, had not yet arrived. When they broke for lunch, Villalón went out to the airport to meet the Frenchman. Once they were all together, they talked well into the evening.

The morning meeting had been, after some initial moments of anxiety, a relaxed and open, almost optimistic one. That was because of Villalón; the suave Argentine believed that people needed to be animated at the outset if fruitful discussions were to result—even if it meant persuading them that conditions were better than they actually were. With the arrival of Bourguet, a tall, skinny, bespectacled man with the appearance of a respectable attorney below the shoulders and a long-haired anarchist above them, the mood changed perceptibly. Here was a man who appeared at once in his element, not so much because he enjoyed the high of international political intrigue, but because something in the expression of his bearded face immediately took on the character of the person whose point of view he was expressing. As far back as he could remember, Christian Bourguet, now forty-five, had wanted to be a lawyer. But whereas for some youths the attraction of the law was its promise of high salaries and prestige, for Bourguet the profession was almost interchangeable with a life of service to humanitarian causes. While still a student, he had worked with a lawyer involved in preparing Morocco for independence, and one of his first jobs in Paris was defending ultra-right-wing activists who had been sentenced to death for trying to overthrow the French Government and maintain Algeria as a French colony. Bourguet didn't share the political ideals of the people he defended at this time; he simply felt that everyone, regardless of his or her political or ethnic persuasion, had the right to be defended by a lawyer. But when his natural tendency to empathize was backed up by belief in the cause for which he was working, as was the case with the Iranian revolution, his earnestness knew no bounds.

The change in mood was partly a consequence of Bourguet's own expectations; for an exercise in diplomacy, he had expected to encounter diplomats. Harold Saunders, wearing traditional dress, taking copious notes throughout, going off alone during their breaks to correct his notes and list his further questions, corresponded to Bourguet's expectations. Jordan didn't at all. He seemed much too casual—he was wearing a blue suit but no tie—and years too young for the role. Instead of taking notes, he stored most of what he heard in his head. The most unusual fact of all was his openness. Bourguet had expected an elaborate, diplomatic exposé of the problem, but Jordan's manner was blunt. "What can we do to solve this problem?" he kept asking in a number of variations. The Frenchman liked the directness of Jordan's approach, and yet the questions of the young American seemed to beg a simple answer, as though a solution could be found simply because they were at last in touch. Everything was black or white. Gray didn't exist. He had to penetrate that sensibility, and the only way to do that was to shock him.

Bourguet began by trying to explain to Jordan what the Shah represented to the people of Iran, and what the United States represented to those people as a consequence of the support it had tendered the Shah, the arms purchases it had permitted and even encouraged, and the manner in which it had intruded itself in Iranian affairs. The extradition of the Shah to account for his crimes, as well as the return of his assets taken from the country, were fundamental problems. If the United States was unwilling to address itself to these questions, Bourguet said, no beginning could be made in the discussion of freeing the hostages.

Up until that point, there had been no surprises. But as Bourguet continued, the American became increasingly alarmed.

"The Shah *must* be brought back to Iran to be tried," Bourguet said. "The Shah returned, or the Shah dead, is the key to the problem. Nothing can be done unless this problem is solved. Regardless of whether it had figured in the original taking of the hostages, now, in the public mind, the Shah's extradition or his death has become the central issue. It's not a question of saying it's good or bad. It's a fact."

What the Iranians want, Bourguet said, is that the problem "disappear." As long as the Shah is alive, there is always the possibility of his return to power. For the Iranians, Bourguet went on, the Shah is a true myth. The Iranian people will never believe that his trip to the United States was for medical reasons; for them, the trip appeared as the beginning of a process designed to return the Shah to power. It had happened in 1953; why should they not believe that it might happen again? Consequently, the request for the return of the Shah to Iran is designed to make the problem "disappear."

Jordan was dismayed. What the Panamanians had told him about the Americans not understanding the Iranians was true. For more than two months they had been dealing with the problem as though it represented the lashing out of a rather primitive people. Only now did he comprehend the depth of the feelings involved, and the symbolic importance of the return of the Shah. The Panamanians had been right to recognize the issue for what it was; their theory that the Iranians really didn't want the Shah, however, was as off base as the Americans' notions that the demand for extradition was nothing more than rhetoric.

Impulsively, Jordan turned to Saunders and blurted, "That's not what the State Department has been telling us."

There was a moment in which the only sound in the room was of the traffic in the street, and in that moment, it occurred to Jordan that he had just made a most undiplomatic admission in the presence of the representatives of Iran. But it occurred to him, as well, that conventional diplomacy had gotten them nowhere for seventy-seven days. He was not a professional diplomat, but he was the man they had asked to deal with because they liked the way he operated. The way he operated was to trust his instincts, and he was going to trust them now. He was a politician who dealt in give-and-take; every bone in his body was telling him that this was a moment to give. He turned abruptly to Bourguet. "We had thought that the real problem was the return of the Iranian assets, and the taking up of relations between the countries on a new level, one of equality, where the Americans would promise not to interfere anymore in Iran. Okay. But we didn't understand that the problem of the Shah was that fundamental."

Much would happen in the ensuing hours, and the next day, when the group would meet a second time, Bourguet would press his advantage, urging the Americans not to impede the attempts for extradition but rather, to instruct the Panamanians to arrest the Shah and decide later what to do on the basis of the evidence. Jordan would say that he was not ready to take such a decision at this time, that he wanted to see if there weren't other ways to tackle the problem. He would raise the prospect of the UN commission to look into Iran's grievances, its appointment to be announced simultaneously with the release of the hostages—a prospect Bourguet would scathingly dismiss, thus: "To imagine that the hostages would be liberated simply because a commission is named is a hypothesis so mindless it is not even worth considering." And Jordan would acknowledge at that point, "We have a feeling that Waldheim is not quite telling us the whole story of what happened during his visit to Teheran." In their most constructive moments, the participants would envision a "scenario" to be worked out between the disputants, by which the release of the hostages would be secured in exchange for some as yet to be defined concessions on the part of the Americans. At the end of the meeting, Bourguet would call Teheran and ask Sadegh Ghotbzadeh whether he was willing to speak directly to Hamilton Jordan, who was standing by, or meet with him in London, in the interest of shortening the process. And Ghotbzadeh would brusquely refuse to talk to or meet with Jordan, declaring, "No Iranian can meet an American face to face."

And so the Americans and the representatives of Iran would part only minutely closer to a break in the hostage crisis than they had been before they met. But one thing had occurred at that meeting that would eventually make all the difference in the world. The guileless honesty of Hamilton Jordan, which had made the professional diplomats catch their breath, had lanced through the lifelong biases of the representatives of Iran. In Hamilton Jordan, they would conclude, they had found a man who exploded all their assumptions about the character of Americans. Villalón, in particular, knew that as a Latin American, he shared a vision of *los gringos* as an insensitive people. Here was a man who seemed totally receptive to others' ideas, eager to learn everything he could and so passionately committed to a solution of the hostage problem that he was willing to put his own life on the line.

During one of those snack breaks, Jordan had taken Bourguet to one side—Bourguet would later conclude that Jordan hadn't wanted Saunders to overhear—and said, "Look, if in order to resolve the problem, a face-to-face meeting would help, I'm ready to take an anonymous airplane and go to the airport in Teheran and meet any leader you want."

Bourguet was stunned. Finally he said, "Don't you realize the risk you'd be taking? You're the White House chief of staff. You could be taken as a hostage."

"I know that," Jordan said. "But we have to get those people out of there."

chapter ten

The Moslem Card

LET US BRIEFLY JUMP TEN MONTHS IN THE NARRATIVE.

In November 1980, after the hostages had been held for more than a year, I received a telegram from Mohammed Heikal, the most prestigious journalist in the Middle East and an old and cherished friend. The telegram said that he and his wife were arriving in Paris the following week and would like to have a meal with my wife and me.

Heikal had been the most trusted aide of Gamal Abdel Nasser and served as Minister of Information and briefly as Minister of Foreign Affairs of Egypt. A trim and dark-skinned Egyptian, he is a worldly and debonair man with a keen appreciation of the good life. When in London, he stays at Claridge's; in Paris his hotel is the Crillon. We had lunch at one of Paris' great restaurants, the Pré Catelan in the Bois de Boulogne. I knew that Heikal had been in Teheran just after the hostages were seized and was a keen student of the Iranian revolution. So I used the early part of the lunch to get his impressions of what was going on in Iran and to get his insight into the philosophy and thinking of the Iranian revolution. Heikal was so forthcoming and so fascinating on this subject that I decided to go farther with him. This was a man I had known for years, and one I knew I could trust. So after receiving his assurances that he would tell no one, I confessed to him that I was working on the biggest story of my life—the secret negotiations to free the hostages. What was so fantastic, I explained, was that I believed I was in touch with all of the intermediaries the

United States Government had employed to make contact with the Iranians.

I waited then for Heikal to register his surprise. But he was silent, and his expression didn't change. At last, he said, "No, you're not in touch with all of the intermediaries the United States has employed."

"How do you know I'm not?" I asked suspiciously.

"Because I'm an intermediary," he replied.

I should have been surprised at that point, but I wasn't. Nothing this extraordinary man does surprises me. Six years before, as an example, he had come into possession of a story that no other journalist could get. The story was from his Arab sources, and was to this effect: Shortly after the election of Richard Nixon, the Arab leaders met to discuss how they might neutralize the pressure that American Jews had historically been able to put on U. S. Presidents. It was high time that the Arabs started exerting pressure on American Presidents, the Arab leaders believed; in Richard Nixon they felt they had an American President who could be bought, and they should figure out some way to get an amount of money to him so large that it would change his views on the Middle East. The figure they decided on was $12 million.

One of the leaders at the meeting, Anwar Sadat, was not very warm to the idea at first, but he subsequently changed his mind and decided to go along. Egypt was to put up $2 million, and Saudi Arabia and Kuwait were to put up the other $10 million between them. The Saudis and Kuwaitis even proposed to lend Egypt its $2 million contribution. The money, they all decided, should be passed to Nixon by an intermediary. But there the story stops. Some sources say the money went to the intermediary. But there is not one shred of evidence that Nixon ever got the money.

All of these details were reported by Mohammed Heikal on the front page of *Al Ahram*, the newspaper he ran at the time. No other newspaper or news outlet picked up the story, because none of them could prove it. Heikal's own proof was irrefutable, however; he had been at the meetings in which the project was discussed.

Heikal, I would learn during our lunch, had been involved in the hostage crisis since the previous January, when he was contacted by the Americans in the hope that he might be able to get their messages to the Ayatollah Khomeini.

In identifying him as a person who could, if he was willing to cooperate, carry messages to Khomeini, the Americans were right on target. No one they might have found was better connected or more respected than Heikal.

He is one of those few journalists whose stories and columns transcend national boundaries. Perhaps only Walter Lippmann and James Reston in the United States have approximated the power that Heikal wields in the Middle East. Almost every article he writes is reproduced throughout the Arab world.

In November 1978 Heikal was in Paris when he received a telephone call from an aide of the Ayatollah Khomeini, who had recently arrived there himself. The aide asked Heikal if he would like to see the Ayatollah. "No," Heikal replied, "because I don't have a newspaper ready to participate in his battles."

"Never mind," the aide said, "the Ayatollah wants to see you."

When Heikal arrived at Neauphle-le-Château, he was surprised by the warmth of the Ayatollah, who greeted him with a broad smile. Before they had even sat down, the warmth was explained. "We've got a mutual friend," the Ayatollah said.

The friend turned out to be Gamal Abdel Nasser, the Egyptian army colonel who overthrew King Farouk, became President of Egypt in 1956 and gained prestige around the world as the champion of Egyptian nationalism. The Ayatollah reminded Heikal then of Nasser's generous response to his request for funds for victims of the Shah.

Their talk that day was theoretical. Heikal identified himself as an advocate of nationalism. Khomeini thought that nationalism was passé. Islam, he said, was the wave of the future.

"I think religion can play the role of heavy artillery," Heikal acknowledged. "Even from Paris here, with heavy artillery you can destroy the old regime. But to achieve victory you have to bring in your infantry—and the infantry of the revolution are the intellectuals, the politicians, the technicians, the bureaucrats, the technocrats, the people who can really make things go and change."

"Yes, I understand that," Khomeini replied. "I'm not pretending that an Islamic revolution will be run by the mullahs [spiritual leaders]. I agree that the revolution needs all that you say. But Iran will definitely be able to mobilize among its sons good Moslems who are educated in the best universities in the West, and who can achieve the aims of the revolution."

It was to see, among other things, whether the country had been able to do that since the revolutionaries had come to power that

Heikal returned to Iran in November 1979. He was fascinated with
the idea of an Islamic revolution, and proposed to write a book about
it. It would be his second book on Iran. His first book on the country—
and his first published book—had dealt with the preceding revolution,
when Iran had nationalized its oil industry.

Heikal arrived on November 25, three weeks after the hostages had
been seized—an action he deplored, even though he favored the revolution itself. The next morning his arrival was reported in the newspapers. That evening, he received a telephone call in his room at the
Hilton Hotel from a young man who identified himself as a representative of the *Moraditun* at the American Embassy. The word the
young man used was rich with historical references, evoking soldiers
of the "vanguard" stationed in outposts meant to guard a town or an
army or a country. The young man told Heikal that the militants at
the embassy would like to see him in order to "exchange revolutionary
experiences."

At first, Heikal dismissed the call as a hoax, but then he thought
better of it and appeared the following morning at the embassy with
his assistant and an Iranian diplomat who had been assigned to aid
him in his work. To the journalist's surprise, a committee of militants
was there to receive him. They issued badges for him and his assistant,
but refused to admit the diplomat.

The students led Heikal to the commercial section of the embassy
and then to a room with a large table. In the center of the table was a
tape recorder. For the next five hours, they queried him, not about his
own revolutionary experiences but about what they had done. They
wanted, above all, to know whether he approved of their action.

It was not an easy question for Heikal. He saw the action not as an
isolated episode but in the context of the countercoup organized by
the CIA, with an assist from British intelligence, in 1953 against the
revolution that had brought the nationalists to power a few years before. That revolution, he believed, had come about through the normal democratic process and according to the liberal rules of the game.
And then the man installed in power by that process and those rules
had been ousted from power with the help of foreign forces. All this
had been admitted publicly; all this the students knew, and so it was
only normal for them to believe that the American Embassy was, even
now, the center of an operation working against Iranian independence
and the current revolution. None of this was justification for their actions, Heikal knew, but he also felt that any judgment against them

must be tempered by an appreciation of the context in which they behaved.

In answering the students, Heikal spoke as diplomatically as he could, lest a too direct response cut them off.

"I think that maybe if I was thirty years younger I myself would have thought to do such a thing," he told them. "I can understand what you have done, but I can't accept it, because it's very dangerous." And then Heikal proceeded to explain to them why it was dangerous: By their action, he said, they had isolated their revolution. They had given the rest of the world a reason to be against what had happened in Iran. "You don't see how they are treating you and using this against you. This revolution started as a human movement, and then it was shrunk into an Islamic revolution and then shrunk again into an Islamic revolution in Iran, and then shrunk still further to only a Shi‘a revolution. Where do you go from here? From a human revolution you have been shrunk to such a point that you are isolated even in your own country."

But the students were too filled with what they had done to be impressed by such a message. It was not what they wanted to hear. They were too certain that the American Embassy was to be the center of a counterrevolution, and as proof, they led Heikal to a storehouse of provisions they had discovered, which, they told him, had been laid in for an expected siege of five to six months. For a moment Heikal was speechless; then nothing he could say could persuade the students that the "storehouse" was the PX.

Heikal spent a month in Teheran, gathering material for his book—as well as impressions about the state of mind of the leaders of the government and the revolution that would prove extremely helpful in his subsequent work as an intermediary. In Bani-Sadr, he found a man congenial to the ideas that he had expressed to the students, as well as grateful that he had expressed them. At a dinner given by Bani-Sadr's sister one evening, the Iranian quoted Heikal to the effect that there was a limit to power, and the more people understood this the safer they became. The United States had learned that in Vietnam, and Egypt had learned that in its long struggle against Israel. Now Iran must learn it as well. The students had made their point; the situation they had created had to come to an end lest it pit Iran against the rest of the world, and thereby destroy its revolution.

But the Ayatollah, whom Heikal saw in Qum the next day, did not share his ideas, and did not seem in a mood to impose discipline on

anyone, the student militants least of all. "Why do you want discipline
and order?" he asked. "If we insist on discipline and order, that means
using the Army and the police, and that shouldn't be done in a revolution. Our people have been in prison for more than thirty years.
Nobody can stop them from breaking the bars of that prison and getting out and doing whatever they want. The people in the streets, with
their ferment, are a guarantee of the continuation of the revolution."

What Khomeini wanted was for all the forces of the revolution to
express themselves, even if the result was chaos. He accepted that the
country would experience a fit of chaos, but he saw no other way to
unleash all of its pent-up emotions.

As to the hostages, it was Heikal's belief that while the Ayatollah
did not completely approve what the students had done, he understood
it. He had no sympathy whatever for Heikal's argument that the action
of the militants had been contrary to international law.

"What is this international law?" he demanded. "Have we participated in it? No. Have we written it? No. Is there anything in the international law that says anything about conducting a coup d'état against
a nationally and freely elected government in a country? No. Is there
anything in this international law against the drainage of the wealth of
the country? No. Is there anything in this international law that would
protect the people of Iran from the Shah of Iran taking all their wealth
to himself? No. I don't recognize this law. I have not participated in
it."

Heikal left the Ayatollah with the hope that his people would "get
rid of the problem as quickly as they can." It was a pragmatic argument. "I know the States," he said. "I happen to know something
about how they act. And I have been reading about situation rooms
and computers and people who are specialized in crisis management. I
can imagine that the high command in the United States dealing with
this crisis has quite a technological setup, something very advanced
that reminds you of guiding a moon landing." Then Heikal gestured
about him at the tiny room in which the Ayatollah was living, from
which issued the guidance that the revolutionary government transformed into fiat. "And then, look at the command post of Iran. You
know the way decisions are made, if they are made at all, and the way
information is passed. You know it's through whispering. How can
these people cope with a crisis management on the other side—which
will definitely outwit them?"

All that was prelude to the events that followed.

On January 10, 1980, Heikal traveled from Cairo to London. He had not been at Claridge's for very long when an old friend from Egypt dropped by to see him. The friend told Heikal that the Americans wanted to contact him. Would he be willing to talk to the Americans about Iran and the hostage crisis?

Heikal reflected for some time before replying. "Yes, all right, I'll meet with the Americans, but I won't meet with the CIA. I'll only be willing to see somebody who has political status—and I want to know his identity before I agree to see him."

The next day the friend was back with a suggestion: would Heikal go to Washington to talk to Secretary of State Cyrus Vance?

"I'm sorry," Heikal replied, "I was just in Washington two months ago. I only go to Washington once every two years."

The friend's reply was immediate, as though he had expected a refusal. "You're going to be here for a few more days," he said. "I'm going to Geneva. When I come back, I'll give you an idea of who you could see."

Several days later the friend was back with a new suggestion, that Heikal should meet with Harold Saunders, the Assistant Secretary of State for Near East and South Asian Affairs.

"I'd be glad to meet with Harold Saunders," Heikal said at once. He had known Saunders when the American was involved in the first disengagement discussions between Egypt and Israel in 1977; he both respected and liked him.

The meeting was arranged for January 19. The Americans wanted Heikal to come to the U. S. Embassy in Grosvenor Square, but he refused. So Saunders, who had just finished his twelve-hour marathon meeting with Hamilton Jordan, Christian Bourguet and Héctor Villalón, sat down with the Egyptian at the flat of a friend. Another American whose name Heikal didn't catch came with Saunders and sat silently through the meeting.

"Can you help?" Saunders asked.

Heikal replied that he would like to help, because he was interested in seeing the Iranians put this problem behind them and get on with their revolution. Whether he could help was another matter. He would first have to clear the matter with the Ayatollah Khomeini. There was this further problem: "mediation" was a discredited word among the Shiᶜites.

There was another problem that Heikal did not disclose to Saunders until later: his own aversion to the circus atmosphere in which mediation efforts are usually carried on. Politicians from all over the world, aware of the instant stardom the American news media could convey on anyone involved in mediation efforts in behalf of the hostages, had besieged Heikal with calls since the crisis began, asking if he could help them secure a mediator's role. If he was to be involved, Heikal determined, it would have to be with the assurances by both sides that his efforts would be kept a secret. Otherwise, they would come to naught.

He could not be a mediator, Heikal told Saunders now, but he would try to be a communicator between the two sides.

After their meeting, Heikal telephoned Ahmed Khomeini, the Ayatollah's son, in Teheran and told him about the American contact. What should he do? Heikal asked. Khomeini suggested that Heikal write at once to his father. Heikal did. In the letter, he stressed that he would not be functioning as a mediator. If he had to choose sides, he said, he would be on the side of Iran. But if the Ayatollah thought discussions might be of some use, he would pursue them.

When Heikal delivered his letter to the Iranian Embassy in London, the chargé d'affaires had already been alerted by Teheran to expect it. A few days later, on Friday, January 25, the chargé called Heikal and said, "There's someone here who wants to see you." But when Heikal got to the embassy he found it wasn't a person; it was a message from Ahmed Khomeini, informing him that he should go ahead and talk to the Americans.

Heikal immediately informed the Americans by means of an intermediary that he was ready to help facilitate communications. A week later, again through an intermediary, he received a printed message from the United States Government. It was unsigned, and presented the essence of the American position that the Americans wished Heikal to convey to the Ayatollah Khomeini in whatever way he felt would achieve the best results. The pertinent portions of the U. S. Government message were these:

"USG declares that the US perception of what is happening in Iran has been changed by developments in Afghanistan. USG urges that the problem of the hostages be resolved so that Washington and the new Iranian government can reconsider their relations. USG assures the Iranian leaders that the United States respects the integrity of Iran, believes that its security is of vital importance to the west and that

Iranians have nothing to fear from US. USG promises that the moment the hostages are freed, the US government will start official negotiations with Iran for future cooperation, including the important matter of military spare parts."

In addition to the printed message, the intermediary gave Heikal some thoughts to pass along. He was to convey to the Iranians that the United States accepted the Islamic revolution as a fact, and was prepared to cooperate with the new regime in a manner unhindered by complexes developed in the past. There was no problem that could not be solved, the message from the Americans said.

chapter eleven

A Sign from Iran

BY JANUARY 22, TWO DAYS AFTER THE CONCLUSION OF THE LONDON meeting, it seemed that the Shah of Iran was going to be arrested by the Panamanians, regardless of anything the Americans might want or decide to do.

For almost three weeks now, the efforts to effectuate that arrest had been proceeding on an orderly course. The basis of the action was Article XX of the Panamanian constitution, which required that any extradition request from a foreign power recognized by Panama be followed by the arrest of the person named. Whether the extradition would occur or not was another matter entirely; it would depend on Panama's assessment of the validity of the petition. Where the possibility of death for the person to be extradited existed, extradition was forbidden. In the case of the Shah, the Iranian Government was to make a simple, ministry-to-ministry request to the government of Panama for his arrest in anticipation of the arrival of the documentation supporting its petition for extradition. Once the request was received, the Iranians would have sixty days in which to file their documents. The arrest triggered by the request would be little more than symbolic, and might last for only ten minutes, after which the Shah would be released on bail. Nonetheless, the symbolism was potent enough for the Iranians, and under their constitution, the Panamanians were obliged to comply.

The feeling—at least on Christian Bourguet's part—was that the Americans would finally conclude that these legal proceedings were being accomplished between two sovereign powers, and there was no way the United States could interfere.

The Panamanians, for their part, were satisfied that in cooperating with the Iranians, they would be improving the climate for discussions leading to the release of the hostages.

On January 11 the Iranian Foreign Office sent a Telex to the Panamanian Foreign Office, indicating that a warrant charging the Shah with certain crimes would be arriving soon by diplomatic pouch. On January 17 the warrant was passed to the Panamanians at the United Nations in New York; it arrived in Panama the next day.

It was 3 A.M. on January 23 in Teheran when Sadegh Ghotbzadeh, asleep in the Foreign Office, was awakened by a call from President Royo of Panama, informing him that the Shah would be arrested at seven in the morning. Ghotbzadeh was transported by the news. He was approaching the end of his campaign for the presidency of Iran and, by all accounts, trailing both Bani-Sadr and Hassan Habibi, another former exile. At least one reason for his poor standing was that his preoccupation with the hostage crisis and the extradition of the Shah had left him no opportunity to campaign. The arrest of the Shah could be the magic the Foreign Minister had been looking for to give his candidacy the boost it needed. That was not just his assessment. The other candidates—there were several on the Revolutionary Council alone—had told the Foreign Minister that if he succeeded in getting the Shah arrested, they would drop out of the race. "If you can really get the Shah arrested, you will be the President of the republic because you are the one who would have gotten him," Bani-Sadr said. That the other candidates were all willing to give way to Ghotbzadeh if he collared the Shah was an indication of how strong the myth of the Shah's return to power was in Iran at this time.

The first thing Ghotbzadeh did after receiving word from Royo was to call Christian Bourguet, who had come to Teheran for conferences with the Iranians following his meetings in London with the Americans. Bourguet had been asleep in his hotel room for only an hour—he had been working at the Foreign Ministry until 2 A.M.—when the excited Foreign Minister awakened him with the news. But he was alert enough to warn Ghotbzadeh, "Don't make any announcements until you've received the Telex confirming the actual arrest."

"I can't wait for the Telex to come," Ghotbzadeh said. "I'm leaving for Meshed at six-thirty. I have speeches to make, and political meetings to attend. I've *got* to go to Meshed." Meshed was one of Iran's two holy cities. Ghotbzadeh had managed to squeeze out a trip to the other one, Qum; not to campaign in Meshed would be an unforgivable slight in the eyes of the Shiᶜites.

"Okay, go," Bourguet said, "but leave very precise instructions not to release the news until the Telex comes."

"I'll take care of it," Ghotbzadeh said.

An hour later Ghotbzadeh received a second call from Panama. This time it was General Torrijos, who confirmed the pending arrest and saluted "the courageous struggle of the Iranian people." The connection was a bad one, and they spoke through an interpreter, but one fact came through very clearly. The arrest would take place at 7 A.M.

Once more, Ghotbzadeh telephoned Bourguet. This time the exhausted Frenchman said nothing about waiting for the confirming Telex. He expressed his pleasure, and then went back to bed, hoping to sleep for another hour before going to the airport to take a plane to Paris.

But Ghotbzadeh couldn't sleep. He was too excited. He knew the announcement of the Shah's arrest would be greeted with jubilation throughout Iran.

Before leaving for Meshed, Ghotbzadeh wrote out a press release and gave it to an assistant, along with instructions to make the announcement at 7:30 A.M.—one half hour, presumably, after the Shah's arrest and the arrival of the confirming Telex.

When no Telex had arrived by 7:30 A.M., Ghotbzadeh's assistant, unable to contact him for further instructions, released the story.

Had the Foreign Minister's instructions been confusing? Had he failed to impress sufficiently on his staff the importance of waiting for the confirming Telex? Whatever the reason, the responsibility was his —and he had made a terrible, irretrievable error. He had neglected to consider the eight-and-one-half-hour time difference between Iran and Panama, and to clarify whether the arrest was scheduled for 7 A.M. Teheran time or 7 A.M. Panama time. The Panamanians had, indeed, scheduled the arrest of the Shah for 7 A.M., Panama time, on January 23. In Panama, as the radio and television stations flashed the news of the Shah's arrest and of the jubilant Iranians pouring into the streets, it was 11 P.M. on January 22, and the Shah was in his home on Contadora Island.

The Panamanians were furious. The premature release of the news had put them in an impossible situation. It would now appear that Panama was backing a decision taken by Iran rather than by Panama, even though that was not the case. Under the circumstances, the Panamanians did the only thing they could. They denied that they had ever planned to arrest the Shah.

On other fronts, however, Christian Bourguet and Héctor Villalón, who had accompanied him to Teheran from London, had made considerable progress. The arrest of the Shah had been only one of three projects on their minds following the London meeting with Hamilton Jordan and Harold Saunders.

The second project had been to animate the "program" they had envisioned with the Americans that might lead to the release of the hostages. At the heart of the program was a scenario by which each side, through a series of carefully orchestrated acts, was to arrive at the point where it would give something away in order to get something back. Precisely what each side would give up and get back had yet to be defined—that Bourguet and Villalón would attempt to work out with the Americans. But before anything, they had to have the accord of the Iranians as to whether they should proceed.

By all means, Ghotbzadeh said, but with one critical proviso. The establishment of any commission to carry through the scenario had to be undertaken at the request of Iran, not the United States. The Americans would then respond to Iran's request. "If that is not the case, there is no point in continuing," Ghotbzadeh said, "because it's essential that at that point we in Iran be able to claim victory by saying we have obtained that."

The third project of Bourguet and Villalón had been to find some means of solidifying their credibility with Hamilton Jordan.

Before they had parted on January 20, Jordan had told Bourguet and Villalón that, in spite of the good feelings he had developed for them, he would be compelled in the next few days to verify their background. He pointed out to both men that they had no mandate from the Iranians to conduct any negotiations with the Americans. It was true, even of Bourguet, who had a legal role as an attorney for Iran. But that legal capacity had nothing to do in a formal sense with the role he was now playing, that of an intermediary attempting to reconcile the viewpoint of people who happened to be his clients with the viewpoint of the people to whom they were opposed. When he and Villalón had originally asked the Iranians for authorization to meet the Americans, Sadegh Ghotbzadeh told them, "Go meet them, but don't forget that you don't represent us. You're meeting them on a personal basis and not in our name, and you are not authorized to speak in our behalf. You are not, in the hostage affair, designated as our attorney."

In London, Jordan had not expressly asked Bourguet and Villalón to provide the Americans with proof of their relationship with the Iranians, but both men had gotten the idea that they would be able to work much more effectively in any future dealings if they could supply such proof. On their arrival in Teheran, they had put the problem to Ghotbzadeh. "We don't know what proof you can give," Villalón said, "but we absolutely must have something which shows that we don't just represent you, the Minister of Foreign Affairs, but the entire Revolutionary Council. How you do that is up to you."

Ghotbzadeh's eventual solution was designed to cure more than one problem.

One of the difficulties Bourguet and Villalón had related to Ghotbzadeh on their return from London stemmed from the visit of UN Secretary-General Waldheim to Teheran. The two emissaries told the Foreign Minister how difficult it had been to persuade Hamilton Jordan, especially, that there was no profit in believing that the hostages could be liberated merely by sending a UN investigatory body to Iran.

"That's not what Waldheim said when he got back from Teheran," Jordan had countered. According to the Americans, Waldheim had told them that, on the basis of his talks with the Iranians, their proposal "wasn't impossible."

"Did you say that to Waldheim?" Bourguet asked Ghotbzadeh.

"Never!" the Foreign Minister said.

When Bourguet and Villalón saw Ghotbzadeh the day before their return to Paris, they asked him what he'd been able to come up with that would certify them with the Americans.

"We talked about the matter at the Revolutionary Council," he said, "and we've decided to give you this." Ghotbzadeh held out a cassette. He told them that the cassette was a tape of the Council's meeting with Secretary-General Waldheim on January 4. The tape, he said, would correct Hamilton Jordan's impression, gained from Waldheim, that the hostages would be exchanged if the UN would only send a commission. And he was quite sure, Ghotbzadeh added, that after the Americans heard the tape, they would have no further doubts as to the linkage of its bearers to the revolutionary government of Iran.

When Bourguet and Villalón returned to Paris, they received word that the Americans would like them to come to Washington. Getting together with the Americans, however, was not uppermost in their minds. They had a major problem to overcome that required their immediate attention: the tattered credibility of the Iranian Government. Four weeks before, they had flown to Panama bearing a gift—the release of three American hostages, a way of demonstrating the desire of the government of Iran to cooperate with Panama. That gift had been snatched from them when Bani-Sadr confided the plan to a French senator who then took it upon herself to announce it. Now the two emissaries had worked patiently for weeks to arrange the arrest of the Shah, and that too had been snatched from them by an untimely release of information.

What were the Panamanians to think? That the Iranians weren't responsible people? Who could blame them for thinking so? Iran's reputation was already besmirched by the seizure of the hostages, an act that had defamed the country with every responsible government in the world. Some fences had to be mended. Bourguet and Villalón determined to return at once to Panama.

They spent a day trying to contact the appropriate authorities in Panama to advise them that they were coming, and to offer their regrets. In addition, they persuaded the Panamanians to send a face-saving Telex to Ghotbzadeh, which said:

"Not yet having received the request for extradition, we give you sixty days to give it to us. In this case, the Shah is placed under the care of the executive power." Then they decided that it might be a good idea to postpone the visit to Panama until after the Iranian elections that weekend. They would see the Americans first.

On January 25 Bourguet and Villalón boarded a Concorde for New York. At John F. Kennedy Airport, they were met by a State Department representative and driven to La Guardia Airport, where they were put on the shuttle to Washington. Once again, they were met by an official car and driven to the Hay-Adams Hotel, just across Lafayette Park from the White House. Although they could see the executive mansion from their rooms and could walk there in less than two minutes, they were driven in an official car. By the time they arrived at Hamilton Jordan's office, they had good reason to believe that Jordan would be happy to see them. But for good measure, they wasted no time in presenting the gift they had brought him—the tape of Kurt Waldheim's meeting with the Revolutionary Council.

F

For Jordan, the tape was dramatic proof that the two intermediaries he was dealing with were legitimate. But he was not uninterested in the contents of the tape, which helped put an end to the misunderstandings which had persisted from Kurt Waldheim's return from Teheran—either because Waldheim's message had been unclear, or because the Americans had failed to understand the Secretary-General.

By this point, Bourguet and Villalón had listened to the tape. As Villalón handed Jordan the tape, he said, "You remember in London you weren't convinced that we were telling you the truth. You thought that the Iranians had said something to Waldheim other than what we told you. Well, we reported that to Teheran, and there seems to be a big mistake. We don't know if you've misunderstood Waldheim. What we do know is that Waldheim never talked to the Revolutionary Council about sending a UN commission with prior release of the hostages."

The tape, Villalón explained, had been made at the meeting of the Revolutionary Council—standard practice. "You'll see that there's nothing in it," he said. "I mean by that, the discussion between Waldheim and the Revolutionary Council is nothing. Just emptiness, wasted breath. It wasn't a negotiation. You're going to see that what we told you was true, that the Iranians never told Waldheim what Waldheim told you they said."

Then Villalón came to the larger purpose of the gift they had brought Jordan. "The cassette was recorded in front of everyone at the Revolutionary Council. There was no way we could have stolen it, and we wouldn't have taken such a risk in any case, so the fact that we have it should be proof enough that the Revolutionary Council agreed to our taking it."

That day, Jordan, Harold Saunders, Bourguet and Villalón began preliminary work on a scenario between the United States and Iran that would be managed by the United Nations. Hours later, when the two exhilarated but exhausted representatives of Iran made their way back to their rooms for some badly needed rest—having arisen on Paris time, they were living a thirty-hour day—Hamilton Jordan, alone in his office, listened to the gift they had brought him.

What had happened was exactly as Bourguet and Villalón had represented it. The Secretary-General had never presented to the Revolutionary Council the American plan for simultaneous release of the hostages along with the creation of a UN commission of inquiry.

The first thing Hamilton Jordan did after hearing the tape was to

order a transcript sent to President Carter, who was spending the
weekend at Camp David. Then Jordan asked himself why the Foreign
Minister of Iran would want the United States Government to know
what had transpired at the meeting between the UN Secretary-General
and the Iranian Revolutionary Council. The answer was evident. It
was not in Iran's interest for the United States to have an impression
of reality different from what existed.

The tape did prove that Waldheim had not pushed the American
position with the Revolutionary Council. Yet Jordan was not upset; he
knew that the Secretary-General had been in a precarious, even dangerous situation throughout his stay in Iran, and he was not sure
whether he himself would have had the courage to put himself in that
position. To Jordan, there was a more significant meaning to the tape:
it convinced him absolutely that Christian Bourguet and Héctor Villalón were intimately connected to the revolutionary government of
Iran.

On January 26, a Saturday, Bourguet and Villalón spent the entire
day in Hamilton Jordan's office with Jordan, Harold Saunders and
Henry Precht of the State Department. The five men did not even step
outside for lunch; it was brought into Jordan's office.

They had begun the day before at an impasse: the United States
would not assist the creation of a commission to inquire into past
American involvement in Iran until the hostages had been released.
Iran, for its part, wanted a public judgment of the Shah as the price of
the hostages' release. Then Bourguet and Villalón presented a compromise that had been proposed to them by Ghotbzadeh: the United
States would permit the commission to go to Iran before the hostages
were released, *but* the commission would be permitted to see the hostages.

For the Americans, that was a heady prospect. The hostages were
now completing their twelfth week of captivity. No one had seen them
since Christmas. Nothing was known of their physical health and mental state, or of the conditions of their captivity. There was even doubt
as to exactly how many hostages were being held, and what their iden-
tities were.

The compromise proposal wasn't what the Americans wanted. But
on the basis of his conversations with Bourguet and Villalón, Jordan
had become convinced that the United States was going to have to

take some chances. On his return to Washington, he had reported to the President that they had to stop believing they could resolve the crisis with halfway measures. They would have to change their approach totally. If they remained adamant about simultaneous release of the hostages with the appointment of the commission, he, for one, was sure that Christian Bourguet was right, that the United States was pursuing "a mindless hypothesis."

Over the weekend, while Harold Saunders went up to New York to confer with Kurt Waldheim on the setting up of a UN commission and on its possible composition, Bourguet and Villalón made a quick trip to Panama to calm some Latin tempers. President Royo, in particular, was still annoyed by Sadegh Ghotbzadeh's premature announcement, but he finally agreed that he would listen to the extradition request when the Iranians presented it. Royo even proposed his legal adviser, Eduardo Morgan, as someone who might represent the Shah—a recommendation Bourguet quickly discouraged.

By January 29 Bourguet and Villalón were back in the White House, putting the finishing touches on the scenario, and meeting several high government officials—Cyrus Vance and Zbigniew Brzezinski among them—who wanted to inspect two such unconventional go-betweens, of whom much had been heard by now.

In their meetings with Jordan and Saunders, Bourguet and Villalón also had a preliminary discussion regarding the possible members of the commission, which would be heavily weighted with representatives from Third World nations.

But the touchiest moment of the day, by all odds, was when Hamilton Jordan broke the news to the two emissaries that six American diplomats had been smuggled out of Iran by Canadian diplomats.

The Americans, who were absent from the embassy when the militants struck on November 4, had first been hidden by members of the British Embassy staff. Then, as tensions between the Iranians and the British mounted, it became evident that the Americans would have to be moved. Arrangements were made to send them to the Canadians. The logistics were worked out by Bruce Laingen, the American chargé d'affaires, who had been sequestered in the Foreign Ministry since the seizure of the embassy. To maintain secrecy, Laingen communicated through a Thai cook he knew—probably the only other person in Teheran, besides himself, who spoke the language.

Jordan had known for several days that the Americans were coming out. He was elated by the development, but worried at the same time that the Iranians might overreact and either harm the remaining hostages or derail what they had managed to get on the track toward their release. "I hope this won't hamper our working together," he said to Bourguet and Villalón when he told them the news. He emphasized that the United States had had nothing to do with the escape, and hoped that they would convey that to the government of Iran.

"I'd better call Teheran and explain it to them in the least troublesome way," Bourguet said, and then, to Jordan's astonishment, he asked if he could place a call to Sadegh Ghotbzadeh. Jordan gladly obliged, and Bourguet even read the Iranian Foreign Minister a communiqué the White House had put out, expressing its satisfaction at the escape of the Americans, but disclaiming responsibility.

What else Bourguet said to Ghotbzadeh Jordan never learned, because the two men spoke in French. But he was sure Bourguet had tried to put a good face on the episode, because other than ripping from the wall the Foreign Ministry telephone Laingen had used since the embassy was seized to converse daily with Washington, the Iranian Government took no reprisals at all.

Before Bourguet and Villalón left Washington, they agreed to meet Jordan and Saunders in Europe after trying out the proposed scenario on their clients. The meeting would take place at a secret site to be arranged by the Swiss. Jordan also asked the two men to bring with them some written indication from Bani-Sadr—who had just been overwhelmingly elected President of Iran—that they were his representatives.

Then Jordan gave Bourguet and Villalón a letter testifying to his pleasure with the work they had done together. It was a formal expression of the genuine feeling he had developed for both men.

"As friends and supporters of the Revolutionary Movement in Iran," Jordan wrote the two men, "you have been forceful and effective in outlining to me the concerns and grievances of the Iranian people. Based on your presentation and these discussions, I have come to understand the depth of the concerns of the Iranian people." At the same time Jordan praised Bourguet and Villalón for the "patient and attentive" way they had listened to the views of the United States: "When you return to Iran, I hope that you will convey to President-Elect Bani-Sadr and Foreign Minister Ghotbzadeh that our government is prepared to work with the government of Iran to resolve the present crisis quickly on an honorable basis and is prepared to proceed toward its resolution through a series of reciprocal steps.

"I believe you to be men of great integrity and intellect whose only interest in this matter is to see the present problems between Iran and the United States peacefully resolved. On behalf of our government, I would be pleased if you could continue and expand on this informal dialogue."

As they left the White House, Bourguet and Villalón carried with them a memorandum that they would read many times on their return flight to Teheran.

In its conception and timing the scenario was like a Hollywood version of Russians and Americans exchanging captured spies at the border. With one hand they trade documents, and with the other they pull their man across.

The pivotal scene in the scenario, when all was said and done, envisioned the transfer of the hostages from the students to the government. Only when this had happened would the Iranians be in a position to make good on their promise to release the hostages, an event that was to take place simultaneously with the release of the UN report evaluating the charges against the Shah and the United States. Then, according to the scenario, there was to be a simultaneous release of statements, one by the United States, the other by Iran, each side acknowledging certain historical errors in its relation with the other.

chapter twelve

Mr. Thompson, Mr. Sinclair and Mr. Prescott

THE AMERICANS WERE NOW ON THE HOOK. ON THE RECOMMENDATION of Hamilton Jordan, they had made the first concession: no prior release of the hostages as a condition for the establishment of a United Nations commission to investigate Iranian grievances. They would have to wait to see what kind of response Christian Bourguet and Héctor Villalón could produce. Could they, in Harold Saunders' stiff State Department language, "stimulate a dynamic which would permit the Iranian government to justify certain movements in relation to the hostages?" In hard terms, could the Iranians get the hostages moved out of the embassy compound, where they were under the guard of the student militants, to some other place—a hospital, an administration building, even the Foreign Ministry—where they would be in the government's hands? That was the absolutely indispensable prerequisite to the hostages' release.

Bourguet and Villalón arrived in Teheran on February 1. They went immediately to the Foreign Ministry, where they reported to Sadegh Ghotbzadeh. It was the first time they had seen their friend since he had lost his race for the presidency. He was so depressed that he could not even bring himself to discuss the hostage issue, dwelling bitterly, instead, on how his preoccupation with that very problem, while Bani-Sadr was out campaigning, had cost him the election. All evening, his two friends worked on Ghotbzadeh, attempting to put a good face on the affair. "Okay," Villalón said, "so you won't be President. You're still the Foreign Minister. You still have an important role to play." At last they succeeded in focusing him on the scenario they had brought back to Teheran.

He hadn't read more than thirty seconds when he said, "No, that's still not right." The problem was in the very first paragraph of the proposed scenario. The paragraph did state clearly that it was Iran calling for the creation of the UN commission "to hear Iran's grievances and to allow an early solution to the crisis between Iran and the United States." That much was fine, the Foreign Minister said. The problem was with the sentence that followed. "This request will state Iran's desire to have the commission speak to each of the hostages." "Out of the question," Ghotbzadeh said. He reiterated what he had told Bourguet and Villalón after London and before Washington: Iran must be able to claim a victory over the United States. The establishment of the commission at its request—apart from any mention of the hostages —would, in his eyes, be that victory.

Now he told Bourguet and Villalón exactly what he wanted. Step One: Iran requests the Secretary-General to establish a commission. Step Two: Waldheim offers to establish a commission. Step Three: Iran accepts the offer, and *then* requests that the commission speak to each of the hostages.

But other than that, Ghotbzadeh was positive—so positive that he determined on the spot that all efforts other than the UN commission and the extradition of the Shah should be stopped.

Until this moment, the three plans conceived by mid-December were still in the minds of the Iranians, the first an Iranian trial of the hostages as symbols of past U.S. interference, the second an international tribunal (the MacBride Commission), the third the UN commission. They had already succeeded in moving the Ayatollah from the first to the second plan, Ghotbzadeh told Bourguet and Villalón. Now, he said, he would undertake to move the imam from the second plan to the third.

Bourguet and Villalón were elated with the Foreign Minister's reception of their work. But their friend Ghotbzadeh was just one of the Iranians they had to sell; there remained the new President, Bani-Sadr, the Revolutionary Council and the Ayatollah Khomeini. The imam represented a special problem; on January 24 he had suffered a heart attack and been moved from Qum to an intensive-care unit at a hospital in Teheran.

Before they could deal with any of these matters, yet another problem presented itself in the person of an old acquaintance.

Nuri Albala, the French Communist lawyer, had not been back to Teheran since late December, when he had attempted, along with Sean MacBride, the aging Irish diplomat, to establish an international tribunal in his confederate's name. Both men had believed from the outset that the UN commission would never get off the ground, but had decided to stay in the background lest they be accused of sabotaging it in favor of their own program.

Albala returned to Teheran on February 2, ostensibly to push a pet project, the publication of documents in the possession of the government that dealt with charges of corruption and crime under the Shah and his links to the United States. But he decided to use the occasion of his presence to inquire as to the status of the MacBride Commission. When his old friend Sadegh Ghotbzadeh told him that they were dropping the idea in favor of the UN commission, Albala sputtered a protest and stormed from their meeting.

Later that day, Albala met with Bani-Sadr. When the President asked him if he had seen Ghotbzadeh, Albala confessed his unhappiness at Iran's decision to drop the MacBride plan.

"Who said *that*?" Bani-Sadr demanded.

"Ghotbzadeh."

"But Ghotbzadeh told us you and MacBride had dropped the project."

Albala denied it. He said that he had sent several messages about the project to the Foreign Minister through the Iranian Embassy in Paris.

"I know nothing about these messages," the President said. In his view, he went on, the MacBride plan was a better one than the UN commission plan—and he would so state that evening to the Revolutionary Council.

Without realizing he had done so, Albala had turned up the fire on a long-simmering feud between the two rivals-in-exile, Bani-Sadr and Ghotbzadeh. It had begun in Paris, where Ghotbzadeh had held the spotlight as the aggressive organizer of the opposition and Bani-Sadr was perceived, to his annoyance, as an impractical intellectual. It had matured with the arrival of the Ayatollah Khomeini and the subsequent jockeying for position, and peaked a few weeks after the hostages had been seized. At that time, Bani-Sadr had seven posts in the provisional government. One of the seven was that of Foreign Minister, a post he had acquired following the ouster of Mehdi Bazargan and his Foreign Minister, Ibrahim Yazdi. In late November 1979 the new Foreign Minister was preparing to go to New York to defend Iran's position during a UN Security Council debate on the hostage crisis, when, out of the blue, the imam ordered him not to attend.

It did not take Bani-Sadr long to learn that the order had not been the imam's idea. He had been persuaded by Sadegh Ghotbzadeh. Iran, Ghotbzadeh had argued, should not go to a Security Council meeting —or to any meeting—that had not been requested by Iran.

Bani-Sadr exploded. "As Ghotbzadeh is so great, as he knows how to run this country's foreign policy, let him take charge of the Foreign Ministry. I resign."

That was how Ghotbzadeh had become Foreign Minister. Two months later he had embarrassed all of them by his careless handling of the prospective arrest of the Shah. Now the election was over; Bani-Sadr had buried his rival—Ghotbzadeh had received less than 2 percent of the vote, against his own 75 percent—and he saw no need to let Ghotbzadeh play his lone hand any longer.

That evening, at his hotel, Albala received a call from Ghotbzadeh. Now it was the Foreign Minister who was storming. He accused the Frenchman of meddling, and demanded that he stop. Then he slammed down the telephone, putting an end to a six-year friendship.

Later that evening the Revolutionary Council, acting on the recommendation of President Bani-Sadr, endorsed the MacBride Commission plan.

By the time Christian Bourguet learned of the Revolutionary Council's endorsement, he already knew that his cause was in trouble. After meeting briefly with the two emissaries, Bani-Sadr had designated Said Sanjabi, the son of the revolutionary government's first Foreign Minister, as his representative, to work out any discrepancies between the proposed scenario and the Iranian Government's position. Bourguet was surprised to find just how contrary Sanjabi was. Bani-Sadr had said that he didn't want to humiliate the United States, and here Sanjabi insisted that the commission's report conclude with a declaration of guilt by the Americans. "They must not only regret what they have done," Sanjabi told Bourguet, "they must excuse themselves; it's apologies we want."

The Iranian Government, moreover, would not be satisfied that the commission's report be simply published as a UN document, as suggested by the scenario, Sanjabi went on. Iran demanded a special session of the UN to discuss the findings. Strange, Bourguet thought. This is something completely new. "No," he told Sanjabi, "on that point your President has already accepted the solution discussed in the scenario."

The issue on which Sanjabi was most intransigent was the method of transferring the hostages. According to the scenario, they were to be handed over jointly to the commission and the Iranian Government. Absolutely unacceptable, Sanjabi said; since the hostages were taken by the students, there was no reason why the government should take responsibility now.

Bourguet found this idea preposterous. "Under whose guard should they be?" he asked. Sanjabi could offer no coherent solution.

The Frenchman felt that Sanjabi was steering matters toward a total impasse, and doing so for a purely selfish reason; internal politics demanded that each Iranian politician appear more revolutionary than the next one.

Bourguet, the lifelong advocate, felt that he understood the Iranian students' position: they wanted the world to know what they had gone through. The only way to achieve that objective, they believed, was through a public trial—and because they held the hostages at gunpoint and threatened to kill them if even their own government interfered, there was great sympathy among key Iranians for such a trial. Not only would it appease the students; it would satisfy their own desire to tell the world about the injustice and torture and theft and the involvement of the Americans.

In the past Bourguet himself had favored a trial—one held by the Iranians, or the tribunal envisioned in the MacBride proposal. But now that he had been with the Americans, and understood their position, he had all but concluded that no solution was possible other than one through the UN.

Strange that he should be understanding the American viewpoint. It was the lawyer in him compelling that, he knew. There were times to defend a client, or even to prosecute on a client's behalf. But there were also times to conciliate, and to do that one had to go beyond the client's biases, and even one's own view.

Bourguet was a "man of the left," but in France that could mean many things. He liked to think of himself as a man apart from political movements. He had never really identified himself with any specific group, nor had he directly participated in the political process. While one of the primary characteristics of the French left is its critical view of the United States, the only given in Bourguet's political lexicon was that American foreign policies were, in his experience, designed to serve the interests of the United States, and its economic interests in particular. It was his observation that in pursuit of those interests, the United States had in the past supported a certain number of dictatorial regimes that had committed acts against the rights of man. That was what interested him.

Bourguet's involvement in the hostage crisis was more complex than a simple desire to help his clients in an unofficial capacity, and it had nothing to do with money because neither he nor Villalón had received a penny for their work. Bourguet, the committed humanist, involved himself because he truly feared that the hostage crisis had the potential to set off a third world war, and because fifty-three people were being kept hostages under conditions he could not accept as a defender of human rights. He wanted to help set them free.

Functioning as an intermediary, with special knowledge of Iran, rather than as an attorney, gave Bourguet certain advantages that he could share with the Americans. Because of his work with the Iranians, he had special knowledge of them. Had he been functioning as their attorney, he could not have shared this knowledge with the Americans; now when the Americans asked him for an opinion, he could answer.

What emerged, as a consequence, were his own sentiments and beliefs, as well as the sentiments and beliefs of the Iranians. He tried to express what the Iranians felt in a less theatrical way than they did. Bani-Sadr, Ghotbzadeh and others had to have an official language concerning the United States. But privately, they spoke a different language—one that, while no friendlier to the United States, nonetheless conveyed a much more comprehensive understanding of the situation and a greater willingness to find some means to end the crisis. His role, Bourguet saw, was to get *that* message across, so that the Americans would know there was something behind the intransigent, take-it-or-leave-it public posture.

The Iranians' attitudes were sometimes so passionate as to be crippling and so unrealistic as to be childish. It was these attitudes that

Bourguet could criticize to their face and attempt to change. Only someone they had known for years and trusted implicitly could have gotten away with such a role in these passionate times. They knew that when he said to them, "You have no right to do that," it didn't mean that he was against them, it meant that he felt it was in their best interests to change their attitudes.

The time had come, Bourguet believed, to change some attitudes, solidify ideas, invest the proceedings with some realism. It was time to stop dreaming of tribunals and Nuremberg-style trials, neither of which the United States could buy, and throw in with the idea of a UN commission. For a while, Bourguet himself had been sympathetic to the MacBride proposal. But any illusions he had harbored in that regard had been swept away by a chance encounter with his French attorney friend Nuri Albala.

Bourguet and Albala went back a long way. They had fought together in many causes. People often confused them for one another, calling Bourguet Albala and Albala Bourguet, because they were both built the same, and wore beards and glasses. Even their ideas were often interchangeable in those days. Then Albala joined the Communist Party and they were no longer close ideologically. Nonetheless, they remained good friends. Together, they founded an association for friendship and solidarity with the Iranian people. Albala was the Secretary-General and Mrs. Bourguet the Assistant Secretary-General. Together, they had warned the Iranians in Paris who were about to return to Iran to take power that they must not now commit the same sins as their predecessors. "On the day that you do, we will be against you," they said. And together, when they had learned to their dismay about the summary justice and executions in the months following the departure of the Shah, they had organized a committee to investigate.

A year had passed; on February 8, 1980, as Christian Bourguet was coming to the end of his most recent visit to Teheran, he met an Iranian lawyer he knew in the lobby of the Intercontinental Hotel. The lawyer, Abdel Karim Lahiji, had worked with Bourguet in the defense of political prisoners in Iran.

"What are you doing here?" Bourguet said.

"I'm going to Nuri's room," the Iranian answered. "Come along."

Bourguet knew that Albala was in Teheran; he had seen him in the coffee shop of the hotel a few days before. When they got to Albala's room, Albala suddenly broke off his conversations, asked everyone

else to leave and confronted Bourguet. He was, he said, furious with
Bourguet's law partner, François Cheron.

"Why? What's he done?" Bourguet asked.

"We've set up a whole system with Sean MacBride to nail the
Americans. We've convinced a lot of non-aligned countries to oppose
the economic sanctions against Iran. We even got France to agree to
throw in with the non-aligned countries—and then Cheron goes off to
the Quai and persuades them to completely change their minds. Now
we've got a bunch of African countries worrying about the meaning of
the French decision, and having second thoughts about going along.
And all because of Cheron. I'm absolutely furious. I can't reason with
him. I can't make him understand that this is a fantastic opportunity
to judge the United States—and we have to seize it."

It was all suddenly so clear. Albala, who obviously didn't know of
Bourguet's and Cheron's involvement in the hostage negotiations,
wasn't concerned about a solution to the hostage problem. All he
wanted was to use the problem to settle some old scores with the
United States. If it took two years, *tant mieux*. To Bourguet, the prospect of a drawn-out tribunal was ghastly. Iran, in effect, would be used
as a political trampoline, with no regard whatever to the country's
own crippling problem: the power of the students and the predicament
in which the students had placed Iran with the rest of the world.

That was the message both Christian Bourguet and Héctor Villalón
labored to convey to the Iranians.

Before presenting the scenario to the Revolutionary Council and
the Ayatollah Khomeini, Bourguet and Villalón redid the front page
to make it appear as though the paper was the work, as well as the
idea, of the government of Panama. Everyone knew who had co-
authored the scenario, but no one wanted to acknowledge it. Nor did
the Iranians, who were refusing to talk directly to the Americans, want
to be embarrassed should the scenario somehow fall into unfriendly
hands.

On February 8 Bourguet and Villalón put their work and their recommendations before the Revolutionary Council, which had already
given its tentative endorsement to the MacBride Commission plan. In
arguing his case, Bourguet pointed out that whereas the idea for the
MacBride Commission had come from outside Iran, the UN Commission proposal was the country's own.

That day, Bourguet and Villalón got a big lift from Hassan Habibi,
one of the founding members, along with Ghotbzadeh, Bani-Sadr and

several others, of the Association of Islamic Students. The MacBride Commission procedure would be a big trial that would go on for months and months, he said. It would serve as a basis for accusing the United States of intervention throughout the world. "We're in agreement on this, but we're not in agreement on the people who have planned the tribunal, because it's a Communist project clearly set up by the Russians."

To everyone's surprise, the Revolutionary Council, which was not known for its unanimity or ability to make prompt decisions, approved the scenario, as amended during the previous week, with only one condition. Its approval was contingent on the Ayatollah Khomeini's blessing.

Finally, the scenario was put before the Ayatollah, who had recovered sufficiently from his heart attack to deal with a few matters a day. He gave the scenario his guarded approval. Before he could commit himself, however, the imam said he must first see what the commission members came up with, so that he could judge whether they had done their work honestly. Had they concluded that the Shah had committed crimes? Had they concluded that the United States had intervened in Iran? If they came to those conclusions, thereby proving their honesty, then he would favor the release of the hostages—provided Iran's money was returned.

Now the only remaining business in Teheran was Hamilton Jordan's request for a more formal statement of Bourguet and Villalón's relationship with the Iranians.

From the beginning, it had been understood by everyone on the Iranian side that Bourguet and Villalón were not the official representatives of Iran. Rather, they were "friends" of the Iranian Government. The difference was a critical one. As friends, rather than representatives, they had no right to sign anything, nor could they commit the Iranian Government to anything whatsoever. Their work consisted solely of setting forth the position of the Iranians to the Americans, and vice versa, and to try to work out a solution that would be acceptable to both sides.

To satisfy the Americans, Bani-Sadr gave Bourguet and Villalón a handwritten note, which said:

"I have looked over the memorandum you submitted to me and confirm to you my agreement for you to continue to develop it, until it is finally approved by both parties."

Ghotbzadeh's letter to both men was much more elaborate. It also deliberately picked up the device by which the origins of the scenario were hidden from anyone who might make trouble with the government officials for dealing, even at arm's length, with the Americans. In all communications relating to the negotiations, the code name for the United States was now "Panama."

The last paragraph of the Foreign Minister's letter clearly indicated that the Iranians wanted the negotiations to continue.

"I beg you, as much in my name personally as in the name of our government and our country, to pursue this effort, and to believe that we will do, for our part, all that we can to help you succeed and in this way permit the end of the current crisis."

On the morning of February 9, three Americans registered at the Bellevue Palace Hotel in Bern, Switzerland, under the names Ralph Thompson, Henry Sinclair and Harvey Prescott. The three men went to their rooms, then gathered in Suite 324–325. As Hamilton Jordan, Harold Saunders and Henry Precht they awaited the arrival of Christian Bourguet and Héctor Villalón.

The arrangements for the meeting had been made by the Swiss Government at the request of the Americans, and were so secret that the United States Embassy in the capital city did not know they were there. The Swiss had even determined to pick up the bill, so that no credit cards or checks would need to be involved.

The Americans were euphoric. They felt that a solution was in sight. The setting in which they would work seemed appropriate to their mood: each window framed a picture-postcard view of the Alps, deep in snow, glowing with the sun's rays.

That afternoon, a Swiss official who was to pick up Bourguet and Villalón asked Jordan what they looked like: "You can't miss them," Jordan laughed.

When Bourguet and Villalón walked into the suite that evening, it was like a meeting of old friends. Smiles flashed and eyes twinkled and there were firm handshakes all around. There was no mistaking the personal bond that had sprung up between them, especially that between Bourguet, Villalón and Jordan. Their time together had been in concentrated blocks lasting only several days, but by now they felt as though they had known one another for years. Much of that feeling was due to the men themselves, but part of it was attributable to the person through whom they were communicating.

Stephanie Van Reidgersberg, thirty-four and the mother of two, was a tall woman whose short, blond, carefully styled hair and classic dress were a cool contrast to the often frantic proceedings in which she was engaged. A State Department translator, she had first worked with the negotiators in Washington late in January. From the outset, it had been evident that she possessed the uncommon capacity, whether speaking French, Spanish or English, to represent each speaker with full conviction. Years of living in other countries had taught her to derive the "true" meaning of others' words, regardless of ideological, cultural or language differences. She had an almost childlike ability to put aside her own patterns and values and identify with those of the speaker. She always seemed to arrive at a true meaning, an exact thought, a precise sentiment, and there were even times when she was able to help the negotiators say what they wanted to say. Van Reidgersberg had interpreted at Camp David and even dealt with Fidel Castro, so she was used to high-powered discussions, but it was evident from her absorption that she considered herself fortunate to be a witness to a vital moment in history.

That it was, but one would scarcely know it from the negotiators once the work got under way. Hamilton Jordan worked in a sweat shirt, and padded about the room in bare feet or moccasins. Bourguet and Villalón smoked almost constantly, mostly cigars, until the atmosphere reminded Jordan of late-night political meetings. From time to time they worked in shifts, one group writing, the other sleeping. Outside their rooms, the mood was more in key with the nature of the event. The corridors were empty except for the Swiss security officers dressed in civilian clothes; in response to a government request, the hotel management had moved guests to other floors. Other security officers patrolled the hotel lobby without arousing suspicion. A few hundred yards away, the Telex room at the Foreign Ministry was being manned around the clock to receive messages from Washington and Teheran.

By this point the Americans had learned that Bourguet and Villalón were not men with whom you dealt quickly. You had to hear their story and philosophy first. But as time-consuming and uncomfortable as that sometimes was, it was also extremely helpful. The Americans had to know what the other side wanted, and to learn that, they had to listen to a great deal of passion. Both Bourguet and Villalón seemed invested with the anger of the people whose views they expressed.

They argued many points in the next two days, but two of them were most critical. The first had to do with the extradition of the Shah, the second with a need for an "apology" from the Americans.

Bourguet and Villalón wanted the Americans to give the Panamanians the green light for the arrest of the Shah by indicating that they would not object if the arrest took place. "It's very nice sending a UN commission to Iran, but you remember what I've told you: you won't resolve the problem of the Shah until the Shah is judged or dead," Bourguet argued. "That's what it is and nothing else. You can't escape it. We're not asking anybody to kill the Shah. We're not asking for his life. I'm not even sure that his extradition wouldn't cause problems in Iran. That's another question. If you don't want the MacBride Commission or something like it, what we come up with here has to be an acceptable substitute. The Shah must be tried somewhere. You've got to do it. It can't be avoided. If you do it in the framework of MacBride it will go on for many months. If you don't want the MacBride project, there'll have to be another trial outside of Iran. He's in Panama. The trial will have to take place in Panama."

Jordan, Saunders and Precht had listened in silence. Now Jordan said, "Everything in its time."

What they wanted, the Americans said, was to treat the matter of the extradition apart from the scenario, and leave the matter of the extradition and arrest out of the scenario altogether.

"Okay," Bourguet responded, "but don't forget that the story of the extradition still exists in a parallel way. You can't forget it. If you don't understand that, we can do all the scenarios in the world, and it won't do us any good."

Jordan smiled lightly. Then he said, "Okay, we won't try to get the Shah out of Panama before the end of the sixty-day period. We can't create a new situation—and the Shah's departure from Panama would make everyone question the whole scenario. We won't ask the Panamanians to make him go, and if no one asks them, they're not going to throw him out." At this point, Carter's chief of staff drew a breath and leveled his gaze at Bourguet and Villalón. "But the day when we have to discuss the extradition problem, you know that's going to be one difficult discussion. That's something you'll have to fight about with the Panamanians, but you'll also be fighting against us."

So the United States was now on record: if the Iranians insisted on going through the process of arrest, that was between them and Panama, and the United States wouldn't interfere. But if the Iranians seriously tried to extradite the Shah, the United States would stop it.

With the Shah's arrest out of the way, the negotiators then settled on the second major problem—the admission of its errors by the United States. That question broke down into two parts: a promise that the United States would not intervene in Iranian affairs, and an apology for past interventions.

The first part was surprisingly easy. Jordan said it for all three Americans: "The Iranians should understand that this crisis has had at least one consequence in the United States. It has made us understand that we can't act in regard to Iran in the same way that we have before. That's clear."

The second part was an entirely different matter. When Bourguet asked for an official apology, Jordan had a one-word answer: "No."

The lawyer shook his head. "I told you and told you and told you, and I'm still telling you that, for the hostage problem to be settled, it will be necessary to wipe out the cause of the hostage problem from the heart of the Iranians. I don't justify the taking of the hostages. I'm against it. But we're not here to discuss whether the Iranians were right or wrong in doing what they did. We're trying to find a solution. You must understand that you're dealing with a revolutionary government in a country where the people had the power to overthrow the Shah. Do you think for a moment that the government would use force against the students, who are supported by the people? It's inconceivable. If the same thing happened in the United States, if American students attacked the Iranian Embassy and took Iranian diplomats as hostages and then refused to leave, what would you do? Would you send the troops?"

"Yes," the Americans chorused at once.

Bourguet was flabbergasted. "That's inconceivable to me," he said at last.

"We can't tolerate that in our system," Jordan said. "We can't let things happen that way. In our country, order has to reign. We would try anything and everything, we would use anybody who might influence them, but if in the end they refused to leave, we'd force them. We'd bring the troops."

Now Villalón spoke. "You would do that because you're an organized country," he said. "But in Iran it's not the same thing. In Iran it wouldn't be possible. A government that would do that would be turned out by the people at once."

Once more they returned to the question of the apology. "You can't destroy the causes of the hostage crisis unless you destroy them in the hearts of the Iranians," Bourguet repeated. "There are two causes— one, the Shah, and two, the past record of the United States."

"No American President can ever say, 'My predecessors behaved wrongly.' That's the way it is, and that won't change," Jordan said. Then, his voice clipped, his anger controlled yet evident, the President's chief of staff added, "We are not about to apologize to a country that has illegally seized and held our people in violation of all precepts of international law."

In the end it was the Americans who came up with a twofold solution to the impasse.

The first idea was to use an ambiguous term in English that the Iranians could translate in any manner they liked. The Americans might acknowledge "grievances of the Iranian people"; in Farsi, that could become "the crimes against the Iranian people." Both countries would be served.

After a considerable discussion, the Iranian and American representatives agreed on language for statements to be issued not only by President Carter but by President Bani-Sadr after the freeing of the hostages. Carter was to "express understanding and regret for the grievances of the Iranian people, including the widespread perception of US intervention in Iran's internal affairs; affirm the right of the Iranian people to make decisions governing their political future and the engagement of the US to respect that right; and to affirm a desire for normal relations based on mutual respect, equality and the principles of international law." The Carter administration would later argue that nothing in this language constituted an apology to Iran. But in Iran, these words would have been read differently—a frank acknowledgment by the United States Government of past interference in the affairs of Iran. For his part, Bani-Sadr was to "admit the moral wrong of holding hostages, express regret, and promise to respect international law and affirm a desire to establish normal relations based on mutual respect, and equality and international law."

A second idea was agreed on to deal with economic problems between the two countries, notably the conflict over the Iranian assets seized by the United States. It was Héctor Villalón, the only businessman in the room, who came up with the most practical suggestion in the meeting for the solution of this problem. The two governments would agree, via the scenario, for the establishment of a joint commission to deal with the financial problems between them after the release of the hostages.

"Unfortunately, I have experience in this matter," the Argentine said. "I was involved in Cuba. I know the consequences of a blockade. There is an enormous quantity of money that belongs to me that has been frozen for nineteen years. We can't have that kind of a situation again. To unfreeze funds frozen by the Americans we'll have to create new dialogues, to begin as soon as the accords are drawn up. There's only one way we can do that. You, the Americans, have sat down at the same table with the Vietnamese. Why couldn't you do the same thing with the Iranians?"

It was a splendid idea—to settle the technical problems after the settlement of the political problems—and everyone agreed.

From time to time as they worked Jordan would excuse himself to go to the bedroom, where he would telephone President Carter with a progress report via a special line installed by the White House Communications Agency.

By the end of the next day, they had hammered out a minute-by-minute "clock scenario" in which each event would trigger off the next. The most minute details had been worked out, down to the text of a Telex to be sent by Sadegh Ghotbzadeh to Kurt Waldheim. They had even managed to decide on the composition of the UN Commission; Sean MacBride's name had been dropped, at the suggestion of Bourguet, and replaced with Martin Ennals, Secretary-General of Amnesty International.

When it was all over, Bourguet telephoned Ghotbzadeh in Teheran and read him the scenario, as well as a series of instructions he had written on the back of several green hotel laundry lists. "You will get a trigger Telex through the Swiss ambassador in Teheran, which will tell you that the Americans have bought this scenario," Bourguet advised the Foreign Minister. "That's how you'll know that what I'm telling you is official."

That night, the negotiators slept the sleep of the just. They believed they had devised a scenario that could free the hostages within weeks.

chapter thirteen

The Play Begins

THERE ARE EVENINGS IN THE THEATER WHEN A WAYWARD GESTURE, a dropped line or an almost imperceptible change in the timing of one of the actors can cause an entire performance of even the most finely tuned play to go to pieces. Imagine, then, the prospects for the diplomatic drama written in Bern, when there were to be no rehearsals and many of the actors would not even be shown the script.

Early on the morning of February 11, the five secret negotiators were driven by the Swiss to Zurich, where they boarded a U. S. Air Force plane for Paris. After they landed, Jordan and Saunders, still traveling under assumed names, took the Concorde back to Washington. Precht remained in Paris, along with Bourguet and Villalón, to try to work out the remaining problems—principally the final composition of the Commission. It was a problem they had not anticipated because, as far as they knew, the selection of the Commission had already been accomplished. But while four nominees had accepted Secretary-General Waldheim's invitation to serve, the fifth, Abu Sayeed Chowdhury, the former President of Bangladesh, was ill, and had declined. The need to find a substitute produced a time-consuming round robin of consultations and negotiations, as well as a severe public relations problem.

By this point, word of the Commission's formation had been leaked to the press. Expectations, as a consequence, were rising for some break in the three-month-old impasse. The negotiators knew that if they didn't firm up the Commission's composition quickly, the entire project could become negatively coated before the scenario had even begun. To compound matters, they were working against a self-imposed deadline that had been established on the assumption that the Commission already existed; the play was to begin on February 18, less than a week hence—and that information had been leaked to the press as well, in all probability by the Americans, trying to get Iran committed.

Late in the week, Ghotbzadeh, who had been on a trip to Athens and Rome, arrived in Paris to take charge of the final arrangements. He holed up in the residence of the Iranian ambassador in the Seventeenth Arrondissement on the north side of the city. Precht sequestered himself at the home of Chris Chapman, deputy chief of mission in the American Embassy. The two sides communicated through Christian Bourguet and Héctor Villalón, working mostly out of Bourguet's unpretentious ground-floor office two blocks south of the Luxembourg Gardens.

After several days and scores of calls to Washington, New York and Teheran, the Iranians and the Americans finally agreed on a fifth member of the Commission, Hector Wilfred Jayewardene, a lawyer from Sri Lanka, brother of the country's President, and a member of a subcommission of the UN's Commission on Human Rights.

The scenario drafted in Bern stipulated that statements written by Presidents Carter and Bani-Sadr would be deposited with UN Secretary-General Waldheim. During the week Henry Precht called Christian Bourguet to communicate a desire on President Carter's part to modify that arrangement. In the first place, the President didn't understand why statements had to be given in advance. "Why shouldn't we let each head of state just give his declaration afterward?" the President had asked. Bourguet, stunned by Carter's naïveté, answered sharply: "Because Iran doesn't trust the United States. It doesn't want to be caught in a trap."

The request that followed, which was not explained, astounded the French attorney. If the statements had to be written in advance and deposited with a third party, rather than have Waldheim hold them, the President wanted them held by Christian Bourguet.

"What? You're crazy!" Bourguet said to Precht. "You want to put such responsibilities in my hands? What if a truck runs over me? That's a terrible responsibility you want to give me."

Precht dropped the matter.

Before the week was over, Hamilton Jordan had returned to Paris, bearing a memo from Carter:

"THE WHITE HOUSE
WASHINGTON
February 15, 1980

To Hamilton Jordan

In your conversations this weekend with Messrs. Bourguet and Villalon, please ask them to convey to President Bani-Sadr and Foreign Minister Ghotbzadeh the following message:

'If, at any time, the Government of Iran desires to release the American hostages at an earlier date than called for in the mutually agreed plan, the Government of Iran has my personal assurance that the United States will abide by all the terms of that plan.'

Convey to Messrs. Bourguet and Villalon our continued appreciation for the useful role they have played in trying to resolve the differences between the United States and the Islamic Republic of Iran."

Now that all the arrangements had presumably been made, the scenario was set to begin. But Jordan's presence in Paris would cause another unforeseen and potentially devastating complication.

The scenario clock was to start running on Monday evening the eighteenth, New York time, with a message from Secretary-General Waldheim to Sadegh Ghotbzadeh in Teheran, confirming his readiness to send a commission to Teheran. But Sadegh Ghotbzadeh wasn't in Teheran that evening, or even the next morning. He was in Paris, dealing with a rumor that, if not quashed, could cost him his job and, conceivably, his life.

The rumor was that the Iranian Foreign Minister and Hamilton Jordan had had a face-to-face encounter.

Three months earlier, a face-to-face encounter with an American had provoked the downfall of the Mehdi Bazargan government. Since then, such encounters had been expressly forbidden by the Ayatollah

Khomeini. In the fervid, summary-justice atmosphere of post-revolutionary Iran, there was no telling what consequences might await an official who violated the prohibition.

There is no denying that a meeting with Hamilton Jordan would have been a great temptation for Sadegh Ghotbzadeh. He was mindful of the prohibition and respectful of the imam, but he was equally mindful of the ruinous economic and political price Iran was paying for the holding of the hostages. He had never doubted that it was in his country's best interest to free the hostages, and as Foreign Minister, had worked to that end almost exclusively since November 4, 1979. But there were personal qualities to Ghotbzadeh that would have an even greater bearing than his official position on the question of whether he should or shouldn't meet with Jordan. For one thing, he had lived for many years in the United States and thought he knew something about the American mentality; he might want to test his ability to negotiate directly. Even more important was his style. For years, Ghotbzadeh had operated as a loner, traveling from country to country, and calling on the media in those countries, offering his dossier against the regime of Mohammed Reza Pahlavi, asking to be "taken seriously," knowing, in most cases, that he wasn't. Now, at last, he *was* in a position to be taken seriously in his country's behalf, and if there was one good thing about an event he otherwise detested it was that the Americans were finally listening. No one had ever questioned the personal courage of Sadegh Ghotbzadeh: if the only way he could solve the hostage problem was at personal risk to himself, he would not hesitate to take the risk.

The prospect that Ghotbzadeh and Jordan did meet in Paris that weekend, therefore, is a fairly good one. Whether the meeting took place is another matter.

On Monday the eighteenth, a young reporter working for Radio Luxembourg, a private station in Paris, broadcast a report that Ghotbzadeh had met with Jordan two nights earlier at the apartment of Héctor Villalón. Jordan will not discuss the matter. As to Ghotbzadeh, when he finally left for Teheran on Tuesday the nineteenth, he was asked by reporters at Charles de Gaulle Airport whether it was true that he and Jordan had met. "Jordan? Who's he?" the Foreign Minister replied. "Until this moment, I never heard his name before." Ghotbzadeh started for his plane, then abruptly turned back. "That's a report being spread by a Communist lawyer trying to destroy the peace process."

The lawyer to whom he referred was the old friend from his Paris days with whom he had had a rupturous battle earlier that month in Teheran—Nuri Albala, still seething because his idea for a Nuremberg-style tribunal had been dumped by the Iranians in favor of the UN Commission.

Meanwhile, the play had begun, and the first scene had all but rung down the curtain.

Days had been spent on that scene because it had meant so much to Iran. The one thing Sadegh Ghotbzadeh had insisted on was that the formation of the Commission be announced in a manner indicating that it was a consequence of a request from Iran. Only in this manner could Iran claim a "moral victory" over the United States. Whether UN Secretary-General Waldheim had not followed the scenario, or press reports of his announcement erred, the message broadcast to the world was that Waldheim had set up the Commission, the Commission had the approval of the United States and Waldheim was now awaiting the reply of Iran.

As far as the Iranians were concerned, the UN announcement made it appear as though the Commission had been the idea of the UN, in conjunction with the Americans. Where was the "moral victory"?

Waldheim's message arrived in Teheran while Ghotbzadeh was still in Paris. The message, accordingly, found its way to Bani-Sadr. The President had been given a copy of the scenario; while he had not been involved in the discussions and was not familiar with the details, it took nothing more than a simple comparison of the first step in the scenario to the message and press reports to persuade him that the scenario wasn't being followed. That being the case, he decided, he wouldn't follow it either.

In the scenario, the response of Iran had been carefully constructed to serve the interests of both sides. The reply was to state that the Commission could see the hostages, but by the use of sufficiently ambiguous phraseology the United States could declare that the purpose of the visit was to determine the hostages' well-being, and the Iranians could give the impression that the Commission was to interrogate the hostages as witnesses to, and even perpetrators of, the "crimes" of the United States in Iran.

All Bani-Sadr needed to do to get the scenario back on track was to say, "Since you're ready to send a commission, we ask you to send it."

But the President didn't do that. In his reply to Waldheim, he dropped all reference to the hostages and simply said that the Commission must come to Iran to investigate the Shah's crimes and the crimes of the United States.

In Paris that day, an alarmed Henry Precht called Christian Bourguet and demanded, "What's this all about?"

As matters stood, the scenario had been abandoned, and the play could not go on.

There followed a hurried conference between Sadegh Ghotbzadeh, Christian Bourguet and Héctor Villalón. Ghotbzadeh, quivering with rage, anguished over his choice: to abort the scenario or swallow his pride. At the urging of his friends, he finally chose the latter. Together, the three men drafted a message that was sent by Telex from Paris to the Foreign Ministry in Teheran and then on to Waldheim at the UN. In this message, Ghotbzadeh confirmed, as Foreign Minister, that the UN Commission would see the hostages.

The play would continue, but the damage had been done. There would be no "moral victory" for Iran in the opening moments, and the Iranians would wonder whether they were being done in by a species of mediation, much like their Shi°ite ancestors many centuries before.

On February 20 the five members of the United Nations Commission —Andrés Aguilar Mawdsley of Venezuela, Mohammed Bedjaoul of Algeria, Adib Daoudy of Syria, Hector Wilfred Jayewardene of Sri Lanka and Louis-Edmond Pettiti of France—departed from John F. Kennedy Airport in New York en route to Teheran. The original plan had been for the Commission to stop briefly in Geneva to gather documents needed for their work, to rest for one night, and then to continue on to Teheran. Instead, the Commission remained in Geneva for two days, because Sadegh Ghotbzadeh needed time to proclaim through the media the moral victory Iran had won by getting the UN Commission to come and because Héctor Villalón discovered that the Commission was not ready to do its work in the manner envisioned in the scenario.

It is possible that two members of the Commission had been shown a copy of the scenario in New York, but none of them acted as though they had seen it. That they were under a complete misapprehension about their function was immediately evident to Villalón when he flew to Geneva to act as a liaison.

Villalón's introduction to the Commission was not a smooth one. Although the co-chairman of the Commission had been advised of his involvement, he could do little more than speak obliquely about his role. What most faulted Villalón in their eyes was that he was not a diplomat, and they didn't understand why they should deal with him at all. Finally, Aguilar agreed to talk to him; from the moment he did Villalón knew they were in trouble.

"You understand that we've been sent by the United Nations to liberate the hostages," Aguilar, the Venezuelan and a co-chairman of the Commission, told him.

"*What?*" Villalón said, unable to believe what he had just heard. "You're completely wrong. You've been designated in the scenario to inquire into the crimes of the Shah, not to liberate the hostages. It's not your problem to liberate anyone."

"But I received instructions from the United Nations," Aguilar protested.

"Who gave you those instructions? Are you familiar with the scenario?"

"No."

"How can you not be familiar with the scenario? Your work is completely spelled out in the scenario."

At that point, Aguilar demanded to see the scenario.

"I'm not authorized to show you the scenario. Call Waldheim. It's an affair between two governments and the Secretary-General."

Villalón told Aguilar that unless the Commission came to an understanding of the role provided for it by the terms of the scenario, he was sure the Iranians would never permit it to go to Teheran.

When Villalón phoned Ghotbzadeh, his suspicions were confirmed. The Iranian Foreign Minister, hearing of the Commission's misconceptions, and still upset by the deviations from the scenario, was ready to abandon it. "It's one more example of the swellheadedness of the UN," he said.

"Listen," Villalón replied, "it's gone off-track, but it would be even worse if the Commission doesn't go at all. Maybe once it's there, we'll be able to get things back together."

Christian Bourguet, who was in Paris, spent the next day trying to convince Ghotbzadeh to temper his pride once more and let the Commission come to Teheran. Finally, Friday night Ghotbzadeh gave the green light.

But even while the UN Commission was flying to Teheran, it became apparent that the leaders of Iran were performing with one eye on the audience. On February 23 the Ayatollah Khomeini had either changed his mind or had never been in accord with the scenario from beginning to end. He declared that the fate of the hostages would be determined by the Majlis, the Iranian parliament, as soon as it was formed.

As if that announcement was not ominous enough for the Americans, they had to deal, as well, with a statement from Bani-Sadr to the effect that the final declaration of the United States called for by the scenario would have to be made before the hostages were released—and he, Bani-Sadr, would make no statement at all.

As the five members of the UN Commission took their seats in Sadegh Ghotbzadeh's office at the Iranian Foreign Ministry, they were surprised to see at either side of the Foreign Minister the elegant-looking Argentinian who had made such a pest of himself in Geneva and a bearded, long-haired Frenchman. In all their years in diplomacy, not one of them had seen anything quite so unorthodox. Not only were the two men flanking the Foreign Minister not diplomats, they weren't even Iranians—and yet they were obviously about to participate in a closed meeting between a duly constituted commission of the United Nations and a ranking representative of the government of Iran.

A minute passed while the Commission members and their staff, seated across from the Foreign Minister and his two counselors, chatted nervously among themselves. Finally, Andrés Aguilar, the Venezuelan, and co-chairman of the Commission, rose to speak. His first words almost ended the meeting.

"Mr. Minister," he began, "thank you for receiving us. We are very happy to be here—but we don't have much time. I have to leave in five days because I have another very important mission. Therefore, we have to start right away on a very clear basis. Although we are from the United Nations, we don't want to talk in circles or use diplomatic language. I'm going to go right to the point. We have already gathered a number of documents in New York and Geneva in regard to the charges against the Shah and the United States. We hope to find others here. But it is certain that we can't start work until we know, first, the date when the hostages will be transferred to the hands of the Iranian Government, second, the assurance that we can see the hostages out of the presence of the students and in the freest possible way, and, third, the date when the hostages will be freed."

Now it was Ghotbzadeh's turn to be speechless. He glared at Aguilar, his face as dark as a storm. When he spoke, his voice was shaking. "It seems that we are not on the same wavelength at all," he said. "You are wrong, you are totally mistaken. You are here because, following the long negotiations in which these two gentlemen have participated, we finally reached an agreement between the United States and Iran. And I must tell you right away that for us, in this agreement, even though it is not signed, something is very clear. The fact that you are here is a victory for us—a moral victory."

Now the storm broke. His eyes flashing contempt, Ghotbzadeh said, "If you think you are here to impose conditions in behalf of the United Nations, you can leave at once, because, in that case, we have nothing more to say to one another. We Iranians have no confidence whatever in the United Nations. For us the United Nations is an organization manipulated by the superpowers. It does not serve the interests of small countries like ours. In all the years I spent in exile, in which I was one of the leaders of the Iranian opposition, I sent perhaps ten letters to Mr. Waldheim to explain the situation of people who were tortured in prison, and the way trials were carried out in Iranian courts. Ten times I asked him for a meeting, and never once did Mr. Waldheim agree to see me. Please understand, neither in Mr. Waldheim nor in the United Nations do I have the slightest confidence. To the degree that the United Nations offers us the means to render public what the Shah and the United States did in this country, well and good. So let that be very clear—or, goodbye, gentlemen, we will be very happy to show you around the country if you so wish."

For a minute, the silence in the room was so complete that the occupants could hear their sharply accelerated breathing. Then Bourguet and Villalón put their heads close to Ghotbzadeh's and began to speak to him so softly that no one else could hear. They were playing for time, trying to calm him down. Finally, they sat back, and Ghotbzadeh glared again at the members of the Commission, almost daring them to speak.

The next moments were subdued. The Commission mapped out a program of work, including visits to the Association of the Victims of Savak and to the Central Bank, to examine documents relating to the asserted frauds of the Pahlavi family. Finally, they returned to the incendiary matter, their visit to the hostages.

"The question of the visit to the hostages will have to be discussed with the Revolutionary Council and then with the students, so that an appropriate date can be established," Ghotbzadeh said.

Now that the atmosphere was calmer, Aguilar once more raised the matter of his restricted time. "With all due respect, I must remind the Foreign Minister that I am obliged to leave on Thursday."

"I doubt that your work will be anywhere near completed," Ghotbzadeh said.

But Aguilar pressed the issue, asking the Foreign Minister to give him a fixed date as to when the Commission would complete its work and be able to depart. Finally, Ghotbzadeh said he was hopeful that the meeting with the hostages would take place on Wednesday, but certainly not before. "I think one afternoon will be sufficient," the Foreign Minister said.

As the meeting was about to end, Aguilar reminded Ghotbzadeh of the international repercussions should their work be questioned in any way. "It's not just our personal reputations at stake, but the reputations of our countries' governments," the Venezuelan said.

An afternoon meeting with President Bani-Sadr was more subdued but no less tense, with Aguilar, once again, pressing for commitments in a manner not foreseen in the scenario. "Mr. Ghotbzadeh has told us that the members of the Commission will be allowed to meet with the hostages. I think it would be appropriate to set up the details of that meeting. The Minister mentioned that Wednesday should be set aside for the meeting with the hostages. I would like to have the opinion of the President concerning the meeting."

Bani-Sadr replied dryly that the Commission would be permitted to visit the hostages to inform themselves of the relations that existed between the Americans and the former regime.

"The Commission should be permitted to ask questions regarding the hostages' health, without taking testimonies," Aguilar replied sharply.

"It is for the Commission itself to decide," Bani-Sadr bowed. "In the last two or three days, the question of the hostages has become secondary. What is essential is to discover whether Iran can liberate itself from American domination. Once Iran has assurances on this issue, the issue of the hostages will not pose too much of a problem."

Aguilar promised Bani-Sadr that the Commission report would be comprehensive and would discuss "Iranian grief." But it would not be possible, he went on, to avoid another question, the illegal seizure of the hostages. "The Commission understands the difficulties of the

Iranian Government and does not expect miracles, but all the same, I would like to ask two questions: The President has mentioned the declaration of Imam Khomeini, in which there are some positive aspects, but there are, as well, some negative aspects, especially where the imam has declared that the final decision concerning the hostages will be taken by the National Assembly, once it has been nominated and seated. I must confess that this has created some uneasy feelings for me. Do you, Mr. President, believe that this is the final decision? My second question is whether it would be possible, in making this decision, to transfer the hostages to the Ministry of Foreign Affairs."

"The Imam Khomeini has declared that parliament will decide the issue," Bani-Sadr replied. "If the United States gives satisfaction to Iran, the hostages will be freed. Everything depends on the attitude of the United States." Then, in answer to Aguilar's second question, Bani-Sadr said that the government did not want to be implicated in the affair of the hostages. "It would be a more liberal act on the government's part not to intervene because of the potential for tension that could create. At the moment it is impossible to transfer the hostages under the authority of the state."

"It was the Iranian Government that asked the members of the Commission to talk with the hostages," Daoudy, the Syrian, reminded the President.

"There will be no deviations in the plan. Iran will execute the plan," Bani-Sadr said.

It was inscrutable talk, right out of the bazaars. But it would have to do.

The arrival of the UN Commission in Teheran had been preceded by a flood of rumors. The most persistent among them was that the members of the Commission were actually spies in the employ of the Americans—and, as "proof," once the Commission set about its work, those who believed the story could point to what they described as the "inhuman" way in which the members treated the victims of the Savak.

The Commission's arrival had prompted a radio appeal to victims who did not reside in Teheran to converge on the city in order to give their witness. By the time the Commission was ready to go to work, 1500 asserted victims, some coming from abroad, had responded to the appeal. Eight hundred of them were housed in the east wing of the

1. Iranian students demonstrating, on November 9, 1979, in front of the American Embassy, where they are holding as hostages the sixty-three members of the embassy.

2. Overhead view of the United States Embassy compound in Teheran.

3. Early in the hostage crisis, some Iranian students show one of the hostages, who is bound and blindfolded, to a crowd.

4. On November 14, 1979, President Carter signs the executive order freezing $12 billion in Iranian assets in United States banks. Looking on are White House counsel Lloyd Cutler (left), Attorney General Benjamin Civiletti (right) and Treasury Secretary William Miller (center).

5. Robert Armao, the chief spokesman for the Shah of Iran, tells newsmen that a decision on whether the deposed monarch will leave the United States will soon be made.

6. Shortly after the embassy take-over, two of the Moslem militant students hurry Monseigneur Annibale Bugnini, the diplomatic representative of Pope John Paul II, into the embassy compound.

7. As Iran's new Foreign Minister, Sadegh Ghotbzadeh announces that he will not attend the United Nations Security Council meeting.

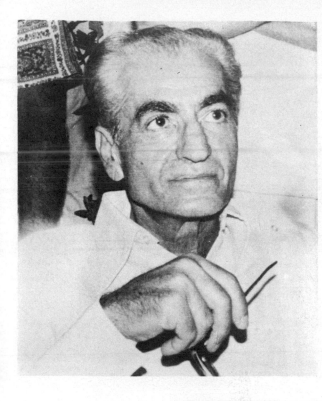

8. On Contadora Island in Panama, the deposed Shah talks to reporters.

9. Atop the roof of his Qom home, the Ayatollah Khomeini waves from behind a giant poster of himself to the crowds gathered below.

10. Secretary of State Cyrus Vance
(left) talks with United Nations
Secretary-General Kurt Waldheim
(right) at the United Nations.

11. Héctor Villalón, one of the key
intermediaries in the secret negotiations to free the hostages.

12. Christian Bourguet, another key intermediary in the negotiations.

13. Kurt Waldheim with Sadegh Ghotbzadeh as he arrives in Iran on his crisis-solving mission.

14. Waldheim on his way to a waiting helicopter after abandoning his planned visit to graves of revolution victims at a Teheran cemetery. Angry demonstrators had mobbed his car.

15. Mohammed Heikal, the Egyptian journalist who played an important role in the secret negotiations.

16. On White House grounds, White House chief of staff Hamilton Jordan and President Jimmy Carter confer.

17. Hamilton Jordan.

18. Iranian President Abolhassan Bani-Sadr.

19. Egyptian President Anwar Sadat (right) and his wife (middle) welcome the Shah (left) and Empress Farah (extreme left) at the Cairo airport.

20. Assistant Secretary of State Harold Saunders (left) and Abdel-Karim Gheraieb, Algerian ambassador to Iran (center), arrive at the State Department to discuss the U.S. reply to Iranian demands for the release of the U.S. hostages in Iran.

21. Bani-Sadr (left) addressing a crowd in the Azadi Square on the first anniversary of the Iranian Islamic Republic as Ayatollah Khomeini's son, Ahmed (right), listens.

25. Hojatolislam Khoeiny, a member of the special commission on the hostage crisis, addresses the Iranian parliament. Listening to him is Hojatolislam Hashemi Rafsanjani, the speaker of the parliament.

26. In January 1981 Deputy Secretary of State Warren Christopher arrives at the U. S. Embassy in Algiers for further negotiations on the release of the hostages.

27. Warren Christopher (left) puts his signature to the formal United States-Iranian hostage agreement early on January 19 as Algerian Foreign Minister Mohammed Ben Yahia looks on.

28. President Carter handing over the reins of power to incoming President Ronald Reagan at the swearing-in ceremony. President Carter still did not know if the hostages had been released yet.

29. Newly inaugurated President Reagan raises his glass in a toast during a luncheon at the capital and announces that the Americans held hostage in Iran have left that country.

Hilton Hotel, which, until the arrival of the Commission, had been closed for lack of guests. The Commission had been installed in the east wing as well, on the fourteenth floor. To the Iranians attempting to organize the inquiry, the sensible solution was for the Commission members to interview the victims, many of them now crippled, some amputees, in the hotel. But the Commission insisted that the victims be brought to the Teheran office of the United Nations, several kilometers from the hotel.

It was cold in Teheran that week, and there was snow on the ground, which made the movement of the victims from the hotel to the UN building that much more difficult. Ninety victims at a time were taken by bus to the small three-story building. Then they stood outside, waiting to be interviewed. To passersby, the sight of so many crippled persons, huddled together in the snow, was overpowering.

There was one other curious decision of the Commission's working against the victims, and that was its determination to function as a team, all five members interviewing the victims one by one, rather than dividing up and taking the testimonies separately. The process, as a consequence, was slow and ponderous, and, given the cold weather and lack of shelter, punishing on the victims. But what was most punishing was the knowledge that the Commission would never see more than a fraction of the victims.

Bourguet and Villalón pleaded with the Commission to reconsider its procedures, to no avail. Upset, they turned to Ghotbzadeh, who immediately decided to form a working group made up of Iranian jurists, to help the Commission. When Bourguet and Villalón took this proposal to the Commission, one of the members asked the obvious question: "How will we know that what your lawyers tell us will be true?"

"In fact, you're being duped right now," Bourguet responded at once. "You know about the little boy with no arms. You believed he was a victim of the Savak. In fact, he lost his arms in an automobile accident, and his mother has been using him to make money."

Reassured by Bourguet's candor, the Commission approved the parallel procedure. Soon thereafter, Ghotbzadeh broadcast a radio appeal, asking all lawyers who spoke or wrote French or English and wished to help with the work to come to the Hilton Hotel. Ghotbzadeh also put out a call for French- or English-speaking secretaries to come to the hotel with their typewriters. Fifty lawyers and as many secretaries responded; working day and night, they managed to take the testimony of all the victims who had not been seen by the Commis-

G

sion. When the interviews had been typed and signed and copied, Ghotbzadeh himself brought them to the Commission. "I beg you," he said, as he turned the affidavits over, "in the name of all the people who made this trip and have not been seen by you, at least see them all at once."

By this point, the Commission's methods had been harshly criticized in the press, and Secretary-General Waldheim had even telephoned his concern to Aguilar. The Commission members finally agreed to a meeting with the victims in the hotel. They too were overpowered by the sight of so many mutilated people. Mohammed Bedjaoui, the Algerian, spoke in the Commission's behalf and in a manner so deeply felt that many in the room wept, the Commission's past actions were forgiven and its moral credibility was established, at last.

As the work dragged on—slowed, in part, by Aguilar's brief absence —there was no more talk on the Commission's part about finishing in five days. That deadline had already passed. Nor had the Commission members been able to see the hostages, and each day that they didn't the pressures mounted. They were felt most, perhaps, by Bourguet and Villalón, who had brought the two sides together, and more than anyone were responsible for the presence of the Commission in Teheran. Although the nature of their work was not publicly known, their presence with the Commission had provoked a series of threats against their lives, and they were now accompanied by bodyguards wherever they went.

At one moment in the proceedings, when their spirits were low, Bourguet and Villalón had called on President Bani-Sadr to ask him if he felt the scenario was still in effect and had a reasonable chance of playing to a successful end. Yes, the President replied, the scenario *was* still in progress, and he saw no reason why its remaining steps would not be taken.

But would there be any hostages to free? As the time for the anticipated release of the hostages neared, Harold Saunders searched frantically for Mohammed Heikal, the Egyptian journalist and unofficial intermediary, and when he finally found him in Geneva, asked him to pass an urgent message to the Ayatollah Khomeini.

"The USG, U.S. Government, is gravely concerned about reports we have received in the past few days indicating that some of the diehard militants at the U.S. Embassy compound may seek to kill some or all of the hostages if they are forced to release them. The U.S. is interested in receiving some form of assurance that the Iranian authorities are able to take measures to prevent this. The murder of the U.S. hostages would be a tremendous setback to stability in the region, would put the U.S. and Iran at odds for some time to come, and would blacken irrevocably the image of the Iranian revolution. If it is true that such action is planned, it is obviously the work of persons who want to further destabilize the situation in the region and undermine the goals of Iran's Islamic revolution."

According to the report the Americans had received, if the government attempted to move the hostages from the American Embassy compound, the militants would kill the hostages and then commit suicide.

Heikal passed the message on to Ahmed Khomeini, the son of the Ayatollah.

By Thursday, March 6, both Bani-Sadr and Ghotbzadeh were in agreement that the UN Commission had fulfilled the scenario commitment to investigate the past. The time had come for the Iranian Government to fulfill its commitment to evacuate the hostages from the embassy and place them under the control of the government.

That task, it was immediately apparent, would take all the skill that Sadegh Ghotbzadeh possessed. The students did not want to give the hostages up, and the government—with the exception of himself and Bani-Sadr—did not want to receive them.

What the politicians all the way up to the Ayatollah Khomeini feared was that in wresting control of the hostages they would be contravening the will of the people—which, in post-revolutionary Iran, could mean instant eclipse. Ghotbzadeh was certain the students understood this, and just as certain that they were bluffing when, on Wednesday night, March 5, they told the Ayatollah Mohammed Beheshti that they had decided to carry out the transfer.

Aghast, Beheshti telephoned Ghotbzadeh to express his displeasure. "The government cannot take such responsibility," he said.

"The students are playing poker," Ghotbzadeh said. "They're trying to bluff. They're making the offer because they're sure we can't accept. They want to play poker, we'll play poker too. We'll tell them we'll take the hostages—and I'll take full responsibility."

Ghotbzadeh had said the magic words: the responsibility would be his. If there was a popular reaction against the move, the head that would roll would be his. The next day, the Revolutionary Council—Beheshti included—agreed to go along.

That day, Ghotbzadeh informed the Ayatollah Khomeini of his plans to transfer the hostages into the custody of the Revolutionary Council. When the Ayatollah made no reply, the Foreign Minister interpreted his silence as approval, and triumphantly announced during a television interview a few hours later that the most powerful man in Iran had "approved" the transfer of the hostages to the Council. "They are all afraid," he confided to Bourguet and Villalón, but he went ahead with plans, nonetheless, to move the hostages to the Foreign Ministry.

The transfer of the hostages was to be made by military helicopters on Saturday, March 8, and the military had already organized the operation down to the last detail, including special markings on their craft that would identify them so that students would not shoot at them under the impression that they were part of an American rescue mission. Trucks had been commandeered for use in case the helicopter operation somehow failed. Ghotbzadeh even brought the military and student leaders together in his office to be certain they would recognize one another when the operation took place.

At the embassy compound, the student militants spoke bitterly about the "betrayal" of the Ayatollah, and some of them conceded defeat. But the diehards among them hadn't quite given up, and they now initiated a maneuver to stall the release until the last possible moment. Before they would agree to the transfer, the students announced, they wanted a written presidential order to do so. By eight-thirty Saturday morning, Ghotbzadeh was on the telephone, trying to get the letter from Bani-Sadr. But the President wasn't in his office, and couldn't be found. An hour and forty-five minutes later, Bani-Sadr finally returned Ghotbzadeh's call, and the Foreign Minister dictated a letter for him to give to the students. For good measure, Ghotbzadeh suggested that the President send the text of the letter to the radio and television stations for immediate dissemination.

By 11:30 A.M., Bani-Sadr had written and signed the letter, and sent it to Ghotbzadeh, who gave it to three student militants who had come to his office from the embassy compound. Still, the students weren't giving up. They had a new demand: a list of the hostages to be released.

Incredibly, no such list existed, although the hostages were now in their 126th day of captivity. When word of this new complication reached the Foreign Minister's office, Christian Bourguet immediately contacted several American journalists to see if they could come up with the names. They couldn't. Bourguet sat down at once and wrote out a questionnaire, copies of which were to be given to each hostage as he or she emerged from the embassy.

At 12:30 P.M., the air force officers in charge of the operation reported to Ghotbzadeh that all preparations for the transfer had now been made and the helicopters were standing by, ready to take off as soon as the order was given.

Thirty minutes later, as the Foreign Minister waited impatiently for the hostage list, the media began to broadcast reports of massive demonstrations throughout the country protesting the release of the hostages. But the pictures on the television screen—and subsequently in the newspapers—were close-ups, and disguised the fact that the demonstrators numbered only a few hundred, a paltry group compared to the kinds of turnouts Iranians usually produced.

Nonetheless, the damage had been done.

At one-thirty that afternoon, Ahmed Khomeini telephoned Sadegh Ghotbzadeh to declare that his father had been misrepresented. Because he had not objected to the transfer did not mean that he had approved it. Within the hour, the Ayatollah's son had put out a statement to that effect.

Now the newspapers were on the streets reporting that the student militants were refusing to turn the hostages over to Sadegh Ghotbzadeh and the Revolutionary Council. In desperation, Ghotbzadeh convoked an emergency meeting of the Council for 6 P.M. No sooner had he done so than calls began coming in from members of the Council, saying that they didn't want to meet—and that the transfer of the hostages was now impossible. Ghotbzadeh became so enraged that he wanted to go on television to address the nation, but Bourguet dissuaded him.

Then came another student demand: eight hours' advance notice, broadcast on radio and television, before the transfer of the hostages— at which point they planned to open the embassy compound gates and let the public in. It was an impossible condition, an invitation to slaughter.

So ended the first round of efforts to transfer the hostages.

On Sunday the Revolutionary Council agreed to a meeting that evening to deal with the problem of the students. The meeting, long, tense and abrasive, focused on Sadegh Ghotbzadeh's call for an ultimatum to the students, and use of force if they ignored it. The Council rejected the Foreign Minister's proposal, and decided to meet the next day with the Ayatollah to ask him to settle the hostage conflict. To the astonishment of everyone present, Bani-Sadr did not show up. He had been convinced by Ahmed Khomeini that his presence was not necessary. The Ayatollah's son was later quoted as saying that he kept Bani-Sadr away as a practical joke. Whatever the intent, the President missed a crucial meeting of the Revolutionary Council.

On Monday morning the Ayatollah listened to both sides, and then came up with a proposal. It was not a compromise, nor even a new idea. It simply fused the present impasse to a statement he had made several weeks before that had been lightly passed over at the time. If the UN Commission did its work "honestly," he had said, then the hostages might be freed. He was not talking about freeing the hostages now, or even of transferring them. What he proposed to the Revolutionary Council was that he would order the students to let the Commission see the hostages *provided* the leader of the Commission first made a declaration of the Commission's findings. If the Commission was prepared to condemn the crimes of the Shah as well as the complicity of the United States, then he would know that the members had done their work honestly, and the matter of the hostages could proceed.

To the Iranians, the idea made capital sense. The Commission members would only be declaring publicly what they had already admitted many times in private: their conclusions did indicate that crimes had been committed and that the United States had "interfered" in the internal affairs of Iran. Furthermore, this brief preview of the Commission's findings would enable Iran to claim publicly the "moral victory" it had been deprived of earlier because of the foul-up over the opening act of the scenario.

It was agreed that the Ayatollah's plan should be presented privately to the Commission, and only announced publicly the following day if the Commission rejected it. In that manner, the Iranians would avoid the charge that they were presenting the Commission with an ultimatum.

Sadegh Ghotbzadeh rushed to the Hilton Hotel to communicate the

proposal to the Commission. The Commission asked for time to think
it over.

And then, suddenly, time no longer mattered. As Ghotbzadeh was
leaving the hotel, a journalist rushed up to tell him that the Ayatollah's
plan had just been broadcast.

The plan, it was later said, had been released "inadvertently" by
Ahmed Khomeini. No one believed that. Ahmed Khomeini was a
leader of the religious wing of the revolution; he stood to gain if Bani-
Sadr and Ghotbzadeh failed. By making the terms of the Ayatollah
public, he had made certain that there would be no backing off by
Iran, and that there would almost certainly be no accord.

That afternoon Bani-Sadr lobbied heavily with Mohammed Bedjaoui, the Algerian member of the Commission and his country's regular ambassador to the UN. By giving its first impressions in Teheran,
Bani-Sadr argued, the Commission would "reassure the Islamic students about its true impressions."

But Bani-Sadr's importuning was of no avail. The UN Commission
cried "blackmail." Not only did the Ayatollah's request violate the accords of the scenario, his proposal would not permit the Commission to
see the hostages in a free atmosphere, beyond the control of the militants.

For the next twelve hours, until 3 A.M. in Teheran, there would be
dozens of calls between Teheran, Washington and New York, as the
Americans and the Secretary-General would plead with the Commission members to stay on. Bourguet and Villalón, in almost constant
communication with first Henry Precht, then Harold Saunders and
finally Hamilton Jordan—with President Carter often standing next to
the phone—would tell the Commission that by leaving Teheran they
were creating a threat to world peace. In a final, desperate effort to
persuade the Commission, Carter would say, "The United States is not
opposed to the Commission doing its duty"—a clear signal to the Commission that it could accept the Iranians' conditions.

But Andrés Aguilar of Venezuela wasn't having any of it. Suddenly, angrily, he drew Héctor Villalón aside and said, "If President
Carter himself asks me to say what I found here, I'm not going to do
it." The French and the Sri Lanka members backed Aguilar.

That was the end. The Commission would leave in the morning—
after experiencing one more example of Byzantine byplay: an attempt

by the student militants to shove the purloined American Embassy documents off on them rather than surrender them to the government. In this manner, the students felt, they would satisfy the Ayatollah's order to surrender the documents while at the same time not appearing to be bowing to the government. And "shove" the documents they did, into the arms of the protesting diplomats, and then into the windows of the cars that were taking them to the airport.

At the American Embassy, the hostages would spend their 129th day of captivity.

Late that evening, alone in his office, President Bani-Sadr commiserated with his favorite journalist, Eric Rouleau, the correspondent of *Le Monde*. How wrong the militant students were, he said, when they charged that the Commission's efforts were directed against their principal objective, the extradition of the Shah. "Once the Commission's report was adopted by the Security Council, we could have used it to demand the Shah's extradition from Panama. We would have benefited from the support of the international community. The international community would have put pressure on the United States, forcing them to recognize their wrongs and to stop being an obstacle to the extradition of the Shah." Bani-Sadr sighed. "By opposing the investigating Commission, the Islamic students have involuntarily proved that the Shah was right. From the beginning, the Shah predicted the failure of the UN Commission."

chapter fourteen

A Turn for the Worse

THE MAN WHO HAD PRECIPITATED ALL OF THE FOREGOING HAD NOW been in Panama for two and one half months. It had not been a happy time, and it was a question in his mind as to which aspect of life plagued him more—his political situation, his physical circumstances or his deteriorating health.

The Shah had been aware of the attempts to extradite him almost from the moment they had begun. Privately, the Panamanians assured him that extradition would be in violation of their laws and that, as a consequence, he had nothing to fear. And yet these same Panamanians did nothing to quash rumors that Panama was negotiating with Iran on the matter of his arrest. The Shah was kept up to date by friends in Europe who would relay press reports to him and ask, "What the hell is going on?" One day the Shah's chief of staff, Robert Armao, received a visit from an American who had dealt for many years with the Panamanians. "They're selling the Shah out," the man told Armao. "I deal with these people. I know all of them intimately. I'm telling you, you'd better get him out of Panama because they're selling him out. Never trust the Panamanians. Royo, Torrijos—forget them! They're selling him out."

At first, the Shah refused to believe such assessments. "Maybe you're wrong," he told Armao when the New Yorker expressed his own suspicions.

"Even a fool can see what's happening," Armao would insist.

"Well, where else could we go? What alternatives do we have?" the

Shah would ask. But Armao's suspicions buttressed his own, and then his twin sister, Princess Ashraf, compounded matters even further with her constant calls for permission to let her try to find him another place.

Then came the announcement by Sadegh Ghotbzadeh that the Shah had actually been arrested. It wasn't true, as the Shah knew better than anyone, but it required no conspiratorial temperament to conclude that Ghotbzadeh must have had something to go on. To add to the Shah's discomfort, almost immediately after the heated public denials by the Panamanian Government that such an arrest had been contemplated, there were local press reports examining the "technical possibilities" of extradition. Once again the Panamanians assured the Shah that there was nothing to the reports. He did not believe them.

One day, at last, the Shah confronted General Torrijos with his suspicions. "You're going to turn me over to Iran," he said flatly.

"No! We will not! There is no way it could happen!" the general assured him.

But the Shah did not believe Torrijos either.

What the Shah ultimately perceived as a charade was being accomplished against a background of increasing dissatisfaction with his physical existence. The small house in which he had been living since December 15 had been accepted for lack of an alternative. But by now, the tight quarters had gotten on his nerves. Then, the location was hardly premium: although the house was on the beach, it was also 200 yards from an airfield. The friction between the Shah's staff and the Panamanians, which had surfaced almost immediately after his arrival and dealt almost exclusively with money, had intensified. Despite the initial assurances of General Torrijos that he would deal personally with anyone who attempted to profit from the Shah's presence in the country, the Shah's staff felt that the bills he was receiving were preposterously high. There were hints that Contadora Island could be bought—for $10 million. Other properties the Shah and his staff were shown seemed equally inflated in value.

The Panamanians continued to make life uncomfortable for the Shah's American staff. Armao and others were charged with leaking false stories to the American press. On one occasion, Armao was not permitted to accompany the Shah on a visit to the American ambassador. Early in March, Mark Morse of Armao's staff was arrested on a charge of interference with Panamanian security. The Shah's inter-

pretation was that the Panamanians were angry about his staff's repeated complaints about overcharges.

But none of this was of any consequence compared to the Shah's
growing conviction, whether it was right or wrong, that he was becoming a prisoner, cut off from the rest of the world.

In appearance, he was a free man. But there were increasing indications that his telephone was tapped. One day, one of his aides complained during a call about the high costs to which they were being
subjected; the next day, the Panamanians protested that too many details about money were being discussed on the telephone, and not long
thereafter, they set up a tape recorder in his house to record all his
calls—and then charged him for the machine. Then, on February 7,
the Panamanian Foreign Minister stated that the Shah was not free to
leave Contadora without the government's permission. Why the Foreign Minister would make such a statement no one could fathom, but
it was true enough. Panamanian security guards still patrolled the island. And the airport was so small that no large plane could land
there; if the Shah ever decided to make a "getaway," he would have to
transfer at Panama City. When an old friend said to him one day,
"Your Majesty, you must leave," the Shah replied, "I don't know if I
could."

To add to the Shah's discomfort, there were the dismaying reports
of violence and destruction and deaths streaming out of Iran. "He is
like a sculptor who made a statue, a beautiful statue and they crushed
it, crushed it down in so little time," Princess Ashraf told Barbara
Walters. And, finally, there were the bitter memories of betrayal. The
person the Shah mentioned the most now in this connection was
Valéry Giscard d'Estaing, the President of France who had told the
leaders of the United States, Great Britain and West Germany at
Guadeloupe that France had written off his regime. "When I think
that this man was calling me 'Your Imperial Majesty' less than a year
ago, and licking my shoes!" he exploded one day to a visitor.

During all this period, there had been only one moment when the
Shah had seemed to warm to life. It was when a mutual friend told
him about an encounter with Princess Soraya, the Shah's ex-wife.
"Are you going to see the Shah?" she had asked him.

"Yes," he replied.

"You know when he was operated on in New York, I sent him a
telegram and he never answered me," she said. "But please give His

Majesty my best regards, and say that I think of him and that I hope everything will be all right."

When the mutual friend recounted this conversation to the Shah, it was as though he had tapped some hidden reservoir of will. The Shah straightened, and smiled, and looked away, deep in some private thought.

These days, the Shah smiled very little. He liked a small segment on the western edge of Contadora Island, where he could sit alone at the water's edge and watch the setting sun.

And then there was the constant preoccupation with his failing health.

When the Shah left the United States in December, it was with the firm understanding that, should he need surgery or any other medical help, such help would be forthcoming. The Americans would make Gorgas Hospital in the old Canal Zone available to him, fly his doctors down, if necessary, and, as a last resort, return him to the United States for any special treatment. A few days after the Shah had settled into Contadora Island, his physician, Benjamin H. Kean of New York, flew to Panama on a plane furnished by the State Department to implement the Lackland agreement providing for the care of the Shah at Gorgas. The first thing Kean did was to put Adán Ríos, a specialist in oncology and member of the Gorgas staff, in charge of the case. Kean also arranged to have laboratory work done at Gorgas. Finally, the doctor organized a surgical team that could be quickly assembled to deal with any emergencies. The Shah was a helicopter trip away from the hospital. Satisfied with the arrangements—all of them approved by General Torrijos' personal physician, Carlos García Aguilera—Kean returned to New York.

For a while, the Shah responded well. He had arrived in Panama still depleted from his surgery, but by the end of January he had gained twenty-four pounds. At dinners given by President Royo or General Torrijos he seemed comfortable, even animated. Then, overnight, his aspect seemed to change. He became, in Torrijos' words, *un muerto vivo,* a living dead man.

What had happened was that the Shah's spleen, controlled for months by chemotherapy, had begun to enlarge again. This development had not been unexpected by his Panamanian doctors, who had noted even during the time that the Shah was gaining weight that the splenectomy should not be postponed for long.

In mid-February, the Shah developed a respiratory infection. The bewildering events that followed flowed from such a confluence of emotions that it is best, perhaps, to trace them from their separate sources.

When the Shah fell ill, according to the Panamanians, Dr. Flandrin, the cancer specialist who had attended the Shah all these years, was summoned from France. He, Dr. Ríos and Dr. Carlos García Aguilera, General Torrijos' private physician, agreed that a splenectomy should be performed as soon as possible.

During the winter—again, according to the Panamanians—the Shah had been persuaded by General Torrijos to have his surgery at Paitilla Medical Center, a new ninety-patient private facility next door to the Holiday Inn in Panama City. With this accord in mind, the Panamanians alerted Paitilla and preparations for a secret operation were begun. The doctors were optimistic. Technically a splenectomy is not usually a difficult operation; it is performed routinely in most of the country's hospitals without major problems. Where the spleen is greatly enlarged, however, as was the case with the Shah, certain complications such as hemorrhaging, infection and thrombosis must be anticipated. Ríos, accordingly, arranged to obtain the most modern blood-separating machine available, one that permits selective transfusion of all blood elements, from M. D. Anderson Hospital in Houston, and invited a specialist, Dr. Jean P. Hester, and an engineer, Peter Greco, to install the machine and participate in the case.

It was at this point, the Panamanians say, that they began to experience difficulty with Dr. Benjamin Kean. According to their account, Kean attempted to intervene through the State Department, the Army medical command and IBM, the manufacturer of the machine, to prevent the blood separator from being shipped to Panama. Failing in this, he presented himself in Panama to integrate the medical group attending the monarch.

On March 6, Flandrin, Ríos and García all recommended an immediate splenectomy to the Shah. The Shah accepted the recommendation of the French and Panamanian doctors and indicated total confidence in his upcoming surgery—or so the Panamanians contend.

Kean tells an entirely different story.

He was, it should be remembered, the physician in ultimate charge of the case. The Shah was "his" patient, and whatever authority Ríos or others possessed had been given to them by Kean. His problems began, he says, when, instead of sending the Shah's blood for tests to

Gorgas Hospital as he had instructed, the Panamanians began to send it to Paitilla, which was partly owned by Dr. García. Next, he began getting secondhand reports that the Shah was not feeling well, but he could not get Ríos on the telephone to confirm them. So he returned to Panama.

At Contadora, Kean, accompanied by Robert Armao, encountered García. "I bring you a message from the general," Kean quotes García as saying. "The Shah will be operated on in Panama and no place else."

"That's no problem," Kean replied. "Since the Canal treaty, Gorgas Hospital is now part of Panama. My agreement with the U. S. Government is that the surgery will be at Gorgas."

"You don't seem to understand," García said. "Gorgas Hospital will not do. It'll be in Panama. Otherwise no operation in Panama."

Kean had difficulty controlling himself. Finally, he said, "Will you say the same thing to the Shah—as directly as you've just said it to me?"

"Yes," the Panamanian said.

The doctors then went to see the Shah. The Shahbanou was with him. The couple listened dispassionately as García repeated exactly what he had told Kean.

When the doctor had finished, Ríos said, "Let's get the best man possible," and started to reach for the telephone. Kean stopped him. "I consider this a betrayal," he said.

At this point, the Shah said, "Good day, gentlemen." He rose and left the room.

But Kean wasn't giving up. When he and Armao were alone, he said, "We've got to get Jordan and Cutler and insist on Gorgas."

Armao wasn't responsive. He told Kean he understood that Gorgas, which had once been clearly superior, was no longer very much better than other hospitals in Panama.

Kean did not agree. He interpreted what was going on as a consequence of Panamanian national pride. For years, Gorgas had been a hated symbol of North American domination. Now, he felt, the Panamanian doctors were making a medical decision on the basis of non-medical factors. How could he regain control of the situation? "We've got to get in a man so famous and powerful that they'll obey him," Kean declared. His first thought was Dr. Michael E. DeBakey, the famous Texas heart surgeon, and within a few hours he had DeBakey's agreement to do the surgery provided he could bring his own team.

According to Kean, he had no trouble selling the idea to the staff at Paitilla, some of whom had been Kean's students at Cornell. But whether the Panamanians completely understood the role DeBakey was to play is a matter of conjecture. As far as Kean was concerned, the surgery would be performed by DeBakey and his team. The Panamanians believed that DeBakey was coming to observe.

What ultimately snapped their patience was a report in the press that DeBakey would arrive in Panama with his own team of surgeons, anesthesiologists and nurses. The Panamanians were outraged. To them, the "invasion" of DeBakey in this manner would make it seem to the rest of the world as though they were medical primitives. The more politic among them asked that "form be respected" and "foreign authority not be imposed." In tougher moments, they fumed that it was their hospital and their country, and a matter of professional pride to them that they perform the surgery. Dr. DeBakey, whom they acknowledged as an important teacher, could look on and offer advice and, in some unimaginable emergency, take an active role, but he was under no circumstances to bring his "team."

On March 14, the Shah, apparently persuaded by General Torrijos, entered the Paitilla Medical Center. What may have been even more persuasive than the general's counsel was the position of the Panamanian Government, communicated to him and his advisers from the outset. He was free to go wherever he pleased, but once he abandoned Panamanian jurisdiction he could not re-enter Panama. A foreign-administered hospital was considered outside Panamanian jurisdiction.

Several members of the Shah's entourage accompanied him to Paitilla and took adjoining rooms. The Shah occupied room 353. Its windows were barred. He kept the door closed and locked. Although the room was air-conditioned, he refused to cool it, preferring to let the temperature rise to a level that made him perspire.

The Shah seemed to get along well with his Panamanian doctors, although he gave them the impression that he was more than mortal. Before they examined him, they were required to ask his permission. They called him "Majesty" and stood in his presence. It gave some of them the feeling that they were attending an audience with royalty rather than performing a medical examination.

Late that afternoon, Kean arrived in Panama with Michael DeBakey.

One other cause of friction between the Panamanians and Kean had been the storm of publicity surrounding the pending surgery. The Panamanians contended that until Kean made some public declarations in New York, the only people who had known about the surgery, other than himself, were the Shah, the doctors attending him in Panama and the administrator of Paitilla. Once the news was out, however, strict security measures had to be taken because of local and long-distance telephone threats against the hospital and its personnel.

Kean and DeBakey immediately fell afoul of those measures. The two doctors checked into the Holiday Inn and then walked to the hospital. But when they tried to enter, they were stopped by an armed guard because they were without proper credentials. It took an acrimonious half hour to straighten the matter out—plenty of time for the Americans to develop some conspiratorial theories.

Another exacerbation: in spite of the Panamanians' wishes, DeBakey had arrived with a team, and done so with a flourish, coming by private plane.

Kean apparently wanted to present the Panamanians with a *fait accompli:* to assert his authority as the doctor in charge, and to move the Shah to Gorgas. He was counting on the ability of the United States to pressure the Panamanians into acceding, and on his ability to obtain consent from the Shah—who was, after all, the final authority as to where the surgery would occur and who would perform it.

Finally, Ríos proposed a meeting between the two factions to see if something couldn't be worked out. The meeting took place in the Paitilla library. The American doctors arrived half an hour before the scheduled time, and the meeting got under way before many of the Panamanians were present. But those who were there vehemently expressed their disgust at the press declarations implicating the competence of Panamanian doctors and hospitals; their feelings that foreign doctors who would not be assuming responsibility for postoperative complications should not operate; their belief that the security of patients and personnel at Paitilla had been jeopardized because of the Americans. And they told Kean flat out that DeBakey had been authorized only as an overseer and consultant precisely because of the heavy-handed publicity that had infuriated the Panamanian medical community. In an especially heated moment, the Panamanians reminded the Americans that they were not in Afghanistan—meaning that they were not in a country where foreigners could do as they pleased.

Later that morning, in a private meeting with DeBakey, the Panamanian doctors attempted to cut him out of the controversy. They told him they were not disgusted with him, only with Kean, and they invited him to join them. DeBakey replied that his role had not been clearly explained to him; he had been unaware, he said, that a Panamanian team was preparing to operate. His preference was to retire from the case inasmuch as he was unwilling to assume responsibility without complete control.

At this point Ambler Moss, the American ambassador, attempted to mediate in an effort to end the dispute. He, Marcel Salamin, Torrijos' political counselor, and Dr. Ríos were informed by the Panamanians that DeBakey was welcome, but that Panamanian doctors did not appreciate being displaced in their own country.

That evening, at a meeting in the Holiday Inn, the factions made peace. DeBakey accepted the Panamanians' invitation to join the team. At the same time, however, the Houston surgeon proposed a postponement so that the Shah could recover even more from his respiratory infection and because the present atmosphere was not appropriate to good work.

At ten o'clock the next morning, Sunday March 16, all of the doctors—Americans, Panamanians and French—assembled at the hospital and accepted the recommendation that the operation be postponed for several weeks. The exact date would be determined by the Panamanian doctors, and closely held for security reasons. The doctors further agreed to refrain from any comments to the press. Then they went *en masse* to room 353 to announce their decision. The Shah, in apparent agreement with the decision, returned to Contadora that afternoon.

Had the doctors made a more attentive examination of their patient's psychological state, they might have gotten some indication of what they would discover only later.

All during this period the Shah, his family and staff had looked on with horror at the infighting of the physicians. The insistence of the Panamanians, in particular, was filtered through the conspiratorial consciousness the Shah and his entourage habitually applied to all matters. Why were the Panamanians so insistent on operating? Had one of the Shah's enemies managed to reach a member of the medical team? Would the Shah be assassinated on the operating table? Or would he be put under heavy sedation—and awaken in Teheran?

As farfetched as such considerations might seem to others, they were uppermost in the mind of the Shah, the Shahbanou and the

Americans, Robert Armao and Mark Morse—who, by this point, had completely taken on the coloration of their clients.

Had the doctors recommended immediate surgery, the Shah probably would have gone through with it. But now, with the postponement, he had some moments to reflect. His assistants, trusted former aides of his friend Nelson Rockefeller, were urging him to leave. But most of all, the Shah knew that he did not have long to live. He wanted to die in peace, on friendlier soil, in a culture closer to his own.

chapter fifteen

The Second Time Around

TWO DAYS AFTER THE UN COMMISSION HAD STORMED FROM TEHERAN, the secret negotiators were back at the Bellevue Palace Hotel in Bern, Switzerland, under the same tight security arrangements and camouflages that had characterized their first effort. They were determined to try again, and at once—a spirit that underlay the letter Jimmy Carter gave to Hamilton Jordan on the morning of his chief of staff's departure.

> "THE WHITE HOUSE
> WASHINGTON
> March 12, 1980

To Hamilton Jordan

In your discussions with Misters Bourguet and Villalón, I would like for you to present this message:

'Please convey to President Bani-Sadr and Foreign Minister Ghotbzadeh our desire to continue our informal discussions and negotiations through Misters Bourguet and Villalón.

We are prepared to pursue reasonable reciprocal steps to resolve the present crisis.

A renewed commitment to this process will be required on the part of both the United States and Iran, and I am sure that it will be understood that we will need evidence of both the willingness and ability of the Government of the Islamic Republic of Iran to fulfill any new commitment that they might make.

Finally, I continue to look forward to the day beyond the present difficulties when we can build a relationship with Iran and its people based on equality and mutual respect.'

Sincerely,
Jimmy Carter"

Once more, Bourguet and Villalón flew to Zurich and were driven by the Swiss Government to Bern. And once more, the Americans awaited them—Jordan, Saunders, Precht and Stephanie Van Reidgersberg, the State Department interpreter who by this point seemed a full-fledged member of the team. But the six of them needed no translator to understand what each of the others was feeling: an overpowering sense of disappointment at having come so close and missed; a profound desire to reassure one another that all had not been lost; a belief that, in sharing this experience, each was evolving an identity transcending previous personal boundaries; and, finally, a certainty that, despite the explosion of emotion that had accompanied the UN Commission's visit to Teheran, the scenario represented not simply a means to end a specific crisis but a desire of Iran and the United States to make up.

Yet how had it come to pass that a collective effort expressing the points of view of both sides had not been able to succeed? Before they could write a new scenario, the negotiators needed to discover why the old one had failed.

UN Secretary-General Waldheim took the heaviest criticism—first, for botching the initial phase of the scenario, then for immediately dispatching the Commission from New York even before Sadegh Ghotbzadeh was back in Teheran, thereby putting unwanted pressure on the Iranians and, finally, inexplicably, for not showing the scenario to the Commission members so they would understand that they were actors with lines to recite rather than policemen on a rescue mission.

The Americans were held accountable for leaking information that not only added to the pressure by raising expectations, but helped produce the distortions in the public mind about what the Commission was supposed to do.

The Iranians were blamed for letting internal politics intrude in an international dispute that most of them truly wanted to resolve. Bani-Sadr was criticized for backing down on two occasions when he could have moved the hostages out of the students' control. Ahmed Khomeini was singled out as a saboteur.

Finally, the Commission itself was criticized for its high-handed manner at the outset and its inflexibility at the end. Had the members mastered their pride and remained one more day, they would have seen the hostages. Of that everyone was certain. The Ayatollah would have *ordered* the students to permit the visit; not a person in Iran would have dared to disobey an order from a religious leader. Once the power of the students had been broken in this manner, the transfer of the hostages to government control would have followed.

That last was conjecture, but Bourguet and Villalón backed it up with information that awakened new hope in the Americans.

Over the preceding weekend, even as the Commission members were preparing to leave, the situation had been changing radically, Bourguet and Villalón said. A high government official had at last had the courage to put his career on the line and stand up to the students, and the repercussions had been profound. The official was Sadegh Ghotbzadeh. On Thursday March 6, he had taped a scathing interview for Iranian television in which he had demolished the students' contention that they were acting in accordance with the imam's wishes. "So they're guarding the hostages. Fine. They're heroes," the Foreign Minister said caustically. "But the important thing is that they're trying to play a political role—and that is none of their business."

By their actions they were interfering in the revolutionary process, Ghotbzadeh charged. And since the revolution was an Islamic one, they were violating Islamic precepts and opposing rather than supporting the imam. "They found documents at the American Embassy which they can alter as they wish, and are using them as evidence to accuse people—even our ministers. Their action is inadmissible. They must give up all the documents to the government."

The interview with the Foreign Minister was broadcast on Friday March 7. Many who saw it felt that Ghotbzadeh had signed his death warrant; at the very least, they felt, he would be taken off to prison. At the same time they could not help admiring a man with the courage to take such a frightening risk, and many Iranians who had previously thought little of their Foreign Minister now rallied to his side.

One Iranian in particular had been moved by Ghotbzadeh's statements—the Ayatollah Khomeini, watching television for the first time following his prolonged illness. "He's right, you know," Khomeini said to his son Ahmed, who was watching at his side.

On Monday March 10—the day before the UN Commission left Iran—the Ayatollah publicly ordered the students to turn over the captured documents to the government. A small demand, perhaps, but enormously important in the context of the problem. This was why the students had tried so desperately—unsuccessfully as it turned out—to force the documents upon the Commission members. Symbolically, the power of the students had been broken.

That, Bourguet and Villalón said, was why they were now so certain that a new effort by the UN Commission would result in the transfer and eventual release of the hostages. President Bani-Sadr had flatly stated that the hostages would be transferred within a week, and his prediction had been communicated to Hamilton Jordan in Washington by Bourguet and Villalón. Although Ghotbzadeh had cautioned that the transfer might take more like a fortnight, he, too, was positive that it would occur.

Bourguet reminded the Americans that an auspicious time was approaching. From Bern he was going to Panama to supervise the filing of papers requesting the extradition of the Shah. That request, as they all knew, meant automatic arrest—and once that happened there would be such rejoicing in Iran that the hostage problem could be quickly ended.

Buoyed by this analysis, the negotiators got to work. If there had been any stiffness in their previous meetings, it was gone altogether now. Whatever suspicions they had harbored as strangers, they were now friends working toward a common objective, acknowledging and tolerating one another's special traits.

The Americans marveled at how Bourguet and Villalón meshed. Whatever disagreements they may have thrashed out when they were alone, in public they invariably took a unified position. Only the slightest sign—a raised eyebrow, a furrowed brow, a darting look— would betray an occasional divergence. What made their seamless partnership all the more remarkable were the obvious differences between them: Bourguet, the bearded, long-haired lawyer; Villalón, the urbane entrepreneur with every hair in place. Villalón was wealthy, Bourguet strictly middle-class. Although no announcements had been made, it was obvious that it was Villalón who was picking up most of the checks, not because Bourguet wasn't generous but because he simply couldn't afford it.

Another difference was in their approach to problems. By now it was clear that Bourguet was the theoretician of the partnership, with the overall strategic view. Villalón was the tactician, proposing means of implementation. Bourguet became bored with details; at times they seemed beyond him. That was when Villalón would take over with ideas for introducing each step in the process, and for the order in which they should come. The Argentine was by far the more optimistic of the two; however bleak the outlook, he would always invent a new solution.

The most significant difference between the Frenchman and the Argentine was cultural. Bourguet had spent the largest part of his life in Moslem countries and was deeply impregnated with their ways. He understood their mental processes, something Villalón did not. For the South American, Iran was another world.

On the other hand, there were many things that Villalón understood about the Americans that were beyond Bourguet's grasp. The good intentions of the Americans had been a revelation. Often, in their work, he would arrive at a point he felt he was going to have to fight for, only to discover that the Americans had already thought of it, analyzed it and accepted it. If they had made mistakes in Iran, it was because they truly hadn't understood what it meant for them politically to support the Shah.

Jordan especially. What had struck both Bourguet and Villalón that first day in London and remained with them throughout was the difference between Saunders, the diplomat, who corresponded to their prior notions of what Americans were like, and Jordan, the informal and accessible chief of staff. Jordan, they observed, trusted Saunders the man but not the institution he represented. At times it almost seemed as if he were trying to say, "These people will never let us work in as direct a way as we'd like." Jordan's astonishing offer to go himself to Teheran had been conveyed to the Iranians and rejected, but neither Bourguet nor Villalón could get over that the young American had been willing to put his own life on the line. Was it a maneuver? they asked themselves. Had he been sincere, or was he simply the best actor they had ever seen? Neither man could explain why, other than as a consequence of their own experience, but both had chosen to believe that Jordan had been sincere.

The basic objective this time, all the negotiators agreed, was to be as explicit as possible about the manner in which events were to occur, and the times when they would take place. They saw now that the previous scenario had not been specific enough, and that the parties, as a consequence, had been able to diverge from its steps or escape them altogether.

Everything this time was to be organized around the transfer of the hostages from student to government control. But when would it occur? That was still the one great question, but this time there was something to go on—the predictions of both Bani-Sadr and Ghotbzadeh. Bourguet explained to the American how they had come about.

At a last-ditch meeting with Bani-Sadr on the eve of their departure, the UN Commission members heard him swear that the transfer would be made "in a week at the very latest."

"Do you realize what you are saying?" one of the members challenged. "You are the President of Iran, and you are committing yourself to the fact that the transfer will be made in a week—by March 18."

"Yes. I can promise you. There's no problem whatever."

Later that evening, the Commission repeated its conversation to Ghotbzadeh. "Look," the Foreign Minister said, "I think Bani-Sadr confuses his wishes with reality. He's making promises he can't keep. It can happen, but not for two weeks."

Now, in Bern, Bourguet said to the others, "There are two declarations—Bani-Sadr's which clearly promises one week, and Ghotbzadeh's, which doesn't clearly promise, which isn't one hundred percent sure but which says, 'I think there's a very good chance it will be before March 25.' So let's use the second estimate and not the first."

Bourguet pointed out to the others that the deadline for the filing of the extradition petition in Panama was March 24. He felt the congruence of dates was propitious. He and Villalón were generally more optimistic than the Americans, whose spirits they frequently worked to shore up. "We almost did it," they would say. "That proves we can." They made certain that the Americans understood that they shared their concern about the hostages, and they frequently reminded them of their abhorrence about what the Iranians had done. At meals, they tried to lighten the atmosphere by diverting everyone's mind, asking dozens of questions about Jimmy Carter, his reelection campaign— they hoped he would win—and his campaign for human rights. If Henry Precht was any measure, these efforts did some good. At first, the Iranian desk officer, like Saunders an incessant note-taker, had reminded them of a CIA agent because of the manner in which he asked the same question a dozen times in different ways to see if the answer would vary. Now Precht, who at the outset refused to use his rusty French, would pass an entire meal with only an odd English word.

It was in this atmosphere that Bourguet and Villalón proposed to Jordan that he write a personal letter to Bani-Sadr, emphasizing the desire of the United States to continue the attempt to resolve the hostage crisis with the help of the two intermediaries. Villalón, who would be returning to Teheran the following week, would hand-carry the letter. As Jordan went off to write the letter, the others put the finishing touches on the proposed new scenario.

This scenario, called the "Second Revision," was comparable to its predecessors. The difference was in the circumstances surrounding it. The UN Commission had failed; this was the "last chance" scenario, its purpose to kick off the negotiations again, starting with the personal letter from Hamilton Jordan to Bani-Sadr. The letter, in turn, was to trigger the return of the UN Commission to Teheran to take up its work again. This time the Commission *would* see the American hostages. From this point, the provisions of the two previous scenarios would be put into effect, leading to the release of the fifty-three Americans. But, burned by the previous failures, the American negotiators were now more prudent. They added a last paragraph to the scenario, taking into account that their previous plans might not work, and suggesting a new solution.

IF THE FINAL STEPS OF THE EARLIER SCENARIO CAN NO LONGER BE FOLLOWED, IT IS NECESSARY FOR BOTH PARTIES TO AGREE ON THE STEPS IN A NEW FINAL STAGE. IN THESE NEW CIRCUMSTANCES, THE UNITED STATES BELIEVES THAT THE COMPONENTS OF THE FINAL STAGE—INCLUDING THE REPORT OF THE UNITED NATIONS COMMISSION, THE STATEMENTS OF PRESIDENTS CARTER AND BANI-SADR, THE ESTABLISHMENT OF AN IRAN-U.S. JOINT COMMISSION TO RESOLVE BILATERAL ISSUES, AND THE RELEASE OF ALL 53 AMERICANS—SHOULD BE TAKEN SIMULTANEOUSLY. IT IS ALSO THE POSITION OF THE UNITED STATES THAT THE RELEASE OF THE HOSTAGES SHOULD TAKE PLACE NO LATER

THAN FIVE DAYS AFTER THE VISIT TO THE AMERICAN
PERSONNEL.

Using hotel stationery, Jordan wrote steadily for an hour. When he
finished, he returned to the group and read them what he had written:

"I am taking the liberty of sending you this personal and private
message through our mutual friend, Mr. Hector Villalón. The only
copy of this letter is in the possession of President Carter.

"Because we have reached a critical point in the process of trying to
peacefully resolve the differences which face our countries, I thought it
was important that I convey my thoughts to you personally and in
complete frankness. I would welcome your frank reaction to these sug-
gestions.

"I was pleased to receive your message of March 10th that the 53
American hostages would be transferred to the custody of the Iranian
government within fifteen days. I conveyed this message to President
Carter, and he considered it an encouraging development.

"I believe that we share a single objective: to put an end to the present crisis and to build a new relationship with your country and government based on equality and mutual respect. But quite frankly, the
possibility of having such a relationship in the future will not be possible unless our hostages are returned to our country at an early date.

"From the outset, President Carter has pursued a policy of patience
and restraint. He did this not only to insure the safe ultimate release of
our hostages, but also to create an atmosphere after their release
which would allow our respective governments to build a new relationship which recognizes the new realities created by the Iranian revolution. This continues to be our objective and our hope.

"However, the atmosphere of restraint created and sustained by
President Carter cannot last forever. A growing number of political figures and journalists who have supported President Carter's policy of restraint are now advocating extreme measures as a result of the Commission's departure from Teheran. Despite this growing frustration,
President Carter has not abandoned his policy of restraint. As soon as
we learned of the Commission's decision to leave Iran, President
Carter called upon the American people and the Congress to be patient. He also conveyed to the UN Commission through Secretary-
General Waldheim and Secretary Vance his desire that the Commis-

sion not abandon their work and be prepared to return to Teheran under the proper circumstances.

"We believe that the process negotiated by Misters Villalón and Bourguet represents an honorable way to resolve our problems. We are prepared to renew our commitment to that process, but must have evidence of your government's willingness and ability to abide by that process. The transfer of the hostages to the custody of the government would be an appropriate gesture.

"After we resolve the immediate problems, I can assure you that our government will adopt a reasonable attitude in resolving our numerous bilateral problems. Misters Bourguet and Villalón have recommended the creation of a joint U.S.-Iranian Commission as the instrument for dealing with these bilateral issues. We would be receptive to this approach and could see the Commission as the means for developing our future relationship.

"Finally, I appreciate the opportunity to be able to communicate directly with you. We are aware of and appreciate your personal efforts to resolve this crisis in a manner that is fair and honorable to both countries. It is my humble judgment that time is working against us.

"I hope to have the honor of meeting you some day."

As the negotiators flew back to Paris the next day, once again in a U. S. Air Force plane, Jordan told Bourguet and Villalón that he wanted to take his letter to Bani-Sadr to Washington with him for some possible modifications as well as President Carter's approval.

On Sunday March 16, a Marine guard from the American Embassy in Paris delivered a sealed envelope to Villalón at his sixth-floor apartment on the Avénue President Wilson, a few hundred yards from the Place du Trocadéro in the fashionable Sixteenth Arrondissement. The envelope was accompanied by a French translation of its contents, which Villalón read. It was the same letter Jordan had written in Bern to President Bani-Sadr.

The next day, Villalón took the letter to Teheran and gave it to the President.

The Americans were not nearly as hopeful as they had led Bourguet and Villalón to believe. By now, they knew that they had been used as political pawns in the power struggle in Teheran. The efforts to resolve the crisis had failed, in the final analysis, at least from their perspective, because certain members of the Iranian leadership, notably Bani-Sadr, did not have the political courage to do what they had planned to do. They had the will and the desire, but not the capacity.

This realization provoked some thorough soul-searching among the Americans. For two and one half months they had had no way to negotiate with the revolutionary government. Now, they knew beyond doubt, they were dealing with men who were trusted by the Iranian leadership. But what leadership was it? Did the nominal leadership of the country truly have the power to resolve the crisis? Or had the United States been dealing with the wrong Iranians?

From the outset, the Americans had known that they were in touch with only a portion of the leadership. It was now painfully obvious that they had to make contact with that other portion which had heretofore remained aloof: the clerics gathered around the Ayatollah Khomeini in Qum.

It was to that end that Harold Saunders went to Geneva on March 16 to talk to Mohammed Heikal, the Egyptian journalist he had recruited as an intermediary in January. The two men met at Château Bellerive, the private residence of Prince Sadruddin Aga Khan, where Heikal was staying while attending a seminar. Saunders explained the problem. "Qum is closed to us. We have no means of contacting Qum —and we know that Khomeini makes the final decisions." Then he said, "Will you go to Teheran and see what can be done?"

Heikal said he would.

While the Americans prayed that one or the other of their initiatives might work, they weren't making any bets. That same day, at their request, Erik Lang, the Swiss ambassador in Teheran, sent a letter to Sadegh Ghotbzadeh at the foreign ministry, asking that arrangements be made for Easter Week services for the hostages.

The new scenario, if successful, foresaw the release of the hostages around April 1. Easter was April 6.

chapter sixteen

Flight

IT IS POSSIBLE THAT MICHAEL DEBAKEY KNEW FROM MARCH 15 THAT the Shah would never have surgery in Panama and that all of his statements and actions from then on were meant to help cover the Shah's flight from Panama. It was on March 15, according to Robert Armao, that the decision was made to leave. "Doctor, we're getting out of here," Armao told DeBakey that day. "Do me a favor. Pack up, go home to Houston and await our instructions. We will tell you where the operation will take place. It will probably be in Egypt." After the several factions had made up, Armao instructed DeBakey, "You just play along with them and say yes, we'll have a cooling-off period and you'll come back to do the operation."

That DeBakey never intended to return is further indicated by a telephone conversation he had with Hamilton Jordan just before leaving Panama City on Monday March 17. Jordan called to urge DeBakey to perform the surgery there, but the surgeon said that conditions weren't optimal, and strongly indicated that he wouldn't be back.

On Contadora Island that morning, Armao said to the Shah, "We're down to our last card."

The Shah reflected for a moment. Then he said, "I'm afraid we're going to have to play it, even though a lot of people say we're going to jeopardize Sadat."

"Sadat doesn't seem to be worried," Armao replied.

Just the day before, Madame Sadat had made one of her frequent calls to Empress Farah. "With your permission," Armao said now, "we'll get Madame Sadat back on the phone and tell them you'd like to come."

They made the call at once. Empress Farah spoke to Madame Sadat. Her reply was immediate. "My husband is here! You are welcome." Then Sadat got on the telephone. "We welcome you. We welcome anybody you want to bring. Bring DeBakey. Bring anyone. Anyone you bring is a guest in our house."

Sadat said he would send his own plane to fly the Shah to Egypt.

It was agreed in the Shah's entourage that the decision to leave would be communicated to no one. Preparations would be made with the utmost discretion, so as not to alert any of the guards. There was to be no mention of the plans on the telephone because they knew that all their calls were monitored. It was conceivable that the conversation with the Sadats had been recorded and then translated; they could only hope that that was not the case. When a day passed with no reaction, they concluded that the Panamanians had decided not to make the extra effort.

But there finally came a time when Robert Armao had to communicate the decision to his office in New York. He did so in words so oblique that they almost passed as code. But it wasn't quite good enough, because within moments after he finished, a Panamanian official called the Iranian colonel in charge of the Shah's security, and said, "Armao says you're leaving."

The colonel promptly called Armao. "Let's get up to the Shah's house," Armao said. "He'll have to call Torrijos."

Soon after, word of the Shah's decision reached the White House. Hamilton Jordan set out for Panama, his purpose a singular one—to try to persuade the Shah to remain in Panama and have his surgery there. But the President's staff chief almost didn't make it. His first plane had radar problems and had to turn back. His second was flying at 30,000 feet when it suddenly depressurized, forcing the pilot to dive to a lower altitude. That plane landed at New Orleans, where Jordan boarded a third plane for an uneventful flight to Panama.

As soon as he arrived, Jordan telephoned Armao, and proposed that he visit the Shah. "Hamilton, you come visit all you want," Armao replied. "We're leaving. The decision is made."

"Are you telling me, Bob, that no matter what I have to offer you, you're leaving?"

"As I talk with you, the luggage is going by right in front of me."

Jordan decided not to visit the Shah himself, lest their contact contaminate him in the eyes of the Iranians and end his secret negotiations with the intermediaries, Christian Bourguet and Héctor Villalón. Instead, he called Lloyd Cutler, the White House counsel, and asked him to fly down at once. Cutler arrived that evening, along with Arnold Raphel, an assistant to Cyrus Vance, and went immediately to Contadora.

Robert Armao was waiting at the airport when the two men landed at Contadora. It was late afternoon; the Pacific Ocean was glazed by the setting sun. Armao led them to the house, where the Shah and Shahbanou awaited them in a screened porch at the end of the veranda.

To the Americans, it was immediately evident that the Shah had been fighting a terrible battle. But despite his physical deterioration, he was alert and vigorous, primed by the knowledge that once again, if only briefly, it was as it had been before: he was receiving the emissaries of the President of the United States. The Shah dismissed Armao, saying that he wanted to meet with his guests alone.

For the next forty-five minutes, the Shah and Shahbanou listened attentively and politely as Lloyd Cutler went over the options available to them, as well as their potential impact, not only on the hostage crisis, but on world events. The United States was concerned about the Shah's forthcoming trip to Egypt, Cutler explained. His presence there could undermine the position of President Sadat, and thereby jeopardize the prospects for peace in the Middle East. The American Government hoped that the Shah would remain in Panama. It was convinced that the Panamanians could be trusted. Torrijos was an honorable man; he would not permit extradition. Panamanian doctors could also be trusted to perform the surgery with skill and care. There was nothing to fear in Panama. There was much to fear in Egypt.

If the Shah was not satisfied with the Panamanian hospitals, Gorgas Hospital would definitely be made available, as the Americans had promised in the Lackland Agreement. If, however, the Shah was determined to quit Panama, then the United States was prepared to stand by its further pledge that the Shah could return to the United States for medical treatment. But if the Shah elected to return, he would first have to renounce any future hopes to the throne. Cutler did not use the word "abdicate," but that was what he meant.

When Cutler had finished, the Shah, with the practiced skill of a man accustomed to directing his own and others' destiny, let his visitors know that nothing they had said would alleviate his concern over the prospect of an operation in Panama. He had no confidence in the Panamanian doctors. Not even DeBakey's presence in the operating room would help. He was convinced that it just wouldn't work out. He intended to go to Egypt.

The Shahbanou agreed. She thought that the Shah's health was in danger in Panama, and she wanted to leave for her own sake, as well. She wanted to be near her friend Jehan Sadat. She wanted to be where she felt welcome.

The prospect of returning to the United States was not a realistic one, both the Shah and Shahbanou agreed. They did not feel welcome there. As to abdication, that was out of the question, the Shah said, once again with the Shahbanou's concurrence. The people still loved him, he went on. He had been deposed by a small group of militants who didn't truly reflect the Persians. He did not want to take from his son the right to rule on the day the Pahlavi family returned to Iran.

After Cutler and Raphel had gone, the Shah told Robert Armao what had happened. Since his exclusion from the meeting, the young lawyer and public relations executive had been seething; he was convinced that the Americans had somehow been responsible. But if he had been upset before, it was as nothing compared to his fury once he learned the substance of the American offer. The United States Government, he believed, was attempting to manipulate a dying man. "You have the right to say, 'Thank you, I'll go to the States tomorrow, and I will take the abdication under advisement,'" he told the Shah. "Then, when you get to Houston, you can say, 'To hell with you.' If you want to play their game, you can do that."

"No," the Shah replied. "I'll feel more comfortable among friends. We'll go to Egypt."

"Egypt is better in terms of the crisis, but I have to caution you—medically we'd be better off in the States."

"I agree with you, but they don't want us. We're going to Egypt."

Christian Bourguet had arrived in Panama the day before, believing that within twenty-four hours he would finally effectuate the arrest of the Shah. He had with him a demand for the extradition of the Shah that had been translated into Spanish and certified by the Panamanian Embassy in Paris. His hopes had been amply fortified by Juan Materno Vásquez, a Panamanian lawyer engaged by the Iranian Government, who met him at the airport in an optimistic mood. Materno

Vásquez was a close friend of General Torrijos, who had just assured him that the arrest of the Shah would be no problem. Even the extradition of the Shah seemed possible, Materno Vásquez told Bourguet—with the understanding, of course, that Iran guaranteed to make up to Panama in economic favors what Panama stood to lose as a consequence of the probable reaction of the United States. That same day, Materno Vásquez had conveyed the very same assurances to Bourguet's law partner in Paris, François Cheron.

The only problem on the horizon was that Farough Parsi, the Iranian diplomat who was to present the papers of extradition, had not yet arrived in Panama from New York. Parsi's presence was indispensable; only an Iranian could present the papers. But even that problem seemed to be approaching a solution; Parsi had telephoned that morning to ask if Bourguet had arrived, and was standing by in New York, waiting to make the trip.

Parsi, Materno Vásquez said, was to call him later that evening, about 10 or 11 P.M., to give his exact arriving time.

It was then that Bourguet made a decision he would come to regret: he entrusted Materno Vásquez to tell Parsi to take the first plane possible in order to arrive in Panama the following morning.

It was like being off a fraction of a degree at the base of an angle; how large an oversight it eventually became can only be seen in terms of the events that followed.

The next morning Materno told Bourguet that Parsi had indeed telephoned—to report that he would not be arriving until the following Monday, three days later. Bourguet was dismayed and said so, but Materno reassured him. Monday was time enough—it was, in fact, the last day for the Iranians to present their petition for extradition; their sixty-day period was up on that date, and Parsi would meet them at the ministry at ten o'clock that morning.

By now it was too late for Parsi to get to Panama that day; there was nothing Bourguet could do but hope for the best. Nonetheless, he remained irritable through the day.

Late that afternoon, as Bourguet was copying the extradition papers in Materno Vásquez's office, Torrijos called the Panamanian. "The general wants to see you," Materno Vásquez said to Bourguet.

"Okay, let's go."

"No, he wants to see you alone."

Half an hour later, a Land-Rover arrived, driven by a member of the general's security service who took Bourguet to the general's

H

home. When Bourguet arrived in the living room, he was surprised to find Hamilton Jordan. The two men greeted one another warmly. "What are you doing in Panama?" Bourguet said in his accented but serviceable English.

"I have a little problem," Jordan said. "The Shah is leaving."

Bourguet turned, open-mouthed, to Torrijos. "That's not possible," he said.

Many times during their meetings Jordan had told Bourguet flatly that the United States would never permit the extradition of the Shah. And Bourguet had replied, "Well, that is your problem. You do your work, I do mine. As the attorney for the Iranians, I can't be reproached for that. I am going to try to get him extradited. I believe that this man has committed crimes and must be judged." Now, as Bourguet recovered from his shock, Jordan said, "I'm not here to prevent the Shah's extradition. I'm here to try to keep him from leaving."

What Jordan worried about most was that the departure of the Shah might have a calamitous effect on efforts to free the hostages. Jordan asked Bourguet to estimate how Iran would react to the five different possibilities: the return of the Shah to the United States for a new bout of surgery; his departure to Egypt for the same reason; his departure for some unspecified country; his transfer to Gorgas Hospital in Panama for surgery (a solution Torrijos immediately labeled impossible because it would put into question his agreements with the United States on the Canal Zone); remaining where he was and having his surgery at Paitilla Medical Center.

The three men talked for an hour, but one response of Bourguet's stuck in Jordan's head: "If the Shah returns to the United States, the hostages are dead." What seemed obvious to all three men was the desirability of keeping the Shah in Panama.

It was an incredibly difficult moment for Jordan. Officially, the United States was committed to preserving the freedom of the Shah, and was therefore against his detention in any form whatever, even a symbolic house arrest. Such an arrest—the automatic consequence of a petition for extradition—set up grave political problems. Since the Shah was refusing medical attention from the Panamanians, his detention there ran the risk that he would die under arrest, an event that would be a calamity for President Carter.

Jordan, on the other hand, was charged with the responsibility of attempting to negotiate the freedom of the hostages. He was certain that the flight of the Shah at this moment would have a disastrous effect on those efforts. For this reason, he wanted the Shah kept in Panama. There he stood now, listening to General Torrijos and Christian Bourguet discussing a way of doing just that.

"Listen, I could keep him, I can arrest him," Torrijos said to Bourguet. "Only you must understand that for public opinion here, it's not possible for me to commit an act like that against the will of the Shah unless I can justify it with a political advantage."

Bourguet considered. "That may be a possibility," he said, "but it's a problem of time. Since yesterday, everyone's on vacation in Teheran. It's the Iranian New Year."

Torrijos told Bourguet he would give him twelve hours. If the Iranians would produce a "spectacular act" in respect to the hostages —either liberation or transfer out of the students' and into the government's hands—he would arrest the Shah.

Hamilton Jordan said nothing.

The Shah communicated his firm decision to leave Panama to Lloyd Cutler when the White House counsel returned on Saturday morning at ten-thirty. Cutler could see the packed bags sitting in the hallway. He did not attempt to change the Shah's mind. What he did do was propose that a chartered jet would make the trip more readily than the plane offered by Sadat, which would most likely have problems in refueling and obtaining landing rights. He offered to arrange the charter, and the Shah agreed.

Early Saturday afternoon, Torrijos telephoned Bourguet. "The Shah absolutely wants to leave," he said. He told Bourguet that President Sadat had even sent his own plane to pick up the Shah and his entourage. The plane was in New York, waiting for authorization to land in Panama—which, thus far, Torrijos had withheld.

Bourguet begged for more time.

"I can't detain him more than another twenty-four hours. If the transfer hasn't taken place by then, I'll have to let him go."

Bourguet telephoned Teheran at once to communicate the extension of the deadline, and the urgency of the matter.

At dawn on Sunday Farough Parsi, the missing Iranian diplomat, finally arrived in Panama to file the request for extradition, an act that would automatically require the Shah's arrest. But he would be unable to do so until the next morning, and by then the Shah would be gone. The Panamanians could have made an exception and opened the appropriate office to accept the papers, but Bourguet knew that Torrijos wouldn't do that. The general had named his price, and he expected to be paid.

Maybe it's for the best, Bourguet consoled himself. Maybe this pressure from Torrijos will be enough to do the trick.

Since the previous evening, Bourguet and Juan Materno Vásquez—brought into the matter so that he could speak Spanish, a language not well known in Iran—had been in communication with Héctor Villalón, who was in Teheran. Through the day and into Sunday much energy was expended and many calls exchanged, but with no "spectacular act" to show for it.

It was now late Sunday evening in Teheran. Eric Rouleau, the correspondent of *Le Monde,* arrived at the home of Bani-Sadr for an interview with the President. But the President, he was told, was in an emergency meeting. Even so, Rouleau's arrival was announced, and, in accord with Oriental custom, he was allowed into the meeting. The scene he found had touches of the theater of the absurd. There was the President of Iran, barefoot and wearing pajamas, sitting cross-legged on a sofa, deep in conversation with Sadegh Ghotbzadeh, Héctor Villalón and several Iranian aides. The topic was the one on which life in Iran had turned for the last eighteen days: how to wrest the American hostages away from the Islamic students.

"Force!" Ghotbzadeh insisted.

"That's not decent!" Bani-Sadr replied. "I'll go myself to the Embassy and try to convince them."

The others shook their heads.

At regular intervals, Villalón would call Bourguet in Panama to get the latest word on the whereabouts of the Shah and the negotiations with the Panamanians. Time was running out. The price hadn't changed: transfer the Americans to government control in exchange for the arrest of the Shah.

At midnight, the telephone rang. Ghotbzadeh answered. From the Foreign Minister's replies, Rouleau gathered that it was General Torrijos calling, speaking through an interpreter. "Please wait until 7 A.M. tomorrow," Ghotbzadeh beseeched the Panamanian. "By 7 A.M., I swear to you, we'll have the hostages out of the students' hands."

Suddenly there was silence. Ghotbzadeh's face turned ashen. He removed the telephone from his ear. "The Shah has left," he said to the others. Without saying goodbye or hanging up the telephone, Ghotbzadeh returned to his place among the group. A long silence followed. Finally, Bani-Sadr said, "I'm going to bed."

The Shah and his entourage had left Panama at 2 P.M. local time aboard an Evergreen Air Lines DC-8 chartered for $275,000. That evening, Christian Bourguet made one final effort to stop him. He sent a message via the American ambassador to Hamilton Jordan and Lloyd Cutler as they were flying back to Washington, proposing in behalf of Sadegh Ghotbzadeh that the Shah's plane be intercepted in the Azores and returned to Panama. If they would do that, the Foreign Minister had sworn, the Iranians would transfer the hostages from the militants to the government. Jordan and Cutler did not consider the proposition for long before discarding it. They didn't believe that Ghotbzadeh or even Bani-Sadr could deliver, and they didn't want anything to happen to the Shah as a consequence of an arrangement made by or with the consent of the United States.

The Iranians had been looking for some proof that international law worked for them. More than that, both Bani-Sadr and Ghotbzadeh needed some dramatic way of showing the nation that there was a serious intention of arresting the Shah, of making him pay, to deliver satisfaction "of a moral nature," as Marcel Salamin put it, that the Shah should not go unpunished for the crimes and the violations of rights attributed to him.

One can speculate that the Shah's symbolic detention in Panama might have been enough to enable Bani-Sadr and Sadegh Ghotbzadeh finally to persuade the Ayatollah Khomeini to command the militant students to release the hostages. But because an Iranian diplomat didn't make it to Panama as scheduled, on Friday March 21 when the extradition papers were supposed to be filed, the Shah was able to flee —and the Americans were held hostage for the 141st day.

The last thing Mohammed Reza Pahlavi did before leaving Panama was to send a hand-written letter to the man who had invited him to come there the previous December.

"Dear General Torrijos,

I want to thank you once more for all the signs of friendship, hospitality and human understanding that you have shown my wife and myself, since you so graciously invited us to come to your beautiful country. It's a pity that we knew only a few places of Panama, but of what we have seen you have a lovely country and a lovely people. I believe that God has chosen you to accomplish great many things, among them the historical treaty for the Panama Canal. I am certain that you will provide all the necessary leadership to accomplish all your historical aims and that Panama and its proud people will go from progress to progress and happiness to happiness. May God bless you.

My wife joins me in sending to Mrs. Torrijos our best wishes for a long and happy life, as well as to all your lovely children.

Your sincere friend,
M. K. Pahlavi"

chapter seventeen

Up Against the Wall

WHEN CHRISTIAN BOURGUET ARRIVED IN WASHINGTON TWO DAYS after the Shah left Panama, it was with the belief that the United States had lost its best chance to that moment to liberate the hostages. He was bitterly disappointed that the Shah had slipped away, and yet absolutely convinced of the good faith of the Americans in trying to keep the Shah in Panama. For whatever reason they had acted as they had, the Americans had not attempted to frustrate the Iranians' objectives.

After the Shah's departure, Bourguet received word that President Carter wanted to meet him. Instead of flying directly back to Paris, he flew to Washington. An official limousine took him to the White House. He spent the next several hours with Jordan, Lloyd Cutler, Zbigniew Brzezinski and other White House figures. Vice-President Walter Mondale also came by. In midafternoon, word came that the President was ready to see him.

"The President's very busy," Jordan apologized. "He may only be able to see you for a few minutes, maybe a quarter of an hour."

"That's up to him," Bourguet replied with a shrug.

Jordan and Stephanie Van Reidgersberg, the State Department interpreter, escorted Bourguet across the Rose Garden into a room on the ground level of the White House living quarters. There, the left-wing French lawyer and the President of the United States found themselves face to face for the first time.

The President was standing when Bourguet walked in. He smiled and started toward him, holding out his hand. "Ah! Christian! Our hero!" he said.

It was a spontaneous effort on Carter's part to convey the gratitude he felt to this heretofore obscure Frenchman for serving as the living link in America's connection to its imprisoned diplomats, but it completely missed the mark. Bourguet immediately tightened, distressed by what he construed as an attempt by Carter to draw him onto the side of the United States.

But Carter's very next words undid the damage. "I'm sorry about what happened in Panama," the President said. He was aware, he added, how the departure of the Shah had complicated the task of the Frenchman and his ally, Héctor Villalón, and he wanted them both to know, once again, how grateful he was for their efforts.

Bourguet, who had approached the meeting with a certain tension—he was, after all, meeting the President of the United States—began to feel exactly what he had felt initially for Hamilton Jordan. Here, obviously, was a well-meaning man, filled with good intentions.

And then, all at once, it really was like London again, because the President was asking Bourguet, albeit in a slightly different form, the same question Jordan had asked in their first encounter: "What should we do?" And suddenly Bourguet was no longer ill at ease, because when anyone, even a chief of state, asked him for advice, he was, in effect, a lawyer counseling a client.

In London, Bourguet had felt that he needed to pierce through some thick misapprehensions on Jordan's part about relations between the United States and Iran. Now here was the man who, by his visit to Iran two years before and his expansive endorsement of the Shah, had helped set in motion a chain of events that had led to the present dilemma. It struck Bourguet that Carter probably still didn't understand that; unless he did, there was no way to answer his question. "I don't know, Mr. President," Bourguet began, "if you realized the consequences and reactions of the Iranian people to the fact that you spent New Year's Eve with the Shah. You may have done it with the best intentions in the world, but you are paying for it today."

"But all those people are innocent," Carter protested. "All diplomats are innocent."

Bourguet shook his head. "Mr. President, I understand when you say they are innocent. But you have to understand that for the Iranians, they aren't innocent. Even if none of them has personally ever committed a crime, they are not innocent because they are diplomats who represent a country that has done a number of things in Iran. You must understand that it is not against their person that the action is being taken. They have not been hurt. No attempt has been made to kill them. You must understand that they are a symbol, that it is on the plane of symbols we have to think about this matter."

Now a great desire took hold of Bourguet, to convey to Carter the understanding that underlay his own passionate conviction. He did not wish to seem to be lecturing the President of the United States, but when would such an opportunity ever present itself again? Conviction overpowered restraint, and Bourguet launched into a disquisition about the Pahlavi dynasty.

"Mr. President, this is, perhaps, a unique opportunity. Maybe no one has ever told you what I'm about to. I don't know if you have the time to read about it in the newspapers, so I'm going to tell you. I can quote from memory the passages in certain testimonies that were taken from victims of the Savak. In March 1979 my wife went to Iran to investigate charges of torture, and she came back with files from the Savak. And in these files you can see in the upper right-hand corner a photograph of the person when he is arrested—a boy or a girl, looking fine—and then at the bottom there is a picture of the corpse, the girls with their breasts cut in bits, no teeth, their eyes closed, cigarette burns all over their bodies. And then there is a statement of the motive for which the Savak claimed the person was arrested, and the cause of death: car accident, twenty miles from Teheran. When you see things like that, Mr. President, and when you tell yourself that things like that may have taken place because it was necessary to defend American interests, it's difficult to accept. After that, are you surprised that American diplomats are taken hostage? I am not. I am sorry, but not surprised."

For another thirty minutes, as the President listened somberly, Bourguet continued with his indictment. When he had finished, he said, "Do you think we can solve this problem?"

"Yes," the President said.

Then Carter began to write in a notebook in front of him. When he finished, he tore the page from the notebook and handed it to Bourguet. "So that there will be no confusion," he said, "so that it is quite clear what my position is, here is what the United States Government wants."

Bourguet read the note:

"What U. S. wants:
a) Captors released unharmed—quickly
b) When desired, normal relations with Iran under the existing government, recognizing the results of the revolution
c) An opportunity for Iran to air grievances through UN, Int. Court
   of Justice, or media.

J. C."

When he finished reading, Bourguet looked at the President and
nodded.

"You can turn this over to Mr. Bani-Sadr and to the Ayatollah
Khomeini," Jimmy Carter said.

Moments after leaving the room, Bourguet looked at the note the
President had given him and saw that he had written "captors" for
"captives." Only then did he realize how upset the President must have
been made by what he had just told him.

In Paris two days later, Bourguet called Héctor Villalón in Teheran to
relay his impressions of his visit to Washington. When they finished
talking, Villalón wrote a long letter to Sadegh Ghotbzadeh.

"Dear Minister,
Christian just arrived in Paris. He asks you to please call him without fail today at 2:30 P.M., Teheran time, so that he can give you a
brief report of his visit to the other party.

He saw the number-one man, the number two, the head of the Security Council and all those dealing with the problem, including Hamilton (who, in addition, phoned me tonight and through the intermediary of his secretary, we had a 1 hour 10 minute conversation
. . . charged to the other party). Regarding the meetings with Christian: I consider it very important that he give you a quick analysis of
the general situation of the other party which is not good and moreover
strikes me as dangerous. The appointment with the number-one man
was expected to last fifteen minutes; it lasted an hour and a half. His
good will, his worry and his desire for a peaceful solution to the question is almost dramatic. It's the worst moment of the electoral cam-

paign and everything is and will be conditioned in the days to come by this fact.

With the exception of Hamilton, the team of technicians considers that there will be no other solution but to take the offensive. They are very skeptical and this team sent last night, through the intermediary of our Swiss friends, a message to President Bani-Sadr, reminding him that the situation is very difficult and begging him to reach a decision before Monday, because, starting Tuesday, it will be very difficult for this team, and this is the reality of things, to be able to attend the monthly meeting of the Security Council Tuesday and approach the Republican members of the Senate and the Congress and force the government to put the planned program into action.

Hamilton phoned me at 6:00 in the morning to tell me that they had given instructions in Bern that this message not be sent in the end. But the order, for some reason, never came, and Mr. Kaiser [Marcus Kaiser, the Swiss chargé d'affaires in Teheran] went to the President's office to see Mr. Bani-Sadr.

In any case, there is nothing sensational in the message, it simply recalls the critical situation and, in establishing a new deadline, in reality it's a question of their own deadlines vis-à-vis the internal American situation.

I promise these men to keep them up to date in the coming hours.

At this very moment Mr. Kaiser just arrived at the Presidential office. It seems Mr. Bani-Sadr has read the message and his reaction is not negative because in the end he feels that the Americans have not up till now cornered him.

Hamilton begged me to tell you the following:

a) He went down to Panama simply to put pressure on Torrijos and avoid the departure of the Shah.

b) He followed the advice of Christian and didn't visit the Shah.

c) Torrijos didn't want to listen to reason because in the end the plans held the risk of creating a huge scandal within the country and the national guard would have had to intervene and upset the whole internal situation.

d) Torrijos put as a condition for keeping the Shah that a very important gesture on the part of the Iranians take place so that he would appear in the eyes of the public in the most honorable way.

e) The Americans never asked Torrijos to make a bargain with the transfer. Nor did they suggest intervening.

f) In regards to the trip to the Azores, it's an obligatory stop. On this island there is only one airport and no one could imagine how the plane could be stopped without transforming it into a huge scandal.

g) Regarding the negotiation with Sadat, it was carried out directly by Kissinger and Sadat was opposed to any modification of his decision in view of Carter's warning that it would end up creating big negative events in the region.

Last message from Hamilton: America today hasn't even the slightest moral commitment towards the Shah, starting from his departure from Panama. They will never intervene, whatever might happen to them . . ."

For 147 days, Jimmy Carter had acted with the caution of a man haunted by the horrible vision that had visited him the moment he heard the hostages had been seized—the student militants shooting one hostage per day in the courtyard of the American Embassy until the Shah was returned to Iran. Now, at last, the President's patience was at an end. On Saturday March 29 he sent a warning to President Bani-Sadr of Iran that was devoid of caution, ambivalence or uncertainty: if the American hostages were not transferred in forty-eight hours from the custody of the student militants to the government of Iran, Washington would inflict further sanctions on Iran.

What had finally triggered Carter's anger was an episode as bizarre as any in the negotiations thus far—the publication in Iran of a letter, under his signature, that he had never sent.

To this day, no one can say with absolute certainty how this "letter" came to exist, but there are several enticing theories.

First, there is Villalón's version. Eighty percent of the "letter" was supposedly identical in content to a puzzling government-to-government message the United States had sent to Iran on March 25. The message, which was probably drafted by Hamilton Jordan, was meant to be presented to the Iranians as a "trial balloon"—an effort to ascertain what kind of words from Carter would unblock the situation in Iran and lead to the release of the hostages.

That the message existed is indisputable. It was received in Teheran and decoded by the Swiss, who had been serving as diplomatic postmen almost since the crisis began. According to Héctor Villalón, Marcus Kaiser, the Swiss chargé d'affaires, telephoned to tell him about the message. Villalón went by the Swiss Embassy to pick up a copy, and brought it to Sadegh Ghotbzadeh's office.

What follows is also based on Villalón's recollection. He and the Foreign Minister read the message and found that it corresponded in tone and intent to the personal letter Hamilton Jordan had addressed to Bani-Sadr ten days earlier. Neither Villalón nor Ghotbzadeh could figure out why the Americans had sent a message so similar to the one that had already arrived. Then Villalón asked Ghotbzadeh if he had brought Jordan's letter to the attention of the Ayatollah Khomeini.

"No," Ghotbzadeh replied.

"Do you suppose it's a trap of some kind to see whether he's kept informed?"

"Perhaps," Ghotbzadeh said. Then and there, he decided to have the message translated into Farsi for delivery to the Ayatollah.

At 6 the next morning Villalón was awakened by a call from Hamilton Jordan in Washington, which produced still further confusion. Jordan told Villalón that the United States had instructed the Swiss not to deliver the message, but the instruction had arrived too late.

It was a call a few days later from Ahmed Khomeini to Sadegh Ghotbzadeh that really complicated the matter. By this point, the message from the United States had been translated into Farsi and delivered to the Ayatollah. "We have a great idea," Ahmed Khomeini said now. "We're going to turn the American message into a letter from Carter to the imam."

Any message coming from the government in Washington was assumed by the Iranians to be a message from President Carter, whether it was signed by him or not. So why not publish the message as a letter? Khomeini argued.

What Ahmed Khomeini, and presumably his father the Ayatollah, found so compelling about the message were two critical "admissions." The first was that the U.S.-Iranian dispute originated in circumstances over which the present administration had had no control. "I would like to inform you," the letter said, "that my Government inherited a very delicate international situation, product of a different policy, of other circumstances which have led us all to commit errors in the past." While not an outright admission of guilt, the statement bordered on the very apology for the errors of previous administrations that Hamilton Jordan had sworn the United States would never make.

The second statement of surpassing interest to the Iranians said, in

effect, that "boys will be boys." "I very well understand that the take-
over of our country's embassy in your country could have appeared to
you as the understandable reaction of Iranian youths."

The letter went on to say that the United States was "ready to recognize the new realities born of the Iranian revolution. This remains
our objective and our hope since, in the final analysis, I consider that
we are pursuing the same single objective—world peace and the establishment of justice for people." Once the hostages had been passed to
the control of the government, "we are ready to adopt a reasonable
and friendly attitude in regard to the numerous bilateral problems
existing between us," the statement said.

Ghotbzadeh was horrified by Ahmed Khomeini's proposal and said
so, but none of his arguments could persuade the Ayatollah's son,
whose dislike for him was well known, to change his mind. The only
reason Ahmed Khomeini would have called to tell him of his plan
would have been at the insistence of his father, whose paternal feelings
for Ghotbzadeh were probably as much at the base of the antagonism
between the two younger men as their political differences.

Both Ghotbzadeh and Villalón understood immediately the destructive potential of this development. Until this moment, the negotiations
between the countries, however removed and bitter they were, had
been carried on in an atmosphere of qualified trust—that is, the messages passed between them by Villalón and Bourguet were faithful
representations of what each party wished to convey. Now chicanery
was about to be introduced into the negotiation.

Villalón was certain that the idea had been Ahmed Khomeini's, not
his father's, and that it represented a power play on the son's part.

That is the story as Villalón reconstructs it. There are other
theories. One is that Ahmed Khomeini had been waiting to get back at
the Americans for a threat they had made months before, and the "letter" presented a tailor-made opportunity to do so. The source of his
anger was a message that had arrived from the Americans via the
Swiss Embassy at the time the UN Commission was in Teheran. The
message was addressed to Christian Bourguet, Héctor Villalón and
three Iranians—Ghotbzadeh, Bani-Sadr and Ahmed Khomeini. It
stated that if things did not go as planned, the Americans would make
the scenario public. Bourguet and Villalón viewed the message as a
heavy-handed attempt to apply pressure, one that could very well
backfire and destroy the negotiations. The two men threatened to bow

out of the negotiations if the United States didn't apologize. The Americans quickly retreated, and Bourguet and Villalón filed the incident away. But Ahmed Khomeini did not forget. In making the "letter" public, he was saying, in effect, "You Americans threaten. We Iranians don't threaten. We do."

Yet another theory about the origin of the letter is that Villalón himself wrote it, or at least rewrote the American message out of a well-meant but brash desire to precipitate a breakthrough in negotiations.

Eric Rouleau, *Le Monde*'s correspondent in Teheran, recalls a dinner with Villalón and Jonathan Randal of the Washington *Post* in which Villalón confided excitedly, "I've just gotten the most sensational message from Carter through the Swiss Embassy. It's going to solve the whole hostage problem."

One high-ranking Swiss diplomat maintains that Villalón wrote the letter on Swiss Embassy stationery, using for reference previous messages sent to Iran by the United States. There are further theories about the letter: that Villalón changed the message, making it even more conciliatory than the White House had intended it; that when he delivered the message, he told the Iranians it was an official message from the White House and not the trial balloon it was intended to be; and that he did tell the Iranians it was not an official communication, but the Iranians decided, for internal political reasons, to act as if it were the real thing.

Whatever the origin of the "letter," its existence was real and had to be dealt with in a manner that would counteract the poison it would surely intrude into the negotiations. The two men agreed that Villalón should advise the Americans not to deny the existence of the message. It would come out in any event; let the Iranians have the moral victory they would claim and had so long awaited.

Villalón argued that case with Harold Saunders in Washington, as Henry Precht listened in. The two men agreed that the idea seemed to make sense. But half an hour later they called back to say that it was too late. Jody Powell, the President's press secretary, had already publicly denied that the letter, whose contents had just been released in Teheran, was legitimate.

In a panic, Villalón called Bourguet in Paris. The two men decided that there was now only one way to keep the negotiations from falling apart. Bani-Sadr must personally call Carter and tell him he had nothing to do with the letter. But would the Iranian President, mindful of the Ayatollah's prohibition of direct contact between Iranians and Americans, do that? He had not shown such courage before.

To Villalón's enormous relief, Bani-Sadr agreed at once to talk to Carter. Villalón himself dialed the White House from the telephone on Bani-Sadr's desk and, in halting English, got Jordan's office. Within moments the President of the United States and the President of Iran were on the telephone together.

Carter was angry, but not so emotional that he failed to see the opportunity afforded by Bani-Sadr's extraordinary call. After Bani-Sadr had disclaimed all involvement in the creation of the "letter," Carter offered to send him a genuine letter, one that would be conciliatory in tone, that would dampen emotions and perhaps keep the negotiations on course.

Within several hours the letter had arrived on the Telex of the Swiss Embassy in Teheran. The message noted Bani-Sadr's "renewed assurance" through the Swiss Embassy that the hostages would be transferred to government control, and it stressed that the United States had "demonstrated good will towards Iran and Bani-Sadr." Carter continued: "In addition, during the past two months we have refrained from harsh statements against Iran and have tried to take into account Bani-Sadr's position. We tried unsuccessfully to have the Shah remain in Panama." Carter concluded that he had noted with interest Bani-Sadr's remarks on American television that "the hostages could be released earlier than the convening of the parliament under the right conditions and a 'change in the U.S. attitude.'" He asked Bani-Sadr for specific ideas in this regard.

Jimmy Carter had kept his cool, but he had not discharged his anger. He did that shortly after sending the message to Bani-Sadr, and he did it with another message—an ultimatum to Iran to transfer the hostages to government control within forty-eight hours or face stiff reprisals from the United States.

The ultimatum arrived in Teheran on Sunday, March 30, and provoked an immediate meeting of the Revolutionary Council. The meeting went on almost continuously through the day and into Monday. At last, late in the day, the Council agreed that it would take over the hostages—provided the United States would publicly acknowledge that the Iranian parliament, which was about to be elected, had the right to decide on the fate of the hostages. It was an effort to legitimize the revolution, to be "taken seriously" by the United States. The Council authorized Bani-Sadr to send the message.

At 7:30 P.M., Héctor Villalón arrived at the foreign ministry to dine with Sadegh Ghotbzadeh. The two men often met alone at that hour to eat a simple dinner of meat, rice and vegetables. This evening Villalón was jubilant. He had just come from Bani-Sadr's office; Ahmed Khomeini had telephoned and told him that the Ayatollah and the students had given their agreement for the transfer of the hostages, and it was now Bani-Sadr's responsibility as President to carry out the order.

Ghotbzadeh listened carefully to Villalón's report. Then he shook his head. "It won't happen," he said. "Bani-Sadr will never make the decision."

"What do you mean?" Villalón protested. "Khomeini has given the go-ahead. The students have given the go-ahead. Now it's just a matter of formalities."

The Foreign Minister smiled faintly. "You are thinking like a Westerner. You don't understand the intricacies of the Iranian mind, and the subtleties of our logic. Bani-Sadr does not want to go before the people and say, 'I, the President of the Islamic Republic of Iran, have taken the decision to transfer the hostages.' He wants to say, 'I declare that the Revolutionary Council has taken the decision.'" The Shiᶜites had a saying, Ghotbzadeh told his Argentine friend: "He who takes the responsibility also takes all the risk." What the Ayatollah and the students were really saying was, "We have given the go-ahead for the decision to be made, but it is you who must take the decision."

The Foreign Minister reflected for a moment. When he spoke, his voice mixed desperation and resignation. "God does not wish it to happen," he said.

"What does God have to do with it?" Villalón asked incredulously. "It's up to Bani-Sadr to carry out the order, not God."

Once more, Ghotbzadeh shook his head. "No," he said. "If God had wanted Bani-Sadr to make the decision, he would already have done so."

For months Erik Lang, the Swiss ambassador, had been continuously frustrated in his attempts to get any sense out of anyone in the Iranian government. Power was fragmented, and each of the power centers constantly interfered with the others. Lang had made no secret of his frustration but he had continued to solicit meetings, nonetheless, just to talk about the situation.

That day Lang had been scheduled to see Bani-Sadr at noon. They did not meet until almost midnight. Nothing in his face, as he entered the President's office, betrayed any feeling on the ambassador's part that this meeting would be any different from all the others. But in fact, Lang had every reason to believe that, after 149 days, the hostage crisis was finally coming to a make-or-break moment. Earlier that day Lang had learned from François Cheron, Christian Bourguet's law partner, who had arrived in Teheran the day before, that Bani-Sadr would be giving him an important message to transmit to the Americans. The message would say that the Revolutionary Council would take control of the hostages within another day.

In addition to receiving this message, which he was to convey at once to ,he United States, Lang had one for the Iranian President from the American Government: This was truly the last chance for Iran. If this effort was not successful, then the United States would know that it was dealing with people who were incapable of freeing the hostages.

As Lang delivered his message, Bani-Sadr burst into tears.

He had finally been cornered. If he did not make the statement, he knew, his ability to resolve the hostage crisis would be nil. If he did make the statement he risked his position and, possibly, his life.

Bani-Sadr gave Lang the statement.

At 2 A.M. Erik Lang called François Cheron at his hotel and asked him to come at once to the Swiss Embassy. When Cheron arrived, Lang handed him a copy of Bani-Sadr's message. "This isn't the message you told me Bani-Sadr was going to send," the ambassador said.

The statement Bani-Sadr had given Lang was an amplified version of what the Revolutionary Council had authorized him to send. It said that if the government of the United States recognized the right of the newly elected Iranian parliament to decide the ultimate fate of the hostages, one of two things would happen:

(1) The Revolutionary Council would take over custody of the hostages. Or

(2) the students would be mobilized into the Revolutionary Guards, keeping custody of the hostages but now under the direction of a triumvirate that would be made up of one member of the Islamic stu-

dents, one member of the Iranian Government, and one member of the Revolutionary Council. The hostages would be allowed greater freedom, greater access to communications, and the right to go out into the courtyard for exercises and jogging.

Only much later would the two men learn what had caused the Iranian President to make the additions that he had. The previous evening, before Lang's visit, Jonathan Randal of the Washington *Post* had dropped by Bani-Sadr's office to show him an advance copy of a speech that Ahmed Khomeini was to deliver in his father's name the following day. The speech was violently anti-American and said nothing in support of the idea of moving the hostages. Worse yet, Khomeini likened President Carter's "letter" of the previous week to a speech made by the Shah in November 1978, when he said that he "understood" the Iranian people and was going to liberalize the government. At the time, the opponents of the Shah had considered the Shah's speech an act of "eating dirt." By comparing Jimmy Carter's "letter" to the Shah's speech, the Ayatollah was suggesting that Carter, too, was "eating dirt" and that the Iranians had the Americans on the run.

As he read the advance copy of the speech, Bani-Sadr paled. He was too far away from the Ayatollah's position for comfort. He would have to do some adjusting.

But when Erik Lang saw Bani-Sadr at the President's office at 11:30 the next morning, there was no indication that he had backed down. To the contrary, Bani-Sadr informed him that a decision had been taken to transfer the hostages to the government. Bani-Sadr told the ambassador that his big problem now was how to guarantee the security of the hostages when they were transferred, and he was going to discuss that problem now with Ahmed Khomeini.

Lang returned at once to the Swiss Embassy and flashed the message to the Swiss foreign office in Bern, from where it was relayed to Washington.

For a while it seemed as if the transfer would take place. The Iranians moved cots and lockers into the Foreign Office, where the hostages would be housed. They notified the Swiss Government to have a plane ready to pick up the hostages and fly them away. The Swiss, characteristically, were ahead of everyone; instead of holding a plane in Switzerland, they sent it to Karachi, a thirty-minute flight from Teheran. Discussions were even held about the safest way to move the hostages from the foreign ministry to the airport; everyone agreed that, as obvious as it was, a middle-of-the-night exodus would be the best.

That morning in Teheran, Bani-Sadr's staff attempted to hold off the publication and dissemination of the Ayatollah Khomeini's acerbic anti-American speech. They failed. The text of the speech was published in the morning editions of the *Kayhan,* a leading Teheran newspaper. That afternoon, Ahmed Khomeini delivered the speech to an audience of half a million persons gathered in the city's largest square.

Then it was Bani-Sadr's turn. He began talking in the early evening. He rambled on and on, his speech laced with anti-American statements, but without any mention of the hostages.

Watching the speech on television in his office at the foreign ministry with François Cheron and Héctor Villalón, Sadegh Ghotbzadeh said, "He's saying nothing. He's scared."

Then, suddenly, Ghotbzadeh leaned forward. "Look!" he said, pointing to the screen. "You see those people near the rostrum? They're Communists. Watch what happens when Bani-Sadr finally mentions the hostages."

Almost two hours had passed. Bani-Sadr was reading to the vast audience the message he had received from the Americans via the Swiss, interspersing the text with his own commentary. At last, he came to the hostage issue. "The night before last the issue was raised at the Revolutionary Council, which decided: If America issues an official statement that until such time as the Majlis is formed and the proper decision is taken that America will refrain from resorting to any propaganda or making any claim or saying anything or making any provocation, then the Revolutionary Council agrees to take the hostages under its care and custody."

Bani-Sadr had finally and publicly spoken the fateful words—not in his name, but in the name of the Revolutionary Council. But the words were drowned out in a cacophony of invective—not from the crowd of half a million, but from the few hundred militants who had gathered near the rostrum and two smaller groups that had positioned themselves at two microphones in the crowd. The screams of the students, picked up by the microphones and intensified by amplifiers, howled from the dozens of loudspeakers set up in the square. "Traitor! Traitor!" the militants chanted, until it seemed as if half a million people were crying for the President's head. Unless you understood such techniques and knew what was happening, that is exactly what you would think, Sadegh Ghotbzadeh knew. He knew, as well, that the Ayatollah was watching the speech on television. He fumed.

It was five o'clock in the morning when President Carter met with his advisers to consider the messages from President Bani-Sadr, as well as the text of his and the Ayatollah's speech. When the Americans cut through the rhetoric, what remained, in however qualified a form, was the pledge of the Iranian Government to transfer control of the hostages from the students to the Revolutionary Council. It was precisely what the Americans had been waiting for for months, but there were no smiles or sighs of relief. Those would come only if and when the Iranians kept their word, something they had consistently failed to do.

The important thing, the Americans all agreed, was to seize upon the positive portion of Bani-Sadr's statement and to offer something in return: the removal of the threat further to tighten the political and economic screws.

The sun had hardly risen in Washington when a message from the White House was on its way back to Teheran, via the Swiss, addressed to Bani-Sadr and Ghotbzadeh.

"Citation:

'The announcement by President Bani-Sadr that the hostages will be transferred to the care and protection of the Iranian Government is a positive step.

Accordingly, we will defer imposing further sanctions at this time.

We understand it is the position of the Iranian Government that the hostage issue will be resolved when the new Parliament comes in. The early release of our people is essential and, as you know, that is the U. S. objective.'

Fin de citation.
Téhéran, le 1er avril 1980."

By late afternoon Teheran time, the White House message, as well as the text of President Carter's early morning press conference, in which he characterized Bani-Sadr's statement as a "positive step," had reached the Iranian President's desk. This reaction was immediately negative. Carter had not used the one word the Iranians were looking for—the "right" of the Iranian parliament to deal with the hostage problem.

Bani-Sadr turned to François Cheron. "Will you try to do something about that?" he asked. "Try to get the United States to make the response we asked them to make."

Cheron called Bourguet in Paris and explained the problem. Bourguet immediately called Hamilton Jordan at the White House, and the Americans went to work at once.

But by 7 P.M. in Teheran there was still no reply from the Americans. Bani-Sadr was increasingly nervous. He had taken the responsibility, but he had nothing to show for it. The Ayatollah's bitterly anti-American speech and the cries of "traitor" were in the forefront of his consciousness. It did not comfort him in the slightest to be so far out on a limb.

At last, Bani-Sadr could take no more. He sought out reporters, echoed the Ayatollah's anti-American bitterness and said that no deal was possible.

At the very moment that Bani-Sadr was giving his interview, the American reply arrived at the Swiss Embassy in Teheran. It said that the American Government recognized the "competence" of the Iranian parliament to deal with the disposition of the hostages. "Competence" was a word the Americans had agonized over. To acknowledge the "right" of the Majlis to deal with the question implied that holding the hostages was a legitimate undertaking; this the United States could never do.

But whether "competence" would have satisfied Bani-Sadr was moot. The Swiss Embassy was closed. The clacking of the Telex machine resounded through empty corridors.

When Bani-Sadr finally received the message the following morning, April 2, he read it aloud to his staff, then stuffed it into his pocket and went off to take part in Iran's Nature Day.

Héctor Villalón made one last, desperate try. On April 3 he delivered a message to Bani-Sadr pointing out that the White House had responded "exactly" to the demands the Iranian President had made.

But the real force of Villalón's letter was in his analysis of the stagger-
ing financial cost of the struggle to Iran.

". . . It must be figured that you are losing at least ten million dollars a day in interest on frozen assets all over the world. This, multi-
plied by the days of freeze starting from the taking of the Embassy,
represents an extremely considerable figure of loss for the Iranian people. If you add to that the loss of international credit, the interest in
damages demanded back from Iran for not having carried out con-
tracts connected to these credits, the paralysis of an enormous economic commercial and financial activity, and all the losses stemming
from the impossibility of obtaining spare parts, the technological support necessary to industrial development and the excessive cost of
merchandise purchased by Iran from exceptional commercial channels, this means to us a daily loss of 50 to 100 million dollars a day
that your country is undergoing since the day of the Embassy seizure.
All that, without counting the true detriment that is the enormous
delay in the technological and industrial development of the country."

The logic of Villalón's arguments was overwhelming, but it was too
late for logic—not only in Teheran but in Washington as well.

chapter eighteen

"Enough!"

JIMMY CARTER DID NOT AWAKEN SUDDENLY ON APRIL 2 THINKING that the time had come to attempt a military rescue of the hostages. The idea had been growing in his mind for weeks.

Although the Joint Chiefs of Staff had told the President categorically after the hostages were taken that no rescue effort was feasible, the military had done a complete turnaround in the intervening months. They knew exactly where the hostages were (a fact they hadn't been certain of at the outset), they had evolved a plan of operation in which they believed, and they had a force in training to execute it.

Given that option, and given all that had taken place, Carter began to feel that he had no other choice. From the perspective of the White House, it seemed clear after the failure of the April 1 initiative that although there were people in the Iranian leadership who had the desire to resolve the hostage crisis, they lacked the capacity and the political courage to do so. Moreover, there were increasing signs of instability in Iran, with indications that several months of drifting leadership would follow in which no decisive figure would emerge who was capable of resolving the problem. There were reports out of Teheran from people who knew Khomeini's doctors that the Ayatollah's health was failing and that he wouldn't live much longer. For all his sins, Khomeini at least had the power to secure the hostages' release. For these reasons, the Administration saw no hope of a diplomatic breakthrough in the immediate future. It might take months, even years, before the hostages would be freed.

Other factors were weighing on the President. Better than anyone, Carter knew how the hostage crisis had paralyzed his administration's efforts in other fields, if only because it had diverted his own attention and energies so greatly. Politically, therefore, he was twice wounded—first by the crisis, and again by its impact on his programs. His campaign for reelection registered the frustrations of the American public. While his political fortunes had risen after the taking of the hostages, he was beginning to slip in the polls and had lost a key primary in New York to Senator Edward Kennedy. Jimmy Carter was now in the midst of a fight for his political life, and it looked as if he was losing. A military operation that freed the hostages would dramatically alter the odds.

The military options ranged from a naval blockade to all-out war. But a rescue effort seemed the only option that had a chance of resolving the problem.

It was in that atmosphere, and in the wake of President Bani-Sadr's retreat on April 1—an event that had frustrated, irritated and even embarrassed the President beyond all previous limits—that Carter said, "Enough!"

The decision to proceed with the rescue operation was made at a luncheon meeting of the National Security Council at the White House on Friday April 11. At that meeting were Vice-President Mondale, Zbigniew Brzezinski, Hamilton Jordan, Lloyd Cutler, Defense Secretary Harold Brown, General David Jones and Warren Christopher, sitting in for Secretary of State Cyrus Vance, who had departed that morning on a brief vacation. The subject had been so tightly held that Christopher had known nothing about it. He made the assumption that Vance had known about it and approved the idea; otherwise the Secretary of State would have remained in town or left instructions for his deputy.

Christopher was mistaken. Vance was aware that a military option had been under discussion for some time, but as far as he knew, Harold Brown and his people at the Pentagon had only been exploring it; he had no idea how serious an option it was until after the decision was made.

Vance learned of the decision when he returned to Washington on Sunday April 20. Very early the next morning he went to see the President. The two men met alone. Vance told the President of his "very deep concern" about what had been decided while he was away, and then he listed his objections:

First, it was an extremely difficult operation with very limited chance of success.

Second, even if it were successful, a number of hostages would be lost in the process.

Third, if any of the hostages got away, others would be seized the next day—American newspapermen and perhaps even British and French. In the end, there would be more hostages than before.

Beyond the matter of hostages was the question of the political impact of the rescue effort. Vance foresaw the possibility of an explosion across the whole of the Middle East, with the added possibility of an Islamic war against the West. Further problems would result with America's allies. In the wake of the April 1 failure the United States, in addition to finally severing diplomatic relations with Iran, had embargoed trade on all but agricultural goods and pressed the Western allies to go along with the sanctions on the promise that the United States was not going to use force. How were these allies, who could not be informed in advance, going to react when they learned that they'd been deceived? Finally, Vance felt that a military action, even one limited to the rescue of the hostages, would push Iran into the arms of the Soviet Union.

When Vance had finished, the President said, "Those are strong arguments. Would you like to present them to the Security Council?"

"Yes, I would," Vance said.

Two hours later, Vance laid his case before the National Security Council. A brief discussion followed, after which the decision taken on April 11 was reaffirmed. His was the only negative vote.

Under the circumstances, Vance told the President, he would be forced to resign. But he promised that he would say nothing until the action was over.

Earlier, the President had cautioned those White House people who knew of the decision to refrain from so much as intimating that anything special was afoot. Jordan, to his intense embarrassment, had to lie flatly to the White House senior staff early in the week. "A rescue mission is impossible and couldn't even be attempted," Jordan told the staff even as the mission was approaching Iran.

Carter, Vice-President Mondale, Jordan and others connected with the election campaign were meeting on the third floor of the White

House on the afternoon of April 24 when a call came in for the President. He listened quietly, and left at once. Minutes later, he called Jordan. "You and Fritz join me in my office as soon as possible, but make your excuses and leave in a way that doesn't alarm the others," the President said. When the two men entered the Oval Office, they found Carter standing behind his desk. "I have some bad news," he said. "I had to abort the rescue mission." Two of the eight helicopters sent on the mission had been lost and a third was not operational, the President told them.

Jordan could not believe his ears. The military had managed to succeed in entering Iran undetected—to his mind, the most difficult part of the mission—only to be undone by mechanical problems.

In moments Harold Brown, Cyrus Vance and Jody Powell joined them. "At least there were no American casualties and no innocent Iranians were hurt," the President said. Just then, another call came in. It was General David Jones at the Pentagon. "Yes, Dave," the President said. Then his eyes closed, and his face grew slack. "Are there any dead?" he asked softly. He listened for a few seconds. "I understand," he said then, and slowly put down the phone. In a shaking voice, he told the others what had happened: a helicopter and a C-130 transport had crashed in a dust storm as they were preparing to withdraw. There had definitely been casualties, and perhaps some dead.

They sat in silence, and misery. At last Cyrus Vance said, "Mr. President, I'm very, very sorry."

Of all the questions asked after Tabas, the most bewildering is the one posed by a secret two-page CIA report given to the CIA director, Stansfield Turner, on March 16, 1980, evaluating the prospects of Operation Eagle Claw. The pertinent portion of that report was its second page:

"6. The estimated percent of loss among Amembassy hostages during each of the five major phases was:

(a) Entry/Staging   :   0%
    Assumes no loss of cover.

(b) Initial Assault   : 20%
    Assumes . . . immediate loss of those under State FSR and
    FSS cover and others.

(c) Location/Identification   : 25%
Loss of State personnel before full suppression of resistance.
Problem accentuated since Amembassy hostages not collocated.

(d) Evacuation to RH-53s   : 15%
Assumes loss from snipers, from inside and outside Amembassy Compound, and from AT and Apers mines.

(e) Transfer—RH-53s to C-130s   : 0%
Assumes maintenance of site security.

7. The estimate of a loss rate of 60% for the Amembassy hostages
represents the best estimate of CA and M&P Staff.

8. It is presumed to be equally as likely that the Amembassy rescue
attempt would be a complete success (100% of the Amembassy hostages rescued), as it would be a complete failure (0% of the Amembassy hostages rescued).

9. Of special note is the fact that *no* analogous large-scale rescue attempts have been mounted in heavily populated urban areas within
hostile territory during the past 15 years. The only roughly similar attempts, (Son Tay—Nov. 1970; Mayaguez—May 1975; Entebbe—July
1976) were all made in lightly populated rural areas of hostile territory."

The American Government, in sum, had undertaken a rescue mission that its own intelligence service had predicted would result in the
deaths of 60 percent of the people it was trying to liberate.

To some of the people who had been negotiating secretly since January to secure the peaceful release of the hostages, the rescue effort
seemed insane. In Paris, Christian Bourguet said to himself, How stupid! It was crazy, it was reckless, because only if you don't know the
Iranians can you believe that you can get them to move by force. They
are a people who are simply not afraid of dying, and particularly not if
their death is to be as martyrs in defense of their faith, which they in-
tertwine in their minds with patriotism. And they would have reacted
—oh, how swiftly they would have reacted—because in Teheran word
passes at the speed of light and the people pour into the streets, no
matter the hour, and there was not one chance in a hundred that the
commandos could intervene before everyone would be aware of what
was going on.

Bourguet had always been afraid of retribution in some form by the

United States, but it was a bombing he had expected, or the occupation of an oil port, or the threat to blow up a refinery in Abadan, or even an attempt to kidnap the imam. What he had most feared was that the Americans would not understand that none of those acts, not even the kidnapping of the imam, would have budged the Iranians. The imam would have preferred to let himself die by fasting rather than order that the hostages be freed. And had he died in that manner, or had the Americans killed him, the Iranians would then have surely killed the hostages.

It was early afternoon in Paris when President Carter, sitting ramrod straight at his desk in the Oval Office, addressed the nation: "I ordered this rescue mission . . . It was my decision to cancel it . . . The responsibility is fully my own." Within the hour Bourguet was on the telephone with Hamilton Jordan. "But what were you thinking of?" he asked. "What were you trying to do?"

"What do you want us to do?" Jordan said. "What else *is* there for us to do?"

His telephone awakened Hamilton Jordan in the middle of the night. He could tell by the moment's delay and the faraway noise on the line that it was an overseas call. Then he heard a voice that had him instantly alert. "This is Sadegh Ghotbzadeh," the caller said.

Ghotbzadeh had obtained Jordan's unlisted apartment number from Christian Bourguet. He well knew the restrictions imposed by the imam on direct contact with the Americans, and the risks for those who violated the prohibition. But this matter, he felt, required direct contact. The Foreign Minister did not waste words. "What the hell is going on?" he said. "What are you guys doing?"

For the next several minutes, Jordan attempted to convey to Ghotbzadeh the same message that the United States was frantically putting out to Iran through all available channels: the raid had not been punitive; its sole objective had been to free the hostages.

In the forty-eight hours after the raid, as the student militants dispersed the hostages to numerous hiding places in and outside the city, dozens of messages passed between the Americans and the Iranians through the intermediaries, Bourguet and Villalón. In addition to assuring the Iranians that the raid had not been intended to punish, the

Americans wanted the Iranians to know that the decision had been taken because they had felt there was no other possible solution. The Iranians wanted the Americans to understand that they had made a monumental mistake, proving that they understood nothing at all about Iran.

What amazed the Americans throughout was the softness of the Iranian response. To a certain extent, it was explained by the resignation of Cyrus Vance; that was a form of self-sacrifice they could understand. But even more important was the mystical perception they applied to the raid. Ghotbzadeh called Bourguet to impress on him that neither the Ayatollah nor he would seek any revenge against the hostages, and to pass that message to the Americans. "They have been punished enough. It's an act of God. Let's start again," the Foreign Minister said.

The Americans did just that. Two days after the raid, Harold Saunders telephoned Mohammed Heikal in Cairo, and asked if he would be willing to meet him in Geneva. Heikal said he couldn't.

The next day, the same well-placed Egyptian who had first contacted Heikal in London to see if he would act as an intermediary appeared at Heikal's lavish apartment at the edge of the Nile River and, without comment, handed the journalist a Telex he had just received from the Americans.

Harold Saunders continues to deny that he or any American official had anything to do with the message, but its authenticity as an American Government message is beyond question. It was a remarkable document, written with a first paragraph that would permit the U. S. Government later to deny authorship. It was an attempt to snatch victory—the liberation of the hostages—from the jaws of defeat—the Tabas raid. The message had many solid ideas, the most important of which was to focus Iranian attention on the more generous aspects of the Koran. But it had one shocking suggestion: that the hostages be taken to the ruins of the Tabas raid before being released.*

* Saunders states: "Regarding the so-called message from me to Heikal after the failed U.S. rescue mission, I never saw, was aware of, nor approved the message reported in the TV narrative. In the course of the hostage crisis there were several cases where intermediaries embellished basic approaches with their own detailed ideas and drafts. I can only assume that is what happened in this instance. I did, more generally, from January on, urge Mr. Heikal to take the line with the Iranians that holding hostages was inconsistent with the principles of Islam. I never suggested or could even have considered having the hostages taken to Tabas to witness the wreckage of the rescue aircraft before release."

The message said:

"Would appreciate following idea be presented to Haykal (sic) as coming from you.

The concept is to have Haykal go to Iran and present to Bani-Sadr a way to use the rescue disaster to get the hostages released and the issue behind him. Haykal would persuade him of the unique opportunity this presents for him to ride the crest of Islamic nationalism to solidify his own position. To the extent Khomeini shares the desire to be rid of the problem, the concept could be presented to him too. Themes which Haykal can draw on are as follows:

a. The success of Iran's revolution has been clearly and finally demonstrated with the humiliating defeat of the U. S. Government rescue mission. God has shown the world that no matter how powerful the enemy, righteousness accrues to the aggrieved party and in this case the moral superiority of the Islamic Republic is there for all to see. Therefore:

b. The American hostages have served the purpose Iran has wanted. They served as a pretext to show the world dramatically the evil of the Shah's regime and the U. S. Government support for it, and America's inability to mount the rescue operation is the second and final attestation to the justness of their being taken (i.e., the Iranian act brought about an American reaction which only underscored, in its failure, the message Iran originally wanted to get across). The hostages just are not needed any longer.

c. The hostages will be released. Iran never intended to harm them anyway. The gesture dramatizes Islam's magnanimity and compassion. There was never any hatred for the American people, only the U. S. Government. (Let the hostages go now and make the Americans look even more foolish and inept. Perhaps fly them out via Tabas, along with newspaper correspondents and note down their disparaging comments, etc.) Iran and the Islamic Republic emerge as both victorious and morally supreme.

d. The captors emerge victorious and are national heroes. They have not hurt anybody, they have honored the dictates of the Imam, will be rewarded amply by the Government and recognized specially by Imam. It may be the last time the captor force can be gotten off the compound without somebody in Iran losing face in the process.

e. The release itself should be announced by Iran as being a dramatic act of clemency and mercy for the hostages which was taken by Khomeini himself. The procedure for release offers Iran tremendous propaganda opportunity, cloaking the whole miserable five months in an aura of decency and mercy. Iran thus refurbishes the image of Islam, something all other Muslims in the world wish to happen. The U. S. Government, as opposed to the American people, is again scored for its enmity toward just causes and the release in no way represents a lessening of Iran's battle with the U. S. Government or a compromise with it."

The message from the Americans could scarcely have come at a less propitious time, or to a less sympathetic source. Since the raid, Heikal had been seething. It was not simply that he had believed the negotiations were finally getting somewhere, in spite of the surface problems, or that the raid had blown everything sky high. It was that he had been unwittingly made a party to a deception. He was one of several people being used by the Americans to set up a smoke screen of false assurances. Now, he knew, the Iranians would believe no one, not even him, and they had all the right in the world not to. This is the moment to stop all attempts to help, he had told himself after learning of the raid, because now it was all nonsense. Continuing would only be disgraceful.

And now this preposterous idea!

When he finished reading the message, Heikal looked up at the man who had brought it to him. "Do they really want me to pass this message to Teheran?"

"Yes, I think so," the man said.

"They must think I'm crazy, then. I'm not going to pass such a message."

There was, then, the matter of the bodies.

In one of the first conversations between Christian Bourguet and Henry Precht, the Iran desk officer—who denied all prior knowledge of the raid, despaired that it had happened and blamed it on Zbigniew Brzezinski—urged Bourguet to do everything he could to help mitigate the shock. One way to do that, Precht proposed, was to attempt to return the corpses of the eight Americans to the United States as quickly as possible. Could Bourguet suggest someone who could take on that mission in behalf of the American Government?

Bourguet thought about it for only a short while before calling

Precht back. He had, he felt, the ideal candidate: Hilarion Capucci, a Lebanese Catholic and the Archbishop of Jerusalem.

Capucci had won worldwide attention when he was arrested by the Israelis in 1974 for running guns to the Palestinians. He had been defended in that case by Christian Bourguet at the request of Sadegh Ghotbzadeh, who at that time was an Iranian exile with close contacts to the PLO. Capucci had no love for the Americans; he was a friend of the Iranian revolution. But he, like Yasir Arafat, saw in the hostage crisis an opportunity to get credits with the Americans for the PLO, and thereby bring them closer to the viewpoint of the Palestinians.

Bourguet and Capucci had not seen each other in years when they found themselves together in Teheran in February. At that time Bourguet persuaded Capucci to ask the Iranians to let him see the hostages, a request the Iranians granted, and it was Capucci, again at Bourguet's suggestion, whom the Iranians approved to conduct Easter services for the hostages. On both occasions, Bourguet was pursuing a request of the Americans to facilitate as many visits as possible so that information on the condition of the hostages could be obtained, and on both occasions Capucci had acquitted himself well. After his first visit, the archbishop had emerged with numerous messages from the hostages to their families. But the Americans had been reluctant to make direct contact with him, fearing that he would try to use the occasion to further the cause of the PLO.

This time, however, there was no hesitation on the part of the Americans. Capucci, they agreed, would be the ideal man to carry out a most distasteful mission, the retrieval of the bodies of the men killed in the Tabas raid. But it was another several days before Bourguet and Villalón could secure the Iranians' approval.

As soon as Capucci arrived in Teheran, he set to work with the Apostolic Nuncio, Annibale Bugnini, and Erik Lang, the Swiss ambassador. Theoretically, it was a simple assignment that should have been accomplished quickly. But there was a health problem: the bodies had not yet been embalmed, and there was a need for doctors to make certain that no risks to public health were involved. There was also a need for lead caskets.

These problems were manageable, however, compared to the one that almost prevented the bodies from leaving. The Americans had said that eight members of the mission had been killed. The Iranians counted nine bodies. (Later, they would insist there were ten.) The Americans had no doubt whatever about the accuracy of their body count. They surmised that the ninth body was that of an Iranian who had been prowling about the American helicopters abandoned in the desert when the Iranian Air Force came to bomb them.

The mullahs were aghast at the thought that an Iranian would be transported from the country and buried in the United States. They proposed that all of the dead be buried in the Cemetery of the Martyrs. For a while, it looked as though this was what would happen. Then Sadegh Ghotbzadeh intervened. "I'll take care of it," he said when Bourguet called him in alarm. "The decision has been made to return the corpses. They have to be returned. We can't create new problems. It's complicated enough as it is."

On May 5 a Swissair jet flew the caskets to Zurich. There they were placed on the tarmac, where Capucci held a brief religious ceremony. But the archbishop refused to turn the caskets over directly to the American diplomats who had come to the airport to receive them; instead, he demanded that the Swiss Red Cross accept them. Then it was the Americans who refused to accept the coffins from the Red Cross until they had been opened and examined for bombs.

Only after the caskets had passed from the control of the Iranians did the two civilians who had observed the proceedings in silence leave the field: Christian Bourguet and Héctor Villalón, who had come to Zurich at the request of both parties to make certain no further problems developed. They were exhausted; they had come to Zurich the night before but been unable to sleep because of the intensity of their emotions. For almost four months they had worked at their own expense to send fifty-three hostages back to America. What they were delivering, instead, was nine coffins.

chapter nineteen

Down to the Depths

FORCE HAD FAILED. THE RELEASE OF THE HOSTAGES, IF IT WAS EVER
to occur, would have to be by negotiation after all.

But how was the process to be started again? Before they could ever
hope to arrive at the plain of understanding, the negotiators would
have to scale a mountain of mistrust.

And before that could begin, the Americans would have to answer
the most fundamental question of all: how was it that a few hundred
militant students could frustrate the wishes of a democratically elected
government—particularly one whose President had, not four months
before, received 75 percent of the popular vote?

Until that question was answered, no further negotiation was possible, because the United States would not understand the problem with
which it was dealing—which meant, in effect, that it did not understand the people who had posed it.

SENATOR STONE: All of these months questions have flooded in
to us and I am sure to you—probably more to you than to us. Who are
these people? Who is counseling them? Who is leading them? Where
are they headed? What are they? Do we have any clearer idea now
than we did six months ago about that? If so, who are they?

Those questions were put to Deputy Secretary of State Warren
Christopher on May 8, 1980, by Senator Richard Stone of Florida as

Christopher testified before a Senate committee inquiring into the abortive American attempt to rescue the hostages.

"Our ideas are still quite misty and vague," Christopher replied. "We believe there is a substantial number of Islamic extremists in the group who previously we had called students but who I think are better described as hard-line, right-line Islamic extremists. Those would numerically be the largest number on the basis of what I know."

There were many in the American Government who assumed that the group was dominated by Marxists. That some of the students were members of the Communist Tudeh Party, or at least supported by it, is highly likely; Hilarion Capucci, the Archbishop of Jerusalem, confirmed after conducting Easter services at the embassy that he had recognized two militants who had been trained in the Soviet Union and were supporters of the most left-wing element of the PLO.

But most of the students, it seems clear, were what Christopher said they were—militant right-wing extremists. This is not so much a political as a spiritual definition, because college students in Iran, for the most part, get as worked up over religion as their American counterparts do about football. The cause in which they had invested their ardor was a spiritually pure society. They passionately rejected accusations that they were opposed to the development of a modern industrial society; what they opposed with such vehemence were the social and political corruptions they believed had accompanied the introduction of such a society to Iran. They had a word for it: "Westernization." One source of their hatred for the Shah was that it was he who had "Westernized" Iran. Western habits were "blasphemous," they said, echoing the invective of the imam. They called themselves "The Students Following the Imam's Line." Each day, five times a day, they prayed to Mecca together in the parking lot of the embassy compound. The sexes were separated, according to Moslem custom, and the women covered their heads.

The militants had been recruited from Islamic student societies at several universities in Iran, principally the Polytechnic. Most of them were the first members of their families to receive a higher education, and they found it difficult to deal with the cosmopolitan atmosphere into which they had suddenly been plunged. For many, the experience had been a case of you-can-take-the-boy-out-of-the-country-but-you-can't-take-the-country-out-of-the-boy. They were much more bound to the religious traditions in which they had been raised than they were to the ideas and customs they found in Teheran.

It is conceivable that this majority of Islamic extremists who seized the American Embassy could have been manipulated by the minority of Marxists among them, although, given the Islamic stamp that existed in all of them, it is perhaps ingenuous to think that they were. But the question, in any case, is moot. The functional identity of these students—Marxist and non-Marxist alike—was created by the event they unwittingly precipitated.

When the students swept into the American Embassy compound, it was with the idea that they would stage a sit-in for three to five days in an attempt to focus world attention on their grievances against the Shah and the United States. Coincidentally, the students hoped to rally support against the present government, which they viewed as too Western. They did not know what to expect from the government, and their first impulse was to wait and see how the government would respond.

The government did nothing—but the people responded with an outpouring of feeling that changed everything. As word of the seizure spread, they rushed to the embassy—first hundreds, then thousands, then tens of thousands—chanting anti-American slogans and crying for the return of the Shah. Suddenly, the surprised students realized that they had been presented a role by the people that exceeded their wildest dreams—to hold the Americans hostage until the Shah was returned to stand trial.

No one—not the students and certainly not the politicians—could be oblivious to this expression of emotion by the people. It was they, not the Ayatollah Khomeini, who had caused the downfall of the Shah. They, not the Ayatollah, were the revolution. Six months had passed since the hostages had been taken; the passions of the people had subsided, the mobs at the embassy gates had disappeared. But no one really knew what the people wanted now, or whether they were ready to respond to a reasoned plea for the release of the hostages in the best interests of Iran. It was against this uncertainty that the politicians—and the Ayatollah must be included among them—were trying to function, mindful that a wrong decision on their part could cost them their positions.

Among the members of the Revolutionary Council only Sadegh Ghotbzadeh and, to a lesser extent, Bani-Sadr, were committed to the release of the hostages. Although almost all of the others agreed that the hostage crisis was an economic and political disaster for Iran, none of them, not even Bani-Sadr, wanted to be associated with the actual

release if they could possibly help it. To compound the problem, while
the leaders of the revolution were united in their allegiance to the Ayatollah, they were deeply divided among themselves. On one side were
the "Occidentals," Bani-Sadr and Ghotbzadeh, and those aligned with
them. On the other side were the religious groups who wished to dis-
credit the "secularists" and take power themselves. Chaos such as that
engendered by the hostage crisis precisely served their interest.

Power, at this moment, did not reside in one place. No decision
could come solely from the President. He had to have the concurrence
of the Revolutionary Council—itself divided between the secularists
and the clerics—and the Council and the President, in turn, had to
have the concurrence of the Ayatollah. While it would seem that ultimate power resided with the Ayatollah, that wasn't the case because of
the manner in which he chose to use it. He, too, often seemed unwilling to make a choice that might be an unpopular one, and so he
often avoided choices by throwing responsibility back to the President
and Revolutionary Council. Give me a unanimous recommendation,
he would say in effect, or I can't make a decision. Whether his ambivalence was opportunistic or an expression of Moslem belief in con-
sensus is difficult to judge.

What it finally boiled down to was a simple formula: those in power
wanted the hostages released, so that they could run a successful government. Those who were not in power did not want the hostages
released, because they wanted the government to fail.

For those not in power—the clerics—the seizure of the hostages by
the students had been tantamount to a gift from Allah. The students
understood that. They supported the clergy and hoped they would
come to power so as to establish a true theocracy that would "purify"
the revolution of any and all Western tendencies. Their support was
undergirded by historical fact: it had been the clergy that had led the
fight against foreign economic domination, be it British, Russian or
American, for more than one hundred years.

On May 9, 1980, the students got their wish. That day the people
of Iran, voting in parliamentary elections, gave their overwhelming
approval to hard-line Islamic candidates. At last the religious leaders
were in a position to gain effective control of the country—and they
had used the hostages to do it.

For Sadegh Ghotbzadeh, the troubles were just beginning.

On the day that the more liberal secular candidates for parliament were receiving a drubbing in Iran, Ghotbzadeh was at the Hotel Bellerive-au-Lac in Zurich with Christian Bourguet and Héctor Villa-lón, trying, once again, to come up with fruitful approaches to the hostage crisis. Several days before, the Foreign Minister had flown in an Iranian Government plane to Belgrade for the funeral of Marshal Tito. From there he had telephoned Bourguet and Villalón, who were already in Zurich, to propose that they join him in Belgrade. On reflection, it did not seem like a good idea; hundreds of reporters were in the city to cover the funeral, and their presence together would be noted. He decided to join them in Switzerland.

On the flight to Zurich Ghotbzadeh had a guest, the Swiss Foreign Minister, Pierre Aubert. "It's important just to keep talking and let time take care of everything," he told Aubert.

In Zurich, representatives of the Swiss Foreign Office joined in the counsels. Harold Saunders was also there, meeting separately with Bourguet and Villalón, and making certain to steer clear of Ghotbzadeh lest he further complicate the Foreign Minister's life. Saunders also met with Hilarion Capucci, who had remained in Zurich after delivering the caskets. What their combined efforts came up with was two expressions of the same idea: the first, an "Islamic initiative," the second, a "Socialist initiative." The Islamic initiative envisioned the creation of a "front" of Islamic nations whose representatives would approach the Ayatollah with a plea that he invoke the tenets of the Koran calling for generosity, understanding and forgiveness. "There has to be forgiveness," they would tell him. "The time has come to forgive and forget and release the hostages." The Socialist initiative would enlist a group of progressive European leaders whose independence of either major political bloc might commend them to the Iranians. The Socialists, too, would attempt to persuade the Iranians to resolve the crisis in their own interest.

The Islamic initiative got nowhere. The Americans, who supported it, wanted to enlist Hilarion Capucci to sell the idea to key Moslem leaders. But Capucci, who was willing, had been forbidden by the Vatican since his arrest by the Israelis to travel to any countries involved in the Arab-Israeli dispute. Saunders told Capucci that he would press the Vatican for permission, but Capucci never heard from him. After other efforts proved equally fruitless, the project was dropped.

The Socialist initiative did not fare much better. Bourguet and Villalón had flown to Madrid to ask the Spanish Prime Minister, Adolfo Suárez, to use Spain's good relations with Islamic countries in support of that initiative. While there, they talked with Felipe González, the leader of the Spanish Socialist Party. González liked the idea, and became even more enthusiastic when he discovered that other major European Socialist leaders had arrived independently at the same notion. In fact, West German Chancellor Helmut Schmidt, Austrian Chancellor Bruno Kreisky and former Swedish Prime Minister Olof Palme had already gathered in Hamburg to discuss the matter. They had an active ally in Teheran, Ali Reza Nobari, the governor of the Iranian Central Bank.

The Socialists who finally made the trip, González, Kreisky and Palme, managed to get through to the clerics, among them Ayatollah Mohammed Beheshti, the leader of the Islamic Republican Party, which had just taken control of the Iranian parliament. The Socialists counseled Beheshti that putting the American hostages on trial was the worst thing the Iranians could do.

But basically, the Socialists found, the power structure in Iran was still so fragile, in spite of the elections, that the Iranians wouldn't budge on their position, and no single leader would come forward to demand the release of the hostages.

A month later, Jimmy Carter would stop off in Madrid on his way home from an economic summit meeting in Venice and a side trip to Yugoslavia to decorate the grave of Marshal Tito. There would be much pomp and ceremony, but Carter's most important visit in Madrid would be with González. Carter would take home a sober message: with the ongoing power struggle in Iran, nothing could be done immediately to bring about the release of the hostages.

One by one, the various initiatives were failing, and the back doors were closing.

On May 30, Mohammed Heikal's efforts as an intermediary ended. That day, Heikal received another message from Harold Saunders via the same Egyptian courier the American diplomat had used several times before. "This is an opportunity for Heikal to go to Teheran while the Parliament is forming," the message said. "He could contribute to a climate which could bring about the release of the hostages and suggest ways in which the U. S. might relate constructively to the political process in Teheran."

Heikal refused. The best way for the United States Government to

get its messages to the Iranians now, he counseled, was through the
Algerians and the Swiss.

More than any single person in the hierarchy, Sadegh Ghotbzadeh had
identified himself, both privately and publicly, with the need to free
the hostages. He was still the Foreign Minister, but each day was a
battle for his political life. Technically that life depended on the whim
of Bani-Sadr who, as President, had the power to appoint and dismiss
the members of his cabinet. But since the election, in which his "Occidental wing" had been all but destroyed, Bani-Sadr had been reduced to a figurehead President. There was no telling how readily he
would succumb to the pressures from the victorious clerics, now in the
progress of organizing the parliament, to "purify" the government by
getting rid of its objectionable members—in particular, Sadegh Ghotbzadeh.

As if he didn't have enough trouble with his own countrymen,
Ghotbzadeh was still fighting a rearguard action against Sean Mac-
Bride, the Irish diplomat, and Nuri Albala, the French Communist attorney, who blamed him for derailing their MacBride Commission in
early February. For a few days in late March, it had looked as though
the proposal were back on the tracks. MacBride had reappeared in
Teheran on March 29, at the height of the efforts by both the Americans and the Iranians to get the hostages transferred from student to
government control. He had come at the invitation of Bani-Sadr, who
sent word through Ali Reza Nobari, the head of the Central Bank, and
Leonard Boudin, a left-wing American lawyer, that he wanted to see
MacBride alone—meaning that he was not to go through the Foreign
Office of Sadegh Ghotbzadeh. For MacBride, the tactic was confirmation of the tension between the two men that he had sensed at his
meeting in December with Ghotbzadeh, when the Foreign Minister
had questioned him closely about Bani-Sadr.

On March 30, MacBride had extensive meetings with Bani-Sadr.
Together the two men drew up a draft message from the government
of Iran to be sent to the United States, proposing, in effect, that the
MacBride Commission become the mechanism for settling the hostage
crisis. The message was approved by the Revolutionary Council the
next day at the same meeting in which the Council was discussing the
American ultimatum regarding the transfer of the hostages.

MacBride left Teheran with a copy of the approved message, and

once back in Dublin sent copies of his copy to UN Secretary-General
Waldheim and Arthur Hartman, the U. S. Ambassador to France. But
the Iranians never sent the message to the Americans—or, if they did,
the Americans never received it.

During his stay in Teheran, MacBride had assured a number of persons, including François Cheron, Nobari and Eric Rouleau of *Le
Monde,* that he was acting with the accord of the American Government. On April 5 the Swiss delivered a message from the Americans
to Bani-Sadr and Ghotbzadeh:

"We have been told that Mr. Sean MacBride spoke of having the endorsement of his proposal from Secretary Vance when he was recently
in Iran. The Secretary has not met with nor communicated with Mr.
MacBride in several months. He is not familiar with his proposal and
certainly has not endorsed it."

Once more, Sean MacBride had been snubbed, and once more he
blamed Sadegh Ghotbzadeh. On May 28 MacBride put his feelings
about Ghotbzadeh into a letter to Olof Palme, who was about to
depart for Teheran. It was filled with the kind of innuendo and false-
hoods rarely found in diplomatic correspondence:

"While I could not say that they had specifically agreed to the setting
up of a tribunal with jurisdiction to try the Shah in absentia, I got the
impression that this could be acceptable, providing the hostages were
released. One of the main difficulties in dealing with the Iranian Government was that the Foreign Minister Mr. Ghotbzadeh was completely unreliable. On the other hand, I found the President [Bani-
Sadr] both reliable and constructive. Throughout the period during
which I was negotiating with the President, Mr. Ghotbzadeh was carrying on parallel secret negotiations with Mr. Hamilton Jordan of the
White House. The two of them heavily disguised with wigs and false
mustaches met in Europe on a number of occasions, denied in Teheran. It was as a result of these bizarre meetings that a letter purport-
ing to come from Carter and addressed to the Ayatollah Khomeini
was concocted and duly delivered. Neither Vance nor Carter had seen
or authorized this letter. The release of the letter by the Ayatollah to
the press had apparently not been anticipated by Mr. Ghotbzadeh and
Hamilton Jordan. The Ayatollah then became convinced that this was

another example of American double crossing. This created an unfortunate atmosphere."

There was no way Sean MacBride could have known whether Cyrus Vance did or didn't know about the existence of the letter that had supposedly been sent in late March, because MacBride hadn't seen Vance since January 9. As to Carter, he and MacBride had never met. And while Hamilton Jordan did carry a disguise with him on his clandestine trips, he didn't use it once. Ghotbzadeh carried no disguise at all.

Still the matter wouldn't rest. Early in June, Albala, whose friendship of many years with Ghotbzadeh had ruptured in February, showed up in Teheran at a conference of left-wing lawyers from fifty countries organized by the Iranians to look into the crimes of the Shah. (This was the same meeting attended by Ramsey Clark over the vigorous objections of the American Government, which had tried to send him to Iran officially the previous November to negotiate for the hostages' release. This time Clark was accused of being a traitor, to which he replied that there was nothing treasonous about trying to understand another people and find a way to persuade them to release the hostages.) Albala told a number of people that he intended to make a speech attacking Ghotbzadeh. Word of Albala's threat reached Christian Bourguet, who passed it along to Ghotbzadeh. Ghotbzadeh sprang into action at once. He appointed himself chairman of the conference, and shunted Albala off to a committee. When the Frenchman tried to make his speech in front of the committee, the chairman ruled him out of order.

The tactic was a good example of the skills Ghotbzadeh had acquired in the fourteen months since he had been transformed from a political exile to a ranking member of the revolutionary government, first as director of Iran's national radio and television and then as Foreign Minister. From the moment he assumed the latter role, he set a style rarely found in diplomatic work, an informality just this side of coarseness. His discourse not only eschewed diplomatic niceties, it was often deliberately brutal in its candor. Two months later, Ghotbzadeh would send a withering letter to Russia's Foreign Minister, Andrei A. Gromyko, denouncing the Russians for asserted intrusions on Iranian sovereignty. The charges were old hat—the kinds of political mischief the Russians have been accused of since the start of the Cold War. What was fresh was the tenor of Ghotbzadeh's letter. "What makes me, as the Foreign Minister of the Islamic Republic of Iran, with a meager record of service, and as the representative of the youngest republic of the world, write this letter in full respect but with revolutionary candor is my desire to state the facts frankly and sincerely, no matter how unpleasant they may be, and to express matters as they appear to me," Ghotbzadeh wrote. "Perhaps this would mark the beginning of a new style of diplomatic correspondence free from lies, concealment and hypocrisy. Who knows, perhaps the future generations will choose this method to save themselves."

Like his countrymen, Ghotbzadeh often spoke under the influence of transient feelings. He would take a certain position with complete conviction and sincerity one day, and then the next day express the opposite viewpoint with just as much conviction. In neither case was he lying.

But over the months, this freewheeling style had been undergoing a subtle transformation. Ghotbzadeh's mentor, Héctor Villalón, had been quietly urging him to take positions after thoughtful study and then to maintain them, to make declarations only after careful checking (his premature announcement of the Shah's arrest had mortified the Foreign Minister), and above all not to succumb to despair. In their most desperate moments during the hostage crisis, Villalón reminded Ghotbzadeh, they had always been able to think of a new approach, invent a new solution or try a new way of acting.

At the outset, Ghotbzadeh had given the impression that even though he was his country's Foreign Minister, he didn't really care what happened outside Iran except in the United States. But as the hostage crisis deepened and Iran's position in the world community deteriorated, he quickly saw that foreign and domestic policies were inextricably bound.

More than a month had passed since the Majlis—the first parliament to be elected since the revolution—had been won by the Islamic Republican Party and those sympathetic to its theocratic objectives. To judge by the priorities of the new legislators, however, the hostage problem didn't exist. Their primary objective seemed to be the reimposition of the strict moral codes that had been abandoned by the Shah, and their ardor was felt throughout Iran. Patrons of restaurants who played music in their establishments were dragged into the streets and beaten. Working women in government offices were commanded to wear veils. Against these pressures, even ranking officials of the government succumbed. One morning a member of the Majlis paid a visit to the Central Bank. "There are women here who are not veiled," he stormed. "I demand that they be veiled. If not you'll all be thrown out."

"I can't accept that! It's inadmissible!" the Central Bank's Nobari protested to his luncheon companion that day. The next day he capitulated.

And then there was the purge of the secularists from government, which the victorious clerics had demanded.

As the pressures for his resignation mounted, Ghotbzadeh had Bani-Sadr to thank for the fact that he still had his job. Bani-Sadr did respond to the demands of the Majlis that someone else take over the foreign ministry, but the only names he would pass on to the parliament were those he knew the parliament would reject.

This rapprochement between Bani-Sadr and Ghotbzadeh had been one of the consequences of the clerics' victory. Whatever rivalries or differences in styles and approaches had divided them in the past, they and those who had sided with either one or the other had been reunited by their common interests.

Those interests went all the way back to the period of their exile when the "Occidental" exiles were as one in the plan they envisioned for Iran. There had been two parts to the plan. Part one had been to use the leadership of the Ayatollah Khomeini to overthrow the Shah and create a revolutionary government instead. Part two had been to assume secular control of the government. Part one had succeeded; part two had failed.

What now? On Bani-Sadr's part, it was to fight a rearguard action as President.

The Iranian constitution provides that the Prime Minister be approved by the President. Before the Prime Minister can form a government, moreover, he must first submit his selection of proposed ministers to the President. The President, in turn, proposes the government to the parliament for its approval. If the President refuses to present a slate of ministers, or even an individual nominee, to the parliament, the parliament cannot give its approval alone. So while the President may not retain any personal power, as was approximately the case with Bani-Sadr following the election of the Majlis, he nonetheless keeps the key.

Frustrated by his own efforts to nominate an acceptable candidate for Prime Minister, Bani-Sadr told the parliament that he would listen to its proposals. But when the dominant Islamic Republican Party presented its candidate, the President rejected him. Only when the party had come up with a man who, in Bani-Sadr's mind, would not be as skillful as the earlier candidates, did the President give his approval.

Even then, Bani-Sadr wasn't through. When the new Prime Minister presented his list of ministerial candidates to the President, he refused to approve the ministers proposed for science, economy, the interior—and the Foreign Office.

For a while, Ghotbzadeh was pleased to retain his uneasy perch, on the assumption that only if he remained in office could he possibly resolve the hostage crisis. But by midsummer he had come to see it differently.

Paradoxically, Ghotbzadeh's role as gadfly, as dangerous and potentially fatal as it was, had caused him to amass a certain power base of his own. Each time he went on television to attack the students and eventually those clerics who supported them, he received the support of the imam, whose basic premise, however fanatical he himself might be, was that everyone who was part of the revolution must be heard, and who, in addition, had always favored his "adopted" son. The more violent Ghotbzadeh became, the more support he won for himself throughout the country—if not for his ideas, at least for the courage he demonstrated.

Such was the situation that Ghotbzadeh believed he could remain Foreign Minister as long as he wished, despite the objections of the clerics. But there came a point when he determined that he no longer wished to do so. "I don't want to collaborate with those people," he confided to Christian Bourguet. "I don't share their ideas. I am against what they want to do in Iran. I am against their comprehension of Islam."

In the back of Ghotbzadeh's mind was the idea that the only way the clerics could be gotten rid of was to let them try to run the government. He was positive they would fail, and that the people, seeing their incompetence, would turn them out.

By early August, with the hostage crisis entering its ninth month without the slightest sign of hope, Sadegh Ghotbzadeh became convinced that the only way to break the impasse was to lance it—using himself as the lance. On August 18, 1980, 289 days after the hostages were seized, the Foreign Minister of Iran presented an extraordinary letter to the Majlis that, in effect, put his life on the line. It was a reasoned, yet passionate plea for an understanding of the economic and diplomatic cost of continuing to hold the hostages. In all the words that had been spoken in Iran since the hostages had been seized, none like these had ever been heard before.

Ghotbzadeh's argument was diabolical. One by one, he took up all the solutions proposed in Iran for dealing with the hostages and, after expressing sympathy for the ideas, demolished them. For example, he discussed the possibility of trials for the hostages, noting that between "eleven and thirteen" of them were "undoubtedly guilty of espionage." But what would such trials accomplish? he asked. They would only convince the Iranians, who were convinced already, of the Americans' guilt. The trials would have no impact on "those who have so far refused to believe that there are spies among the hostages. On the contrary, such summary trials will create in the world public opinion the impression that our claims so far have been empty and we lack internationally acceptable evidence. In this case, we will have proved to a world arranged against us the injustice, not the justice, of our cause."

Inexorably, Ghotbzadeh destroyed the idea of an international tribunal of the type suggested by Sean MacBride:

"Even if sufficient evidence is presented and some hostages are found guilty, then two problems will arise. First, we will have on our hands some hostages who are found innocent of the charges, but have remained in captivity more than nine months. Who will defend against the claims of such hostages? Second, all diplomats caught in the act of spying throughout the world so far have been expelled from the host country. Not even a single diplomat has so far been tried and punished for espionage anywhere in the world. So, if we do so, our confrontation with the world will continue. Especially, we shall not be able to restore our U. S.-usurped rights. Whether we hold one or fifty-two hostages will make no difference in this respect."

Finally, Ghotbzadeh added up the financial and diplomatic cost to Iran of holding the hostages, and concluded that in every domain Iran found itself isolated. He closed his letter with a stirring peroration.

"Dear sisters and brothers, hear my sincere plea," the Foreign Minister concluded. "I know well that writing such a letter to the Majlis will prompt a new wave of libel and defamation against me and provide ammunition for biased critics out to justify their unfounded accusations of the past. I have exposed myself to diverse attacks and prepared myself for martyrdom whether political or otherwise. Scorn and torture are the necessary consequences of choosing this way."

That same day, August 18, 1980, Sadegh Ghotbzadeh, "the son-in-law of the Prophet," tendered his resignation as Foreign Minister to his spiritual "father," the Ayatollah Khomeini. Less than three months later, prayer rug in hand, he went off to jail. But by then the impasse on the hostage crisis had long since been broken—at least in part as a consequence of his lance.

chapter twenty

A New Season

". . . we must especially note that one of our main conditions, the extradition of the deposed Shah, has become irrelevant."—Sadegh Ghotbzadeh, in his August 18, 1980, letter to the Majlis.

IT HAD NOT BEEN AN EASY DEATH.

The Shah's spleen had finally been removed on March 28, five days after his arrival in Egypt. Michael E. DeBakey performed the surgery at Maadi Hospital, a military facility along the banks of the Nile near Cairo.

For a while after the operation, the prognosis seemed favorable. There had been no visible evidence that the lymphoma was still present in the Shah's body, Dr. DeBakey reported. The Shah had apparently responded well to drug therapy. But the spleen had had to be removed in any case, because it was producing anemia and depressing platelets and white cells; as soon as it was out, the platelet and white-cell counts returned to normal and the anemia began to recede.

Reviewing the surgery a few days later, DeBakey said that it had gone well from a technical point of view. The operation had been easier to do in Egypt than it would have been in Panama, he added, because he had had the full support and cooperation of the Egyptians. As an indication of the positive mood, President Anwar Sadat conferred his nation's highest civilian award on Dr. DeBakey in a televised ceremony, and secondary awards on the American, French and Egyptian doctors who had assisted him.

The optimistic mood did not last. The Shah never fully recovered from the surgery, and before long it was evident that the lymph cancer had spread to other parts of his body. On June 27 he was rushed back to Maadi Hospital with a high fever, and underwent emergency surgery to deal with a pancreatic abscess. Once again, as in Panama, the air filled with medical innuendo, with Egyptian doctors muttering about the presumption of the Americans and the Americans wondering about the competence of the French and the Egyptians, until it seemed at times as though the process had become more important than the patient. An Egyptian newspaper, *Al Ahram,* reported that a surgical instrument had grazed the Shah's pancreas, which is adjacent to the spleen, during the initial operation, causing damage that led to the formation of a cyst. Newspaper reports, probably abetted by Egyptian physicians, pointed out that Dr. DeBakey was best known as a heart surgeon rather than an abdominal surgeon. In Houston, DeBakey denied that there had been a surgical error; he blamed the problem on anti-cancer drugs, which, he said, had damaged the Shah's ability to withstand infection. There were other newspaper reports—stimulated, perhaps, by the Americans—that the Egyptian doctors had prescribed too strong a chemotherapy program.

The charges and countercharges were as useless as they were unseemly. There was no way to apportion blame, and no point in trying. The truth was stark and simple: it was time for the Shah to die.

Medically, the Shah had been between the proverbial "rock and a hard place" ever since his treatment began. The objective of the extraordinarily powerful chemotherapeutic agents he had been receiving for eight years was to kill the young cancerous cells that were multiplying in his body. In the process, however, the chemotherapeutic agents also killed everything else in the body that divides and multiplies: lymphoid tissue, which produces the proteins in the body that resist infection, and white cells, the first line of defense against infection. The Shah's illness, histiocytic lymphoma, can be checked for a long time if caught early enough, but eventually either the disease or the treatment will overpower the body. At some point in the treatment, the white-cell count will fall to such low levels that the medication can no longer be given; then the body must be permitted to replenish itself with white cells. In the interim, the cancer grows.

Essentially, it's a contest that can't be won. The treatment can only stave off defeat—for a while.

When chemotherapy is given, resistance to disease is essentially abolished. Under these circumstances the slightest infection can become rampant and kill within twenty-four hours. Normally, the body's white cells attack and destroy the bacteria as the blood goes through the spleen and liver. But when white cells have been diminished to such low levels that there aren't enough to fight the bacteria, "blood poisoning" occurs. That is how the Shah would die.

He underwent three operations in three days, one of them to remove three pints of pus and water that had accumulated beneath his lungs. From that point on it was accepted, even by him, that he would not leave the hospital alive.

He spent much of his last month of life alone. The Shahbanou and Princess Ashraf visited him regularly, but none of the children came, and two of them went to Alexandria to remove themselves from the sadness. Only two people maintained a constant vigil—Mark Morse of Robert Armao's staff, and Ardeshir Zahedi, the former Iranian ambassador to Washington.

Morse was there to help the Shah prepare the American version of his book, *Answer to History*. They were working from the transcript of ten hours of taped interviews the Shah had made with Morse the previous month. As the Shah's strength ebbed, his voice faded until it was barely audible, and Morse would have to lean close to hear him. But the dying monarch remained coherent throughout. "Don't use that," or, "Forget about that," he would instruct Morse on hearing statements about personalities that he had made in anger and wanted eliminated from the book.

Zahedi was there out of love and remorse. The Shah had bitterly denounced the diplomat after his ouster, which he blamed in part, at least, on Zahedi's advice. For more than a year Zahedi had been trying to reestablish himself at the Shah's side, to no avail. The Shah had spurned him in the Bahamas, and sent him packing in Mexico with the observation, "The man is crazy." But Zahedi turned up in Egypt just as the Shah's condition grew grave. This time the Shah, knowing that he had only a few weeks to live, let his repentant former confidant stay.

Three weeks after the final surgery, Mark Morse telephoned Robert Armao in New York to report that the Shah seemed progressively weaker even though the French doctors were saying he was getting better and better. Morse urged Armao to assemble a new team of American physicians and fly them to Egypt. "It's too late," Armao said. He, himself, made plans to fly to Cairo to be with the Shah at the end. But he would arrive too late.

For weeks, the Shah's temperature had been above normal. On July 26 it suddenly rose precipitously as the bacteria proliferated throughout his defenseless body. At ten o'clock that evening he went into shock. The family and few remaining retainers gathered quickly: the Shahbanou, Princess Ashraf, his son Reza and eldest daughter Farahnaz, a military aide, Colonel Kiomars Jananbini and, finally, his valet of twenty-five years, Amir Pourshoja, whose violent grieving worried the others because he had a weak heart. Through the night they waited, as the Shah's breathing became more and more labored. Morning came. Death seemed moments away. The family gathered at either side of the bed, Morse and Zahedi at the foot, the colonel and Pourshoja off to one side. Seven members of the Shah's medical team were also standing by.

At last the Shah stopped breathing. Mark Morse looked at his watch; it was 9:56 A.M.

For a moment, there was silence. Then Pourshoja put his head against the wall and began to wail so violently that the others feared for his life.

An Egyptian doctor removed the needles from the Shah's arms. The Shahbanou removed the wedding ring from his finger, and then withdrew a small version of the Koran that her husband had kept beneath his pillow. Then she closed his eyes, and she and Reza kissed him on the cheek.

The Iranian newspapers carried massive headlines that day, but there was no explosion of joy. As one resident of Teheran put it, the Shah might be an abominable man, but it was never appropriate to rejoice over someone's death. The only good thing one could say was that the myth was dead, at last. The Shah would not return.

"The Shah returned or the Shah dead is the solution to the problem," Christian Bourguet, the French lawyer, had told the Americans in London. The Americans could only hope that Bourguet had been right, and they set out to see if he was.

Iran had a Prime Minister, at last: Mohammed Ali Rajai, a former primary-school teacher who had been arrested and tortured by the

Savak. On August 31 Secretary of State Edmund Muskie, who had succeeded Cyrus Vance two weeks after Vance's resignation, sent a letter to the newly appointed Rajai. In the letter, Muskie asked Rajai to take a new look at the hostage situation. He promised that the United States would recognize Iran's revolutionary regime and not interfere in Iran's internal affairs if the hostages were freed.

But Rajai did not reply.

It was 8 A.M. on September 9—the normal starting time in the office of Secretary of State Muskie—when his secretary, Carole Parmalee, received a telephone call from Fredo Dannenbring, the first minister of the West German Embassy in Washington. Dannenbring told Parmalee that he had a message for Muskie from the West German Foreign Minister, Hans Dietrich Genscher. The message was urgent, Dannenbring said, but he did not explain why.

Parmalee put Dannenbring's call on hold, conferred briefly with her boss, and then came back on the line. Dannenbring could see the Secretary within the hour.

A call of that kind always prompts some immediate organizing at the upper echelon of the State Department, so that the Secretary of State will have a backup group with him for the interview. The organization of the group fell to Arnold Raphel, one of Muskie's two executive assistants. Raphel, an expert on Iran who speaks fluent Farsi, called Leon Billings, Muskie's other assistant, whose area of expertise is Europe. "Do you want to take this? It's a European matter," Raphel said.

"It doesn't sound that exciting," Billings said. He had more pressing matters on his agenda. He asked Raphel if he would sit in, and Raphel agreed.

With Muskie when Dannenbring arrived at 9 A.M. were Warren M. Christopher, the Deputy Secretary of State, George Vest, the Assistant Secretary of State for European Affairs, Raphel, and a junior desk officer who had recently been assigned to the German desk. The desk officer was there to take notes, and was mildly nervous at finding himself in the office of the Secretary of State in his first weeks on the job.

Dannenbring did not waste time. He unfolded a one-and-a-half-page communiqué in German that had come in overnight from Bonn, and proceeded to translate it for the group.

The message had nothing to do with Europe. It reported that a high-ranking official in the Iranian Government, who was also a close friend of the Ayatollah Khomeini, had been authorized by his government—with Khomeini's approval—to meet secretly in West Germany with a high-level official of the United States Government, with a view to solving the hostage problem as rapidly as possible.

The Iranian was Sadegh Tabatabai, a state secretary in the Iranian Government. He had been Deputy Premier of Iran during the government of Mehdi Bazargan. Tabatabai had spent his exile in Germany; he was married to a German woman, and spoke German fluently. The most impressive fact about him to the Americans concerned his sister; she was the wife of Ahmed Khomeini, the Ayatollah's son.

The Americans received the news with reserve. Their mood did not change even after Dannenbring had left. They had been burned too many times by the Iranians in the preceding ten months to get excited. And yet they couldn't help but wonder if this time might be different. The message was genuine, no doubt about that. It had come from Tabatabai himself, forwarded to Bonn via Gerhardt Ritzel, the West German ambassador to Teheran. Arnold Raphel, the only man in the room with experience in Iran, was impressed. "I think this sounds good," he said.

Then Muskie telephoned President Carter to inform him of the news.

"Come on over," the President said at once.

Both Muskie and the President agreed, however, that it would be wise to have the message from the Germans translated so that they could study the entire text. The task was given to the young desk officer, with the strictest instructions that he was not to talk to anyone or use a secretary to have the translation typed. The young man paled; he, himself, did not know how to type. It did not help his concentration to be reminded by jest on two occasions that morning that he was not to talk to anyone, or that he was keeping the President of the United States waiting.

While the text was being translated, Arnold Raphel wrote a covering memorandum for the President in the secretary's name. Point one was that they shouldn't get too excited. Point two was that the information should be "tightly held." Point three was that in all the negotiations to free the hostages, this was the first time that an Iranian had attempted to contact an American, rather than the other way around.

At four o'clock that afternoon, Muskie and Christopher finally saw the President. When Carter finished reading the message from the Germans, he looked up at Christopher. "Chris," he said, "I want you to go yourself."

Warren Christopher is a Californian who goes against the grain of that state's reputation for ebullient behavior. Taciturn, at times severe, he looks exactly like what he has been for most of his adult life—a utility company lawyer, with a head for complex issues and figures. Christopher had served in the administrations of John F. Kennedy and Lyndon B. Johnson; his nomination as Deputy Secretary of State was one of the best political appointments Jimmy Carter had made. If negotiations with the Iranians were truly about to materialize, the casting couldn't have been better.

That day, with the President's approval, Christopher established an interagency task force to work out an American position in anticipation of the coming negotiations. The group consisted of Lloyd Cutler, counsel to the President; G. William Miller, Secretary of the Treasury; Robert Carswell, his deputy; Benjamin Civiletti, the Attorney General, and his deputy, John Harmon; Harold Saunders of the State Department; Roberts Owen, who had argued America's case against Iran at the World Court in The Hague; Douglas Dworkin, Warren Christopher's assistant; and Arnold Raphel.

Together, they drew up a response to the West Germans, indicating the willingness of the United States Government to meet in West Germany with Sadegh Tabatabai. Warren Christopher would be the American representative.

The Americans added a kicker to the response. While they believed the Germans were relaying the message from Tabatabai in good faith, they wanted some form of reassurance as to his authority to negotiate in behalf of the Iranian Government.

Normally, the Secretary of State or Deputy Secretary would sign off on such a message. But this one was taken to President Carter for his review after Muskie had approved it. It was late that evening before Arnold Raphel had delivered the American response to Fredo Dannenbring at the West German Embassy. Dannenbring immediately translated it himself and cabled it to Bonn.

Tabatabai's response was back, via the Germans, in less than forty-eight hours. It informed the Americans that the Ayatollah Khomeini would deliver a major address the following day. In that speech, there would be a paragraph listing the four major points to be satisfied before the hostages could be released: the return of the Shah's wealth; the cancellation of U.S. claims against Iran; a guarantee of no U.S. military and political intervention; and the unfreezing of Iranian assets held in U.S. banks.

There is a radio monitoring service in the Department of State's cavernous building at Foggy Bottom that the professionals refer to as "Fibis," after its initials, FBIS. Its official name is the Foreign Broadcast Intercept Service. When the Ayatollah Khomeini spoke in Teheran on September 12, Fibis was on the job, taping the broadcast for anyone who might need to listen to it, translating the speech from Farsi to English and putting it on the teletype machines for distribution to the operations centers of the State Department and the various country desks.

Early that morning, Arnold Raphel dropped into the office of the Iranian working group adjoining the operations center to read the text of the Ayatollah's speech. Within minutes, the sense of expectation he had felt began to ebb. No big deal, he thought. It was another typical Khomeini speech, full of revolutionary fervor and anti-American invective.

Suddenly, Raphel straightened. In the heart of the speech was a paragraph so different in tone, it was as though someone had put a piece of paper in front of the Ayatollah and ordered him to read:

"On the return of the deposed Shah's wealth and the cancellation of all the United States claims against Iran, a guarantee of no United States military and political interventions in Iran and the freeing of all our investments, the hostages will be freed."

Raphel tore off the copy from the teletype machine, raced through the halls and burst into Warren Christopher's office. "I think we've got somebody we can talk to," he said.

The implication of the first message from the Germans had been that Sadegh Tabatabai had come forward to identify himself the moment the Iranians decided they wanted to make a deal. That was not the case at all. What would prove to be the first major breakthrough in the hostage crisis since negotiations had been abandoned the previous April had been under development for many months, in a textbook example of diplomatic initiative by the German ambassador, Gerhardt Ritzel.

Except for his impeccable dress, Ritzel looks more like a contented burgher than an experienced foreign service officer. He is in his late fifties, a heavyset man with a round face, white hair and a most undiplomatic lack of reserve. His stories betray concern and affection for the people they portray. That capacity for empathy helped him to pick up, early in his tour of duty in Teheran, that a revolution was coming.

The moment of truth for him occurred in early October, 1978, during the period when the Shah, in an effort to stem the floods of protest, eased up on his censorship of the opposition. One consequence was a program of lectures by Iranian writers and poets, all of them anti-Shah, that was to run over seven nights. The organizers anticipated a nightly turnout of three hundred. The first night two thousand persons appeared, forcing a move to a larger auditorium. By the fourth night, the crowds were so large that no hall could hold them. The lectures were moved outdoors. The audience overflowed onto the streets, obstructing traffic, unmindful of the rain and the cold as they listened to the lyrics of opposition.

Public identification with opposition elements was still risky business at that time. Yet 80,000 Iranians had effectively risked it by the time the lecture series ended. To Ritzel, who had played a behind-the-scenes role in the organization of the event, the message was unmistakable. From that moment on, he did what any good diplomat does under such circumstances—what the Americans should have done and would have done had they not been compromised by their relationship with the Shah. He made contact with the opposition.

At first, it was strictly a cloak-and-dagger operation—standing under the third tree from the corner on a certain block, waiting for a blue car to come along, then driving for two hours through the streets of Teheran, followed by a sudden transfer to a black car and another hour's circuitous drive until the driver was satisfied that they had not been followed. Finally, Ritzel would be driven to the meeting place, where he would be met and inspected by an armed guard.

In such manner did Ritzel meet with some of the men who would become the leaders of the country once the Shah was toppled. One of those men was Mehdi Bazargan, the first post-revolutionary Prime Minister. Two others, Mahmoud Araghani and Hazrat Shirazi, were ayatollahs. By the time the opposition took power, Ritzel was the best-connected diplomat in Iran. When the Ayatollah Mahmoud Taleghani, a major force in the revolution, died on Setpember 10, 1979, the German ambassador was the only Westerner invited to the funeral.

Ritzel's popularity with the new regime was due to more than his early interest and the contacts he had made. To his dismay, he discovered what he described to friends as an "irrational German reputation" in Iran. There were two aspects of the Third Reich of Adolf Hitler that these Iranians found congenial. The first was the war against Great Britain, which helped to loosen that country's hold on Iran. The second was the "Final Solution," Hitler's massacre of the Jews. Whenever Ritzel heard such commentary, it tested all his diplomatic skills. He himself had emigrated from Nazi Germany in protest against the policies of the regime.

Another factor complicating Ritzel's work was that he did not speak Farsi. But he quickly developed, nonetheless, an acute feel for the extraordinary communication patterns existing in Iran. Contacts were rarely direct at the outset—rather, one exposed one's interests to, say, half a dozen persons over tea in the bazaar. One of those persons might know someone who might know someone, in turn, who could lead you to the individual you needed. It was a process of tying off a thousand little knots so that by the time you found the man capable of making the decision, he had a carpet to stand on.

Before such an intercession could take place, a prospective intermediary would have to be persuaded by your line of reasoning. Only then would he argue in your behalf.

The one man in Iran whom Ritzel most needed to reach was the Ayatollah Khomeini. On two occasions during the hostage crisis—in December 1979 and again in February 1980—he was offered an audience with the imam. But he had seen on television what happened during such audiences: his diplomatic colleagues would sit cross-legged on the floor, listening to the imam's lecture, understanding nothing. Ritzel, accordingly, set forth some conditions of the prospective audience: he was to be allowed his own interpreter, there must be a dialogue, not simply a monologue by the imam, and there was to be no television coverage. The audience did not materialize.

But Ritzel's objective remained the same—to reach the Ayatollah, and in a telling way.

One of the tasks the ambassador had set himself on being appointed to Iran was to make a thorough study of the Koran, and of Islamic law in general. In the ninth chapter of the Koran he had found a passage stating that a foreign envoy in an Islamic country must be treated gently, even if the country of that envoy declares war on the Islamic country. One day in June, Ritzel took that information with him to Meshed, the holy city, where he had arranged an audience with an ayatollah who was close to Khomeini. Portraying himself as a student of Islamic law, Ritzel asked the ayatollah to discuss with him the meaning of three words or phrases: truth, justice and the way to treat guests. Two and one half days of discussions ensued. "Why do you come?" the ayatollah asked the ambassador at last.

"I would like an interpretation of those words," Ritzel replied

"Why do you come?" the ayatollah insisted.

"Do you really want to know?"

"Yes."

"I know now that you are against truth, justice and the gentle treatment of guests."

"You are right," the ayatollah sighed.

What Ritzel had succeeded in drawing from the ayatollah was the admission that the holding of the hostages was a betrayal of Islamic law. That interpretation, he would subsequently learn, eventually made its way to the Ayatollah Khomeini.

It was in this same indirect fashion, styled on the ways of the bazaar, that Ritzel finally managed to deliver the most critical message of all to the Ayatollah Khomeini via Sadegh Tabatabai.

Tabatabai's credentials as an intermediary could scarcely have been better. In addition to being related by marriage to the Ayatollah, he had been profoundly involved, himself, in the Islamic revolution. Twenty years before, as a university student, he had helped his friend Sadegh Ghotbzadeh found the Islamic Students Association. When the Islamic students fell afoul of the regime of Mohammed Reza Pahlavi, many of them were imprisoned, tortured and then sent into exile. Sadegh Ghotbzadeh and Ibrahim Yazdi went to the United States. Abolhassan Bani-Sadr went to France. Sadegh Tabatabai went to Germany, where he learned German, married a German woman and remained until the Ayatollah Khomeini came to France at the end of 1978. Tabatabai thereupon joined his fellow exiles and friends, and assisted in the final push from abroad that helped to topple the Shah. When the imam returned in triumph to Iran on February 1, 1979, Tabatabai was with him.

Soon Tabatabai was the Deputy Premier of Iran. For Ritzel, he was a find—a highly placed Iranian who spoke German. Tabatabai enjoyed their association as well; it helped him maintain his German. The two men would meet twice a week to discuss Iran and the revolution. Ritzel found Tabatabai's mind young and fresh and open, but he was tough all the same, and preferred toughness in return. The two men grew to like each other not simply as professionals but as friends. The closeness they developed made possible the frank and sometimes brutal exchange of views that was needed once the hostages had been seized.

On November 4, 1979, two hours after the embassy had been overrun, Ritzel called Tabatabai. "Now what's this?" he asked.

"If we ever get out of this we'll be lucky," Tabatabai replied.

From that moment on, the two men were in constant touch, and their contacts were all clandestine. Once again, Ritzel would take a circuitous route to their meeting place. Tabatabai would do the same. Nor were there witnesses to the crucial portion of their talks; if ever a third party was present at the rendezvous, he would leave when the discussions began.

From the outset, Tabatabai acknowledged that the seizure of the hostages had been detrimental to Iran. But he sympathized completely with the students in their grievances against the United States. His arguments were the classic ones: the United States had reimposed the Shah; the Shah had stolen Iran's wealth; his policies had set back Iranian development.

Ritzel, for his part, would attempt to explain the role of the United States in the context of the geopolitical struggle between East and West. But his arguments would be blunted to an extent by his own firsthand knowledge of some of the excesses to which Tabatabai referred. One example: the Shah had bought from the United States more than five hundred Bell helicopters that had been used in Vietnam, at a cost in excess of $500 million. You could see them everywhere, but they never flew.

Ritzel's major argument with Tabatabai was that Iran needed the world's approval for its revolution and could not, therefore, afford the hostage issue. Tabatabai agreed. But how the issue should be resolved was another matter. On this, their arguments were violent.

"They have to apologize," Tabatabai would insist.

"Never. It can't be done," Ritzel would reply.

"They have to return the money. You can't even raise the question of a solution with me until the money is returned," Tabatabai would say.

"You must prove that that money was transferred illegally out of Iran," Ritzel would argue.

As the dialogues continued, Ritzel kept his own government informed, but he balked about telling the Americans. When Bonn suggested that the ambassador go to the United States for direct contacts, Ritzel vetoed the suggestion; he did not want his passport stamped by U. S. Immigration lest it end his usefulness. Even the offer of a second passport did not persuade him; he felt the most important thing was to keep his distance to be certain his usefulness wasn't compromised.

Ritzel did see Edmund Muskie at the end of May, when Muskie, newly appointed as Secretary of State, came to Bonn. Ritzel had been evacuated from Teheran earlier that month after running such a high fever that he couldn't speak. The two men met for coffee at the residence of the American ambassador. The ambassador was not unknown to Muskie because he had been in almost daily communication by cable with Warren Christopher since the beginning of the hostage crisis. A month had passed since Tabas. Ritzel told Muskie that he could try to be helpful in the future, but that he would have to be assured that there would be no second rescue attempt. Muskie nodded his head.

As soon as he returned to Teheran, Ritzel resumed his dialogues with Sadegh Tabatabai. Gradually, the issues in the dispute between Iran and the United States began to sort themselves into two categories: those that were negotiable, and those that were not.

There were three concessions that Iran had no business even asking for, Ritzel argued: the return of the Shah's money without legal process, the right to sue the U.S. diplomats who had served in Iran, and an apology from the United States.

There were four points, however, that could be discussed: the return of the Shah's wealth by legal means, the cancellation of all claims by the United States against Iran, guarantees against future American involvement in Iran's internal affairs, and the return of embargoed funds.

Ritzel wrote out the four points and handed them to Sadegh Tabatabai. Tabatabai gave them, in turn, to his brother-in-law, Ahmed Khomeini, along with all the arguments, so carefully worked through with Ritzel, as to why these points, and only these points, could possibly be negotiated.

In due time Ahmed Khomeini passed the four points on to his father, and eventually the imam accepted them. But before he would permit them to be passed on to the Americans, he insisted that they be approved by a committee of the Majlis. Because the imam had accepted them, their approval was foreordained. But which members of the Majlis would serve on the committee? To avoid any ambiguities or questions, there could be no liberals on the seven-man committee. They all had to be hard-liners.

They were. And they endorsed the four points.

On September 14, 1980, Warren Christopher and his interagency group—minus Lloyd Cutler, who remained in Washington as the group's contact man with President Carter—boarded a huge Air Force transport for a flight to Europe. The plane was loaded with military personnel and other government employees going to various parts of the Continent on official missions. As far as any of them knew, Christopher's group was on a routine economics mission. The Deputy Secretary of State would also confer with British Prime Minister Margaret Thatcher, West German Chancellor Helmut Schmidt and French President Giscard d'Estaing on the crisis in Poland, which was just beginning to develop. In the next several days, the press would be told that Christopher's discussions with the world leaders had extended to plans for new U.S.-Soviet disarmament talks. All of these were cover stories meant to disguise the one purpose of Christopher's mission: to meet with Iran's representative, Sadegh Tabatabai, in the hope of resolving the hostage crisis at long last.

The Americans were hopeful. There were reasons, they felt, why the Iranians might want to get rid of the problem. The most important of these was that the political value of the hostages had ended; with the grudging appointment by President Bani-Sadr of Mohammed Ali Rajai as Prime Minister, the long struggle for power between the liberals and the clergy was over. The clerics had won. Now that they were in power and had control of the Majlis, moreover, the responsibility to perform was theirs. In that context, the hostage problem was a diversion. There was no further public relations value to be gained within Iran by holding the hostages. The external reaction had always been negative. Finally, as even the hard-liners had been reminded on August 18 by Sadegh Ghotbzadeh, the sanctions against Iran were hurting the country.

For the first time since the hostages had been seized more than ten months before, the Americans at last had something to go on. Once four specific conditions for the release of the hostages had been stated, they could develop a position that responded to those points.

But what most buoyed the Americans was an idea that *hadn't* been expressed. The four points listed by the Ayatollah Khomeini in his speech did not include a demand that the Americans apologize to Iran. That was the best sign yet that the Iranians were ready to deal.

In the days before Warren Christopher was to meet with Sadegh Tabatabai, Arnold Raphel gave him a crash course in the Persian mentality, particularly as it exhibited itself in negotiations. What it boiled down to was that Persians did not like to deal with details. They preferred to reach a broad understanding of a problem and work out an agreement in principle. The details would be elaborated by the technicians.

There were two possible tracks he could take, Raphel advised Christopher. He could do a "cut-and-dry job," attempting to pin down everything, in which case he would probably "lose" Tabatabai. Or he could try to reach an agreement in principle.

"Let's take the second track," Christopher said.

When the Americans arrived in Germany, they were driven directly to a government villa outside Bonn where, they supposed, the meeting with Tabatabai would take place. But the schedule was still up in the air and several members of the group decided to go sight-seeing. Christopher and Raphel remained behind and were just sitting down to a late lunch when they received word from Hans Dietrich Genscher, the West German Foreign Minister, that the site of the meeting had been changed for security reasons, and the meeting would take place in one hour and a half. When the Germans came to pick the Americans up, the others still hadn't returned. Christopher and Raphel went to the meeting alone.

Only much later would it become apparent that the Americans might have been set up. The change in scene and time might not have been for reasons of security at all, and the sudden setting of the appointment might not have been an accident. Tabatabai, who had come alone to Germany, did not want to feel overwhelmed in a room filled with American negotiators, and the Germans may have maneuvered the Americans in such a way in order to meet the Iranian's demands.

They drove out of the city for twenty minutes in an unmarked German car. Finally, they arrived at a one-story country house that looked as if it might be some government official's hideaway. They were admitted to a foyer, and then to a living room with a row of glass doors leading to a terrace. On the patio terrace were Genscher and another man they presumed to be Tabatabai. It was.

As they walked outside to meet him, it struck Raphel at once that here was a Frenchified Iranian wearing a French silk suit—nothing at all like the tough revolutionary he had expected. To Christopher, he looked like any well-dressed, successful American businessman in his early forties.

As they were introduced and shook hands, Tabatabai smiled lightly, and then exchanged pleasantries for a few moments in English. After all the bluster and acrimony and arm's-length exchanges of the last ten months, this first direct encounter between official representatives of the governments of Iran and the United States seemed totally out of key.

Then it was time to negotiate. As they turned to go inside the house, there was a moment's awkwardness as Christopher and Tabatabai each gestured for the other to go first. That awkwardness vanished as soon as they began to talk.

Christopher began. "We both probably have a number of speeches that we might want to make to each other," he said. "But I think it would be more efficient if we focused on the conditions for the return of the hostages."

Tabatabai nodded. His response was in German, which was translated by Genscher's interpreter. In any language, it was music. "My government wishes to resolve the problem of the hostages quickly. If an agreement can be achieved, the Americans will be free in a relatively short time."

Heartened, Christopher moved quickly to the four points. For the Americans, one of the demands presented no problem. The United States would pledge not to interfere in the internal affairs of Iran.

The return of the Shah's fortune was another matter. "You want the Shah's assets. It's not in our power to give them to you," Christopher explained. "We don't know where they are, and we couldn't give them to you if we did know. Our legal system proscribes that kind of seizure without due process."

However, Christopher went on, if Iran wished to engage in legal proceedings to discover and lay claim to the Shah's wealth on the grounds that it had been illegally expropriated, the United States would offer what counsel and assistance it could.

On the matter of unfreezing Iran's assets in the United States and in U.S. banks abroad, there was no problem for the American Government. President Carter had frozen the assets by executive order; he could countermand that order at any time. But the American Government had no control over whatever legal actions might be taken by its

citizens, and American citizens had already filed three hundred lawsuits against Iran, asking judgments of some $6 billion. Those lawsuits
envisaged the settlement of claims out of Iran's $8 billion in frozen as-
sets.

The United States could renounce its own claims against Iran for
holding its diplomats hostage, but whether the U. S. Government
could deliver Iran and its assets from private American claims was another matter altogether, Christopher told Tabatabai.

Throughout, Tabatabai listened intently. He let Christopher do
most of the talking. When he did reply, his manner was curt,
reaffirming Arnold Raphel's initial judgment that he was not a typical
Persian. The typical Persian spoke in a deferential and roundabout
manner, and with a certain flowery style. On the other hand, if Tabatabai was a Frenchified Iranian, he was also one tough revolutionary.

The meeting broke up after almost three hours, with an agreement
to meet in two days after both sides had had an opportunity to talk to
their respective governments.

The Americans thought they had done well, and the Germans
agreed. Their assessment was reinforced two days later when the same
group sat down for breakfast at 7 A.M. on September 17 in the same
small country house.

When Tabatabai spoke, it was in Persian, with a classical Persian
phrase. The American response to the four demands, he said, was "not
an unwelcome position."

Tabatabai told the Americans that he had some speeches to make in
Germany, and would not be returning to Iran until September 22. But
as soon as he was back, he said, he would take up their response in
earnest.

The Americans were pleased to hear this, but what stuck in their
minds was that Persian phrase, "not an unwelcome position."

Before going to Germany, Warren Christopher had figured that the
prospects of gaining the early release of the hostages were about one
in ten. Now, in the wake of the Iranians' response, he raised the odds
to fifty-fifty.

But on September 22, the day Sadegh Tabatabai was to return to
Iran, the prospects were suddenly nil. Sadegh Tabatabai was stuck in
Germany, and the Iranians wanted nothing to do with negotiations to
free the hostages.

They were at war with Iraq.

K

chapter twenty-one

A Matter of Money

IT WAS AN OLD SCORE THAT IRAQ, ENCOURAGED BY WHAT IT PER-
ceived as the disintegration of leadership in Iran, had chosen to settle.
Years before, the Shah, armed to the teeth by the Americans, had
been able to impose his will on the Iraqis by claiming sovereignty over
some disputed oil-rich territories on the border that separated the two
countries.

"Our only hope is that the two nations can resolve the situation
peacefully," Secretary of State Edmund Muskie told the UN General
Assembly. But the Iranians didn't believe him. Was there not a conspiracy behind everything? To them, this one was clear: the United
States had pushed Iraq into war with Iran in order to force Iran to free
the hostages.

On September 23, one day after the proclamation by Iraq of "full-
scale war" against Iran, Iran Radio announced the formal decision by
the Majlis to freeze the hostage issue. The hostages, the announcement
said, had been moved to a new secret location.

Never had a solution to the crisis seemed further away.

The Americans did not stop trying. In mid-October, they learned
that Mohammed Ali Rajai, the Iranian Prime Minister, would be arriving in New York momentarily to plead Iran's case against Iraq before the UN Security Council. They quickly drew up a list of Third
World diplomats who might conceivably intercede in their behalf and
arrange a meeting for them with Rajai. One name stood out, that of
Mohammed Bedjaoui, the Algerian ambassador to the UN.

If any nation would seem congenial to the Iranians, that nation was
Algeria. It was an Islamic country, to begin with; it was a revolutionary country as well, having won its independence from France in
1961, and it had been among the first countries to acknowledge the
new government of Iran by sending an ambassador to Teheran. Finally, the Algerians had been representing the interests of Iran in the
United States since the preceding April, when formal relations between the United States and Iran were severed.

On October 15 Warren Christopher and Arnold Raphel made a
quiet trip to New York to meet with Ambassador Bedjaoui. Two days
later, Bedjaoui went to Kennedy Airport to meet Rajai as he arrived
from Teheran. He handed Rajai a note from the Americans expressing
their desire to meet with the Iranian Prime Minister. Rajai refused; he
was under strict orders from the Ayatollah Khomeini not to see any
representatives of the U. S. Government.

Rajai's trip, however, was not without its consequences. No one had
foreseen the impact his presence at the United Nations would have on
the schoolteacher turned Prime Minister. Not only was he without previous political experience, he had scarcely traveled before. With his
two-day growth of beard and his white shirt buttoned to the collar, he
seemed completely out of his realm. It was possibly in response to
these circumstances that Rajai, beset by numbers of diplomats, four of
them from Moslem nations, counseling the immediate release of the
hostages, indicated publicly that a decision was "not far away." The
United States, he said, had already apologized "in practice" for its
support of the Shah.

The Americans were encouraged. It had obviously registered on the
Iranian Prime Minister that his country was diplomatically isolated.
But in Iran, there was consternation. What Rajai had said in New
York did not accord at all with the facts as they existed in Teheran.
Had the Prime Minister been attempting to establish his inde-
pendence? Numbers of Iranians thought so, principally because Rajai
had pointedly left for the United Nations without informing the presi-
dent of the country, Bani-Sadr, that he was going.

The last thing those who had been closest to the efforts to free the
hostages wanted was for the Americans to develop a false sense of
hope. They knew that it would only cause the hard-liners to get their
backs up—which, in fact, was exactly what had happened in Iran following Rajai's pronouncements at the UN.

Even though he had not been actively involved in specific negotiations since the previous April, Héctor Villalón, the Argentine expatriate, had remained in touch with the situation, principally through his protégé Sadegh Ghotbzadeh. Watching Rajai on television in the library of his sixth-floor Paris apartment overlooking the Seine and the Eiffel Tower, Villalón was overpowered by the feeling that he was once again a relay station in the battle between the United States and Iran. His instincts were more than confirmed in a call to Ghotbzadeh in Teheran. The former Foreign Minister not only confirmed the adverse reaction by the hard-liners to Rajai's pronouncements, he indicated that unless the United States made some kind of dramatic effort, it would be months, even years, before the hostage negotiations would be back on the track.

"What should they do?" Villalón demanded.

"They should make a statement on the war that shows they have a just position," Ghotbzadeh answered at once. "With this statement, I could go to the Ayatollah and unblock the situation."

Villalón immediately contacted Bourguet, and the two men called Henry Precht at the State Department in Washington. Bourguet put the matter into a sentence: "If you really didn't encourage the war, and you consider Iraq the aggressor, you should say so."

Villalón told Precht that the quickest way to communicate the American position would be for someone in the U. S. Government to telephone Sadegh Ghotbzadeh. It was a risk for Ghotbzadeh, whose situation since his resignation had become more delicate than ever. His telephone was tapped by Iranian internal security as well as by buggers employed by the Majlis. If heard talking to an American, he could be accused of being an American spy. Nonetheless, he was willing to take that risk if it would help bring the hostage crisis to an end.

On October 19 Harold Saunders, the Assistant Secretary of State, telephoned Sadegh Ghotbzadeh from Washington and said, "The United States had no responsibility for the Iraqi invasion of Iran, and considers Iraq the aggressor in the conflict." For good measure, Secretary of State Edmund Muskie issued a public statement several hours later: "The United States has nothing to gain by taking sides in this conflict. We are working for an end to the fighting between the two nations. We believe that this conflict can and must be resolved through respect for cardinal principles of international law . . . that territory must not be seized by force of arms; that disputes should be settled by peaceful means. We are opposed to the dismemberment of Iran."

For a few days, it seemed as though the public and private statements of the Americans had done the trick. A special meeting of the Majlis was called for Monday October 27, to consider the hostage issue. A number of members of the parliament—some of them Islamic Republicans—let it be known that they were anxious to reach a quick agreement based on the four points pronounced by the Ayatollah Khomeini on September 12.

But by October 27 the members of the Majlis were once again totally preoccupied with the war. An Iranian town, Desfoul, had been heavily bombed by the Iraqis, and many Iranians had been killed.

As they filed into what had once been the Imperial Senate, the deputies offered a vivid cross-section of the components of the revolution. Some checked their pistols in the cloakroom. Others were accompanied by ferocious-looking bodyguards carrying machine guns. The members of the religious community in their black-and-white turbans seemed anachronistic next to the young people in sport shirts, the bourgeoisie in their three-piece suits and the women wearing veils. All of the deputies sat in luxurious garnet armchairs arranged in a semicircle, underneath crystal chandeliers hanging from a graceful dome. The walls, alternating green marble and beige leather, offered a final, incongruous touch.

The deputy from Desfoul, a young, bearded man wearing a light blue sweater, gave an emotional recounting of the bombing and its aftermath. Then he almost stopped the hostage debate in its tracks. "I propose that we postpone the debate indefinitely," he said. "It would be scandalous to discuss the condition of the American hostages while our citizens are being massacred."

"The hostages should stay in detention until the end of the war!" another deputy cried out.

But there were other deputies in the chamber who insisted that there were practical matters to confront, and before many hours had passed it was clear that there was much sympathy for the adoption of the Ayatollah's four conditions as a basis for a settlement.

Finally, it seemed, the realities had sunk in. The Iranians were worried about the consequences of a continued confrontation with the Americans, and realized that the embargo on trade as well as the freezing of Iranian assets in American banks would prevent Iran from importing the very equipment it needed to wage war.

On Tuesday October 28, the Ayatollah Khomeini gave a speech in which, for the first time in memory, he omitted his usual references to "the Great American Satan." The following day, an Iranian radio commentator noted that "the imprisonment of the hostages has no meaning anymore" because "America has just capitulated" and a good lesson had been given to "whoever would dare meddle with our domestic affairs."

The same day, the Ayatollah Khalkhali, whose summary judgments in the preceding year and a half had been responsible for the execution of several hundred persons, confided to journalists his personal belief that the hostages would be freed before the U.S. presidential elections on November 4, now less than a week away. "We should take advantage of the feigned generosity of Carter in order to obtain the delivery of spare parts which we have bought and paid for," Khalkhali declared. "It's a question of our national security and the lives of our citizens."

Early the next morning, the galleries of the former Imperial Senate filled with journalists and spectators in anticipation of a public debate on the hostages. The session was scheduled to begin at 8 A.M.; there was no reason to believe that it wouldn't because Islamic personalities, unlike politicians elsewhere, are noted for being on time. But by 8:30, the deputies' seats were still less than half filled. The galleries buzzed with rumors. At 8:33, Ali Akbar Hashemi Rafsanjani, speaker of the parliament, announced that the absent members were in the halls of the building but refused to be "formally present." For lack of a quorum, he said, the hostage debate was postponed.

For a moment, there was absolute silence. Then the voice of the Ayatollah Khalkhali rang through the chamber. "Quorum or no quorum, we must begin our work immediately. The problem is crucial for us. There can be no postponement."

"Be quiet!" chorused the dissidents, who by now had penetrated into the assembly and were standing at the rear.

Khalkhali's head jerked around so quickly that the turban flew from his head. "Our brothers and our children are falling by the hundreds on the battlefields!" he bellowed. "You have no right to such miserly acts! Your boycott is revolting! You're traitors, yes, traitors to the nation!"

The uproar that followed was finally silenced by the persistent ringing of Rafsanjani's hand bell. "No one here is responsible for this morning's incident," he said at last. "We were so close to a solution of the hostage affair when America and its allies set off the war against Iran. The anger of the members is understandable." For just a fraction, he paused. Then he said firmly, "The Majlis will meet again this coming Sunday at 8 A.M."

On Sunday November 2, two days before the American elections, the Majlis passed a bill setting out the four conditions under which Iran would release the hostages. Basically, they were the same four conditions announced in September by the Ayatollah Khomeini. But now they were in a much more elaborate form and used highly complicated language, as though a lawyer had become involved. That is exactly what had happened.

Ironically, the lawyer was an American: sixty-eight-year-old Leonard Boudin, a New York City attorney associated for many years with extreme left-wing groups. For twenty years, Boudin had represented Cuba's legal interests in the United States. Much of the legal work involved was as a consequence of the freezing of Cuban assets in the United States by the Americans in retaliation for the expropriation of American businesses in Cuba. Boudin considered himself a ranking expert on the legal aspects of frozen assets. It was because of this experience that Boudin had been recommended to the Iranians in the first month of the hostage crisis by Sean MacBride. Now, almost one year later, the complications produced by Boudin's involvement were, in effect, Sean MacBride's last revenge for the rejection of his MacBride Commission.

It was 4 A.M. in Chicago when Jimmy Carter, asleep in his hotel room following a day of campaigning, was awakened with news of the Majlis action. The President flew back to Washington at once. As he stepped from his helicopter on the South Lawn of the White House, Zbigniew Brzezinski gave him a copy of the Majlis bill, translated into English. Carter read it as he walked toward the White House. Before he was across the lawn, he knew that he was not going to be able to announce a solution of the crisis before the election on Tuesday.

A few hours later, a subdued and badly disappointed Jimmy Carter announced to the nation that the response of the Iranians had been a positive one, but would require negotiations. The United States would continue to seek a solution, he said, regardless of the outcome of the elections. "I wish I could predict when the hostages will return. I cannot," Jimmy Carter said.

Tuesday November 4, Election Day, was also the first anniversary of the seizure of the hostages. The symbolism was too much for the American people; they rebuked Jimmy Carter, whose decision to admit the Shah of Iran to the United States for medical treatment had led to a year of frustration, anguish and humiliation.

The Majlis had made one other decision on November 2, to approve the Algerians as the mediators in the coming negotiations. Despite the role the West Germans had played in putting the United States on the right track, the Iranians now in power saw West Germany as an ideological and political ally of the country they considered "The Great Satan," and preferred to deal through the sure friends they believed the Algerians to be.

The Algerians would soon find out that as difficult as their work would be, it had been made fractionally easier by a number of Americans who had been quietly working to break through the glacial postures. Many of these people, who, from a distance, seemed like do-gooders or glory hounds, were actually experienced crisis mediators—a loose network of professors, clergy and others who had developed their skills in the riot-torn streets of urban America and in confrontations between labor and management. They were the advocates of a new social science known as crisis intervention. They journeyed to Iran with the help of the Departments of State and Justice, carrying with them carefully prepared scripts okayed by the government that they hoped would produce a breakthrough in Iran-U.S. relations.

Their work was almost universally misunderstood by their fellow citizens. They were called "amateurs," "meddlers" and "subversives." One of them, a University of Kansas professor, lost his job. The family of another received bomb threats. Several American ministers were accused of allowing themselves to be used as propaganda tools. As anger and defensiveness over the international affront mounted in the minds of Americans, so did their suspicion and resentment of the private business that was taking these people to Iran. The often positive and highly visible reaction of the Iranians to these missionaries was proof to their American critics of their duplicity.

A key figure in these sub-rosa negotiations was Roger Fisher, a Harvard law-school professor whose specialty was international mediation. Fisher had once mediated a dispute involving the Iranians. He was also well connected, having taught many Iranian students who subsequently became key figures in the present government.

Shortly after the hostages were taken, Fisher sent the State Department a memo arguing against the imposition of sanctions. When the sanctions were imposed he was openly critical of the action, and said so in articles for *Newsweek* and *Time*.

But Fisher was an inveterate follower of international conflicts, and he watched with avid interest and mounting apprehension as the negotiations floundered. The author of a textbook that detailed the potential problems in any negotiating situation, he knew that this one had them all.

Fisher's experience had taught him that the only way to overcome certain problems in negotiations was to change the players and return to "Go." What was needed before anything, he believed, was a change of emotional climate; what was also needed was a mediator capable of helping the combatants identify the problems, and who could get them to engage in small acts of good will—small acts that, with little cost, would produce a constructive emotional impact.

By late summer of 1980, with the negotiations at a standstill, the Americans became concerned to the point of distraction about their apparent failure to understand the Iranians' point of view. They had long accepted that the Iranians hadn't the slightest clue as to what the problem looked like from the American point of view. Who was better equipped to do something about this basic negotiating problem than Roger Fisher? the Americans asked themselves. Would he be willing to go to Iran? they asked him. And did he think he would be accepted by the Iranians?

Fisher had let it be known that while he never wanted to be an official representative of the United States, he would like to get involved. Yes, he said now, he would go. And he believed that the critical articles he had written for *Newsweek* and *Time* would prove to the Iranians that he was not the voice of America.

Fisher made his interest known through the Algerian Embassy in Washington. Soon after, he spoke by telephone to the Ayatollah Mohammed Beheshti, the leader of the Islamic Republican Party. "I'd like to come and talk to you," Fisher told the religious leader. "Would I be welcome? Will you give me an appointment?"

"Yes," Beheshti responded. "I don't want to be sponsoring an American initiative, but if you come I will be happy to see you."

The State Department authorized Fisher's travel to Teheran. Now all he had to do was acquire a visa from Iran. He sent his request to the Ministry of Foreign Affairs in Teheran, and waited for what he believed to be a formality to take place.

The first thing Sadegh Ghotbzadeh did when he found Fisher's visa application on his desk was to call the Ayatollah Beheshti. It was now early August 1980; Ghotbzadeh was still Foreign Minister, still looking for ways to fight back against the clerics who were pressing to have him removed from the government. "I'll be happy to get this Fisher a visa," he said to Beheshti, "if you will ask for it in writing."

"It's not my job to give visas to people," Beheshti replied.

"You're the one who asked him to come, aren't you?" Ghotbzadeh said.

But Beheshti wouldn't bite, and Fisher, caught up in a joust between two men trying to get each other to accept the responsibility for inviting an American, never went to Iran.

Some good had come out of Fisher's efforts, however. In the next weeks, he received several calls from the Ayatollah Beheshti, and gave him a crash course in crisis management. Many of the ideas he planted would prove helpful in the coming months.

And now it was up to the Algerians.

The men whom Algeria assigned to the hostage negotiations were admirably suited to the task. Two of them had impeccable revolutionary credentials. Redha Malek, the forty-nine-year-old Algerian ambassador to the United States, had been in charge of the Algerian National Liberation Front's propaganda during its war with France and had participated at the final peace talks that led to Algerian independence. Mohammed Seghier Mostefai, the governor of the Algerian Central Bank since independence, had been the financial expert of the Algerian revolution. The third senior member of the team, Abdel-Karim Gheraieb, had been Algeria's ambassador to Teheran since the Ayatollah Khomeini came to power, and had the closest contacts of any foreigner with the leaders of Iran's revolution.

From the outset, the Algerians determined to serve as "active intermediaries" rather than originators of ideas, to, in Harold Saunders' words, "help find solutions to problems without ever suggesting the solutions."

Not only would they attempt to explain each side's position to the other, they would tell each side, in advance, how they felt the other side might react to various proposals.

In the persons of the Iranian negotiators, the Algerians were dealing with three powerful egos. Behzad Nabavi was a thirty-eight-year-old revolutionary who had once worked for IBM as an engineer and was now the Minister of State for Executive Affairs. The Ayatollah Beheshti, leader of the Islamic Republican Party (the same Beheshti who had spoken with Roger Fisher), was an extraordinary maneuverer who managed to collaborate for years with the Shah's secret police, the Savak, and still become one of the most important figures in revolutionary Iran. Ali Akbar Hashemi Rafsanjani, the speaker of the Iranian parliament, was a former moneylender in the Teheran bazaar, and a close ally of Beheshti.

Once the talks got under way, the Algerians quickly realized that they would have to educate the Iranians to an understanding of the American political process.

The Iranians supposed that Jimmy Carter could act in the same peremptory manner in his country as the Ayatollah Khomeini did in Iran. Not only did they have to be given lessons about the American Constitution, they had to be taught in a manner that did not offend them. They were extremely touchy, suspicious of everyone and everything, and easily confused by even the most rudimentary financial matters. But they had the hostages, and so they could disguise their own frustrations—even from themselves—by toying with the Algerians as well as the Americans, alternately raising, then dashing hopes.

But not all of the educating took place with the Iranians. Over and over again, the Americans had to be reminded that the Iranians were understandably xenophobic. For as far back as they could remember they had been taught that foreigners had been stealing their wealth. True or not, that assumption was as fundamental to them as their Shiᶜite faith.

Within forty-eight hours after the Majlis had created the conditions for the release of the hostages and the Algerians had begun their mediation efforts, I received word from Sadegh Ghotbzadeh through Christian Bourguet that the Iranian would be willing to do an interview on television with me. The timing was propitious. At last, it seemed, there had been a significant break in the crisis. My questions to Ghotbzadeh would be organized around that very prospect.

I could not, of course, go to Iran. Instead, by one of those space-age miracles that never fail to amaze me, Ghotbzadeh would sit in a television studio in Teheran, where he would hear my questions broadcast from a television studio in Paris. His answers, as well as his picture, would be picked up by an Iranian ground station, bounced off a satellite and caught by a French ground station. The process would be instantaneous.

I reserved time on the satellite, and at the appointed hour was in the studio in Paris. Ghotbzadeh was in the studio in Teheran. But nothing happened. As the first moments of the time I had reserved passed with neither sound nor picture, the technicians in the Paris studio informed me that their counterparts in Iran had refused to turn on their transmitter.

And suddenly the other end of the year-long drama became real for me as it never had before. The exile-turned-Foreign-Minister I had known in Paris had once again become an exile—this time, within his own country.

I can't prove a cause-and-effect relationship for what happened next, but knowing something about Sadegh Ghotbzadeh, I have to believe that the frustration he surely felt as a consequence of being thwarted provoked him to some abnormally rash conduct in the following days. On November 7, two days after I was to have interviewed him via satellite, he gave a speech on the government-owned television network he had once run, and in that speech he roundly denounced the Islamic Republican Party. That same day Ghotbzadeh was arrested and taken off to prison, although no formal charges were filed against him. Nor would there be, because Ghotbzadeh had not broken any laws and could not be brought to trial. The real risk was that, in the vigilante atmosphere of post-revolutionary Iran, he would be killed in prison.

The next day, police ransacked Ghotbzadeh's living quarters and confiscated all of his papers. But as word of his arrest spread, a curious reaction set in. Sadegh Ghotbzadeh, the "Occidental," might not be the kind of man they wanted in office at the moment, but many Iranians remembered the courageous way in which he, and he alone, had publicly stood up to the student militants, and then sacrificed his position in an effort to awaken the country to the perils of its course.

For two days, demonstrations in support of Ghotbzadeh were carried on television. The imam saw the broadcasts; on the third day he made it known that he didn't agree with the arrest of the man he thought of as a son.

On November 12, Sadegh Ghotbzadeh went free.

And it finally came to pass that Héctor Villalón was right: regardless of the leftist or rightist persuasions of governments, at the center of everything was business.

Now that the emotions had cooled and the demand for an apology had been dropped, the freeing of the hostages became a matter of money.

On November 10, an American delegation led by Warren Christopher arrived in Algiers to deliver the U.S. response to the four-point demand of the Iranians. The Algerians were there in full force to receive them. Foreign Minister Mohammed Bejahia put everything else aside to work with the three already designated mediators, Malek, the ambassador to the United States, Mostefai, the governor of the Algerian Central Bank, and Gheraieb, the ambassador to Teheran.

Half a dozen Americans were backing Christopher up, but they were along for consultations. At the meetings themselves, Christopher did all of the talking, sometimes for several hours at a stretch, as he attempted to respond to all of the subordinate demands the Iranians had made in connection with the basic four points.

The next day the Algerians flew to Teheran to convey the American response, and the Americans flew home.

In the next weeks the Algerians set themselves a punishing pace, flying between Teheran, Algiers and Washington. On transatlantic flights, they flew the Concorde. All other trips were in private jets. In Teheran, their dark blue Mercedes with its police escort quickly became a familiar sight as it passed between the Hilton Hotel and the office of the Prime Minister in the center of the city.

One act of the Algerians did much to give a no-nonsense temper to the negotiations. On their first trip to Iran, they made a six-hour trip to various sites outside Teheran to make an inventory of the hostages and assure themselves that they were alive and well.

Still, days passed with no visible sign of progress. The public interpreted the silence as indication of a stalemate. That was not the case, as the negotiators well knew. They were bargaining and, despite some negative public pronouncements by the Iranians, seemingly making steady progress.

And then on December 19, day 412 of the hostage crisis, the Iranians stunned both the Americans and the Algerians with an extraordinary new demand. Before they would free the hostages, they wanted $24 billion. Fourteen billion was to cover their frozen assets as well as interest since the preceding November 14; ten billion was their estimate of the Shah's wealth held in the United States. The $14 billion, plus interest, was to be returned at once; the $10 billion was to be put in escrow in the Central Bank of Algeria, in anticipation of an accounting of the Shah's true wealth and discovery of its whereabouts.

The Americans felt utterly helpless against such a demand. They had only a sketchy idea of how much the Shah had invested in the United States and where the money was located. In 1958 the Shah had set up the Pahlavi Foundation of Teheran for the announced purpose of returning to Iran the wealth he had inherited from his father. The assets of the foundation included real estate and commercial enterprises such as banks, insurance companies and hotels. These were all contained within Iran. But a branch of the foundation was created in New York to provide aid for Iranian citizens studying in the United States. The initial endowment of the branch was $30 million. Out of this money, the foundation built a skyscraper on the corner of Fifth Avenue and Fifty-second Street.

All this Warren Christopher knew. What he didn't know was to what extent the foundation and the Shah's wealth could be considered one and the same.

The house on Beekman Place where the Shah's twin sister, Princess Ashraf, lived, as well as several neighboring buildings were other question marks. There were reports that the Shah had converted the title records to show that the properties belonged to Ashraf, but that, in actual fact, they all belonged to him. Christopher had no way to verify these allegations at once; if it was possible at all, the discovery might take years.

But the value of these properties didn't come close to the $10 billion the Iranians were maintaining had been removed to the United States by the Shah.

The only people who really knew how much the Shah had invested in the United States and what form those investments took were those who had handled his affairs at the Chase Manhattan Bank. They weren't about to talk.

Christopher and those working with him had reason to believe that the Shah's assets in the United States were not remotely as large as they were imagined to be. One of the things they had told Sadegh Tabatabai in Germany the previous September was that they considered the return of the Shah's assets a "non-issue." They were certain that the Shah had been intelligent enough to get all of his assets out of the United States. Tabatabai had agreed with this assessment.

Still, regardless of how much the Shah had in the United States, and even if it could be identified and legally seized, the American Government could not become the agent of any such transfer. In effect, the Iranians were asking the United States to pay ransom, and that was something the American people would not allow. With the inauguration of Ronald Reagan only a month away, Christopher was tempted to drop all the negotiations and let the new Administration handle the problem.

And yet there was one positive aspect to the Iranian demand. For the first time, it seemed that they were ready to accept guarantees instead of cash. Perhaps there was some basis for negotiation, after all.

The frozen assets of Iran held by the government and the banks made up the bulk of the $24 billion figure. The actual value of those assets could be determined. There were, for example, 1.6 million ounces of gold stored in the vaults of the Federal Reserve Bank in New York City, according to press reports. There was a Boeing-747 the Iranian Government had purchased and never received. According to the Americans' calculations, such tangible assets totaled $13 billion —not that far off from the figure contained in the Iranian demand.

Claims against Iran would surely reduce that figure. There were already more than 330 of them, according to the Treasury Department, amounting to some $6 billion. Roughly, the claims fell into three categories: defaults on bank loans, contracts broken by the Iranian Government and illegal seizure by the Iranians of American-owned companies.

For the Algerians, the new demand by the Iranians presented them with their most severe test to date. Privately they were dismayed, but they couldn't say so in public. Nor could they say to the Iranians, "There is no way that you're going to get $10 billion from the Americans for the Shah's assets." What they could and did say was, "This is how the Americans have explained the situation regarding the Shah's assets."

Jimmy Carter himself gave the Algerians a response to Iran's demand for $24 billion. The answer was, "No." However, Carter attempted to cash in on the Iranians' apparent willingness to accept guarantees by submitting a proposal of his own.

The United States, Carter said, would commit itself to the turning over of all Iran's frozen assets except those needed to secure claims under a claims settlement procedure. It would also pay off all loans and be willing to submit unresolved issues to binding international arbitration.

The Americans did not propose a new figure to replace the one they had rejected. But they did introduce a suggestion that would eventually make a final agreement easier. The idea was Warren Christopher's. He could already foresee Iran's reluctance to sign an agreement directly with the United States. What he proposed was that Algeria draw up an accord that would specify the promises made by both countries. It was this accord that both countries would sign.

At first the Algerians balked at the idea. They'd portrayed themselves as "postmen" and didn't want to enlarge their role. But eventually they found Christopher's logic irresistible, and went along with it.

On January 4 the Iranians at last made a move that Warren Christopher interpreted as a sign that they were ready to make a deal. On that day, the Iranians took U. S. Chargé d'Affaires Bruce Laingen and the two other diplomats who had remained with him out of the foreign ministry, where they had been since the embassy was seized, and put them with the other forty-nine American hostages. Christopher was convinced that this was an attempt by the Iranian Government to assert control in anticipation of the forthcoming release of the hostages.

Two days later, Christopher's analysis proved right. The Iranians dropped their demand for $24 billion. The amount they were now prepared to accept, they let it be known through the Algerians, was $9.5 billion. The Iranians also hinted that they might accept the Americans' proposal for binding arbitration.

The Americans were encouraged, but their own estimate of what could be unfrozen quickly without lengthy court battles was $7.8 billion.

The disputants were still far apart, and time was running out for Jimmy Carter, who wanted more than anything to bring the hostages home while he was still in office. To complicate matters, the Algerians found the American position unclear and said that until they understood it they couldn't explain it to the Iranians.

On January 7, Warren Christopher abruptly decided to return to Algiers with his team—Roberts Owen, Harold Saunders, Arnold Raphel and a secretary, Dorothy French—to try to dispel the confusion. Once there, he decided to stay on in order to tighten the negotiating process. Until this point, ideas had been making the round trip between Iran and the United States in approximately two weeks; if a deal was to be made before Jimmy Carter left office on January 20, negotiations must move more quickly.

By January 15 Christopher's strategy seemed to have paid off. Not only had he straightened out the Algerians' problems and gotten a new American reply to Iran, he had received an astounding offer from the Iranians, more generous by far than anything they had previously suggested to the Americans. They would pay off, in full and with interest, all uncontested loans given in the past by the United States to Iran. In addition, the Iranians trimmed their demand for financial guarantees to $8.1 billion.

White House lawyer Lloyd Cutler was attending a farewell dinner for Jimmy Carter on Thursday evening, January 15, when the Iranian proposal came through. He spent the rest of the night, along with Treasury Secretary G. William Miller, rounding up the representatives of the twelve American banks that held Iran's frozen assets. By eleven o'clock the next morning, all the bankers had assembled with the government officials in a State Department conference room to examine the proposal the Iranians had made the day before.

While on the surface the proposal seemed promising, this impression suffered on inspection. Many of the Iranian assets were tied up in loans that were not immediately retrievable. Then there was the question of how much interest should be paid on the Iranian accounts once they were unfrozen. The bankers said 13 percent. Iran wanted 17 percent. The difference was $670 million.

The Bank of America, with the biggest share of frozen assets, stood to lose the most, and its representatives were reluctant to compromise. All day Friday the bankers and lawyers debated the issues, sitting around a huge conference table littered with an increasing array of half-eaten delicatessen sandwiches, coffee cups, overflowing ashtrays and loose-leaf binders. Most of the bankers, summoned abruptly from their homes in the middle of the night, were without slide rules and calculators and had to multiply and divide by hand.

Late that evening the exhausted, disheveled bankers agreed to pay Iran nearly 17 percent annual interest on its frozen accounts. That raised the American offer to $7.9 billion—and trimmed the difference to $200 million.

Under normal conditions, the logistics of a financial transaction that would involve the transfer of billions of dollars by twelve different banks would take months to work out. The American bankers would now try to do it in three days.

They resumed work at ten o'clock on Saturday morning January 17. For the next nine hours they drew up documents that laid out the procedure for the transfer of funds back to Iran. Although they were working with open telephone lines and Telexes, the process went slowly because each step had to be transmitted to the Iranians for their approval before the next one could get under way.

Time weighed heavily. New Yorker John E. Hoffman, Jr., Citibank's principal outside counsel, had been urgently summoned to Washington by the President's chief counsel, Lloyd Cutler, on Thursday. His departure had been so hurried that the only things he had taken with him on the three o'clock shuttle were his briefcase and the little pocket calculator that was now propped in a glass on the table in front of him. As he stared almost accusingly at the calculator, Hoffman reflected on those last hours when they had discovered that nobody had a calculator big enough to total the sums of money involved in the transaction, let alone figure the interest. His own calculator went up only to eight digits. They had finally gotten a big office machine, but no one in the group knew how to work it. Hoffman had finally turned to Citibank's senior executive vice-president, Hans Angermuller, and said, "Hans, you're a banker. You do it."

But with all its frustrations, the working had been easier than the waiting.

On Sunday morning, the bankers took the Eastern Airlines shuttle to New York. The major terms of the transfer had been agreed upon; it was now a matter of the finishing touches, and these were to be made at a meeting in the offices of Shearman and Sterling, a Wall Street law firm. There they worked up an eleven-page appendix to the basic agreement, dealing with the technical specifics.

At the end of the morning all the completed documents were transmitted to Iran. Now all that awaited the transfer of funds by the Federal Reserve Bank in New York was the approval from Teheran.

In order to overcome any problems of mistrust, the negotiators had worked out a plan whereby the unfrozen assets of the Iranians would be moved first to an American account at the Bank of England, then to an escrow account in the same bank of the Central Bank of Algeria.

While the American bankers had been haggling in Washington on Friday and Saturday, similar discussions had been under way in London, where the frozen assets of the Iranians would eventually wind up if and when the deal was consummated. The usually staid offices of Citibank's British lawyers, Coward and Chance, overflowed with representatives of all twelve American banks meandering about the premises in various stages of undress. Salty jokes were communicated via open phone lines to Washington, New York and Algiers. One lawyer, aware of the historic nature of the moment, snapped pictures of his colleagues as they worked, phoned, napped, chatted and changed clothes. At the Bank of England, meanwhile, where the money was to flow, the executives trying to cope with the anticipated influx of nearly $8 billion in the space of a few hours got precious little sleep. Nonetheless, certain forms were preserved. Servants in long coats and top hats made up cots for their employers, and dutifully served refreshments.

That Friday, two of the Bank of England's most senior officials had flown to Algiers in an American Air Force plane to join Warren Christopher. Although it was the Islamic Sabbath, the British bankers and the Americans—Christopher, Harold Saunders, and Ulric Haynes, Jr., the tall, bearded American ambassador to Algeria—worked at the Bank of Algeria well into the evening, sifting details of the money transfer.

The focus was on Christopher. Since his arrival on January 8 he had worked almost around the clock, principally with Algerian Foreign Minister Ben Yahia, a probing and penetrating, yet discreet, diplomat, in an effort to speed the process up. He, too, wanted the release of the hostages to occur during the Administration of Jimmy Carter, the man who had appointed him Deputy Secretary of State. Except for a daily early morning tennis match, Christopher seemed unable to relax. Like the other American diplomats, he was staying at the ambassador's residence; on several occasions Haynes had brought mes-

sages to him in the middle of the night, expecting to awaken him, only
to find him lying in bed staring at the ceiling, unable to put the problems from his mind.

The negotiators did manage to take time out for a dinner party on
Saturday evening given by Ambassador and Mrs. Haynes at the residence, which, with all the visitors, had been temporarily converted into
a boardinghouse. That evening, Harold Saunders raised his champagne glass to toast Warren Christopher, who had just been awarded
the Medal of Freedom in absentia in a ceremony in Washington that
he had listened to on the telephone.

At 7 A.M., Monday, Foreign Minister Ben Yahia informed Warren
Christopher that Iran had at last agreed to the American proposal.
Christopher, still wearing the clothes he had worn to the dinner party
on Saturday evening, hurried to the Algerian Foreign Ministry. A few
minutes later, Christopher straightened his tie, sat at a table and, while
hundreds of cameras recorded the moment, signed the Declarations of
Algiers, using a pen borrowed from Harold Saunders to commemorate
Saunders' fourteen-month effort to free the hostages. At the same moment, the Declarations were signed in Teheran.

In signing, the United States agreed to waive hostage claims against
Iran, and Iran agreed to waive political claims against the United
States. The United States further agreed to unfreeze military items
blocked from shipment to Iran since the hostages were taken. The
greater part of the agreement consisted of a detailed plan for the dis-
bursement of almost $8 billion in frozen assets that both governments
agreed were properly Iran's. The agreement ensured:

• That $7.97 billion would be placed immediately in an escrow ac-
count in Iran's name in the Bank of England.
• That $3.67 billion of that account would be tagged as a loan
repayment fund to pay off in their entirety all syndicate loans made to
Iran by the United States and foreign banks.
• That $1.41 billion—plus anything remaining in the loan repay-
ment fund once syndicate banks had collected on their loans—would
be placed in a loan security fund for disputed loans claimed by U.S.
banks.
• That $2.88 billion would be returned to Iran.
• That unresolved disputes would be settled by an international ar-

bitration tribunal consisting of members appointed by each of the two countries plus a neutral member.

• That arbitration would be binding on both parties.

A section of the Declarations pertaining to another three or four billion dollars—funds whose amount was only estimated and whose ownership was questionable—set forth a plan for settling claims. It ensured:

• That the United States would unfreeze the balance of Iran's assets on the basis of binding third-party arbitration.

• That $1 billion of frozen assets would go into a security fund in escrow to pay off awards resulting from that arbitration.

• That as the security fund was consumed, Iran would replenish it, maintaining at all times no less than a $500 million balance.

Still another section pertaining to any assets the Shah and his family might have in the United States ensured:

• That Iran would be free to take legal actions in U.S. courts for retrieval of any such assets.

• That the United States would freeze any such assets in order to prevent their removal before lawsuits had been decided.

In Washington, Jimmy Carter, after sleeping for only forty-five minutes, made his way to the White House press room. "We have now reached an agreement with Iran that will result, I believe, in the freedom of our American hostages," he told reporters.

Only one question seemed to remain: would Jimmy Carter have the satisfaction of greeting the freed hostages while he was still President of the United States? His presidency would last only another thirty-one hours.

Before many of those hours had passed, however, the question once again was not when but whether the hostages would be freed. The Iranians had found a condition in the technical addendum to the Declarations of Algiers that they refused to accept.

chapter twenty-two

Free at Last

THE OFFICIAL EXPLANATION WAS THAT BOILER-PLATE BANKER'S LAN-
guage had thrown a hitch into the proceedings. What the Iranians
were objecting to was a standard banking clause that would have
prevented future claims by Iran against the U.S. banks.

Unofficially—and completely unknown to the Americans—it was far
more serious than that. A last-ditch power play was under way in
Teheran that could derail the proceedings.

All that weekend, I had been keeping tabs on the negotiations by telephone with sources in Washington, New York, London and Paris. It
seemed to me, as it did to everyone else, that a deal could not be far
off. But then I received a call from Christian Bourguet, and after listening to him with mounting disbelief I said, "Are you telling me that
the hostages may not be released?"

"I wouldn't bet on it," Bourguet said.

His first inkling of the problem, he explained, had been several days
earlier when he had cabled the Bank Markazi—Iran's Central Bank—
for confirmation of a meeting that was supposed to take place in London on Friday January 16 with the bank's counselors. As the bank's
attorney in France, where $400 million of Iran's assets had been fro-
zen by branches of U.S. banks, Bourguet was expected to attend.

But the bank did not reply to Bourguet's query. Puzzled, he called
directly to Ali Reza Nobari, the governor of the Central Bank. No-

bari's response stunned him. "I have no knowledge of such a meeting," Nobari said.

What kind of financial agreement could be worked out between the banks of Iran and the United States that did not include the governor of the Central Bank of Iran? All but bewildered by this point, Bourguet telephoned Teheran once again, and this time he spoke English to be certain that language had not been a barrier to understanding at either end.

Friday evening, the mystery deepened. The Central Bank's London lawyers passed on to Bourguet a message they had just received from their counterparts in New York: Nobari had just canceled the meeting.

First, Nobari doesn't know about the meeting. Then he cancels it. In the name of God, what was going on?

Bourguet was so disturbed by these communications—in such obvious contrast to the public story—that he immediately telephoned his partner, François Cheron, the firm's banking specialist, who was on business in Uruguay, and asked him to return to Paris at once.

The following morning, Bourguet received word from the English that the meeting was on again. It would be held in Algiers either later that day or the next day, Sunday. When no confirmation had come by late Sunday afternoon, Bourguet and Cheron, now back from Uruguay, telephoned Teheran. What they learned confirmed their worst forebodings. The negotiations were in danger of being compromised by a Byzantine intrigue.

The Americans had taken it as an encouraging sign that the men now negotiating in behalf of Iran were all religious hard-liners. All previous "deals" for the release of the hostages had been negotiated with secular leaders who turned out not to have the power to deliver. This time, the Americans felt, Iran's negotiators were those with power to implement their word.

There was one major problem with this reckoning, however, and it had been overlooked not only by the Americans but by the clerics who were eager to negotiate the deal independent of the secularists. The only official in Iran empowered to implement a financial agreement was Ali Reza Nobari, a secularist and ally of President Bani-Sadr.

Suddenly it was all in focus: Nobari and other secularists, most notably Bani-Sadr, hadn't *wanted* to participate in the accords with the United States—because they had wanted to be in a position to criticize those accords after they were made. By not participating, they could not be accused of obstructing a deal. At the same time they could attack the deal as an unfavorable one for Iran, and reap the political profits.

Anti-Americanism was still the most potent political weapon in Iran. The clerics had been so persuasive in convincing the people that anyone who dealt with the Americans was a traitor that in dealing with the Americans now, even indirectly, they were suspected of being traitors themselves. What a bonanza it would be for the secularists if they could tar the clerics with their own brush.

Armed with this insight, Bourguet called London once more. Was there any trouble with the financial deal? he asked. Yes, a Markazi lawyer replied. Ali Reza Nobari had refused to sign the document needed to open an account in Iran's name at the Bank of England in London.

Iran could open the escrow account called for in the financial transactions only through the Iranian Central Bank.

The Central Bank could be represented in such a transaction only by Nobari.

Nobari's refusal to affix his signature to the escrow account application could collapse the financial accords *and* the agreement to release the hostages.

On Monday January 19, a few hours after the signing of the Declarations of Algiers, the Iranians charged that American banks were attempting to trick them by slipping a clause into the appendix with which they weren't familiar.

The agreement reached between the United States and Iran provided that Iran's assets would leave the United States for an Algerian escrow account in the Bank of England. Once the funds were in place, the hostages would be released. But to trigger the transfer of funds, Iran—like any depositor—had to request it. U.S. officials sent the Iranians a copy of the suggested transfer order.

But the boiler-plate language attached to the transaction stipulates that the depositor, in agreeing to the transfer, "signs off" on any future claims against the bank. There had been major disagreements over how much interest was due Iran on its deposits in the banks and, in fact, an escrow account had been established until the dispute was settled. The Iranians and their New York lawyer, Leonard Boudin, felt this clause not only would hurt their case in getting additional interest, but also would hurt their claims for any additional principal that might be found by the banks.

That same day, Treasury Department officials made emergency calls to officials of all the U.S. banks. Would they eliminate that standard banking clause?

The banks said they would.

Hastily, the Americans relayed this commitment to the Algerians, and the Algerians passed it to Iran.

Inexplicably, the Bank Markazi did make an effort to trigger the funds that day, sending a Telex that said, in effect, "send what you have," and ignoring the question of future claims. But since the form of the Telex didn't conform to what the bankers had expected to receive, they didn't do anything with it.

That evening, Leonard Boudin's assistant, Eric Lieberman, and Bank Markazi's London counsel, Roger Brown, drafted a transfer order that corrected the problem and left open the possibility of future claims by Iran on unfound assets.

But there was still no official word from the Iranians.

It was nearly midnight on January 19 in Algiers, where Warren Christopher had been waiting with mounting concern for the message that Iran had accepted the revised financial terms and agreed to release the hostages. In a little more than eighteen hours—6 P.M. local time—President Carter would become a private citizen. No one knew what would happen to the negotiations once Ronald Reagan took office. For weeks now, that very mystery had served the American negotiators like a trump card held in reserve. It was time, at last, to play that card, because in less than a day its value would be nil.

Christopher reached for a U. S. Embassy telephone that linked him directly to the White House. In moments he was put through to the President. Briefly, Christopher reviewed the situation with Carter, and then explained what he proposed to do. Carter embellished the plan.

As soon as he hung up, Christopher instructed his aides to have his State Department plane readied for takeoff at exactly 6 P.M. the following day. "My authority expires then, and then I'm going," the Californian announced to the startled Algerian mediators.

As he spoke, Christopher's face revealed no sign that this gambler's bluff was anything more than a tired man's desire to quit the game.

Word of Warren Christopher's ultimatum reached Iran immediately via the dismayed Algerians. Now all attention turned to Ali Reza Nobari, the one man whose signature was needed to set the deal in motion.

"It's a bad deal for Iran," Nobari protested. But the clerics didn't agree, and the clerics were in power. By this point, the desire to bring the crisis to an end was almost universal. Nobari could resist no longer; he signed the enabling documents.

It was now late Monday evening in Washington. A score of bone-tired, scruffy-looking bankers, lawyers and bureaucrats sat, limbs askew, around the big conference-room table at the Treasury Department. Most of them had been there since Friday morning. Earlier that evening, members of the regular office staff had been packing up the residue of the soon-to-be-replaced Administration, but they had left hours ago and now the offices were quiet.

The work they had done in the preceding four days had been difficult, but it had been as nothing compared to the waiting. It hurt to sit. It hurt to stand. They catnapped on couches in relays.

Then, suddenly, it seemed as though the waiting was over. At ten o'clock a message arrived: Iran was ready to transmit. Now it was time to act. The group prepared to set in motion the final steps in the process of transferring funds.

At midnight they were still waiting.

Tuesday, January 20, 1981: the last morning of Jimmy Carter's presidency. A time for an outgoing President to reflect on his administration and his last hours in the White House. For Jimmy Carter, no such luxuries.

As the big grandfather clock in the Oval Office struck 1 A.M., Carter sat at his desk on his second all-night vigil in a row. From a distance, he looked relaxed and comfortable, clad in a white sport shirt, a blue cardigan and jeans, his feet swung up on the desk. But up close, he appeared drawn and haggard. He had last slept on Sunday night.

Walter Mondale sat in an armchair across from the President, his suit coat still on, his tie loosened and collar unbuttoned. He had been invited by the President to spend his final night as Vice-President with his wife Joan in the Lincoln bedroom. Instead, Joan was upstairs alone. Mondale could not bring himself to leave his political partner.

Jody Powell and Hamilton Jordan, Carter's two closest aides, were there as well. Powell in his shirt sleeves, Jordan still in his coat, with his tie in place. Both watched the President with concern, wondering how much more he could take. My God, let it be over, Jordan kept thinking.

Carter picked up the red telephone on his desk and dialed the White House situation room, where developments around the world are monitored on a twenty-four-hour basis. "Well, I was wondering if you had any report to give me," he said. There was a pause. "Nothing concerning the effort?" He listened a moment and hung up.

There was still no news that Iran had accepted the agreement. There was still nothing to do but wait.

At 2:30 A.M. the Telex machine at the Treasury suddenly came alive. Instantly the battered lawyers and bankers and bureaucrats were on their feet and rushing to the machine.

But there was no message from Iran, just the idle banter of two operators signaling each other that they were on hand.

"Are you there?"

"Yes, I'm here."

And then, for another hour, nothing.

From time to time eyes would meet, heads would shake, chests would heave. It wasn't going to happen.

At last, at 3 A.M., the message began, but it was as though a maniac had claimed the Telex keyboard. As the Americans watched in horror, one error after another appeared. Letters were transposed, at least one name was wrong, numbers were inaccurate. One order for the Bank of Chicago to transfer hundreds of millions into the escrow account came through as a row of zeroes. The Treasury officials relayed the news to G. William Miller, the Treasury Secretary. "What do we do now, wait for another Telex?" one of them asked.

"Screw the Telex!" Miller shouted, his patience finally snapped. "You have the President's order. You know what they have on deposit. Send the goddam money!"

Ten hours had passed since Warren Christopher's ultimatum. At the American Embassy in Algiers, Christopher, Harold Saunders, Arnold

Raphel and the others continued their vigil. Their bags were packed. If word didn't come through in another eight hours, they would take off.

And then, at 11 A.M. local time, the word came: "Telex deemed authentic, and the funds are transferred . . ."

Had the gamble paid off? Had Christopher's ultimatum nudged the Iranians into action? None of them could be certain. But it didn't matter. They had won. Their cheers rang through the embassy halls. Then they sent out to a bakery for a celebration feast of *croissants au beurre*.

Five-fifteen in Manhattan. A winter wind swirls the paper littering Fifty-third Street. Nothing else moves; the street is empty. Then, one by one, twenty-five haggard men appear, their collars turned up, their faces gray with stubble. They do not look like men of means, but they are. The bankers have finished their work, and now they are going home.

By 6 A.M. the twelve American banks had completed the transfer of funds. For the men in the office at the Treasury Department, there was no more to be done except to toast the conclusion of a difficult transaction. Someone brought out the wine they had stored for this occasion. The bottles were opened and the glasses filled. But they remained on the table, as the celebrants asked one another whether they weren't being premature. Shouldn't they wait until the hostages had cleared Iranian air space?

They waited awhile and then, unable to endure another period of waiting, wearily lifted their glasses.

By 6 A.M. the ticking of the grandfather clock was the loudest noise in the Oval Office. Jimmy Carter remained in his command post in a reclining chair behind his desk, periodically putting his feet up in an attempt to relax. From time to time he stared expectantly at the red telephone on the desk, as though willing it to ring.

Half an hour later, it did. Carter listened, then hung up, beaming, new energy in his face. "It was Algeria," he said. "Chris has signed the agreement."

The President called his wife Rosalynn to tell her the good news. "All that's left is for the funds to be transferred to the escrow account," he said. He sat to his desk, straightened the recliner and began to draft a statement.

An aide suggested he call Ronald Reagan to advise him of the newest development. Carter agreed, and placed the call at six-fifty. But the President-elect had just gotten to sleep after a night of champagne toasts and dancing, and was not to be disturbed.

At 7 A.M. the red telephone rang. It was Treasury Secretary Miller. "The funds have been transferred to the escrow account and the Bank of England is engaged in the process of certifying the transfer," he reported.

"Right on, man, that's great," Carter said, waving a clenched fist and breaking out, at long last, in a full-bore grin. Then Carter walked across the room to where Jody Powell was standing, to instruct him on what to tell the press. "The money's in the bank. Our action is complete. Iran is being notified that the money's there. That's all we need to tell them."

It would be another fifteen minutes, thirty at the most, for the certification process to be completed, Carter believed. The time had come to break out the champagne.

Moments later, Jimmy Carter lifted his glass. "To freedom," he said.

An hour later, the red telephone rang once again. Carter picked it up. "It's Chris," the voice at the other end said. "Two Air Algeria Boeing-727s have been cleared for takeoff from Teheran."

Carter beamed again. He turned to Vice-President Mondale and delivered one of his last presidential orders. "Tell Congress that release is imminent."

At eight thirty-one Ronald Reagan returned Jimmy Carter's call, and the outgoing President told his successor the good news. Then, buoyed by the auspicious turn of events of the last few hours, Carter turned to his chief of staff, Hamilton Jordan, and asked him to arrange for the lights on the national Christmas tree, which had been kept unlighted as a sign of sympathy for the hostages, to be turned on as soon as they were free.

At nine-thirty, Hamilton Jordan looked anxiously at the grandfather clock. What were the Iranians up to? he wondered. "They clearly don't know the inauguration schedule," he said under his breath. Or did they? Was this some last-minute humiliation they meant to inflict on Jimmy Carter? "Give it ten more minutes," he kept saying to himself. But when no word had come by ten-twenty, Jordan decided to take control of the situation. "The President needs some time alone," he told the rest of the group. Quickly they filed from the Oval Office— Jordan, too—and Jimmy Carter finally had that moment to reflect on his four years as President. A few minutes later he left the Oval Office for the last time.

Both the television set and the radio were on in Christian Bourguet's home in Paris. There was a bottle of champagne in the refrigerator that he wanted desperately to open. But as welcome as a soothing drink would be, he could not bring himself to do it. For him there would be nothing to celebrate until the hostages were not only out of Iran but safely on the ground in Algiers. Until then, something could still go wrong. In the meanwhile, for the first time since the hostages had been taken, there was nothing, absolutely nothing, that he could do.

What bothered him most was not knowing. Throughout the crisis, he had been on the inside. For all that time, he'd been ahead of the news. Now, in this final hour, he called me in New York every fifteen minutes, accepting as fact reports he heard on television and radio only after they had been confirmed by me.

Ronald Reagan was sworn into office at 11:57 A.M. The hostages still had not been freed. As Jimmy Carter listened to the new President's inaugural address, his eyes shut for a moment. Watching him, Hamilton Jordan wondered if the ex-President had fallen asleep. He hadn't. Carter was praying for the safe return of the hostages.

Carter and Mondale did not linger once the speech was over. They walked immediately to a gray limousine for the ride to Andrews Air Force Base where Carter, Mondale and a number of members of his administration would join for the ride back to Georgia.

They had been under way only moments when, at 12:38 P.M., the telephone in the limousine rang. Carter answered. It was Navy Captain Gary Sick, the Iran expert on the National Security Council, calling from the situation room at the White House. The former President listened intently, then hung up, turned to the former Vice-President and said, "They're out. Thank God."

epilogue

JANUARY 20, 1981, WAS FOR ME A DAY OF HIGH AND MIXED EMOTIONS. Seeing Ronald Reagan arrive at the White House for the ritual cup of coffee with the outgoing President, Jimmy Carter, took me back twenty years in my own life. That day, January 20, 1961, wearing a morning coat and top hat for the first and only time in my life, I headed for the special stands at the Capitol to watch the inauguration of John F. Kennedy. How different the personalities, how historically similar the events I was watching that morning in Suite 1001 of the Plaza Hotel in New York. Virtually without a break, I had been working in that room, littered with television cameras and equipment, for thirty-two days to produce the ABC News Special—*America Held Hostage: The Secret Negotiations.*

Our work, too, had been a secret, not simply for those thirty-two days, but for all the months that I had known about the negotiations and been able to share that knowledge with only the top executives of ABC and a few trusted associates. I would not compare my own frustration during all this time to that of Jimmy Carter or any of the other persons directly involved, but it had been formidable just the same.

And then, at last, it happened! The hostages had been liberated! A loud cheer went up in the room. We were overjoyed that the hostages had been freed. But we, too, were now liberated from the secret we had been protecting for so many months. At last, we could tell the American people the true behind-the-scenes story of the secret negotiations to free the hostages.

Historical judgments are always easier to make in hindsight. I, myself, had many times complained about certain judgments made about the Kennedy administration ten or fifteen years later, pointing out that those judgments were easier to make when removed from the crucible of decision-making. I shall try to remember this in trying to analyze what went wrong in Iran.

There are, to begin with, several incontrovertible facts. American intelligence failed in a dramatic way to foresee the imminent downfall of the Shah. Partly because of this, partly because Jimmy Carter and people around him at the highest level were so involved with other major problems—Camp David and the Middle East, SALT—it would take the White House an uncommonly long time to recognize the danger to the United States in what was happening in Iran. It never did develop a coherent policy to deal with the coming storm.

The fall of the Shah produced one of the major failures in crisis management by a postwar American government. Nor did the Carter administration ever fully understand where the Iranian revolution was going and what was its true intent. Having refused a direct contact with the Ayatollah Khomeini while he was in exile in Neauphle-le-Château in France, having made the judgment that no American official should talk to Sadegh Ghotbzadeh because he was believed to be a Communist agent, or with Abolhassan Bani-Sadr because he was believed to be too anti-American, the United States Government had cut itself off from channels of communication that would have been extremely valuable in the early days of the hostage crisis. It took the U. S. Government more than two months after the hostages were taken to establish real contact with persons able to talk directly to the Iranian Government.

It has been written, and I once believed it myself, that one of the problems of the hostage negotiations was that the Americans were talking to the wrong people in Iran. That, indisputably, became true. But it was not the case in the beginning. The key figures in the Iranian revolution just after the hostages were taken and the Bazargan government fell were Khomeini, Ghotbzadeh and Bani-Sadr. The latter two were also the only two men who sincerely wanted to do something about the hostage crisis. At the beginning, they understood and even sympathized with the motivations of those who had taken the hostages. But they also understood the grave implications for Iran in keeping the Americans, and set out to create a situation in which they could be freed. But their efforts to free the hostages were system-

L

atically used against them by the religious leadership in Iran to whittle
down their power. By April 1980, Ghotbzadeh and Bani-Sadr no
longer had real power in Iran. But from November 6, 1979, the day
Bazargan resigned, until that moment in April, they were the men in
the key power positions and the only Iranian leaders with whom the
American Government could deal.

There has also been the tendency in some quarters to deride the secret negotiations as essentially useless. That is both unfair and untrue.
Whatever else can be said about the Carter administration, it made an
all-out effort to free the hostages. Hamilton Jordan, particularly, gets
high marks for breaking out of the stifling mold of State Department
wariness and boldly trying to strike through to the heart of the questions that had so perturbed U.S.-Iranian relations.

There is a terrible irony in the fate of all the persons who touched
the hostage crisis in a significant way.

Jimmy Carter went down to defeat. He might have anyway, but the
hostage crisis contributed in a significant way to the perception of
Americans that he was incapable of resolving crisis.

Christian Bourguet was virtually bankrupted by his effort in behalf
of the Iranians and the Americans. This highly moral man, whose
commitment to the ideals of the Third World had been proved on
many occasions, refused to accept one penny from the American Government for his efforts. The Iranian Government, his client, has also,
at this writing, failed to pay him for the considerable out-of-pocket ex-
penses he incurred while trying to resolve the hostage matter and
regain Iran's frozen assets. During all this time, Bourguet sacrificed
the legal fees he would normally have earned.

Héctor Villalón, who is not poor, nevertheless put some $300,000
out of his own pocket on behalf of the secret negotiations. His opportunity cost—the money he might have made in business during that
time—was at least five times that. Villalón's motives were different
from Bourguet's—he felt the failure to solve the hostage crisis might
lead to a Communist takeover in Iran—but his work on behalf of the
hostages was as significant as Bourguet's.

Abolhassan Bani-Sadr was stripped of his presidency and forced to
flee Iran to save his life; Ayatollah Beheshti, the religious leader who
led the onslaught against Bani-Sadr, was assassinated. And Omar
Torrijos, the Panamanian leader who used the Shah as bait to try and
free the hostages, was killed in an air crash.

And finally, Sadegh Ghobzadeh, whose life, at this writing, remains in constant danger. If it had not been for the Ayatollah Khomeini, who still holds him in esteem, he would not have been freed so quickly from prison after being arrested last November. How long even that relationship will protect him, given the increasingly ominous circumstances in Iran, remains in question.

A number of other questions remain, as well:

Why did it take so long to free the hostages?

There is no evidence, even today, that people in the United States Government ever really understood the mentality and motivation of the Iranians. As a corollary to that, there is no real evidence that the leaders of Iran ever understood the United States, its Constitution and its laws. The dialogue between the United States and Iran during the hostage crisis represented a massive culture gap. We based our thinking on traditional Judeo-Christian ethics, and what we professed was a respect for international law. But in the eyes of the Iranians, as we've seen, international law was a creation of the West, made irrelevant by what it perceived as steady violations by the United States Government. Most of the people now in power in Iran spent years in prisons being tortured by the Savak, which was notoriously linked up to the CIA. Their hatred of America was and is practically as virulent as their hatred for the Shah and the Savak. The Americans—at least some of the policy-makers in the government—just did not understand this.

Finally we cannot overlook the geopolitical reasons why it took so long to free the hostages. When the Russians invaded Afghanistan six weeks after the hostages were taken, it was suddenly in their interest to encourage turmoil in Iran. Working through people inside and outside Iran, the Soviet Union did everything possible to block release of the hostages and inflict maximum humiliation on the United States. In the last forty-eight hours before the hostages were finally freed, the Soviet media made the outrageous charge that the efforts to liberate the fifty-two Americans was a cover for a United States invasion of Iran. The Tudeh Party, the Iranian Communist Party, constantly opposed the freeing of the hostages, on the grounds that it would lead to new and better relations between Washington and Teheran, something which was not in the interest of the Soviet Union. (That has not happened thus far, but the pressures on Iran to break out of its self-imposed isolation are building. As rage against the United States recedes in Iran, and as memory of the hostage crisis begins to fade in the American mind, the possibility of new relations between the United States and Iran become more possible.)

There are those in America who believe the United States should have walked away from the hostage crisis. They point out that the Iranians are used to haggling in the bazaar. Their argument is that it takes two to haggle, and if the United States had refused to deal, the Iranians would have come running after them. But Americans are not used to the idea of sacrificing human life. And this negotiating tactic, which was never seriously considered by the American Government, would have been unacceptable to the great majority of the American people. So, we negotiated. And in the end we freed the hostages. It was a victory for the human spirit. But it was not a victory for America.

The Iran problem did not cease the day the hostages were freed, even if it did disappear for a time from the front pages of our newspapers and from our television screens. But as the country moved from one revolutionary spasm to another, Iran once again became a major story. The volatility of the situation in Iran makes it almost impossible to predict in what state the country will be when this book appears. It would be foolish to hazard such a guess. But there is one factor which merits our continuing attention. Did the United States learn a lesson in Iran and is it adjusting some of its concepts of foreign policy to accommodate the necessary change? The answer to that question is a loud *no!* There are already several vital countries on this globe where the events of Iran are starting to duplicate—almost as if they have come out of a powerful photocopy machine. The personalities are different; and in some cases the conditions. But the basic thrust of our policy is the same. We still believe we can buy time with economic largesse and that we can prop up unpopular leaders with our presence. We still believe it is an insult to a leader we are supporting to maintain some civilized dialogue with his adversaries. We let our policies be dictated by others, when clearly it is against our long-term national interest. Somewhere else on this globe another violent revolution is inevitable. And when it comes, as in Iran, we will have nobody to talk to.

Les Pins, France
August 11, 1981

chronology of events

Nov. 4, 1979, Day 1 — Iranian militants seize the U. S. Embassy in Teheran and take hostages, including Americans. They demand the United States return the deposed Shah of Iran, Mohammed Reza Pahlavi, who is in New York Hospital. The United States refuses.

Nov. 5, Day 2 — The United States rejects Iranian demand to turn over the Shah. White House Press Secretary Jody Powell says the Shah's stay in the United States is a matter of "humanitarian concern," and he underscores "the genuine desire" on the part of the United States to have "productive and mutually respectful relations with Iran."

Nov. 12, Day 9 — Carter orders a halt to oil imports from Iran.

Nov. 14, Day 11 — The United States freezes all official Iranian assets in American banks on Carter's orders.

Nov. 17, Day 14 — Khomeini orders the militants to release all women and black hostages if they are absolved of "espionage."

Nov. 19, Day 16 — Three of the hostages—two black Marines and a white woman secretary—are released.
Ten American hostages who are scheduled for release appear at press conference in Teheran.

Nov. 20, Day 17 — Ten more Americans are freed.
White House issues statement that says the United States prefers a

peaceful solution to the standoff with Iran, but has other "remedies" provided by the UN Charter.

Nov. 22, Day 19 — Thirteen American hostages released in Teheran on Nov. 19 and twenty arrive in Washington for Thanksgiving Day welcome.
Five non-American hostages are freed from the U. S. Embassy in Teheran.

Nov. 25, Day 22 — UN Secretary-General Kurt Waldheim calls for an emergency session of the Security Council on Iran.

Nov. 27, Day 24 — The UN Security Council meets in a sixteen-minute session to hear Waldheim appeal to the United States and Iran to avoid any action that could "inflame" the situation. Another session is called for December 1.

Nov. 28, Day 25 — Abolhassan Bani-Sadr, considered a moderate on the hostages after having said he does not believe they should be held indefinitely, is replaced as Foreign Minister by Sadegh Ghotbzadeh, who advocates releasing the Americans only after the Shah is returned.

Nov. 29, Day 26 — The United States files suit in the International Court of Justice (World Court) in The Hague for an emergency ruling against the seizure of the hostages in Iran. The suit claims Iran has violated its "international obligation to protect U.S. diplomats."

Dec. 1, Day 28 — UN Security Council begins debate on the Iranian crisis.

Dec. 2, Day 29 — The Shah leaves New York Hospital for the military hospital at Lackland Air Force Base near San Antonio, Texas.

Dec. 12, Day 39 — The U. S. State Department orders the expulsion of 183 Iranian diplomats. They must leave the United States within five days.

Dec. 13, Day 40 — Khomeini permits Ghotbzadeh to invite independent observers to visit the hostages.

Dec. 15, Day 42 — After four days of covert diplomatic maneuvering with Panama's General Omar Torrijos by presidential assistant Hamilton Jordan, the Shah flies to "temporary" exile in Panama. He is flown to the private island of Contadora, thirty-five miles from the Panamanian coast in the Pacific Ocean.

Dec. 21, Day 48 — Carter says the United States will ask the UN Security Council to impose economic sanctions on Iran.

Dec. 23, Day 50 — Tree is delivered to the hostages as militants prepare for the Christmas Eve arrival of three U.S. clergymen invited to lead the Americans in holiday prayer.

Dec. 24, Day 51 — Rev. William Sloane Coffin, Jr., Rev. William Howard and Auxiliary Bishop Thomas Gumbleton of the United States arrive for Christmas services inside the U. S. Embassy compound. They are joined by Cardinal Léon-Étienne Duval of Algiers.

Dec. 30, Day 57 — UN Secretary-General Waldheim tells the Security Council he is going to Teheran in an effort to negotiate the release of the hostages. Ghotbzadeh says Waldheim is welcome, but the militants accuse him of being untrustworthy and say they will not negotiate with him.

Jan. 1, 1980, Day 59 — Waldheim arrives in Teheran but is told he cannot negotiate the release of the hostages. Ghotbzadeh reiterates his position that Waldheim's visit is a fact-finding mission only, not one of mediation and negotiation.

Jan. 3, Day 61 — Khomeini refuses to meet with Waldheim, but Iranian and UN spokesmen say progress was made in talks with other Iranian leaders.
The Secretary-General pledges that the United Nations will investigate alleged human rights violations during the regime of the Shah.

Jan. 4, Day 62 — Embassy militants call on Iranian officials to turn over to them U. S. Chargé d'Affaires L. Bruce Laingen.
Waldheim departs Teheran for New York.

Jan. 14, Day 72 — The Revolutionary Council orders all U.S. news correspondents to leave Iran because of what it calls their "biased reporting."

Jan. 17, Day 75 — Letters written by U.S. hostages at Christmastime reach the United States. One from Robert C. Ode asks the U. S. Government for "prompt action to free us from this terrible situation."

Jan. 20, Day 78 — UN Secretary-General Waldheim says he has a formula to resolve the hostage crisis but adds it will be a "long process."

Jan. 23, Day 81 — Ghotbzadeh announces that Panamanian President Royo has informed him that the Shah "is under arrest" and that Panama is awaiting further documentation before proceeding to extradition hearings.

Jan. 30, Day 88 — Six Americans who escaped from Iran with the assistance of the Canadian Government arrive at Dover Air Force Base in Delaware.

Feb. 4, Day 93 — Khomeini swears in Bani-Sadr as President.

Feb. 7, Day 96 — Bani-Sadr formally takes over as head of the Revolutionary Council, making him the Number 2 man in authority. He is approved by Khomeini. Bani-Sadr again assails the embassy militants, calling them "rebels against the government."

Feb. 15, Day 104 — UN sources say the United States and Iran have agreed on the make-up of a five-member commission, selected by Secretary-General Waldheim, to go to Iran to investigate Iran's charges against the Shah and the United States.

Feb. 19, Day 108 — Bani-Sadr cables formal acceptance of the Waldheim commission and says Khomeini has accepted the final terms set forth by the Waldheim commission.

Feb. 24, Day 113 — Teheran: 10:30 A.M.—UN Commission meeting with Ghotbzadeh.

Mar. 11, Day 129 — The UN Commission leaves after seventeen days in Teheran. They say they will not now be presenting a report on their investigation of the Shah's alleged crimes.

Mar. 21, Day 139 — White House adviser Hamilton Jordan flies to Panama amid reports that he will attempt to settle a dispute between Panamanian and U.S. doctors on the Shah's operation.

Mar. 23, Day 141 — The Shah leaves Panama for Egypt where he will undergo further surgery, ending a 100-day residence on a resort island.

April 1, Day 150 — In a move Carter calls a "positive development," Bani-Sadr offers to take custody of the hostages if the United States agrees to a truce in what he calls its "war of words" and economic and diplomatic pressure against Iran. Carter says he is deferring imposition of new economic sanctions and other punitive measures against Iran.

April 6, Day 155 — Easter services are held for the hostages inside the U. S. Embassy by the three American clergymen, who report later that the hostages seem to be in good condition.

April 7, Day 156 — Khomeini rules the hostages must remain in the hands of the militants. In response, the United States breaks diplomatic relations with Iran, expelling thirty-five Iranian diplomats remaining in the country and imposing a series of economic sanctions.

April 18, Day 167 — Carter orders new economic sanctions against Iran and says that if they don't result in the release of American hostages, "the next step will be military action."

April 25, Day 174 — The White House announces that a U.S. military force flew to a remote desert site in Iran in hopes of carrying out a rescue of the hostages in Teheran, but the plan had to be aborted because of the failure of three helicopters. Eight American servicemen were killed in a ground collision of a C-130 and a helicopter as the aircraft were preparing to leave the area.

April 26, Day 175 — Iran announces the hostages are being moved from the U. S. Embassy to other parts of Teheran and to other Iranian cities to foil another U.S. rescue effort.

April 28, Day 177 — Secretary of State Vance resigns in protest of the attempt to rescue the hostages.

April 29, Day 178 — Senator Edmund S. Muskie is named to succeed Vance. Carter says it was right to order the hostage rescue mission.

May 24, Day 203 — The International Court of Justice calls for release of the hostages and says that Iran should compensate the United States for the seizure.

June 2, Day 212 — Defying a U.S. ban on travel to Iran, former Attorney General Ramsey Clark and nine other Americans attend opening session in Teheran of a "Crimes in America" conference of delegates from fifty nations.

June 17, Day 227 — The Iranian parliament is not likely to consider the hostage question until mid-September, a Teheran newspaper says.

June 25, Day 235 — Ayatollah Beheshti, a leading member of the Iranian parliament, says there is "just a possibility" U.S. hostages judged to be innocent of spying would be freed, but he gives no timetable.

July 10, Day 250 — Khomeini orders the release of hostage Richard Queen, a twenty-eight-year-old vice-consul.

July 18, Day 258 — An attempt is made in Paris to assassinate Shahpur Bakhtiar, the last Iranian Prime Minister under the Shah and leader of an anti-Khomeini exile movement.

July 22, Day 262 — President Bani-Sadr takes formal oath of office before the new parliament.

July 27, Day 267 — The deposed Shah dies in a Cairo military hospital. U.S. officials express doubt that the death will speed the release of the hostages.

July 29, Day 269 — The Shah is buried in a Cairo mosque after a state funeral attended by President Sadat and former President Nixon, there in a private capacity.

Aug. 10, Day 281 — Secretary of State Muskie says the United States is considering new diplomatic initiatives for the release of the hostages.

Aug. 27, Day 298 — Chancellor Helmut Schmidt of West Germany appeals to Prime Minister Rajai to help bring about the release of the U.S. hostages.

Sept. 7, Day 309 — Muskie says in a U.S. television interview that there is evidence of "increasing awareness" by Iranian leaders that the hostage issue should be settled.

Sept. 12, Day 314 — Khomeini lists four conditions for the hostages' release but omits a previous demand for a U.S. apology. The conditions: return of the late Shah's wealth, cancellation of U.S. claims against Iran, unfreezing of Iranian funds in the United States and U.S. guarantees of no interference in Iran. Washington's immediate reaction is guarded.

Sept. 13, Day 315 — Iran's former Foreign Minister, Sadegh Ghotbzadeh, says that Khomeini's four conditions "unlock" the hostage issue and that Secretary of State Muskie's August 31 letter asking for resolution of the hostage issue was "positively received" in Teheran.

Sept. 16, Day 318 — Full debate of the hostage issue is delayed in the Majlis. A special committee is to be chosen to deal with the question. Carter now says "There is no prospect at this time for an early resolution" of the crisis.

Sept. 19, Day 321 — Air and ground battles break out between Iran and Iraq, Teheran Radio says.

Sept. 22, Day 324 — The war between Iran and Iraq becomes official.

Sept. 28, Day 330 — UN Security Council votes unanimously to call for a halt to the fighting between Iraq and Iran.

Oct. 8, Day 340 — Militants holding the U.S. hostages in Iran say that they are "all right" and that the parliament still is studying their fate.

Oct. 16, Day 348 — Prime Minister Rajai leaves Teheran for New York to attend a UN Security Council meeting on the Iran-Iraq war.

Oct. 18, Day 350 — Rajai tells a New York news conference that he believes the United States "in practice" has already apologized for its support of the Shah and a decision on the release of the hostages is "not far away."

Oct. 20, Day 352 — In a campaign speech, President Carter says he will lift U.S. sanctions against Iran if the hostages are freed.

Nov. 2, Day 365 — Majlis sets first official release terms, closely following lines of Ayatollah Khomeini's four demands on September 12 but with new complications for U.S. compliance.
Khomeini says the parliament will make the decision on freeing the hostages.

Nov. 5, Day 368 — The hostage crisis will be prolonged because of Mr. Reagan's election, according to the spiritual leader of the Moslem militants occupying the American Embassy in Teheran.

Nov. 6, Day 369 — Iran appears to have sharply slowed its efforts to deal with the hostage crisis since Mr. Reagan's election victory.

Nov. 10, Day 373 — Deputy Secretary of State Warren Christopher leads a party of Americans to Algiers and delivers the U.S. response to Iran's four conditions for release of the hostages.

Nov. 20, Day 383 — The United States confirms that it has accepted in principle the four conditions "as a basis for resolution of the crisis."

But both governments stress that they are still not in accord on the details of a settlement.

Nov. 27, Day 390 — According to a spokesman for the militants, the hostages have been turned over to the Iranian Government and the militants no longer have anything to do with them.

Dec. 6, Day 399 — Iranian Government spokesman says "it won't take long" to complete assessment of latest U.S. response to release terms.

Dec. 15, Day 408 — President Bani-Sadr says that the fate of the American hostages rests on the return of Iran's assets in the United States, frozen after the embassy's seizure and the subject of numerous lawsuits.

Dec. 19, Day 412 — In exchange for freeing the hostages, Iran demands that the United States deposit in the Algerian Central Bank the Iranian funds impounded by President Carter following the seizure of the Americans in Teheran more than thirteen months ago.

Dec. 21, Day 414 — Iran announces that the United States must deposit with the Algerians the equivalent of $24 billion in cash and gold, representing its estimate of the Shah's wealth and frozen assets, before the hostages are released. Secretary of State Muskie calls the demand "unreasonable."

Dec. 25, Day 418 — The hostages spend their second Christmas in captivity.

Dec. 28, Day 421 — President-elect Ronald Reagan says today that Iran's request for the immediate payment of billions of dollars in frozen Iranian assets as a part of an agreement for eventually freeing the fifty-two American hostages is unacceptable.

Dec. 29, Day 422 — Washington serves notice on Iran that it will not alter its "basic position" on the terms for the release of the hostages despite Iran's insistence of financial guarantees in advance of freedom for the fifty-two Americans.

Jan. 2, 1981, Day 426 — The latest American proposals for freeing the hostages are brought to Teheran by the Algerian intermediaries after four days of talks in Washington. The United States and Iran appear to have reached general agreement on the conditions for the hostages' freedom.

Jan. 6, Day 430 — Hopes in the hostage dispute rise again as Ayatollah Khomeini gives approval to Algerian assistance in effort to free the fifty-two American hostages in Iran.

Jan. 8, Day 432 — Deputy Secretary of State Warren Christopher confers in Algiers with Algerian Foreign Minister Mohammed Ben Yahia on questions raised by the Algerian intermediaries over Washington's proposals to Iran.

Jan. 10, Day 434 — Iran is told by the United States in its last set of proposals for freeing the hostages that within several days following their release it could probably recover 70 percent of its multi-billions of dollars frozen in American banks.

Jan. 16, Day 440 — Terms of a final agreement with Iran are drafted by the United States, and officials say if it is accepted the release of American hostages could come as soon as Sunday.

Jan. 18, Day 442 — The United States and Iran agree on freedom for the fifty-two American hostages in Teheran and the return to Iran of billions of dollars of its assets frozen by this country. Deputy Secretary of State Warren M. Christopher signs the document in Algiers hours after Behzad Nabavi, the chief Iranian negotiator, has signed it in Teheran.

Jan. 19, Day 443 — United States Deputy Secretary of State Warren Christopher and Algerian Foreign Minister Mohammed Ben Yahia sign the Declarations of Algiers.

Jan. 20, Day 444 — Last-minute difficulties with the exchange of funds are ironed out. The Declarations is officially accepted and the hostages are released, one half hour after Ronald Reagan becomes President of the United States.

appendix

The following are the various scenarios and the Declarations of Algiers in their entirety.

This is the scenario hammered out at the White House January 25–29, 1980, to attempt to create the conditions for the setting up of a United Nations investigative commission that would lead to the release of the American hostages. The principals who wrote this and the two subsequent scenarios were Hamilton Jordan, Harold Saunders and Henry Precht on the American side, and Christian Bourguet and Héctor Villalón representing the Iranians.

SECRET/SENSITIVE
A POSSIBLE SCENARIO

Two important steps have already been taken:

1) Foreign Minister Ghotbzadeh has responded to the Jordan/Saunders trip to London by authorizing Messrs. Villalón and Bourguet to travel to Washington carrying tangible evidence of Iran's serious intentions and good will to discuss practical stages to end the crisis.

2) The United States has conveyed through private channels to the President-elect, Mr. Bani-Sadr, and to the Foreign Minister, Mr.

Ghotbzadeh, a message confirming to them the importance which the United States attaches to our conversations.

I. Principles and Procedures
The United States and Iran agree:

1) to accept the principle of the establishment of a scenario, the first stages of which would be defined precisely, and the subsequent stages would be defined in detail as events evolve;

2) to manage this scenario with the help of persons agreed to by both sides;

3) to proceed, within the framework of this scenario, by stages each involving reciprocal actions to be defined in advance;

4) that these agreed points are intended to allow the earliest possible resolution of the present crisis by peaceful means.

II. Establishment of a Commission of Inquiry

1) Request by Iran that the Secretary-General of the United Nations establish a Commission of Inquiry "to hear Iran's grievances and to allow an early solution of the crisis between Iran and the United States." This request will state Iran's desire to have the Commission speak to each of the hostages.

2) Removal by the United States of its objections to the establishment of this Commission.

3) Mr. Waldheim's role:

  a) appointment of a chairman and members of this Commission;

  b) preparation of the terms of reference, which will state that the Commission will not be a tribunal but rather a fact-finding mission, and establishment of deadlines for the Commission's work;

  c) official announcement by Mr. Waldheim of the Commission's establishment and simultaneous publication by him of the Iranian request.

4) Public statement by the United States recalling that the Commission is going on a fact-finding mission to Teheran, to hear Iranian grievances, to meet with each of the hostages, and to report to the Secretary-General. The United States would object publicly to having the Commission subject the hostages to interrogations in connection with its inquiry during any of its meetings with them. The United

States would recall that it is important for it to ascertain the condition of each of the hostages.

5) The Imam would present the establishment of the Commission of Inquiry as a success, would interpret the visit to the hostages as being one of the elements in the investigation into Iranian grievances, and would state his desire to see the Commission conclude its work rapidly.

(would ask government administrations to place their documents at the disposal of the Commission)

III. Work of the Commission

1) The Commission will not leave New York for Teheran until the announcement provided for in paragraph II 5) above had been made.

2) The Commission will hold its meetings in private and will receive evidence and documents to be submitted to it by Iranian authorities.

3) The Commission will visit the embassy as soon as possible to meet with the hostages;

4) As soon as the Commission has concluded its work and drafted its report, it:

> a) will announce that it is ready to return to New York to submit its report to the Secretary-General;
>
> b) will present to the Revolutionary Council (or to the new Government if it has come into being) the part of this report which concerns the conditions of confinement of the hostages; and if these conditions appear inadmissible, the Commission will state that its full report will not be submitted to the Secretary-General until the conditions of confinement have been changed and the hostages transferred elsewhere.

IV. Final Stages

1) The Revolutionary Council (or the Government) will submit to the Imam the section of the report referred to in part III 4) b) above.

2) The Imam, having taken cognizance of this report, will make a public statement on the hostages' actual conditions of confinement thus revealed to him and will order the transfer of the hostages to a hospital under the shared custody of the Iranian authority and the Commission.

3) The report of the Commission will be submitted to the Secretary-General on the occasion of the religious holidays celebrating the

1500th anniversary of the Hegira in Iran (planned for February 11).

4) The freeing of the hostages will take place on the same occasion.

5) The other elements in dispute between Iran and the United States will be studied and discussed by a joint commission formed by the two governments.

This is the refinement of the first scenario written in the White House in January. This document, which took into account the reactions of top Iranian officials such as President Bani-Sadr and Foreign Minister Sadegh Ghotbzadeh, was worked out in a hotel room in Bern, Switzerland, on February 9, 10, and 11, 1980. This scenario was much more precise than the White House draft, setting forth specific times for events to take place that would lead to the creation of a United Nations commission that would go to Teheran and eventually bring about the release of the American hostages.

REVISED SCENARIO

I. Principles and Procedures (no change from earlier draft)
The United States and Iran agree:

1) to accept the principle of the establishment of a scenario, the first stages of which would be defined precisely, and the subsequent stages would be defined in detail as events evolve;

2) to manage this scenario with the help of persons agreed to by both sides;

3) to proceed, within the framework of this scenario, by stages each involving reciprocal actions to be defined in advance;

4) that these points are intended to allow the earliest possible resolution of the present crisis by peaceful means.

II. Establishment of a Commission of Inquiry (changes show detailed sequence of events—all times below are New York time)

1) It is agreed in the approval of this scenario that the Secretary-General of the United Nations should establish a Commission of Inquiry "to hear Iran's grievances and to allow an early solution of the crisis between Iran and the U.S." and that Iran desires to have the Commission speak to each of the hostages.

2) Monday night: Secretary-General Waldheim sends a message to Ghotbzadeh confirming his readiness to send to Iran within a week the

M

Commission of 5–7 members which he discussed in Teheran early in January "to hear Iran's grievances and to allow an early solution of the crisis between Iran and the United States."

3) Tuesday: Ghotbzadeh would respond by agreeing that the Commission should come to Teheran within a week and stating Iran's desire to have the Commission speak to each of the hostages.

4) Tuesday night: the U.S. would remove its objections to the establishment of this Commission by a direct private communication to the Secretary-General. In that communication, the U.S. would state importance that Commission look into the grievances of both sides and work for early release of the hostages. At this time, the U.S. would take the following position publicly: the U.S. will discuss with the Secretary-General the concept of a Commission. The U.S. will reserve its comments until it knows what the terms of reference of the Commission will be. The U.S. has stated its position many times before and need not repeat it. While we have opposed the formation of a Commission under past conditions, we would support any steps by the UN that might lead to the release of the hostages while protecting essential international principles.

5) Tuesday night: Secretary-General Waldheim sends a second message to Ghotbzadeh which would (a) state briefly the purpose of the Commission as a fact-finding mission (not a tribunal) to help end the crisis and (b) recommend the membership of 5–7 for the Commission. In proposing the membership, the Secretary-General would propose Aguillar as Chairman plus 4–6 members, including (1) M'Bow (UNESCO Director), (2) Bedjaoui (Algerian PermRep at UN), (3) Petitti (former head of Paris Bar Association and Association of Catholic Jurists), (4) Martin Ennals (Amnesty International Secretary-General), (5) Abu Sayeed Chowdhury (former President of Bangladesh), (6) Daoudi (Advisor to President Assad of Syria) or Sabah el Rikabi (Head of Union of Syrian Bar Associations). If any of the proposed members is not acceptable to Iran, Iran could suggest that one or two be dropped.

6) Between Tuesday and Friday: Either Bani-Sadr himself would confirm by telephone to the Secretary-General or the Imam would issue a statement that he has authorized the Revolutionary Council to resolve the crisis. The Secretary-General would not proceed until he has received confirmation in one of these forms from Iran.

7) Friday at 1600 hours: the Secretary-General would announce establishment of the Commission and its purpose, including Iran's

desire to have the Commission speak to each of the hostages.

8) After SYG Waldheim's announcement: The President of Iran would publicly present the establishment of the Commission of Inquiry as a success of Iranian diplomacy, would interpret the visit to the hostages as one of the elements in the investigation into Iranian grievances, and would state the desire of the Imam to see the Commission conclude its work rapidly. The Iranian President would instruct government administrations to place their documents at the disposal of the Commission.

9) After the Iranian statement: the U.S. would state that the Commission is going on a fact-finding mission to Teheran, to hear the grievances of both sides, to meet with each of the hostages, and to report to the Secretary-General. The U.S. would object publicly to having the Commission subject the hostages to interrogation in connection with its inquiry during any of its meetings with them.

III. Work of the Commission

1) The Commission would not leave New York for Teheran until the U.S. announcement above has been made. It would aim to begin work in Teheran early next week.

2) The Commission will hold its meetings in private and will receive evidence and documents to be submitted to it by Iranian authorities.

3) The Commission will visit the embassy as soon as possible to meet with the hostages.

4) As soon as the Commission has concluded its work and drafted its report, it: (a) will tell the Revolutionary Council that the credibility of its report would be seriously limited unless the hostages are released immediately or at least moved from the compound to a hospital; (b) will inform the Revolutionary Council that it is ready to return to New York to submit its report to the Secretary-General.

IV. Final Stages:

1) Transfer of the hostages to the protection of the Government of Iran either in a hospital or in the Embassy compound after the "students" have left the premises. (Day Number 1)

2) Return of the Commission to New York. (Day 1 + 1)

3) Submission to the Secretary-General of the Commission's report which will contain findings and recommendations. Publication of the

report as a UN document. The report would express inter alia the following principle as a recommendation to all governments:

—Governments should respect and facilitate within the framework of their internal laws the right of Iran:

a) to file suits against the Shah, his family or associates on the basis of the grave presumption of any serious crimes set forth in the report;

b) to file suits to recover assets which in the report are presumed to have been illegally taken from Iran by the Shah, his family or associates.

(Day 1 + 2)

4) Release of the hostages and their departure from Iran. (Day 1 + 3)

5) One hour after their departure, the SYG will release statements by President Bani-Sadr and President Carter both previously agreed by Iran and the U.S. and, before the Commission left Iran, deposited privately with the SYG.

(a) The Iranian statement will admit the moral wrong of holding hostages, express regret, promise to respect international law and affirm a desire to establish normal relations based on mutual respect, and equality and international law.

(b) The U.S. statement will:

(1) Accept the principle stated in (3) above;

(2) Express understanding and regret for the grievances of the Iranian people, including the widespread perception of U.S. intervention in Iran's internal affairs;

(3) Affirm the right of the Iranian people to make decisions governing their political future and the engagement of the U.S. to respect that right;

(4) Affirm a desire for normal relations based on mutual respect, equality and the principles of international law.

6) Establishment of a Joint Commission to resolve all unresolved bilateral problems. (On a date to be determined by Iran and the U.S. within one month after Day 1.)

This scenario was written in Bern, Switzerland, on March 12, 13 and 14, 1980, in the immediate aftermath of the failure of the UN Commission, which left Teheran on March 11. It was an attempt to restructure a plan that would lead to the release of the hostages, including the return of the UN Commission to Teheran to finish its assignment.

SCENARIO—SECOND REVISION

I. Principles and Procedures
THE UNITED STATES AND IRAN RENEW THEIR COMMITMENT TO RESOLVE THE CRISIS BETWEEN THEM THROUGH COMPLETION OF AN AGREED SCENARIO. THE FOLLOWING IS A SUGGESTED DEVELOPMENT OF EVENTS IN THE DAYS AHEAD:

II. Transfer of the Hostages (Objective: March 15–25)
   A. MARCH 15 OR 16: ELECTION RESULTS ARE ANNOUNCED.
   B. MARCH 16: V [VILLALÓN] RETURNS TO TEHERAN WITH A PERSONAL MESSAGE FROM JORDAN TO BANI-SADR WHICH WOULD MAKE THE FOLLOWING POINTS:
      PRESIDENT CARTER APPRECIATES PRESIDENT BANI-SADR'S MESSAGE STATING THAT THE TRANSFER OF THE HOSTAGES TO THE CONTROL OF THE REVOLUTIONARY COUNCIL WOULD TAKE PLACE NO LATER THAN MARCH 25.
      PRESIDENT CARTER APPRECIATED THIS DIRECT COMMUNICATION AND HAS ASKED JORDAN TO DISCUSS WITH B AND V [BOURGUET AND VILLALÓN] AGREED STEPS THAT COULD BE TAKEN TO MAKE POSSIBLE AN EARLY END OF THE CRISIS BETWEEN THE TWO COUNTRIES AND ALSO ASK THEM TO REPORT TO PRESIDENT BANI-SADR STEPS THAT THE U.S. HAS TAKEN.
      THE U.S. IS PREPARED TO CONTINUE RESTRAINT IN ITS PUBLIC POSTURE FOR A FEW MORE DAYS, DESPITE THE INCREASE IN PUBLIC PRESSURE FOR IT TO ADOPT STRONGER MEASURES.
      THE U.S. HAS URGED THE UN COMMISSION TO COMPLETE ITS WORK AND TO BE PREPARED TO RETURN TO IRAN TO DO SO IN COORDINATION WITH THE IRANIAN AUTHORITIES. UNTIL THE TIME IS RIGHT, WE HAVE URGED THE COMMISSION ALSO

TO MAINTAIN RESTRAINT IN ITS PUBLIC POSTURE.

WHEN THE HOSTAGES ARE TRANSFERRED, THE
U.S. WILL REGARD THAT AS A CLEAR INDICATION
OF PRESIDENT BANI-SADR'S WILLINGNESS TO CON-
TINUE, THROUGH THE SERIES OF AGREED RECIP-
ROCAL STEPS, THE PROCESS TO ALLOW AN EARLY
END TO THE CRISIS, INCLUDING RELEASE OF ALL
53 AMERICANS NOW HELD IN TEHERAN.

THE U.S. LOOKS FORWARD TO A PERIOD BEYOND
THE PRESENT DIFFICULTIES WHEN WE CAN BUILD A
RELATIONSHIP WITH IRAN AND ITS PEOPLE BASED
ON EQUALITY AND MUTUAL RESPECT.

C. MARCH 15–17: THE COMMISSION WOULD LIMIT ITS
PUBLIC STATEMENTS TO AN ANNOUNCEMENT THAT IT
IS REVIEWING THE MATERIAL COLLECTED. BUT, IN PRI-
VATE MESSAGES TO BANI-SADR AND GHOTBZADEH, THE
COMMISSION WOULD RECALL IN PARTICULAR THAT IT
WILL BE UNABLE TO COMPLETE ITS REPORT UNTIL IT
HAS SEEN ALL THE HOSTAGES, AND THAT IT WILL BE
READY TO RETURN TO TEHERAN AS SOON AS THE IRA-
NIAN AUTHORITIES INDICATE TO IT THE DATE AND THE
CONDITIONS UNDER WHICH THE VISIT CAN TAKE PLACE.
AS THE COMMISSION DISCUSSED WITH BANI-SADR, IT
WOULD SUGGEST THAT THE VISIT TAKE PLACE BE-
TWEEN MARCH 21–25, AND COULD ASK THE FOREIGN
MINISTER TO PLACE AT ITS DISPOSAL ALL THE REMAIN-
ING DOCUMENTS IT WISHES TO SUBMIT TO THE COM-
MISSION.

D. TRANSFER OF THE HOSTAGES TO THE AUTHORITY
OF THE FOREIGN MINISTRY AND OF THE REVOLUTION-
ARY COUNCIL.

III. The Return of the Commission to Teheran—Promptly After the
Transfer of the Hostages to the Custody of the Government (Objec-
tive: March 21–25) (The following would be agreed in advance by
Bani-Sadr, Ghotbzadeh, and the commission.)

A. ON ARRIVING, THE COMMISSION WOULD STATE: IT
HAS RETURNED TO COMPLETE ITS MISSION. IT HAS
ASKED THE FOREIGN MINISTRY TO PLACE ALL REMAIN-
ING EVIDENCE AT ITS DISPOSAL.

B. THE FOREIGN MINISTER, AS THE IMAM REQUESTED, WOULD COLLECT ALL REMAINING DOCUMENTS AND EN-ABLE THE COMMISSION TO EXAMINE THEM.

C. THE COMMISSION WOULD MEET WITH THE REVO-LUTIONARY COUNCIL TO REVIEW THE ALLEGATIONS AND SUMMARIZE THE EVIDENCE, AND TO STATE THAT WITHIN —— DAYS IT WILL BE ABLE TO PRESENT A RE-PORT TO THE SECRETARY-GENERAL GIVING THE FIND-INGS AND RECOMMENDATIONS THAT IT HAS BEEN ABLE TO DERIVE FROM THE EVIDENCE PRESENTED.

D. PRESIDENT BANI-SADR, ON BEHALF OF THE REVO-LUTIONARY COUNCIL, WOULD MAKE A STATEMENT ON ITS MEETING WITH THE COMMISSION AFTER THAT MEETING HAS BEEN CONCLUDED.

E. THE COMMISSION WOULD THEN VISIT EACH OF THE HOSTAGES UNDER THE CONDITIONS WHICH THE COM-MISSION WILL PRESCRIBE.

F. THE COMMISSION WOULD MAKE ANOTHER REPORT TO THE REVOLUTIONARY COUNCIL ON THE CONDITION OF THE HOSTAGES. IT WOULD ALSO TELL THE REVOLU-TIONARY COUNCIL THAT THE CREDIBILITY OF ITS RE-PORT WOULD BE SERIOUSLY LIMITED UNLESS THE HOS-TAGES ARE RELEASED. IT WOULD ASK IRAN TO SET A DATE FOR RELEASING THE HOSTAGES AND WOULD COMMIT ITSELF TO PUBLISH ITS REPORT ON THAT DATE. (THE SIMULTANEITY INDICATED IN THE LAST SEN-TENCE IS SUBJECT TO REVIEW AS THE FINAL DATES ARE REVISED.)

IV. Final Steps (Objective: Five days after the visit of the commission to the hostages) The Previous Scenario Agreed to by Both Parties En-visioned a Final Stage of Reciprocal Steps Leading to Release of the Americans Held in Teheran.

HOWEVER, THE SEQUENCE OF STEPS ENVISIONED THEN HAS CHANGED BECAUSE IN THE NEW CIRCUM-STANCES THE COMMISSION WILL RETURN TO IRAN AFTER THE REVOLUTIONARY COUNCIL HAS TAKEN CUSTODY OF THE AMERICAN PERSONNEL. BECAUSE OF RECENT DEVELOPMENTS, THE FINAL STEPS OF THE SCE-NARIO AGREED EARLIER SEEM NO LONGER TO BE COM-

PLETELY APPLICABLE. IF THAT ASSUMPTION IS NOT CORRECT, THE U.S. IS PREPARED TO ABIDE BY THE PREVIOUSLY AGREED SCENARIO.

IF THE FINAL STEPS OF THE EARLIER SCENARIO CAN NO LONGER BE FOLLOWED, IT IS NECESSARY FOR BOTH PARTIES TO AGREE ON THE STEPS IN A NEW FINAL STAGE. IN THESE NEW CIRCUMSTANCES, THE UNITED STATES BELIEVES THAT THE COMPONENTS OF THE FINAL STAGE—INCLUDING THE REPORT OF THE UNITED NATIONS COMMISSION, THE STATEMENTS OF PRESIDENTS CARTER AND BANI-SADR, THE ESTABLISHMENT OF AN IRAN-U.S. JOINT COMMISSION TO RESOLVE BILATERAL ISSUES, AND THE RELEASE OF ALL 53 AMERICANS—SHOULD BE TAKEN SIMULTANEOUSLY. IT IS ALSO THE POSITION OF THE UNITED STATES THAT THE RELEASE OF THE HOSTAGES SHOULD TAKE PLACE NO LATER THAN FIVE DAYS AFTER THE VISIT TO THE AMERICAN PERSONNEL.

This document was handed to American newsmen in Wiesbaden, Germany, by Jody Powell, the press secretary to President Carter. Carter had flown overnight to Wiesbaden to see the American hostages, who had been freed a half hour after he left the presidency. The document was intended to explain the highly complicated transactions that had finally led to the release of the hostages on January 20, 1981.

Mr. Jody Powell
Wiesbaden 1/21/81

THE DECLARATIONS OF ALGIERS

I. *The Declarations of Algiers*
  A. *Background*
The Declarations were the result of four months of intensive negotiation. Because Iran refused direct contact, it was necessary to negotiate through an intermediary government. Fortunately, the Popular and Democratic Government of Algeria was acceptable to both sides and was willing to assume the intermediary role. Algeria became fully engaged, devoting the full attention of its Foreign Minister and a senior

negotiating team. There were great complexities to this three-way negotiating process. There were movement problems, problems of differing languages and legal systems and problems of time required for each exchange. The Algerian negotiating team made numerous trips to Teheran and Washington. Because it was taking about two weeks to complete each cycle of offer and counter-offer, Deputy Secretary Christopher moved to Algiers on 1/8 and remained there until the end.

Algeria played a critical role in explaining each side's position to the other and in closing gaps between them. The Algerian team was also able to verify the status of all 52 hostages.

B. *Main Points of the Declarations*

1. *Basic principle*—when Iran releases hostages, US restores Nov 1979 financial status quo insofar as practicable.

2. *Elements*

a. Iran restores freedom of hostages.

b. US releases Iran's frozen assets.

c. Claims resulting from hostage seizure and assets freeze are dropped.

d. Iran's agreed debts to US lenders are paid.

e. International arbitration replaces existing legal actions on all other preexisting economic claims.

3. *The Basic Agreement*

a. The hostage release and the unfreezing of assets would be simultaneous.

b. Of Iran's $11–12 billion of frozen assets, about $8 billion would be placed in escrow before hostages released. This 8 billion breaks down as follows:

Deposits in overseas branches of US Banks	$ 5.5
Gold, securities and other assets in Federal Reserve.	$ 2.5

c. When the hostages are released, this $8 billion would be applied as follows:

$3.67   billion to pay off loans
from US and other banks

	1.42	billion to remain in escrow
		to secure payment of disputed claims
		between US banks and Iran.
	2.88	billion to Iran
TOTAL	$7.97	

d. Remaining frozen assets (over $3 billion) would be un-frozen, and attachments on these assets dissolved.

e. The underlying economic claims would be submitted to international arbitration by a Iran-US claims tribunal.

f. Of these US assets, $1 billion would be placed in another escrow fund to secure payment of arbitration awards against Iran. As awards are paid, Iran would be obligated to refresh the fund so that it does not drop below $500 million.

g. Iran would be free to initiate litigation in US courts to recover assets of former Shah and his family alleged to belong to Iran. US would agree to assist by freezing any such assets pending outcome of litigation, by requiring reports from holders, and in other ways. Ultimate determination would be left to US courts under applicable US law.

II. *The Closing*

The "Closing" involved three governments, four central banks, twelve US commercial banks and literally hundreds of officials and lawyers in Washington, New York, London, Algiers and Teheran. Throughout the closing period, beginning on the evening of January 18 and continuing into the late morning of January 20, President Carter directed the US closing team. He and his advisers were in virtually constant communication with team members in the Treasury, State and Justice Departments and with Deputy Secretary Christopher and his team in Algiers. The main steps in the Closing are described below:

A. *Signing of the Declarations and Related Undertakings*

1. President Carter signs statement of adherence and nine executive orders.

2. President Carter and Secretary of State Muskie authorize Deputy Secretary Christopher to sign Declarations and Related Undertakings in Algiers.

3. Government of Algeria notifies US and Iran that both are ready to sign.

4. Secretary of State delivers statement of adherence and copies

of 5 executive orders to Algerian Embassy in US which advises Algiers.

5. Iran's Minister of State, Nabavi, signs separate counterparts of Declarations and Related Undertakings on behalf of Prime Minister Rajai of Iran in Teheran in presence of Algerian negotiating team which advises Algiers.

6. Christopher signs Declarations and Related Undertakings in Algiers.

7. Algeria notifies US and Iran that each has adhered and proclaims the two Declarations of Algiers. (2:17 a.m. EST 1/19)

B. *Signing of the Escrow Agreement and Related Documents*

(These documents required signatures by the US, Iran and three central banks—Federal Reserve, Central Bank of Algeria (the escrow agent) and Bank of England.)

1. Christopher signs in Algiers for US at same time he signs Declarations on 1/19.

2. Iran signs separate counterpart in Teheran at about 3 a.m. on 1/19 in presence of Algerian negotiating team. However, Iran refuses to approve or sign attached annex containing detailed instructions defining responsibilities of escrow agent and also containing text of Bank Markazi's instructions to US deposit banks to pay over deposits to Federal Reserve for transfer in escrow.

3. Iran's failure to approve or sign attached annex causes concern to US deposit banks and issue is subject of further negotiations.

4. These negotiations continue throughout 1/19 and into the early morning of 1/20. Iran denounces US banks for "underhanded" maneuver in proposed text of Bank Markazi instructions.

5. The disputed instructions include conventional statement that transfer of specified deposit amounts to Federal Reserve will release deposit banks from further liability. But since Bank Markazi's records of deposits are incomplete as result of freeze and aftermath of Iran's revolution, Markazi's figures do not tally with US bank figures. Markazi therefore wants to reserve right to dispute correct amounts after transfer.

6. US deposit banks agree and submit corrective language. But Markazi declines to approve language or submit satisfactory language of its own. Meanwhile, Iran continues to attack the instructions as underhanded. Entire closing hangs in balance.

7. During the night of 19/20, a solution emerges, as follows:

a. The US deposit banks and the US agree to detach Markazi

instructions as an annex to the Escrow Agreement, and to accept separate instructions if language is adequate.

b. Markazi's English solicitor prepares modification of US bank draft that Markazi agrees to accept. Says at 10 p.m. 1/19 it will be transmitted immediately by telex if US banks approve. US and US banks tell him to begin transmitting.

c. From 10 p.m. to 3:15 a.m., telex of instructions is prepared, test-checked and finally sent at 3:00 EST, giving instructions to 12 banks to transfer precise amounts of deposits, broken down by principal and interest, aggregating $5.5 billion to the Federal Reserve.

d. When the full telex was received, Secretary of the Treasury Miller delivered an Executive Order to the US bank officials present in his office, together with a Treasury instruction to pay over the frozen deposits in overseas branches to the Federal Reserve in New York.

e. The full telex as transmitted contained numerous material typographical errors including one in the initial identifying code number, although the terminal code number is correct. Under normal precautionary procedures for such transactions—this was the largest private transfer in history—all the errors required further correcting of the telex until the text was perfect. This would have taken several hours more.

f. The telex was being received in the office of the London solicitor for the 12 US deposit banks. Lawyers and officials of all 12 banks, the Federal Reserve and the Treasury were present. They were connected by open telephone lines to their counterparts at the Treasury Department in Washington and their counterparts at the US Embassy in Algiers.

g. The US bank officers and lawyers conferred to decide whether the imperfect telex was satisfactory for such a large transfer, but could not reach unanimity. At 3:45 a.m., Secretary Miller, who was at the Treasury end of the open lines, gave verbal instructions to the US banks to make the transfers, and on the basis of this legal direction, they agreed to do so. By 4:10 a.m. the US banks had transferred most of the $5.5 billion to the Federal Reserve Bank of New York. The Federal Reserve Bank of New York then transferred the entire amount to its account in the Bank of England. (Two hours earlier, the Fed had completed the transfer of its own Iranian funds to its Bank of

England account.) The balance of the $5.5 billion (consisting of securities and foreign currency deposits) was transferred by 5:20 a.m. EST.

h. With $7.977 billion now on deposit in the Fed's account in the Bank of England, these funds were ready for transfer to the escrow account of the Algerian Central Bank at the Bank of England. But that transfer could not be made until the Escrow Agreement had been signed by the Algerian Central Bank and the Federal Reserve and until a related Depository Agreement had been signed by the Algerian Central Bank and the Bank of England.

i. At this point (4 to 5 a.m. EST on 1/20) a further snag developed. Since Iran had refused to approve and sign the Annex to the Escrow Agreement containing the Technical Instructions, the Algerian Central Bank, mindful of its intermediary role, also declined to sign the Annex, and insisted that it be removed from the Escrow Agreement. The Annex contained provisions important to the Federal Reserve Bank of New York. The Fed's representative in Algiers decided to consult his superiors in Washington.

j. In a series of telephone conferences lasting over an hour, President Anthony Solomon of New York Fed decided on the advice of his counsel to authorize the signing of the Escrow Agreement. At 6:18 EST on 1/20, the Escrow Agreement and the Depository Agreement were fully signed in Algiers.

k. The New York Fed then transferred $7.977 billion from its account in the Bank of England to the escrow account in the Algerian Central Bank. This transfer was completed at 5 a.m. EST on 1/20.

l. The Bank of England then certified to the Algerian Central Bank that the escrow account had been opened and contained $7.977 billion. Because this had to be done by open telephone line from the Bank in London to its Deputy Governor in Algiers, and then painstakingly verified, typed, proofread and signed, the formal certificate was not delivered until 8:04 a.m.

m. At 8:06 a.m., the Algerian Central Bank certified to Iran and the US that the escrow account contained $7.977 billion.

C. *The Delivery of the Hostages*

1. The Declarations of Algiers provide that when the Algerian Central Bank certifies that not less than $7.977 billion has been placed in the Escrow Account, "Iran shall immediately bring about the safe departure of the 52 US nationals detained in Iran."

2. Iran received this certificate at 8:06 a.m. EST on 1/20.

3. At 12:33 p.m. EST, the first aircraft was allowed to take off. At 12:42 p.m. EST, the second aircraft was allowed to take off. The planes departed Iranian airspace approximately one hour later, and proceeded over Turkey to Athens. After a refueling stop, they arrived in Algiers at 7 p.m. EST on 1/20. In a ceremony combining diplomatic correctness with high emotion, Foreign Minister Ben Yahia of Algeria turned over the 52 hostages to Deputy Secretary of State Christopher shortly after 8 p.m. EST.

4. The hostages will remain at Wiesbaden for several days, and will then be flown to the US to rejoin their families. Every effort will be made to smooth their return to a normal life. As one of his last official acts, President Carter signed an Executive Order appointing a Commission on Hostage Compensation, to consider and recommend an appropriate form of legislation to compensate the hostages and their families for the ordeal they have endured. President Carter has appointed four of the nine Commission members, leaving the appointment of the other five and the designation of the Chairman to President Reagan. The four appointees are:

Henry Bellmon of Oklahoma
Cyrus Vance of New York
Robert Giaimo of Connecticut
Patricia Harris of the District of Columbia

D. *Funds Move From the Escrow*

1. At 1:35 p.m. EST on 1/20, the Government of Algeria certified to the US and Iran that the 52 US nationals had safely departed from Iran.

2. About 2 p.m. EST, on the instructions of the Algerian Central Bank, the Bank of England disbursed $3.67 billion to the Federal Reserve Bank of New York, (which then disbursed the funds to the Agent banks for the loan syndicates), and $2.88 billion to Iran. The balance of $1.42 billion remains in escrow pending settlement or arbitration of disputes between US banks and Iran concerning the remaining amounts owed.

index